thetime-savinggarden

thetime-savinggarden

published by THE READER'S DIGEST ASSOCIATION LTD
LONDON • NEW YORK • SYDNEY • MONTREAL

Make time to enjoy the garden you have created

There is much pleasure to be had on a fine summer day – pottering among your plants, deadheading, coaxing, harvesting and pruning. But when you are assailed by competing demands on your time, it can be impossible to find an afternoon or even an hour to sit back and admire the fruits of your labours.

The Time-Saving Garden can give you back your weekends. In these pages you will find hundreds of ways to make your gardening life easier, with short-cuts, expert tips, time-saving techniques and design secrets that will help to cut down on maintenance. If you want to grow a formal hedge, some pruning is unavoidable, but you'll find ways to make the job quicker and less frequent. A lawn will always need mowing, but a little time spent at the design stage will reap dividends in hours saved trimming the edges thereafter.

You don't need to dig up your entire garden and start again. The book's expert advice will guide you through designing, planning and planting everything from a small group of perennials to a whole new garden – all carefully thought out to make it easy to get it right and to keep your garden looking gorgeous.

To make a great start, next time you go to the garden centre take a look at the directory of 220 easy-care plants at the back of the book first. Choose from these recommended varieties – guaranteed to be the easiest of their kind to look after – and get ready to put your feet up and relax …

The Editors

Contents

Planting solutions for all situations 68

Redesign now to save time later 240

The very best easy-care plants 266

Ten golden rules for

Do you feel you spend **too long maintaining** your garden and not enough time **enjoying it?**

Follow these **10 rules** to growing a **time-saving garden.**

1 Plan carefully

Whether starting from scratch or redesigning parts of your existing garden, think about how much time you will be able to devote to maintaining it and plan solutions that will minimise unnecessary work.

2 Garden naturally

Get to know the climate and soil conditions in your garden, so that you choose plants which will thrive naturally, and not need constant feeding and nurturing or replanting at a later date.

3 Buy the right plants

Always buy plants from a nursery that has a good reputation and sells quality plants. For low maintenance – and to save you time and money – give preference to native species and tried-and-tested reliable varieties.

4 Plant with foresight

Remember that plants grow, so always allow sufficient space between plants for them to spread. Even if you don't like to see gaps in a newly planted bed, it will avoid the tedious business of thinning out – and you can fill temporary gaps with fast-growing summer annuals.

5 Cover the ground

Always keep your ground covered with a layer of mulch, which will suppress weeds and help to keep moisture in – to save the time and trouble of unnecessary weeding and watering.

the time-saving garden

6 Water wisely

Depending on the amount of rainfall your garden receives, water your plants less often, but more thoroughly – it will save both time and water.

7 Feed with care

Use the right fertiliser at the right time for your plants, and always apply it sparingly to avoid excessive growth and extra maintenance.

8 Make use of nature's help

Make useful animals such as birds and insects feel at home in your garden, and they will help to control pests and diseases for you – saving you time doing it yourself, avoiding the use of chemicals and minimising the loss of plants.

9 Use the right equipment

Always use suitable tools and use tried-and-tested methods – you will save energy as well as time, and so benefit your health.

10 Garden at the right time

Grow and maintain plants at the right stage in their growth at the right time of year to lessen the likelihood of failures and to avoid having to do jobs again too soon.

Inspirations for easy-care gardens

Whatever your situation, in sun or shade, in the city or in the country, there are simple solutions for every garden that can help to reduce the amount of maintenance that would otherwise be necessary. Take inspiration from the pages that follow and prepare to take it easy.

A natural garden for wildlife

An oasis for people, plants and animals

Gardens that take their lead from nature require little work but give great pleasure. Just let nature take its course and only interfere when absolutely necessary.

Gravel beds provide sunny spots for plants, birds and small reptiles, and require little maintenance.

Bog zones form natural transitions from water to land and require little help from the gardener.

Birds and bats
eat insects and help gardeners to reduce pest damage.

Containers
can be used to incorporate even exotic annuals into a natural planting scheme.

Gaps between paving slabs
make room for wildlife and can be planted with undemanding and drought-resistant cushion-forming plants, such as scented thyme.

Dead wood
provides a sought-after hiding place for amphibians and reptiles.

Practical solutions for a small space

In a **small garden** behind a terraced house, access is awkward for bringing in plants and materials. **Choose** the right combination of plants and the garden will need **little looking after.**

Variegated leaves
like those of a hosta can add flashes of light to darker corners.

Many fuchsias
are fully hardy and can spend the winter outdoors; they need little maintenance in a border and their vivid colours provide long-lasting interest.

Evergreen shrubs
provide privacy
and need little
maintenance.

Miniature ponds
in buckets or other
containers are quick to
plant and take little
looking after.

Lady's mantle
(*Alchemilla mollis*) is
a robust perennial for
the edges of pathways
and flower beds.

A dry stream effect
is easy to create.
It looks attractive, can
be walked on and is
low-maintenance.

A garden on a slope
Making the most of a natural arena

Sloping gardens do not have to be difficult. Terraced and with appropriate planting, they can be relatively **quick** and **easy** to look after.

Good lighting
at the side of paths makes your garden safer as well as helping it to look attractive at night.

A dry slope
planted with deep-rooting geraniums needs virtually no attention at all.

A rock garden
with undemanding
cushion-forming plants
growing between heavy
stones and boulders is
ideal for stabilising and
supporting steeper slopes.

A dry stream
planting at the foot of the
slope is low-maintenance,
but also provides essential
drainage if the garden
slopes towards the house.

Plants spilling out
over the top of
retaining walls can be
maintained while
standing up, just like
raised beds.

**Steps with no
raised edges**
are quick and easy
to sweep, brushing
leaves and other
debris into adjacent
flowerbeds.

Classic variations on a green theme

The many different shapes and colours of foliage can **add variety** even to a shaded garden, especially if you make use of any sunny spots to highlight **low-maintenance** splashes of colour.

White water lilies (*Nymphaea*) flower in semi-shaded ponds and pools, just as they would in the wild.

A practical ramp formed of granite setts makes an alternative way of climbing a slope next to a flight of steps.

A bamboo hedge
is a low-maintenance
backdrop to a decorative
feature, like this water
pump, and conceals an
unsightly shed behind.

Containers
with shade-tolerant
plants can create
splashes of colour in
darker areas.

**Shade-tolerant
ground cover plants**
like barrenwort
(*Epimedium alpinum*)
can save you from
having to weed any bare
ground between plants.

Ground covering
Petasites suppresses
any weeds in the area
around the base of a
well and reinforces the
impression of a
naturally damp
habitat.

The dead trunk
of a tree provides
good support for
low-maintenance
climbing roses.

A garden that is stylish and modern
Attention to detail makes the difference

'Less is more' makes a practical motto for designing a modern, **low-maintenance** garden. Take care with a few interesting and quirky **details** and use **simple materials**, such as metal, wood and stone to create a stylish and modern overall effect.

The edge of the decked area is level with the lawn, making it easy to mow right up to it without having to trim the lawn edge separately.

Decking provides an enclosed space, inviting you to sit down and admire the view of the garden and beyond.

Simple shapes
give a stylish modern look
to a planting scheme.
Choose globe shaped
blooms, such as
agapanthus or alliums and
broad-leaved hostas.

Grasses
need little or no maintenance.
Choose pond or garden
varieties to create wispy
screens and the sound of
gentle rustling in the breeze.

**A modern dry
stone wall**
made of regular
blocks of stone and
interspersed with
planting pockets
gives a cutting edge
to a natural material
and style.

Running water
is a welcome addition
to any garden. A
simple waterfall
spilling out of a metal
rill is an unfussy
alternative to a
traditional fountain.

Pretty, productive – and trouble-free

A cottage garden can be **brightly coloured**, luxuriant and abundant and yet need **little** maintenance if you plant it **skilfully**.

Swiss chard
(*Beta vulgaris* Cicla Group), like its relative lettuce, is an undemanding leafy vegetable, which graces gardens with its shapes and colours.

Wood chips
make an attractive, low-maintenance covering for pathways. They are also soft to walk on and a cheap option if you have a shredder to make chippings from your prunings.

Vervain
(*Verbena officinalis*)
and other herbs thrive
on neglect. They look
attractive alongside
flowers in a bed and
are useful, too.

Home-made
features, such as this
scarecrow, are unusual
and eye-catching.

A garden tree
can bear succulent
fruit in addition to
looking decorative.
Many fruit trees are
easy to look after.

**Planted next
to the fence**
tall cottage-garden
perennials such
as these dahlia
do not need any
extra support.

A roof garden with Mediterranean flair
Turn up the heat on a sultry terrace

A small roof garden is like an outdoor room. You can rearrange it at will and even take the furnishings and decoration with you when you move.

Raised beds
are easy to look after without bending or kneeling. The plants here must be able to survive hot, dry summers and hard winters.

It is easy to propagate
many container-grown plants. You can take cuttings to grow on in small pots, even if space is at a premium.

Cushion-forming
perennials of drought-resistant plant species can be planted in the gravel between paving slabs and need little care.

If you have nowhere to shelter container plants for the winter, they may need to be protected from frost.

Decoration adds to the visual appeal of evergreen shrubs. A shapely urn evokes memories of hot Mediterranean holidays.

Upright plants with narrow leaves form a striking contrast with plain walls.

Large-leaved perennials planted next to the pond reinforce the impression of a naturally damp zone.

The intricate foliage of undemanding ferns will be reflected in the surface of the pond.

A practical family garden
Create a space built for living in

Small gardens are often used heavily during the **summer months** and little during the rest of the year.

Design the garden as an **outdoor living room** and furnish it as **practically** as possible.

Fold-up furniture
is a versatile choice for a small garden, where there is no room to have the furniture permanently out.

Decking
is an easy-build option for a patio. It is low-maintenance and a comfortable, safe surface for children.

Fix a small work table
to the shed wall at a convenient height to turn it into a handy miniature potting shed.

Garden tools
need to be stored safely and kept close to hand. Even a small shed is big enough for the bare essentials.

A privacy screen
made of robust larch wood does not need to be painted or stained to look attractive.

Retaining walls
built from natural stone look good even in the winter and are also easy to look after.

A dense layer of mulch
between woody plants and perennials saves on watering and weeding.

Careful planning makes life easier

Whether you are designing a garden from scratch or want to change your existing garden to cut down on its maintenance, careful preparation and planning will make your task much easier.

Choices and changes
The benefits of careful planning

Thoughtful design can help you to avoid a range of common mistakes and drastically **reduce the amount of time-consuming** maintenance your garden will require.

✗ WATCH OUT!

Don't be tempted to buy plants before you have finished designing your garden. Bought on impulse, what may seem like a bargain could turn out to be a hindrance to achieving a harmonious, successful planting scheme.

Compile a wish list
Begin by making a list of the wishes and requirements of all those who will use the garden, both in practical terms and general design and plant selection. Note down the suitability of various locations and what maintenance will be involved. Putting it on paper will help you to order your initial wide-ranging thoughts and to reject less suitable ideas – and create a harmonious concept out of the rest.

Remember, it is not enough to base a long-term garden design solely on the immediate needs of its users. Children grow up, householders grow older, external work pressures vary – and the house may even need to be extended eventually. It is unrealistic to expect a garden design to allow for every eventuality, but if you make provision for as many as you can, any future changes will involve considerably less upheaval.

The sand pit built when your children are young, for example, could be converted into a pond once they have outgrown it. And a swing could be constructed in such a way that the space could be transformed later into a garden shed, greenhouse or pergola. While such careful planning is more time-consuming at the start – and more expensive to realise – it will result in savings on both counts in the long run.

Family decision
Involving the youngest garden users early on in the planning stages will give them an incentive to help when it comes to turning their ideas into reality. It will also encourage them to look after their own part of the garden.

30

Just planted

Columnar-shaped evergreens

Bushy shrub

Bare-based shrub

Dwarf shrub

Conical evergreen shrub

Deciduous tree

10m

10m

After a few years

10m

Creating a hedge Initially, there will be gaps between the individual hedging plants (top), which should be spaced at intervals. After a few years, the hedge will have closed up (above) and grown in height.

CHOOSING THE RIGHT POSITION

REQUIREMENT	POSSIBLE SITE	MAINTENANCE NEEDS
Flowering shrubs	Sun or shade, around the garden perimeter	Low depending on variety; less than formal hedge
Entertaining, dining, barbecuing	Large terrace; possibly under cover	Moderate
Hobby area; tool storage	Close to house or garden boundary	Low; take installation requirements into account
Wildlife pond	Semi-shade; away from falling leaves	Low
Fruit trees	Sun and shelter	Moderate
Space for wildlife	Almost anywhere	Low
Quiet seating area	Covered corner of garden between shrubs	Low
Children's play area	Within easy view of the house; some shade	Low if natural design
Clothes-drying area	Breezy spot near the house	Low; could be covered; hard landscape surface useful
Natural shrubbery	Sun to shade	Low to moderate

Small plants grow tall

It is important to take account of your plants' growth when planning, particularly in the case of trees and shrubs, which define the garden's structure. Although dwarf varieties grow less quickly than standard shrubs, all your plants will grow upwards and fill out over time. Hard pruning is one way of counteracting this, but a better and easier way is to start off by planting varieties that will not outgrow their space.

The same applies to perennial plants, which take between two and four years to fill out completely and merge together. When planning a planting scheme, try to strike a balance between living with initial gaps in your flowerbeds and cutting back or removing plants at a later date. While you wait for your plants to mature, you can fill gaps with fast-growing annuals and summer bedding (see pages 142–3).

Tackling older gardens

Transforming an overgrown garden is not easy, since it can be difficult to envisage a tamed alternative. Overgrown gardens are often dominated by poorly managed shrubs that can make it hard or even impossible to get machinery in to clear the space. But once cut back, older gardens often reveal a delightful and workable ground plan and healthy soil. Decide, first of all, which plants and elements of the garden's infrastructure – walls, pathways, a rockery and garden sheds – you want to retain and which to remove.

You may find it useful to enlist the help of a garden designer, who will look at your garden through objective eyes, advise on any technical work involved in the redesign, such as tree-felling, and estimate how long the project is likely to take.

Identifying weak spots in your garden layout

If you are not happy with your garden, the first step in a major redesign is to make a **systematic** and **honest appraisal of your current space** to identify its **weak spots** and its **good points.**

Under the microscope

It is often difficult to pinpoint exactly why you feel dissatisfied with your garden. There is just a vague awareness that this or that could be different or better. But, after some thought, this sense of dissatisfaction can generally be linked to weak spots in the garden's design, which may also make it difficult to maintain.

The best approach is to take a long, hard look at your garden and examine it objectively as if it

WATCH OUT!

Any raised edges on a patio or path are potential trip hazards – ensure that the surface is level where different surfaces join, such as paving slabs set into a lawn. Where levels change, install clearly visible steps.

Major paths
Particularly on well-trodden routes, a clear definition between paths and planted areas – such as a solid, raised edging strip – helps to prevent people taking short cuts across your flowerbeds or lawn.

Minor paths
Paths made of a series of stepping stones provide greater flexibility. It is easy to alter their route or to adapt them to new requirements.

belonged to someone else. Wander round it attentively and note down anything you dislike. Start at the garden boundary and record any external influences, such as lack of privacy from the neighbours, traffic noise, unfavourable growing conditions (such as very exposed or shady), and so on. Then move on to the heart of the garden itself, inspecting all the steps and pathways, paved and seating areas, as well as plant groupings and any garden buildings.

Do the paths run where you need them to? Is the paving completely level or does standing water collect here and there? Does that untidy area between the path

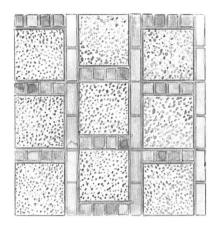

New from old You can make a paved area look brand new simply by rearranging the old paving slabs and stones in a new pattern.

and border annoy you? Do you miss not having a watering tap right at the end of the garden?

Next, turn your attention to the bigger plants – the trees, hedges and shrubs. Finally, study the herbaceous borders and the lawn and note down anything you don't like about them at different times of the year.

Problems in the life of a garden

Every garden has its own life cycle. A young garden will probably still have plenty of gaps and it is not always possible to discern a clear structure. Impatient gardeners may fill beds with plants as quickly as possible to create an instant garden but, after a few years, they discover that the plants have been positioned much too close to one another and they find themselves having to decide which ones to remove. Far-sighted planning and a little patience can save both

unnecessary expenditure and considerable amounts of time. After about five to seven years, most gardens will have emerged from their youthful stage and may be regarded as established. Shrubs, hedges and climbing plants may have reached their optimum height and even the trees should be a good size. The soil should be well cultivated and there should have been time for most early mistakes to have been corrected.

At this stage, plans for redesign are most likely to focus on supplementing or altering the planting schemes beneath shrubs and trees, where light conditions will have altered. Feature shrubs may need to be rejuvenated by pruning. It might even be necessary to replace some of the paving if an inferior quality of material has been used.

As long as they have been properly maintained, mature gardens usually only require redesigning when family circumstances or the owners' lifestyle change. Perhaps the children have grown up and left

TIME-SAVING TIP

■ If you are patient enough to allow plants to develop naturally at their own rate, you will avoid having to rework your planting schemes and save yourself a great deal of time.

home? Maybe the owners have taken up a new hobby or no longer have the time or stamina for time-consuming maintenance work.

Mature gardens

When structural features begin to deteriorate or plants reach the end of their life, it is wise to intervene before they become unsafe. Cracked or uneven paving, large trees with branches that have died and rotten fence panels are all potential hazards and should be dealt with promptly when you notice them.

MAKE LIFE EASIER

■ If old paving slabs have become uneven, you must level the footings before relaying the old slabs or laying new ones. You can also use this opportunity to enlarge paved areas or widen pathways. Instead of taking away all the old materials and buying new slabs, the old ones can be recycled and relaid in a new pattern, using only a small amount of new materials – paving, bricks, setts or even gravel – to fill the extra space.

THE MOST COMMON GARDEN PROBLEM AREAS

PROBLEM AREA	SOLUTION	ADVANTAGES
Raised edges along beds and paths; steps difficult to maintain	Level off adjoining areas.	Easier to clean, mow and sweep.
Plants in the wrong place; pest infestation	Improve soil or location; restock with better suited plants.	Easier soil and easier plant care.
Standing water; muddy areas	Renew substructure; incorporate drainage.	Less need for cleaning; easier plant care.
Soil erosion; problem plants on slopes	Landscape slope into terraces; improve soil; replant.	Far easier to maintain.
Bare, mossy or dense patches in lawn	Remove damaged turf and plant ground-cover plants.	Lower maintenance than unsuitable grass.
Old, overgrown herbaceous plants	Rejuvenate by dividing and improving the soil.	No more unproductive maintenance.
Uneven surfaces to paths	Re-lay paving.	Easier to sweep.
Weeds in beds and borders	Plant ground-cover plants or spreading shrubs; mulch.	No more weeding.
Trees which have grown too large	Radically prune or fell trees.	More light.

Draft your design on paper

Always sketch your garden plan before you start work. A **simple scale drawing can be an invaluable aid** when embarking on new designs or alterations. It is impossible to represent everything on paper, but a plan makes even the bare bones clearer and **easier to visualise**.

30-MINUTE TASK

▶ Sketch a garden plan and make a note of all measurements.
▶ Show any intended changes on the plan

How to produce a garden plan

The first stage is to measure your plot and set out the shape of your garden on paper. Garden planning software for your computer can help you to visualise the finished result, but you will still need to do this first stage manually.

Choose an appropriate scale for the plan, such as 1:100, where 1cm on paper is equivalent to 1m. Draw out the length and breadth of your plot and indicate which direction it faces, as well as the location of your house and that of your neighbours.

Next, make a note of all your house's main windows and doors, as well as patios, paths, paved areas and steps. If you are considering major excavation work or tree planting, you may have to think about the position of underground utility supply cables, gas, water and drainage pipes, cisterns and tanks.

Armed with a tape measure, enlist a helper and make a note on the plan of the main building

Example of a planting plan: herb bed with tall fruit bushes in the centre.
Using a plan drawn to scale and different symbols to depict different types of plants, you can produce a clear planting plan. The symbols for shrubs and summer-flowering plants, can be supplemented with information on colour and flowering periods.

structures in the garden and the location of plants worth keeping. If precise measurements are not easy to obtain, use two fixed points as references – the corner of the house and the corner of the plot, for example – and measure the length from both to the desired spot.

Showing differences in ground levels

Make sure that your plan reflects the contours of your garden, too. Minor uneven areas can be ignored and slight slopes indicated with an arrow on the plan, but steep slopes

and major changes in level should be measured and noted on the plan. A cross section of the relevant area may also be useful for planning terraced beds.

Rest one end of a length of timber on the top of the slope and place a spirit level on it. Get a helper to hold the timber level while you measure the height of the timber above the lower ground level. Make a note of the length of the timber and the height difference over that distance and repeat the process further down the slope if necessary until you reach the bottom. You will

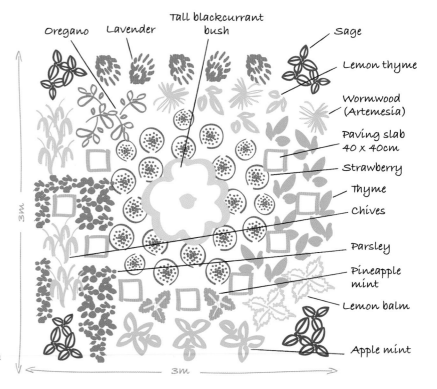

USE OF SPACE FOR FEATURES IN THE GARDEN

FEATURE	SPACE REQUIREMENTS OR VISUAL EFFECTS
Broad-canopied trees	Should have trunks over 2 metres high so that you can pass beneath the branches without ducking.
Open, undivided areas	Can appear smaller than gardens split up into different sections.
Steps and paths	Consider the comfortable stride of all the garden users.
Hedge or walls	Seem much smaller outdoors than the walls of a room, so don't be frightened to plan large features.
Long paths	Can be visually shortened by varying their width, paving cross-wise and introducing curves.
High retaining walls	Can be intimidating; landscape the slope into terraced beds, each around 1 metre in height instead.
Posts for pergolas, carports and play equipment	Choose generous sizes for strength and stability and to avoid the feature looking too delicate.
Path widths	Consider their usage: is it a main or a side path? Will it be used by one person or two people side by side?

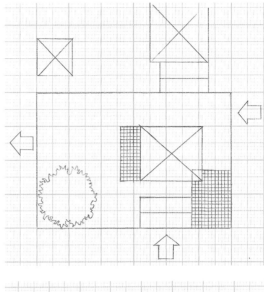

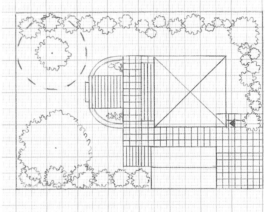

The basic plan (top): a house, car parking area, patio and a tree are included in the plan, as well as important surrounding features: the neighbours' house (above), noise from the road (arrow on the right), direction of a westerly wind (arrow below) as well as a view to a particularly attractive part of the garden (arrow left).

The redesign (below) includes the finished paved areas. In front of the patio a semicircular slope incorporates two steps. A hedge formed of shrubs (for privacy, and a windbreak) and shrub and herb beds on the terrace help to make the garden low maintenance.

then know what the total change in level is over the measured distance.

Once you have completed your outline plan, it is a good idea to make several copies so that you can experiment with different designs without redrawing the bare bones each time. Alternatively, draw your design ideas onto sheets of tracing paper and lay these over the outline plan.

Creating a new design
There are two ways to approach a redesign: either commit your ideas to paper first, before checking the planned locations in the garden itself, or do your planning in the garden, then transfer the information onto your draft plan.

If it is difficult to envisage your plan on paper, you can mark out the positions of different elements in the garden itself. Improvise by using pegs hammered into the ground to indicate the

positions of the corners of sheds and other planned structures. Indicate trees with canes or even a sunshade. The positioning of paths and ponds can be simulated using tiles, a long garden hose or canes laid end to end. Look at your proposed planting scheme from different angles, including from inside the house and from its upstairs windows, taking into account where the shadows will fall at different times of the day and year and the eventual height and spread of any trees.

A planting scheme
Plants for beds and borders need to be planned carefully, particularly if you are to include groups of trees and bushes. Before choosing the exact location for plants, check on their height and spread at maturity so that they will look good together in a few years' time and will be easy to maintain. When planning

hedges, take into account how far apart the plants must be positioned from one another and how much they will spread, remembering to leave enough room for access for maintenance. Make a note of the colour of any existing flowers and their flowering period to help you to plan a coherent and harmonious scheme around them.

Once your design is complete, you can move on to thinking in more detail about any garden buildings you need to buy and construct and choosing and calculating the quantity of the materials you will need.

Tackling a redesign, step by step

A design on paper is just the beginning of **your new garden**. Even at this stage, **effective planning of the tasks ahead** is still crucial and will **save you time**, money and effort.

Hand in hand Many jobs are accomplished more easily if there are two pairs of hands. Tree-felling, in particular, is one which should never be tackled alone.

Calculating quantities

Detailed plans will enable you to calculate precisely the amount of materials you will need and help you to monitor costs. Draw up a list for each part of the garden to be redesigned and itemise the materials required for each stage of work. This will give you a good overall sense of the project, help to determine the order of work and be useful when it comes to requesting cost estimates.

Delivery and storage

Delivery charges for bulky materials such as sand and gravel can often be high so, if you have space to store them, organising for all the materials to be delivered at one time will save money. Check that there is room for a large lorry to access your property and unload the pallets or sacks of materials. Redesign projects are often restricted by limited access and room to manoeuvre.

New from old

When designing a new garden, don't forget about the old material you will be removing. The easiest way of dealing with it is to recycle it in the new plan. Most things can

⏱ 30-MINUTE TASKS

► Before starting work on implementing your new design, check that all your equipment is in good working order.

► Lay out and connect an adequate length of garden hose and place some buckets in readiness – these will be handy for jobs such as watering in plants or mixing cement.

► Spread tarpaulin on the ground ready to store sand or excavated soil and to protect the ground.

THE RIGHT TIME FOR GARDEN REDESIGN PROJECTS

JOBS TO DO	WHEN TO DO THEM
Concreting, wall-building	Frost-free weather
Sowing lawn seed or meadow grass	March–May or September–October
Digging; paving	Frost-free weather
Planting trees and shrubs with a rootball or grown and sold in containers	Frost-free conditions, ideally in spring or autumn, but not in mid-summer or when follow-up watering cannot be guaranteed.
Planting bare-rooted trees and shrubs	Mid-October–December and February–April, while the plants are dormant, as long as the soil is not frozen.
Painting; varnishing	Dry weather; over 12°C outdoor temperature
Laying pond liner	Dry, warm weather
Dividing herbaceous perennials; moving plants	Best done in early spring to stimulate growth, or for spring-flowering species, after flowering.
Planting bulbs	Mostly in late summer or autumn.

A GARDEN REDESIGN

STAGE	MATERIALS
1 Preparing the green roof	Insulating fleece, roof foil, roof underlay, roof plants.
2 Renovating the steps	Concrete, steps, balustrade, lighting and cabling.
3 Removing the lawn	None, but disposal of excavated turf required.
4 Building the path	Gravel, chippings, edging and paving stones.
5 Planting shrub beds	Compost, soil-conditioner, plants, mulch.
6 Planting trees	Supporting stakes, ties, trees.
7 Planting and tying up climbing plants	Trellis or garden frames, stakes or posts, plants, ties or garden twine.

Garden transformation Before and after photographs show how a garden was successfully redesigned (see table, left), incorporating existing buildings into the plan with the addition of a 'green' roof.

be re-used with a little imagination, from earth excavated while digging a pond to the trunk of a tree that has been cut down or old slabs and stones.

Surplus soil that has been excavated can be used to create a mound, level hollows or fill raised beds. Hardwood tree trunks make useful retaining edges for borders, slopes and raised beds. Branches can be stacked up to form a screen, used as supports for perennials, chopped up for kindling or firewood or chipped to use as a mulch. Old paving slabs can be integrated with new ones to make fresh patterns or even used to build a dry-stone wall or edge borders. Gravel and small pebbles can provide useful drainage for dry-stone walls, a rockery or raised bed. You can recycle almost anything in a garden unless it

contains some contaminating material, in which case it should be disposed of safely.

Dividing the work into stages

Plan your work efficiently so that stages run in a logical order. If soil excavated from one area is going to be used to fill a raised bed, for example, prepare the site for the raised bed before you dig out the first area, so that the soil can be moved straight to its new position.

The weather is another important factor and one which will affect some projects, as not all jobs can be carried out in all weathers. For some building and excavation work, if you do not carry it out at the right time you may miss the correct time for planting and end up losing an entire year.

Asking for help

Some jobs require help. Good planning and organisation are key in making efficient use of paid help or keeping your team of volunteers happy. Make sure you have enough tools and equipment to keep

volunteers busy and ensure that all materials are delivered in time for each stage of the work to start.

Call in a specialist firm for projects requiring a high degree of expert knowledge and experience, particularly if heavy machinery is required. Get estimates and book a time for the work well in advance so that you are not held up waiting for the professional to become available or have to use your second or third choice of contractor because only they are free.

Providing a good support network in your garden

A well-planned **infrastructure**, including paths, boundaries, electricity and water supply, will help to make **caring** for your garden as **straightforward as possible**.

⏱ **30-MINUTE TASKS**

► Walk along all the paths in the garden, noting their course.

► Think about the various lighting and power sources you may need and plan your electricity supply accordingly.

► Plan all water outlets and coordinate them with the domestic supply.

Enclosing your garden securely

The infrastructure of a garden includes the way its boundaries are marked out and the garden is enclosed. Ideally, the enclosure of your garden should be planned at the same time as any paths and paved areas. There are various ways to mark the boundaries, and you should be clear about what you want to achieve. Is the boundary primarily to keep unwanted guests out or pets in? Do you want it to provide privacy or act as a windbreak or noise barrier? Do you intend it to be permanent or temporary? Should it be plant-based? And, finally, how much maintenance are you prepared to give it? Look at how much space is available around the perimeter of your property. A fence might occupy a depth of just 30cm, while a trimmed hedge could take up a metre and a natural, untrimmed one as much as 2.5 metres.

Whatever type of boundary you choose, you will need access through it, so think about the size, form and security of gates: the best fence is only as secure as its weakest point – normally the gate. The size of a gate is crucial. To accommodate regular deliveries of materials and large goods, for example, a gate should be at least 2.5 metres wide, but for occasional access some fencing panel systems allow a whole panel to be removed and then

The busy patio Often the most well used part of the garden, this area will benefit from both water and electricity supplies.

replaced. For day-to-day pedestrian access a gate should be at least 900mm wide.

A practical front garden

Front garden design is generally dictated by practical considerations. You may need a garden gate, paths to the front door, areas of level hardstanding for off-road parking and dustbin storage areas.

Depending on circumstances, you may need to install a ramp for a pram, bicycles, or for moving dustbins or garden equipment. The ideal angle of slope for wheelchairs is 1 in 12, but this is not always feasible, and a gradient of 1 in 6 will be adequate for occasional use. Steps should be well lit and fitted with a sturdy hand-rail.

Around the house

The house, from which all entrances, exits and paths in and out of the garden radiate, is the hub of the garden. It is also the source of the electricity and water supply and may provide storage facilities for garden maintenance equipment. Lights, power points and taps can easily be installed on any accessible part of the house wall or the supply can be routed to a paved area or convenient bend in the path.

Ideally, any electricity cable or water pipes taken into the garden

PRACTICAL GARDEN INSTALLATIONS

FEATURE	LOCATION IN GARDEN	INSTALLATION
Work area with table	Close to the house or garden shed.	Water and electricity supply (pages 42–43), shelf, wall hooks for tools.
Lighting features	House or garage wall, paths, steps, patio, paved areas, garden shed.	Think about type of lighting, height of light fixtures and the possibility of an automatic control system.
Boundary fixtures, privacy screen and noise barrier	Garden perimeter, front garden and back.	Check building regulations and planning restrictions with regard to material and height.
Tool shed, greenhouse	Next to the house or vegetable garden.	Water and electricity supply, high enough to store long-handled tools.
Compost area	Hidden but accessible corner of vegetable garden.	Power point for shredder, space for compost bin and wheelbarrow.
Log store	Not too far from access door into the house.	Level, covered area, with adequate delivery access.
Play area	Site in view of house with adequate shade.	Storage facilities for toys, shelter from sun and rain.
Electricity supply	Outside walls, adjacent buildings, patio, workshop.	Strictly regulated; see page 43.
Water supply	Wherever water is most needed.	Water tap, hosepipe holder, possibly drainage.
Water cistern, water butt	Below rainwater drainpipe from house or other building roof.	Possible powerpoint for pump and hosepipe holder; include overflow diverter back into drains.

interest to a long path and also provide sites for features such as containers or seats, but you should avoid creating steps where you will be wheeling lawnmowers or wheelbarrows.

The materials used for the surfaces of paths and seating areas have a big influence on the overall look of a garden. By making use of appropriate materials, unsightly features such as manhole covers can be incorporated into paved areas (see page 248).

(see page 248)

ROOM ON THE PATIO

Just a few square metres of patio are needed to create a seating area adjacent to a house or on which to install a summer house. Remember to leave enough room for people to push back their chairs from the table.

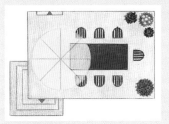

A patio adjacent to the house should have room for tables and chairs and a sun umbrella without blocking access into the garden.

itself should be buried underground at least 600mm deep: beneath or alongside a path is a good location, where damage from digging is unlikley. Use armoured cable or protect standard cable by running it through a protective conduit. Cable carried overhead must be fixed at least 3.5 metres above the ground.

All wiring work in the garden is governed by Part P of the Building Regulations. Notify your local Building Control Office before you start work and have the installation checked and certified by a certified electrician.

Practical paths and patios

For moving heavy garden equipment you will need suitable pathways that follow a logical route, without ruining the look of the garden. Small, paved areas, wider sections of pathway, changes in direction or flights of steps will add

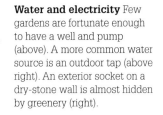

Water and electricity Few gardens are fortunate enough to have a well and pump (above). A more common water source is an outdoor tap (above right). An exterior socket on a dry-stone wall is almost hidden by greenery (right).

Planning paths and paved areas

Paths not only form a physical and visual link **between buildings** and the different parts of the garden, they also **divide the garden** into smaller segments. Paved areas are not just places for setting out tables and chairs, they also **offer visual contrast** with the cultivated areas.

Sculptural staircase Clean curving lines complement the informal clash of colours in the border (above).

A place to pause A circular patio, created using specially designed slabs where the path changes direction, makes an inviting space in which to linger for a while.

Designing paths

Paths are an important element of a design and do not always need to follow the shortest route. Winding paths tempt you to stroll along them and the point where two paths intersect can be an inviting place to stop and look at the plants.

Paths play their own role in giving a garden character and they should be planned carefully. The layout of paths and paved areas and the choice of material depends both on how much they are likely to be used and upon the visual effect desired.

Planning a path

The first task is to decide where you want to site features such as an arbour, an area for sitting or a summer house. Then think about

A solid base A path and any edging stones must be set on firm foundations to make them as maintenance free as possible over a long life.

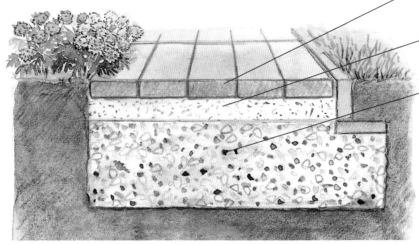

Paving slabs or paving stones are a neat option for the surface of paths and seating areas.

A level bed of sand or grit approximately 5cm deep should be laid to provide a smooth and level base.

A layer of hardcore generally 10–30cm deep (depending on usage and ground conditions) needs to be put down before the sand and compacted to make a firm base.

what sort of path you would like to lead you to it. A main path should be at least 1.2 metres wide and minor paths at least 60cm. The slope of a path and drainage should also be taken into account.

Any type of material can be used on level ground, but where there is an incline of over 6 per cent a solid surface is best. Decide whether you want a porous path (such as gravel) or a solid paved one, and whether or not it should have brick or other decorative edging. Will the path be straight or curved, and will you need to deal with a slope? A path could wind up a slope, or a straight path will need to incorporate steps or a ramp.

Quiet corners

Plan and lay paths and paved areas at the same time, and use materials that complement one another. Two or three different materials are all you need to create an interesting design – too many will give a fragmented effect. If your design involves different surfaces, make sure the transition occurs in a logical place, such as at a point where steps begin or the path widens or changes direction.

The size and shape of a paved area depends on its intended use. You do not need much space to put a garden seat, but a table with chairs will need enough room to allow the chairs to be pushed back. Adjacent planting beds must also be taken

into account: overhanging bushes can shrink the area, but aromatic plants, such as lavender, that will release their scent when brushed against, can be a delightful addition.

Steps and stairs

A quiet corner for relaxing or sitting can be positioned one or two steps higher or lower than surrounding planting areas. Decking provides an ideal base. Textured boards with a

non-slip finish, laid at right angles to the direction of the path, will not become slippery even in wet conditions. Giving some thought at the design stage also to the direction in which the decking will be swept will ultimately make it that much quicker and easier to keep clean.

Any steps needed to link different levels should be well lit and, depending on who will use them, fitted with a solid handrail.

30-MINUTE TASKS

► Sketch the proposed route of the path on a draft plan then mark out the path in the garden itself using two long lengths of hosepipe to represent its edges.

► Walk along the path on your own, pushing a wheelbarrow, and then beside another person, making any necessary adjustments to its width as you go. Remember to allow for the spread of trees and shrubs in the adjacent borders.

Suitable for wheels and rollers A ramp will be needed wherever wheelbarrows or lawnmowers need to negotiate a slope. Here, a slab of slate makes a broad stepping stone across a rill of water.

Water, electricity and light supply

A good garden design will incorporate the provision of **water and electricity** to all parts of the garden. Since the cables and most of the pipework will be sunk into the ground, you can **save time and money** by installing them as you lay paths and other paved areas.

Water in the garden

The main demand for water in the garden is for watering plants. It can also be used to clean equipment and garden furniture, to wash down garden paths and seating areas and to top up ponds.

Since drinking water is precious, and summer hosepipe bans are increasingly common, most gardens will benefit from the installation of a water butt to collect rainwater runoff from guttering from the house, shed or garage. The water collected is free of chlorine and the right temperature for watering plants. Heavy users of water in the garden might consider installing an underground tank to store rainwater, from where it can be pumped up to the surface.

One outside water tap in a garden is very useful, but in a large garden more than one is a real boon. Even if you intend to install an automatic sprinkler system, it will reduce the time taken to unwind and rewind long hosepipes.

If you want to be able to fill a watering can, a tap installed on an outside wall is convenient, while an outdoor sink is an additional bonus for washing pots, tools and muddy boots.

Automatic watering

A time-saving method of watering is to install an automatic sprinkler or drip irrigation system, but both can be wasteful of water. Automatic sprinklers are fed by pipes buried underground. Water pressure causes sprinkler heads to pop up from the lawn or bed when switched on. Drip irrigation systems deliver water to your plants through small nozzles attached to a network of small bore pipes held in place in the flowerbed by spikes stuck in the ground. Alternatively, seep hoses of plastic or rubber, with small perforations along their entire length, are laid on the surface of the soil. They allow water to sprinkle (if the holes are big enough) or trickle out.

Hose timers fitted between an outside tap and hosepipe can be programmed to switch the water on

Rain on tap Position water butts around the house and garden outbuildings to collect rainwater run-off from roofs and you can have a year-round supply of rain for the garden.

MAKE LIFE EASIER

■ Instead of using a spade to dig the trench in which cables or pipes are to be sunk, you can hire a mini excavator from a tool-hire specialist. If you are digging a trench in the lawn, however, cut out the sections of turf first and place them alongside the trench. They can then be re-laid later, once the trench has been filled in again, and you will hardly notice the join.

30-MINUTE TASKS

▶ Decide on suitable positions for low-voltage lights.

▶ Position solar-powered low-voltage lights around the garden. Provided each light has its own solar panel, it can be moved around as you wish.

and off. Most automatic irrigation systems can be controlled and programmed manually or electronically, or even remotely via the internet or telephone.

Power and light

Garden lighting provides security, highlights specimen plants or individual features and can create a welcoming ambience in the evening. The simplest way to add electrical light to the garden is to use self-contained solar-powered lights that can be pushed into the ground on spikes. They do not cast a bright light, but are sufficient to mark the edges of a path or highlight a feature plant and can also be fitted in containers. Remote garden sheds can be lit using simple lights powered by a solar panel fitted to the shed roof, or you could install battery-powered or rechargable lights.

Power points are needed to run electrical garden equipment, mains-powered light installations and other automatic systems. Plan the installation of cables for power points, water filters, pumps and lighting fixtures all at the same time so that you can route and install all the cables together.

Begin in the front garden and decide what lighting you need for the entrance, the paths leading up to the house, automatic gates and any other security features that are in the garden.

Next, plan your lighting for paths and steps around the house. When planning a patio, make provision for an adequate power supply if you need electricity for lights or to power a pump in a water feature. It would be better to install one power point too many rather than one too few.

A summer house will need power and lighting and ideally you should have a power supply on hand in all the main parts of the garden for any electrical equipment, avoiding the tedious and potentially dangerous task of having to run out extension cables.

Safe installations

Underground cable should be sunk at least 600mm deep in a gravel bed. Make the route of the trench as short as possible and keep it well clear of obstacles such as tree roots or rockeries. Following the route of a path is a good option.

A professional electrician may use MICC (mineral-insulated copper-clad) or armoured cable but installing these requires specialist tools. Instead, protect cable with a PVC conduit that will withstand accidental contact with a spade or other garden tool. The cable should also be wrapped in special insulating material so that it is easy to spot if it is accidentally exposed during digging. Always get any outdoor electrical installations checked by a certified electrician (see box, above).

PRACTICAL CHOICES FOR GARDEN LIGHTING

GARDEN LOCATION	SUITABLE FIXTURE AND HOW TO CONNECT IT
Entrance, front garden parking area	Light-sensitive dusk-to-dawn lights or PIR-activated security lights, directionally mounted above head height (mains supply).
Individual plants, garden features, water features, pond	Spotlights or underwater lights, low-level mounting, non-glare (low voltage).
Greenhouse	Supplementary lighting to boost growth (mains supply).
Main paths, steps	Post lights, sunken ground or step lighting, low-level spike lights, glare-free with central switch (mains supply).
House walls, pergola, patio, car port	Wall lamps with energy saving bulbs, glare-free, opaque glass, central switch (mains supply).
Side paths, pool surround, planted beds, stone features	Ornamental globe lights, rock lights, remote control or switched from the house (low voltage).
Pavilion, summer house, tool shed	Wall light, ceiling light, spotlight (mains supply) or solar-powered roof light.

Creating ambience A garden becomes a welcoming space, even at night, with some carefully thought out lighting.

Practical tips for storing garden tools

Buy good quality garden tools and take care with their **storage and maintenance** to protect your investment. Tools that work well **save time** and trouble – as does keeping your garden shed **well organised**.

Organise and save time

Wherever you keep your tools, make sure that they are well organised and stored safely. A jumble of tools in a garage or shed is impractical and potentially dangerous.

Different clamps, hooks and brackets for long handled tools, designed for fixing to walls, can be bought from garden centres or DIY stores. If you don't want to drill holes for each bracket, fix a batten of wood in a suitable place and screw the brackets and hooks to that. Or custom-make a wooden storage units (below) from which to hang tools – with sharp points and cutting edges pointing upwards. If you have space in a corner, you can build a tool stand from ready-made lattice panelling (below right).

Mobile storage

Garden caddies with holders for long handled tools can be pulled along behind you, so everything you need is within easy reach. Different types of trolleys and carts are available to help you transport heavy or bulky items and folding wheelbarrows are useful and easily stored. Mobile storage must be stable, whether fully laden or not, and tools should be stacked safely while you are moving the caddy about. Some mobile tool racks can be pulled with just one hand. Others are strong enough to move bags of compost or tubs and containers. If you do not need many hand tools, these can be kept on the caddy too.

Smaller hand tools are best kept in a basket or a bucket. A mop bucket with a wringer compartment makes an ideal and accessible storage container for small items such as garden twine and wire. Keep an S-shaped hook (sometimes known as a meat hook) handy so that you can hang the bucket, if necessary, from a ladder, tree or

Portable, tidy and safe A garden cart will save you time going back and forth to the tool shed. Load it up with all the tools and materials you will need and simply roll it to where you will be working. Put tools back on the cart when you have finished with them to prevent losing them or causing accidents with tools left lying on the ground.

Safe storage Gardening equipment should always be stored as securely and neatly as possible. If you cannot find an adequate ready-made system and are ready to attempt a little DIY, build your own wall holder or tool rack.

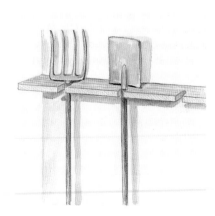

sill can be an obstacle when rolling equipment in and out, but installing low ramps will take care of this. The doors should open outwards and, if possible, should be lockable. Natural lighting is ideal but you may want to include a light and perhaps a powerpoint. A workbench is useful

ergonomically designed and are therefore much kinder to backs and joints.

It is worth taking time over choosing new tools and seeing how they feel in your hands before you buy them. Try them out by simulating the familiar sequence of movements and see how they affect your back and your hands. Feel the weight and try them for size – is the handle shaft long enough for you to use the tool comfortably and without stooping? Is the tool heavy, even without the addition of a spadeful of earth? You will find variations in weight and size as you work your way along the tool rack in the garden centre and it is important to choose the ones that suit you best.

garden fence. Belt holsters are practical for carrying secateurs or a garden knife (never keep bladed tools in a pocket), leaving your hands free for other tasks.

Built in a trice
Once the foundations have been laid, a prefabricated summer house can be erected in no time.

Neatly stored
The area beneath a projecting roof makes a practical place for storing garden tools.

Practical garden sheds
If there's not enough room in your garage for storing garden tools and equipment, the best solution is a garden shed. A wide range of ready-made sheds is available, from small patio storage cupboards to larger walk-in buildings.

The traditional image of the shed is one made from wood, but sheds made from plastic (PVC) and metal are also available, or you could opt for a sturdy brick-built store. The type you choose will depend not only on the number and size of your garden tools but also on how much space is available – and your budget. When making your decision, take into account the following requirements:

The shed door and interior should be high enough for you to be able to enter without banging your head. The walls should be solid enough to allow you to hang up long-handled tools. Ideally, there should also be room for shelving, the storage of large containers and any garden equipment such as a lawn mower, strimmer or shredder.

The door or doors should be wide enough for a lawnmower to pass through comfortably. The door

for small jobs such as cleaning or repairing garden tools in the dry. A water tap on the outside wall of a brick-built shed is also very useful.

Caring for your tools
If you value your tools, take good care of them. Tools will last a long time and you will find that after years of use, old garden tools will fit your hand like a glove, and working with them becomes a pleasure. Grips and handles are now

30-MINUTE TASKS

► Clean all garden tools before putting them away for winter.

► Before or after each use, rub all metal parts with an oily cloth, using a general purpose oil to keep them clean and sharp.

► Treat wooden handles once a year with linseed oil or beeswax, sanding down any splintered parts beforehand.

► Wipe blades of secateurs, knives and saws with surgical spirit after each use or, better still, between plants to prevent disease spreading.

Understanding the soil in your garden

If any of your favourite plants **look sickly,** they may be planted in unsuitable soil. A **soil analysis** may be able to diagnose the problem so that you can remedy it – or save you time and money by **choosing plants suited to the soil** in your garden.

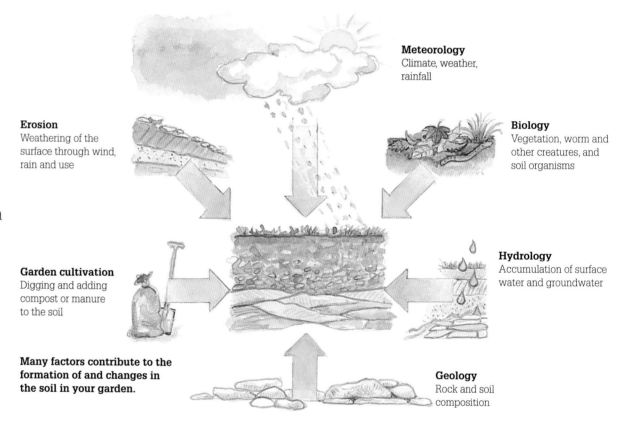

Meteorology
Climate, weather, rainfall

Erosion
Weathering of the surface through wind, rain and use

Biology
Vegetation, worm and other creatures, and soil organisms

Garden cultivation
Digging and adding compost or manure to the soil

Hydrology
Accumulation of surface water and groundwater

Many factors contribute to the formation of and changes in the soil in your garden.

Geology
Rock and soil composition

A dynamic system

Soil consists of weathered rock and decaying vegetation. Soil formation is the result of a combination of continued physical, chemical and biological processes, triggered by climate conditions and organisms living in the ground (see illustration above). As rocks are eroded by wind or rain or by being walked on, minerals are released, while plant and animal waste from micro-organisms in the soil are being broken down and absorbed at the same time. In turn, the soil exercises an influence on these organisms: its physical structure helps to determine what lives in it.

Garden topsoil consists of mineral and organic elements, such as limestone and decayed vegetation, as well as water and air. The ratio of these elements is what dictates the soil's characteristics. Other key factors include the shape, size and distribution of soil particles, the soil's porosity – the amount, size and distribution of air spaces – and the thickness of the different layers within the soil.

Understanding your soil's profile

Soil consists of several horizontal layers. The vertical arrangement of these layers – the soil profile – is important in differentiating between the various common types of garden soil. The key layers are the top cover (leaves, mulch), the topsoil (parent soil and humus-rich intermediate layer) and the subsoil. Large trees and deep-rooting shrubs will force their roots deep down into the subsoil, while smaller plants take root in the topsoil.

In some gardens, the original soil profile may have been altered totally, for example in the garden of a new-build house, where excavation and heavy machinery can turn the area into heavy clay. Removing and replacing soil can expose the subsoil or mix up the layers. The parent soil, with its living compost (humus) layer, may have been pushed aside or buried under the subsoil. All these situations can cause plants to wither for apparently no reason.

Advantages of soil analysis

Just looking at what grows naturally in any given location will tell you something about the condition of the soil. Dry, sunny slopes, for example, suit an entirely different kind of plant from damp, nutrient-rich hollows; plants that thrive in loose, friable soil differ from those better suited to heavy clay.

It is impossible to control a garden's climate, but you can do a great deal to influence the make-up of its topsoil. To do so, you need to know about the soil type. Kits to test the soil yourself are available from DIY stores and garden centres (see page 48). Or you could pay to have your soil analysed at a laboratory, which involves examining samples taken from the upper 30cm of soil from various places around the garden. This tells you all about the soil's physical and chemical composition as well as its pollutant content.

Light and heavy soils

Light soils drain freely because of their high sand content, and are consequently easy to cultivate. They warm up quickly in spring and are well aerated. Their disadvantage is that they do not hold water or nutrients well and quickly dry out.

Heavy soils have a high clay content. They are dense, poorly aerated, tend to hold water, form clumps and are difficult to work; they are also slow to warm up in spring. On the plus side, they retain water and nutrients well.

Most garden plants like conditions somewhere in between. Ideally, soil should be easy to dig, well aerated, able to retain moisture and fairly rich in nutrients. This can generally be achieved by working some sand and compost into the top 30cm, especially if the soil is heavy. Good soil preparation at the outset will save a lot of time and effort later. Once the soil is planted, roots and organisms living in the soil will keep it loose.

To prevent your precious topsoil washing away in the next heavy downpour, simulate a natural top layer with a covering of mulch. This will also protect the topsoil from severe changes in temperature.

A sign of good health Dandelions are an unwelcome sight on your lawn or in your flowerbeds, but they are a welcome indicator that the soil is rich in nutrients and has a high nitrogen content.

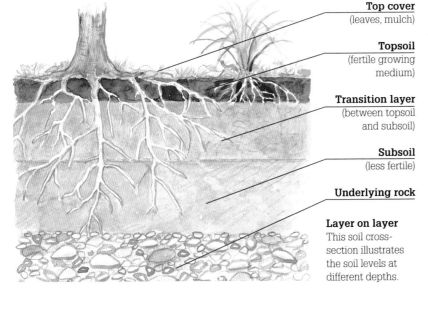

Top cover
(leaves, mulch)

Topsoil
(fertile growing medium)

Transition layer
(between topsoil and subsoil)

Subsoil
(less fertile)

Underlying rock

Layer on layer
This soil cross-section illustrates the soil levels at different depths.

SOIL ENVIRONMENT AND CONDITION

Soil can be differentiated according to the following factors:

Degree of moisture:
Dry, moderately dry, normal, damp, wet

Soil pH value:
Very acidic (3.5-4.5)
Acidic (4.5-5.5)
Slightly acidic (5.5-6.5)
Neutral (7)
Slightly alkaline (7.5)
Alkaline (7.5-8)
Strongly alkaline (8-8.5)

Soil type:
Sandy, peat, clay, chalk, silt

Analysing and improving your soil

It is not difficult to **improve poor garden soil** and it will **save you time** in the long run. Before you begin, be clear about your intended **planting scheme**.

Getting to know your garden's soil type

The composition of your topsoil is vital to the health of your plants. You can perform a rough and ready analysis by simply using a spade. Cut out wedges of earth, roughly 30cm deep, from several different places and look at them closely. A crumbly, sandy soil is normally light in colour, while friable, humus-rich soil is dark. If the soil is light-coloured and sticks to the spade, it is clay. Touching and smelling the soil give further clues: sandy soil with a low clay content crumbles between the fingers; humus-rich soil smells of mushrooms. The higher the clay content, the more malleable and sticky the soil is when wet. The ideal garden topsoil consists of one third sand, one third clay and one third humus (compost) so work in more of what your particular soil needs to improve the balance.

Improving the soil

If a soil is too heavy and full of weed, start by digging the ground thoroughly or turning it with a rotavator. Once the ground has been dug over roughly, any large stones and weeds can be removed. Then sand, compost or both can be added to improve and enrich the soil – concentrating particularly on areas where plants are to be grown. Spread the sand or compost over the surface and work it into the top layer by digging and hoeing. Once you have levelled off the surface, the ground is ready to be sown with seeds or planted. Very sandy soil can be made heavier by enriching it with bulky organic matter such as well-rotted horse manure. Very poor soils can be fertilised effectively by working in blood, fish and bone – at a rate of 50–100g per square metre – in addition to compost.

Humus – plants love it It is quick and easy to plant in soil that is friable and rich in humus, or organic material.

Soil as part of the environment

Most plants depend on very specific soil conditions to do well. Along with other physical factors, such as the porosity and humus content, the pH-value is important; this determines whether a soil is alkaline, neutral or acidic. If more nutrients are leached from the soil than are added to it, then the soil will be more acidic. Acid rain compounds the process and leads to a disruption in the important transportation of ions in the soil. This, in turn, causes a delay in the mineralisation process, locking up nutrients that plants need.

Easy analysis
A simple test produces clear evidence of soil type. Sprinkle a handful of garden soil into a glass filled with water and wait until the particles have settled. Sand will sink to the bottom, with clay settling above this. Humus floats to the surface. The individual soil types (from left to right) are: sandy clay soil, pure sand, and humus-rich soil.

THE RIGHT SOIL FOR THE RIGHT PLANT

PLANTING	NUTRIENT SUPPLEMENTS	ACTION
Sandy Soils		
Trees	Lots of compost (1:1)	Mix in the planting hole.
Specimen shrubs; vegetables	Compost (1:2)	Rake in or mulch.
Lawns	A little compost (1:4)	Rake in.
Natural garden; grass	Unnecessary	None
Shrubs	A little compost (1:3)	Rake in or mulch.
Dwarf trees or shrubs	A little compost (1:3)	Dig in, mulch or add to planting hole
Clay soils		
Trees	Small amount of compost (1:4 to 1:3)	Mix into planting hole.
Specimen shrubs; vegetables	A little sand (1:3) and some compost (1:3)	Rake or dig in.
Lawn	A little sand (1:3)	Dig in before laying or sowing.
Natural garden; grass	Lots of sand (1:1)	Rake or dig in.
Shrubs	A little sand (1:3)	Dig in or mulch.
Dwarf trees	Small amount of compost	Dig in or add to planting hole.
Humus-rich soils		
Trees	None	None
Specimen shrubs; vegetables	None	None
Lawn	Sand (1:1)	Rake in.
Natural garden; grass	Lots of sand (3:1)	Rake in.
Shrubs	A little sand (1:3)	Dig or rake in.
Dwarf trees	A little sand (1:3)	Dig or rake in, or add to planting hole.

The most common soil deficiencies are calcium and magnesium, and these can be spotted easily by characteristic leaf changes in many plants. Adding mineral supplements such as calcium (contained in mushroom compost, for example) or calcium-rich ground rock or even compost will soon replenish the soil. Working in lime also helps, though this will make the soil alkaline and unsuitable for heathers, azaleas and other acid-loving plants.

Giving plants what they need

Always read the information on the label detailing preferred position and requirements for moisture, alkaline or acid soil, and soil type. Although you can change your soil's composition to a degree, you can reduce your hard work by choosing plants that are suited to your garden's natural soil and situation.

A garden with fresh, neutral clay soil is ideal for growing a broad spectrum of plants. If you have poor or sandy soils, look for plants such as herbs, *Stachys* or broom (*Genista*), that will thrive in the conditions you have.

Easy steps to rich and nutritious compost

Making your own compost is immensely satisfying. Using it in your garden will **save you time and money** and benefit your **garden** and the environment.

Creating a compost area

Compost that is ready to use does not smell nasty and constitutes a valuable organic fertiliser for your garden. To make your own, you will need a sheltered spot in semi-shade with room enough for at least two containers. You will also need a reasonable amount of room in which to work, and a flat surface to stand a wheelbarrow and a rainwater butt. A good place to site a compost area is next to the garden shed and near vegetable beds, if you have them. If this is also where you

NITROGEN USERS AND PROVIDERS IN YOUR COMPOST

TYPE OF GARDEN WASTE	EFFECT ON COMPOST
Stoned fruit waste	Nitrogen provider, makes it dry.
Tree and hedge leaves	Nitrogen user, wet.
Nettles	Nitrogen provider, wet.
Chopped straw	Nitrogen user, makes it dry.
Potato leaves	Balanced.
Kitchen waste	Nitrogen provider, moist.
Grass clippings	Nitrogen provider, moist.
Sawdust, wood shavings, pulp, paper	Nitrogen user, dry, aerating.
Straw manure, pets' droppings	Nitrogen provider, moist.

Compost profile
A working compost heap comprises well-rotted compost in the bottom section, semi-rotted compost in the middle and fresh garden and kitchen waste on top.

store your fertilisers, collect rainwater and use your shredder, it is the perfect place for your compost-making activities.

The equipment you need depends largely on what kind of garden you have, what sort of material it accumulates, your compost requirements and which techniques you use to maintain the garden. If you use all your grass cuttings for mulch, for example, sweep all the leaves under the hedge and heap any chopped wood into piles, all you will need, even if you have a large garden, is a thermo-composter for kitchen waste.

If you plan to compost all your garden waste material and use a lot of matured compost, you will need to allocate a larger area in which to collect the material together and to accommodate more compost containers.

Balanced recipe Thin layers of coarse and fine, and wet and dry material should be alternated in a closed compost bin (left).

Chop finely before adding A garden shredder (right) is useful if you have lots of trees and shrubs to prune. Shred tough stalks and twiggy prunings to produce a useful mulch or to add to your compost.

Which container?

Compost bins are available as both open or closed containers. Open composters (often sold as self-assembly kits) are either made entirely of wood or have metal corner struts and slatted wood sides, or sides made of non-perishable recycled plastic.

You can construct your own open composter, either using bricks with holes in them or incorporating a gap under the base of the construction to allow air to reach the compost. Wire containers are particularly airy but do not retain the heat produced by the rotting compost. They are best suited to composting grass cuttings and leaves. Once the compost is well rotted, it can be reached simply by lifting the lightweight wire frame from the heap. Some form of opening at the base must be incorporated in all other containers in order for easy access to the mature compost.

Closed compost bins retain heat and moisture well. The composting process is fastest in insulated thermo-composters, ideal for composting kitchen waste and small amounts of organic material, though if the raw materials you put in are too wet, the contents may rot.

Closed compost bins tend to be unattractive, but you can screen them from view – or buy a good looking bin, such as one that looks like a beehive. If you plan to compost large quantities of leaves, grass cuttings and shredded twigs, you will need an additional couple of open compost containers.

Compost composition

The changes that occur as the humus layer of the soil rots down also take place in the compost heap. Organic materials are broken down by small organisms and are eventually absorbed by fungi and bacteria. For this, they need warmth, air and moisture. The raw materials composted must also have the correct balance of carbon and nitrogen (approximately 30:1) for the compost to rot down properly. Wet, green materials tend to provide nitrogen and dry, brown ones, carbon (see table, opposite). You can keep the composting process going in summer by watering the compost – but if it gets too wet or too tightly packed, it will be deprived of air.

A compost heap should stand on loose, well-drained soil to encourage earthworms to work their way into it. The bottom section can consist of a 20cm thick layer of coarse materials such as the hard stems of shrubs or coarsely shredded branches, followed by further 20cm layers of various organic materials. Try to alternate layers of nitrogen-rich and nitrogen-poor materials. Layers of dry and wet, and coarse and fine material should be alternated, too. It is best to restrict the kitchen waste you put on the compost heap to raw vegetable and fruit peelings and waste – cooked leftovers may attract mice and rats.

Mulching feeds the soil and keeps weeds at bay

Every gardener dreams of **weed-free beds,** light soil and an abundance of plants that need neither watering nor fertilising. **Mulching can,** to a large extent, turn these **dreams into reality.**

Effective ground cover

The only way to deal with perennial weeds is to prevent them from flourishing by using systemic weedkillers or a physical barrier, but both methods may also restrict the spread of your plants. Hoeing or pulling up perennial weeds can actually encourage growth as most can regenerate from even the tiniest root segment. They may be discouraged by using ground-cover plants that suppress the germination of weed seeds, or by applying a 5–10cm layer of weed-free organic mulch, such as leaf mould or processed bark.

These methods are not ideal in beds of perennials: physical barriers prevent perennials from spreading as they should, while bark mulch can be just as harmful to plants as the weeds themselves: if allowed to touch plant stems it can burn them, and it also locks up nitrogen in the soil. The best type of control for perennial weeds is to crowd them out with the plants you do want, as this will deprive the weeds of both space and light. Since many weeds thrive in heavy soil and lots of sun, a strategy of dense planting on friable soil is a good way to keep them at bay.

Spread stone Mulching with gravel, shingle or other stone chippings looks particularly effective in sparsely planted areas.

Bark chippings Pulverised pine bark contains chemicals that inhibit germination, making it an effective means of keeping weeds at bay. It is not tolerated by all garden plants and will eventually acidify the soil. It must not touch the stems of the plants as it may burn them.

WATCH OUT!

Never allow weeds to reach the seed-producing stage or they will end up taking over the furthest corners of the garden. One year's seed is seven years' weed.

Annual weeds complete their life cycle in one year, propagating by seed and then fading. They are fast growing and invasive, and like exposed soil in well-cultivated beds. They can be effectively suppressed by laying mulch to inhibit germination – the mulch can be either organic (lawn clippings or leaf mould, which will decompose) or inorganic (plastic sheeting or stone, which will not). Choose the

Garden tools for soil cultivation
Spade, garden fork, cultivator, draw hoe, Dutch hoe, rake and spring-tined rake (from left to right) – this array of garden tools is all you need to cultivate your garden successfully.

MULCHES FOR DIFFERENT SITUATIONS

PLANTING	MULCH MATERIAL	THICKNESS
Vegetables; herbs	Mulch sheets	a few mm
	Chopped straw, grass clippings	3–8 cm
Semi to full shade with woodland shrubs and trees	Wood chippings, bark mulch leaves	5–10 cm
	Leaf mould, mulch compost, grass clippings	10–20 cm
Mediterranean gravel beds; scented paths	Limestone gravel, shale, slate chippings	5–15 cm
Sun to semi-shade with shrubs, trees and fruit trees	Grass clippings, chopped straw, bark mulch	3–8 cm
	Leaf mould and mulch compost, manure	5–10 cm
Dry, sunny open areas with ornamental grasses, low and dwarf shrubs	Sand, gravel, stone chippings, chalk	5–15 cm
	Gravel, shale, slate chippings, small pebbles	5–10 cm

Wood mulch for feeding or weeding
Depending on the raw material and the way it has been shredded, mulch may vary in colour and structure. Coarse chippings are good as a mulch to deter weeds, but to feed your soil choose a finer grade, which will decompose faster.

right type of mulch for the plants in the bed: do not use leaf mould, which is rich in calcium, in a bed of acid loving plants.

In the absence of any open soil, many self-seeding varieties of plants will also be unable to spread. Choose a mulch that will allow the plants you want to seed and regenerate naturally. In areas of acidic soil, where birch and sorrel seeds proliferate, cultivate beds of alkaline, lime-loving plants beneath a thick mulch of limestone chippings that will provide an unappealing environment for the native weeds. An acidic mulch layer will have a similar effect on lime-loving weeds.

Mulching benefits the soil

Not only is mulching a good means of weed control, it also benefits the soil. It helps soil to retain moisture and reduces the amount of watering needed during summer. It also prevents bare earth from 'panning' or forming a hard surface in heavy rain. Mulched soil will remain light and friable even when heavy rain is

followed by hot weather, since water can only seep slowly through the protective layer and will not turn the soil into a solid mass. A layer of mulch – whether leaf mould, felt, gravel or wood shavings – also insulates against intense heat and cold, providing stable conditions that will benefit any plant. Using an organic material, such as leaf

Polythene or fabric sheet mulch
Mulch sheets are practical for vegetable beds. Cultivated plants are watered through the planting slits cut in the sheet.

mould, grass clippings, your own homemade compost or shop-bought bark compost, has the additional advantage of enriching the soil as it rots down, so removing – or at least reducing – the need to fertilise.

Ground-cover plants offer protection

The ideal form of low-maintenance soil protection is ground cover. Incorporate a dense covering of this type of plant into your planting scheme from the outset or sow seeds over all areas of bare soil. Bear in mind that ground-cover plants cannot be planted so closely together that the entire surface will be covered right away, so a thick layer of mulch will have to be applied between the young plants until they spread.

MAKE LIFE EASIER

☐ When planting a number of new shrubs, apply the mulch as you plant each one and not after you have finished the job. This will help to avoid accidentally treading on the new plants as you step back into the bed. Water each plant before you apply the mulch and you will lock the moisture in. You can see from the layer of mulch exactly where you have already planted and watered.

Work with local weather conditions

Knowing the climate in your region allows you to use **good design and clever planting schemes** to create a **pleasant micro-climate** in your garden all year round. This will benefit you – and your plants.

Sun and shade

The angle of the sun's rays alters dramatically over the course of the year and even throughout the course of the day, changing the shadow pattern cast by the house. When planning and designing a garden, it is important to take into account the position of any large objects and their shadows. This will save you the time and effort of relocating plants or garden features because their position is unsuitable.

If you have lived in your home for a while, you will already be familiar with the areas of sun and shade in the garden, and how they differ as the seasons change. If you are working on a new garden or have just moved house, it is harder to predict where the shadows will fall, but remember that shadows are longer in winter and spring, when the sun is lower in the sky than at the height of summer. Computer garden-planning software can help to predict shadow patterns through the year, alternatively, put stakes in the ground where you plan to plant large shrubs or trees and use them to help you to imagine the shadows that the future plants will cast.

Draw a plan of your garden, noting areas of full sun and shade. Shady areas may not be ideal for planting but they make excellent, sun-safe children's play areas, so site a sandpit or the swing there. If you can only use the garden at the end of the day, you will want to make

Natural paving as a source of warmth
Dark paving stones heat up in summer and will radiate heat until well into the evening.

Know your shadows At different times of the year, depending on the level of the sun, your house and other things in the garden will cast shadows of varying lengths. Take these into account when deciding what to plant where.

N

Shadow on February 20
At 3 pm, the length of the shadow cast by the house to the northeast is approximately three times the height of the house.

Shadow on May 20
By 7.15 am, the shadow to the west is around twice as long as the height of the house.

Shadow on June 20
At 6.30 pm, the length of the shadow to the southeast is around five times the height of the house.

SCREENING FOR SHELTER AND PRIVACY

MEASURE	SUITABLE PLANTS	MAINTENANCE
Foliage-covered wall	Ivy, climbing hydrangea, wild vine, climbing roses	Low. Root barrier may be necessary, needs winter protection from wet snow.
Planted dry wall (foliage-covered base of wall)	Trefoil, broom, *Spiraea*, speedwell thyme	Low. Gaps to be left in the base to allow for planting.
Planted dry wall (plants on top of the wall and in gaps)	Wall rue, houseleek, *Sedum*, dwarf bell-flower, basil thyme, ivy-leaved toadflax	Very low. Plant overhanging dwarf or small woody plants on top of the wall and small perennials in the gaps.
Foliage-covered fence	Clematis, trefoil, climbing roses	Low. Plant only slow-growing climbers.
Foliage-covered screen	Various types of bamboo	Low. Do not plant fast-growing species; may require root barrier.
Free-growing deciduous hedge (single row)	Cornus, hazel, hawthorn	Low. First cut required after approximately 10 years.
Free-growing deciduous hedge (2 to 3 rows deep)	As above, plus roses, willows	Low to moderate. Cut after about 10 years, or gradually prune back individual plants.
Summer deciduous hedge (trimmed)	Copper beech, hornbeam, *Berberis thunbergii*	Low to moderate. Trim once or twice a year.

Protective hedges Beech and privet hedges hardly lose any of their leaves even in winter and provide good all-year-round privacy and wind protection.

Garden thermometer The temperature at ground level can vary considerably from the forecast air temperature, which is measured at a height of 2 metres. Soil thermometers measure the temperature in the earth giving a more accurate gauge for planting.

the most of the evening sun, so avoid planting anything that is likely to cast a shadow over the areas where this is strongest.

Warmth and cold

The height of the sun in the sky not only determines the levels of light but also the temperatures in the garden. The higher the sun is, the more intense the heat. At ground level, this warmth can either be stored or reflected. Dark paving, for example, absorbs the heat and can become so hot in summer that you cannot walk on it barefoot. It also heats the area around it, creating a warmer micro-climate on the patio than in the surrounding garden. Pale, light-coloured wood and porous stone, on the other hand, scarcely heat up at all.

The stiller the air, the hotter we feel. And while some form of wind protection may be welcome in autumn and winter, in summer we may crave a breeze. When buying a sun umbrella or a gazebo, choose a fabric that breathes and does not trap the heat. Tree canopies allow air currents to pass through them, which is why it is always cooler sitting in the shade of a tree than under a parasol.

The best forms of shelter

Walls, screens and hedges can all provide effective protection against the wind. Solid barriers, such as walls and buildings, can create an uncomfortable wind tunnel effect when strong winds blow over the top. Screens and barriers that are not solid and which allow the wind to pass through – such as trellis or shrubs and hedges – offer protection from the wind without creating unpleasant currents.

A tall wind-break situated along a western boundary will also provide some shelter for the garden from any heavy downpours coming from this direction. A sunken seating area will be well protected, and if it is backed by a south-facing wall, this will retain the heat for the evening. If you enjoy sitting outside in the evening, a covered roof will help to prevent warm air from escaping, as will a patio awning extending from the house. During the day, this also provides shade, but remember that it will also make any adjoining rooms seem dark.

30-MINUTE TASKS

► Install a thermometer in your garden.

► Set up a weather station and rainwater measuring device.

Consider the climate when choosing plants

Becoming familiar with **your garden's individual climate** will enable you to decide which plants are best adapted to these conditions. This way you can encourage their **healthy development with minimum interference**.

Frost, shade and damp These factors must be taken into account when choosing plants for your garden. Only certain types of plant will thrive in frosty (top), shady (bottom left) or damp conditions (above).

Study the planting environment
The main environmental factors in a garden that effect the plants within it are exposure to light (whether the plant is sited in sun, semi-shade or full shade) and the soil conditions (dry, normal, damp or wet). Consider all a plant's growing requirements before you buy it if you want it to thrive. It is easier to choose suitable plants than to attempt to change the situation in your garden.

Remember that large trees and bushes also exert an influence on the climate and soil in their immediate environment. Mature trees not only cast shade, but are greedy feeders on the nutrients in your soil. Shallow-rooted trees, in particular, will also suck up a large proportion of the moisture in the ground and can deprive other nearby plants of essential water.

Garden climate
The composition of soil is determined by geological factors as well as by rainfall, and some soils naturally retain moisture better than others. Even if you don't mind regular watering, there is no point trying to create a damp garden in a naturally dry region.

Frost pockets are also common in some parts of the country and may be a problem in just a particular corner of your garden. If you are planting in an area prone to hard frosts, consider the frost tolerance of the plants you choose. The frost tolerance of trees increases with age, so saplings should be protected. Evergreens are less susceptible, but can dry out during periods of sunny weather in winter. This is because they are unable to draw water out of the frozen earth yet continue to lose moisture through their leaves.

The influence of trees
It is not only the size but also the shape of a tree and its leaves that influence a garden's climate. Slender trees cast narrower shadows than spreading ones, and it is darker under a dense canopy than under a light one. Moisture levels under trees vary considerably: light canopies, such as that of a birch tree, allow rain through close to the trunk, whereas rain only penetrates at the very edge of a dense canopy. Where the ground is moist, the root

Environments within the garden Different soil conditions and the amounts of sunshine, wind and rain will determine individual growing environments.

Exposed areas Sun to semi-shade, dry to moist soil

Rocky, stony sites Hot, sunny conditions, very dry and warm soil

system will develop close to the surface; under a dense canopy, the roots will penetrate deeper into the soil in search of water.

Some plants can also react adversely to too much rain, developing root rot, especially in autumn and winter. Others relish a site on boggy ground. Moisture-loving plants generally have broad, tender leaves, while shade-loving varieties tend to have dark green, glossy leaves of all shapes and sizes. Sun lovers often have narrow silvery or hairy leaves. Plants that dislike wind grow low in height; light-hungry varieties strain upwards towards the sunlight. If sited inappropriately, many plants will adopt an uncharacteristic growth pattern, perhaps growing leggy due to lack of light, or suffering scorch in strong winds.

The root system is similarly determined by the prevailing soil conditions: in poor, dry soils, plants produce a dense fibrous root system, far more extensive than their growth above ground. Some plants put down a single deep tap root, thereby outmanoeuvring any rivals for the water supply.

Around trees Moist soil in the shade, dry soil in the sun

Prairie or ornamental grass garden Base of wall, sun to dappled sunlight, dry chalky soil

Try to mirror nature

Look around at wild plants that grow well nearby and try to mimic their characteristics when choosing plants for your garden. Doing this will help you to find species and varieties that will grow happily side-by-side and will thrive with little intervention from you.

This is particularly important beneath trees and hedges, where any large root system automatically results in plants competing for scarce water and nutrient requirements. Allow autumn leaves and dead wood to be left where they fall. This will supply the upper soil layers with extra nutrients, while the warmth given off by the decomposing leaves and wood will provide a winter habitat to numerous creatures, which are useful in controlling garden pests.

Heather garden Full to half-sun, sandy, acid rather than alkaline soil, nutrient poor

Bog garden Sun to semi-shade, damp or wet soil

Beneath deciduous trees Sunny in winter, shady in summer, humus-rich soil, cool

Beneath conifers Shady to dark, dry, acidic soil

Devise your own garden calendar

Early spring can be as warm as summer while June can be quite chilly. **Studying the natural changes that occur in specific plants** over a period of time will allow you to create what is known as a **phenological calendar** directly related to the seasons and growth cycles that affect your garden.

A reliable weather forecaster

The astronomical calendar only recognises four seasons. But the cycle of nature's seasons is not determined solely by the sun's height in the sky, the length of the days and major weather systems. It is also influenced by local temperatures, humidity and other variable factors.

Plants respond to variations in local climate conditions, making native trees and shrubs reliable indicators of the changing seasons. Yellow forsythia and pink apple blossom signal the arrival of spring; and oak leaves change colour in autumn, for example. By taking note of the average conditions across the different seasons over a period or years, it is possible to produce localised weather and 'season' maps for different regions. Through these maps, you can discover a great deal about your own regional climate and use this knowledge to your advantage in your garden.

Defining the seasons

Phenology, the study of seasonal natural phenomena, divides the year into 10 seasons. These are a more accurate reflection of the cyclical evolution patterns in nature than the traditional four calendar seasons. Biologists and meteorologists have selected a range of reasonably common plant species to study, the specific growth stages of which clearly signal the development of vegetation over the course of a year.

By the light of the moon
Many gardeners believe that certain tasks will be better rewarded if carried out during specific phases of the moon.

The changing seasons can likewise be tracked by observing the habits of wildlife. Seasonal occurrences – including the return or departure of migrating birds, the breeding season of birds, the pupation of butterfly larvae or the emergence of butterflies from the chrysalis stage, the moulting season of birds, their autumn migration to traditional over-wintering areas and the arrival of winter migrants – can all be used as reliable markers of nature's cycle.

If you take careful note of these seasonal shifts, you will soon see the natural pattern of the seasons emerging. This will help you to avoid time-consuming mistakes when it comes to sowing, planting and over-wintering your plants.

The power of the moon?

Some gardeners are convinced that the best time to sow, plant and harvest in their garden are determined by the cycles of the moon. But there is no scientific proof that the moon affects plant growth. Scientists believe that its light, even when full, is too dim and its magnetic forces are too weak to have any perceptible influence.

The phenological seasonal calendar
This diagram illustrates the differences between phenological and astronomical seasons. The start of each season is signalled by certain indicator plants in the garden.

10 Winter
Late varieties of apple (*Malus*): leaf fall

9 Late autumn
Oak trees (*Quercus*) and horse chestnuts (*Aesculus hippocastanum*): leaves begin to turn colour

8 Mid-autumn
Horse chestnuts (*Aesculus hippocastanum*): first conkers

7 Early autumn
Common elder (*Sambucus nigra*): first ripe berries

6 Late summer
Rowan (*Sorbus*) and early varieties of apple (*Malus*): first ripe berries

5 Mid-summer
Lime trees (*Citrus aurantiifolia*): start of flowering

4 Early summer
Common elder (*Sambucus nigra*) and grasses (*Robinia*): start of flowering

3 Spring
Apple trees (*Malus*) and lilac (*Syringa*): start of flowering

2 Early spring
Forsythia and pussy willow (*Salix caprea*): start of flowering

1 Pre-spring
Snowdrops (*Galanthus*) and hazel (*Corylus avellana*): start of flowering

WINTER SPRING SUMMER AUTUMN

December January February March April May June July August September October November

59

Jobs for spring

Once **spring** arrives, it is time to get to work. Careful **forethought now** will save time and effort later – and pave the way to a **successful gardening year.**

Trees and shrubs

MARCH

- Prune roses when dormant, just before new buds break, but not if frosty. In colder areas, remove any winter protection first.
- Plant out new bare-rooted trees and container plants, such as pot-grown climbers, unless the soil is frozen.
- Thin out late summer flowering shrubs, remove any frost-damaged, diseased or rubbing stems.
- Prune vigorous growing shrubs, such as willows and dogwoods.
- Give hedges a final trim before bird-nesting season starts.

APRIL

- Cut back early and winter-flowering shrubs after flowering.
- Prune dwarf and small varieties of trees and shrubs (heathers, lavender, buddleja).
- Take soft-wood cuttings and pot them up.
- Tie up new shoots of climbing plants.

MAY

- Give new plants a good watering and lay mulch.
- Remove any newly sprouted suckers (such as *Rhus*) or runners (such as dogwood).
- Non-hardy, container-grown trees can be moved outdoors once the danger of frost has passed.

Flowering plants

MARCH

- Prepare ground for planting perennials: dig in any layers of mulch, loosen and manure the soil.
- Plant hardy, early-flowering shrubs.
- Sow early-flowering biennials and hardy annuals.
- Divide or transplant early-flowering perennials, such as clumps of snowdrops (unusually, this should be done while bulbs are in flower), as well as May-flowering shrubs.
- Sow summer and half-hardy annuals on a windowsill or in a frost-free greenhouse.

APRIL

- Deadhead flowers from spring-flowering bulbs.
- Plant late-flowering shrubs.
- Plant out hardy annuals.
- Divide any perennials which have become ungainly or are reluctant to bloom.
- Bring on dahlias in pots (split any excessively large tubers).
- Sow hardy summer annuals straight into the ground.

MAY

- Plant out chrysanthemums and dahlias.
- Plant out early annuals grown from seed or bought as finished plant, but only after risk of frost has gone.
- Sow perennial seeds, finish outdoor sowings of annuals.
- Stake tall-growing plants, as necessary.
- Remove dead blooms of flowering bulbs.
- Pull up weeds and mulch beds.

Lawns

MARCH

- The lawn's first cut is now due, certainly by the time the grass is 7–8 cm in height.
- Repair waterlogged or bare patches in the lawn.
- Trim the edges of the lawn.
- If making new beds, remove sections of turf and use to repair any damaged areas or to make compost.

APRIL

- Aerate the lawn with a rotary spiked roller and feed.
- Prepare seedbed for new lawns and sow seed during warm weather, keeping moist afterwards.
- Remove thatch and mossy patches from lawn, fill with sand, re-sow with good quality grass seed. Sprinkle with lawn sand to prevent moss build-up.
- Give the lawn its second cut. Use the grass cuttings for mulching around newly planted shrubs or vegetables, providing they are free of weed seeds, or compost.

MAY

- Mow the lawn on a weekly to fortnightly basis; feed as necessary.
- Pull out thistles and other weeds by hand.
- Repair damaged areas and re-sow.
- Delay mowing grassy areas planted with bulbs until the foliage has died back.

Ponds and water features

- Check equipment, such as pumps or pool lighting, for frost damage; service, repair or replace if necessary.
- Check edges of pool lining for frost damage; repair or replace if necessary.
- Remove leaves or floating debris with a net.
- Clean decking and wooden walkways, check for frost damage and tighten up screws.

- If required, varnish any wooden areas during dry conditions.
- Pull up early weeds from around the margins of the pond.
- If the water temperature has reached 5.5°C, begin feeding fish small amounts of food.
- Begin planting new pond plants or marginals.
- Remove weeds from around the perimeter and spread a fresh layer of mulch.

- Divide water lilies.
- Split any overly vigorous plants around the water's edge and re-plant.
- Remove excess algae (blanket weed).
- Check that water features are in working order.
- Treat dry walkways and wooden decking with linseed oil.
- Clean pools and check filter equipment.
- Place miniature water features in position and plant surrounding areas.

Fruit and vegetables

- Spread manure around the base of fruit bushes and mulch around the base of trees.
- Treat fruit trees before they blossom with biological pesticides, such as Bordeaux mixture.
- Prune blackcurrant and gooseberry bushes hard.
- Prepare vegetable beds for sowing and planting.
- Sow hardy vegetables and herbs in early beds. Chit (sprout) seed potatoes indoors.

- Plant onion sets and seed potatoes.
- Sow kitchen herbs.
- Sow lettuce in rows and other types of salad either in rows or scattered, but give frost protection.
- Plant out lettuce and vegetable seedlings, but give frost protection.
- Prick out vegetable seedlings.
- Continue to protect delicate plants at night with a fleece covering.

- Tie up new shoots of trained fruit trees.
- Place a layer of straw mulch around strawberry plants.
- Prepare beds for cucumbers, courgettes, tomatoes and peppers.
- Sow beans and prepare supporting canes for runner beans.
- Plant early vegetable plants grown from seed outdoors once the danger of frost has passed.

Tubs and containers

- Organise tubs and containers for the new season.
- Clean existing tubs and containers.
- Organise drainage material and growing compost.
- Increase watering of container plants while they are still in their winter quarters.
- Check all container plants for pests.

- From the middle of the month, place container plants outdoors during the day and gradually harden off.
- Re-pot any plants which have become pot-bound into larger containers.
- Replace mulch layers on containers, such as grit on alpine trough.
- Feed fuchsias and pelargoniums and water well.
- Plant up new containers and keep in greenhouse till risk of frost has passed; delay planting until May if you do not have a greenhouse; pot up begonia tubers.

- Cut back shrubs once they have finished flowering.
- Remove flowering bulbs from containers and tubs and store.
- If required, line planting containers with a fresh, water-retaining liner and add compost and a slow-release fertiliser.
- Plant hanging baskets, tubs and window boxes with summer bedding.
- Remove dead flowers from evergreen topiary bushes and azaleas and prune after flowering.

Tools and installations

- Check your garden shed carefully (you might find wildlife such as bats or dormice still in hibernation, which should be left undisturbed).
- Check paths and paved areas for frost damage and repair where necessary.
- If you have not already done so, clean and service all garden equipment.
- Check your irrigation system if you have one.

- Check all children's play equipment, tighten screws and, if necessary, replace the sand in the sandpit.
- Bring garden furniture out of winter storage and give it a good clean. Oil hinges and wooden parts and tighten up screws.
- Turn over autumn compost. Half-rotted compost can be used for mulching; use well-rotted material for planting in tubs and beds, provided it contains no weed seeds.

- Arrange the terrace or patio, setting out garden furniture in seating and dining areas.
- Check sun umbrellas, gazebos and sun shades, clean and patch up any damage, if necessary.
- Clean the barbecue.
- Turn on your outdoor water supply.
- Buy stakes in readiness for fruit trees, runner beans, tomatoes and tall shrubs.

61

Jobs for summer

How much gardening you do **in summer** is up to you. A keen **fruit and vegetable** grower will have plenty to do in the garden. **Keep track** of how much time you spend gardening in any one season and decide which jobs you could drop **in future**.

Trees and shrubs

JUNE
- Snip off the dead heads of rhododendrons and azaleas after flowering.
- Cut back broom after flowering.
- Reduce long shoots of climbing plants.
- At the end of the month, trim topiary and hedges.
- Feed roses and deadhead regularly.
- Prune plum trees in June or July when growing strongly.

JULY
- Take semi-ripe cuttings from suitable plants.
- Remove dead blooms of hybrid tea and floribunda roses.
- Prune fruiting bushes after fruit has been harvested, tie up new shoots of espaliers. Prune espalier trees in mid-July.
- Trim box (*Buxus*) and thuja topiary features into shape.
- In dry weather, water trees generously around the root area and mulch the ground (such as with grass clippings).

AUGUST
- Re-trim cut hedges if necessary.
- Stop feeding roses or you will diminish their winter hardiness.
- Plant clematis and evergreens, watering them in well.
- Prune dead material from roses, with the exception of climbers.
- Water trees thoroughly during extended periods of drought.

Flowering plants

JUNE
- Plant the last of the annuals.
- Stake tall-growing varieties to prevent them being flattened by wind and rain.
- Pull out weeds and mulch the beds.
- Cut back early-flowering species, such as delphiniums, to a hand's height above soil level (they will flower again in late summer).

JULY
- Dig up spring-flowering bulbs and tubers and store in a dry place.
- Divide and transplant dwarf iris and other varieties of iris and cut back the foliage to about 15cm.
- Plant meadow saffron (*Colchicum autumnale*) and Madonna lilies (*Lilium candidum*) now.
- Fill gaps in the herbaceous border with clump-forming summer annuals.

AUGUST
- Cut back any seed-producing plants if you do not want them to self-seed (although some seed heads look attractive in winter, and they make good winter bird food).
- Begin planting autumn-flowering bulbs.
- Cut and dry flowers and grasses for dried flower arrangements.
- Check plants for mildew and cut off any affected parts. Do not throw these onto the compost heap; dispose of them in the dustbin or burn them.

Lawns

JUNE
- Mow the lawn when the grass is 7–8cm high.
- Check for any places where water collects and repair these and damaged patches by loosening the soil, filling in the areas with fresh soil and re-seeding.
- If you plan to mow a wild-flower meadow twice a year, carry out the first mow in mid-June.

JULY
- Aerate and feed the lawn.
- If creating a new lawn, prepare the seedbed.
- Do not cut the grass too short or it will scorch in sunny weather.
- Do not waste drinking water by sprinkling it onto a lawn – even dry brown grass regenerates once the wet weather returns.

AUGUST
- Sow grass seed for new lawn from mid-August to mid-September.
- Mow the lawn on a weekly basis but do not feed any more.
- Pull out any thistles or other weeds by hand, or use a selective weedkiller.
- Carry out the second mow of a wild-flower meadow towards the end of the month. Leave the cut grass to dry as hay for 2–3 days so that any spring-flowering grass or wildflower seeds have time to drop out.

Ponds and water features

- Remove any excessive growth of water plants, but keep a look out for any clinging pond creatures.

- Top up with fresh water if necessary and ensure an adequate oxygen supply.

- Test water features to check that they are in working order and top up reservoirs if necessary.

- Water bog gardens and remove weeds.

- Be economical and make efficient use of water when watering the garden.

- If your children's paddling pool is on the lawn, move it regularly so that the grass has an opportunity to regenerate.

- Remove algae and pond weed regularly from all garden water features.

- Put out a supply of water for thirsty birds and insects.

- Check the drain-aways of ponds, which rely on rainwater for replenishment. A heavy summer storm can result in it overflowing.

- Make any water features safe before going away on holiday – they still pose a danger to children and animals.

Fruit and vegetables

- Separate and plant up any strawberry runners.

- Thin out the developing fruit on fruit trees after the June drop.

- Fertilise vegetables as necessary and keep them watered, mulched and weed-free.

- Plant any vegetables pre-grown in the greenhouse outdoors.

- Tie up tomatoes and pinch out side shoots regularly.

- Harvest herbs and early potatoes.

- Harvest berries (such as blackcurrants, and gooseberries) and early fruit.

- Prune back raspberry shoots to the ground after the fruit has been picked.

- Tie up blackberry shoots.

- Add more mulch, if necessary, to vegetable beds.

- Refill the gaps, from which vegetables have been harvested, with sowings of carrots, radishes and winter vegetables.

- Plant onion seed and potatoes for Christmas.

- Pick fruit and vegetables for storage, freezing or preserving.

- Remove any dead, diseased or damaged branches of fruit trees.

- Cut back any branches of morello cherry, nectarine and peach trees, which have finished fruiting.

- Harvest herbs for drying, take cuttings, if desired, and plant in a propagator.

- Tie up any new espalier shoots.

Tubs and containers

- Finish off planting tubs and containers, feed with slow-release fertiliser and mulch, if desired.

- Check for pests and treat if necessary.

- Turn hanging baskets to ensure that plants grow at the same rate.

- Remove tulips that have finished flowering; carefully dig up the bulbs, remove excess soil and store them in a cool, dry place until autumn.

- Apply a liquid feed if the slow-release fertiliser in the soil appears to have been exhausted.

- Deadhead regularly to ensure repeat flowering.

- Water morning and evening, trying not to get the leaves wet.

- Trim shrubs and evergreens into shape.

- Cut back over-vigorous container plants.

- Take and pot up cuttings of fuchsias, pelargoniums and other hybrids.

- Stop applying fertiliser.

- Plant winter-flowering heathers and chrysanthemums in containers.

- Organise an automatic irrigation system or come to an arrangement with neighbours before going away on holiday.

Tools and installations

- Finish getting the terrace or patio ready and decorate with tubs and containers.

- Ensure there is shade for the children's play area.

- Clear out the greenhouse and disinfect it.

- Organise your supply of compost and manure.

- Sort out somewhere to put grass and hedge clippings and fruit tree prunings.

- Check garden lighting in preparation for outdoor evening entertaining.

- Start off a new compost heap for grass cuttings and debris leftover after fruit has been harvested.

- Check that irrigation systems are kept in good working order and continue to collect rain water on a regular basis.

- Organise jars and preserving sugar for making jams.

- Keep a stepladder handy for picking fruit, clean shelves and clear areas where fruit is to be stored.

- Buy freezer bags, empty the freezer before defrosting and cleaning it.

Jobs for autumn

Autumn gives us the **last warm days** of sunshine – time to **tidy up** the garden. Don't be too thorough. Think about the **animals**, which have to store up some winter fat and will need **a place to hibernate.**

	Trees and shrubs	Flowering plants	Lawns
SEPTEMBER	▪ Give hedges and topiary a final trim. ▪ Take semi-ripe cuttings of any plants you want to propagate. ▪ Cut back spent summer-fruiting raspberry canes. ▪ Fit fruit trees with grease bands, prune any damaged branches. ▪ Harvest late-season pears, apples and walnuts.	▪ Plant iris and spring-flowering bulbs. ▪ Sow hardy annuals such as larkspur, poppies and cornflowers. ▪ Feed dahlias, stake and tie up tall autumn-flowering plants. ▪ Plant out biennials, which have been growing on. ▪ Plants that have grown too big, can now be divided (and transplanted).	▪ Aerate, if necessary, and remove any moss. ▪ Re-sow damaged areas of lawn or repair with sections of turf. ▪ Cut wildflower meadows one last time using a scythe or mower. ▪ Loosen any water-logged or hard-packed areas in the lawn and sprinkle with sand. ▪ Neatly edge the borders of the lawn.
OCTOBER	▪ Plant new trees and climbing plants. ▪ Thin out or prune deciduous trees and climbing roses. ▪ Pile up autumn leaves and garden debris in a quiet corner for hedgehogs. ▪ Harvest plums and quince and the last of the late apples. ▪ Begin pruning harvested fruit trees (but not apples – this is done in winter when dormant). Clear the bed around the base of the tree and cover with half-rotted compost.	▪ Continue to dig up, divide and transplant any overly vigorous herbaceous plants and rooted runners. ▪ Final planting of bulbs. ▪ Dig up non-hardy bulbs and dry them off. ▪ Cut back dead or withered summer flowers close to the ground. Leave grasses and other sturdy plants that provide winter structure or seeds for birds. Some dead flowerheads look especially attractive when dusted with frost.	▪ Rake fallen leaves regularly from the lawn and pile up beneath the hedge. ▪ Mow only once every 2–3 weeks. ▪ Give the lawn its final cut of the year. ▪ Fallen leaves will be shredded as you mow – add them to the compost or use as mulch. ▪ Plant bulbs under trees in the lawn to naturalise – when left undisturbed, many bulbs increase.
NOVEMBER	▪ Stake young saplings, firm down loosened root balls well. ▪ Complete pruning of fruit trees (except apples and plums) before the first frost. ▪ Trim hedges and shrubs, if necessary, one last time after they lose their leaves or cut down to the ground. ▪ Plant new bare-rooted trees and shrubs now. Water thoroughly, make a well around the base of the plant to hold water and cover with a layer of mulch.	▪ Mulch flower beds with a layer of leaves. ▪ Prepare new beds by digging over the ground, working in compost and spreading a protective layer of leaves. ▪ Check any stored tubers or bulbs. ▪ Bind up any tender clumps of grasses to protect them from becoming too wet and rotting. ▪ Cut back dahlias after first frost has blackened them, then lift tubers and store in a frost-free place.	▪ Treat waterlogged areas with sand and use a garden fork to make drainage holes in compacted areas. ▪ Consider making a path along well trodden routes. ▪ Consider replacing damaged areas of lawn in heavily used areas with paving or else transform it into a gravelled area.

Ponds and water features

- Remove dead, soft plant material from the bog garden, but leave any attractive dry plant stems or grasses standing for winter interest.

- Remove algae from the water; fish out dead water lily leaves.

- Reduce the amount of food you are feeding the fish.

- Leave natural ponds alone, if possible, as this is the time when many insects, such as dragonfly larvae, are hatching.

- Fix a net over the pond to catch falling leaves or remove them from the water on a regular basis.

- Protect guttering from becoming choked with fallen leaves.

- If you have a pond, you can help to prevent it from freezing and algae build-up by standing thick bundles of long-stemmed straw in the pond.

- Stop feeding fish. Any food will end up rotting on the bottom of the pond, reducing oxygen levels.

- Remove any electrical equipment which could be damaged by frost, such as pumps, empty water pipes and turn off the supply.

- Store lifted non-hardy water plants in containers in a frost-free place.

- Lower all plants, including marginals, below the ice zone to protect their roots.

Fruit and vegetables

- Continue to harvest vegetables, store in a dry place.

- Bring any remaining tomatoes indoors to ripen; get rid of tomato plants.

- Blanch chicory. (Forcing young plants to produce plump leafy heads from roots kept in dark in winter months.)

- Split up any herbs that have grown too large, such as lovage, hyssop, chives and mint, and transplant.

- Cut the last of the herbs and hang up to dry.

- Dig compost or well-rotted manure into beds which have been harvested.

- Cut down the remains of runner beans and pea plants and remove.

- Dig up the last of the potatoes.

- Dig up beetroot and horseradish.

- Plant winter and spring lettuce plants.

- Sow lamb's lettuce and spinach.

- Tidy up the herb garden, loosen the soil and add compost. Mark position of non-hardy herbs and cover lightly with a light mulch.

- Plant garlic.

- Protect beets (such as Swiss chard and spinach beet) from frost with fleece or under cloches.

- Check fruit and vegetable stores for rotting items.

- Delay harvesting winter vegetables, such as sprouts and green cabbage, until after the first frost.

Tubs and containers

- Plant spring-flowering bulbs.

- Plant up window boxes with spring-flowering plants such as pansies, primulas and forget-me-nots, as well as small-leaved ivy.

- Dig up herbs and plant into pots.

- Take cuttings of fuchsias, and pelargoniums.

- Plant autumn-flowering plants, such as heathers and chrysanthemums, in tubs, along with grasses and ivy.

- Collect together any frost-sensitive container plants and stand them in a sheltered place and cover with fleece or place in a greenhouse.

- Plant up tubs and containers with dwarf conifers, ivy, heathers and other hardy dwarf shrubs.

- Clean empty pots and containers, dry and store in a frost-free place.

- Transplant hardy plants growing in containers out into beds. Container plants in plastic tubs can be dug into the ground in their pots.

- Bring any Mediterranean-type plants in tubs into the greenhouse.

- Pot up any frost-sensitive garden plants into tubs and stand in a sheltered place for the winter.

- Transfer outdoor herbs into pots and bring indoors so you can enjoy a continuous supply throughout the winter.

- Water hardy, evergreen container plants very sparingly, place against a house wall and protect from intense sunshine on frosty days.

Tools and installations

- Sharpen tools, check mower.

- Empty compost bin, using any well-rotted compost for herbaceous plants and vegetables. Half-rotted compost can be placed around the base of fruit trees and beneath fruit canes.

- Clear a spot for storing leaves, cut meadow grass and other compostable garden waste.

- Prepare the greenhouse for the winter.

- Organise material to use as winter protection, such as bubble wrap, fleece and straw.

- Have ready the necessary materials for tying up climbing plants and trees.

- Put a net over the pool to catch autumn leaves.

- Fit mesh over the guttering and drainpipes to stop them becoming choked with leaves.

- Clean and tidy up the tool-shed for the winter.

- Clean, repair and oil all garden tools.

- Clean garden furniture and store away safely for the winter.

- Clean out nesting boxes, first checking that they are not being used by hibernating animals, such as dormice. If not, fill with fresh straw, wood shavings or sheep's wool.

Jobs for winter

There is **little** for you to do in the garden during winter. Like the animals and plants, you can **use the time to rest.** Reflect on the **past year** in the garden and make **fresh plans** for the forthcoming season.

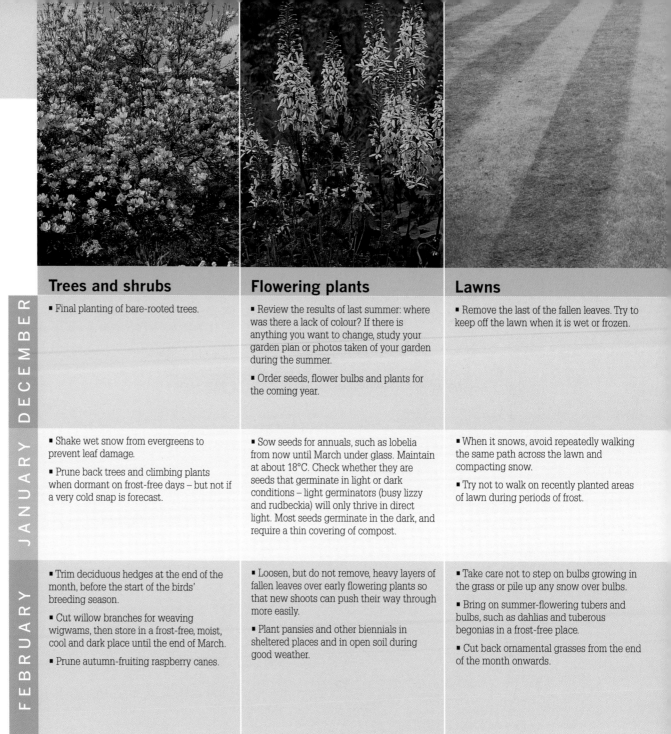

	Trees and shrubs	Flowering plants	Lawns
DECEMBER	▪ Final planting of bare-rooted trees.	▪ Review the results of last summer: where was there a lack of colour? If there is anything you want to change, study your garden plan or photos taken of your garden during the summer. ▪ Order seeds, flower bulbs and plants for the coming year.	▪ Remove the last of the fallen leaves. Try to keep off the lawn when it is wet or frozen.
JANUARY	▪ Shake wet snow from evergreens to prevent leaf damage. ▪ Prune back trees and climbing plants when dormant on frost-free days – but not if a very cold snap is forecast.	▪ Sow seeds for annuals, such as lobelia from now until March under glass. Maintain at about 18°C. Check whether they are seeds that germinate in light or dark conditions – light germinators (busy lizzy and rudbeckia) will only thrive in direct light. Most seeds germinate in the dark, and require a thin covering of compost.	▪ When it snows, avoid repeatedly walking the same path across the lawn and compacting snow. ▪ Try not to walk on recently planted areas of lawn during periods of frost.
FEBRUARY	▪ Trim deciduous hedges at the end of the month, before the start of the birds' breeding season. ▪ Cut willow branches for weaving wigwams, then store in a frost-free, moist, cool and dark place until the end of March. ▪ Prune autumn-fruiting raspberry canes.	▪ Loosen, but do not remove, heavy layers of fallen leaves over early flowering plants so that new shoots can push their way through more easily. ▪ Plant pansies and other biennials in sheltered places and in open soil during good weather.	▪ Take care not to step on bulbs growing in the grass or pile up any snow over bulbs. ▪ Bring on summer-flowering tubers and bulbs, such as dahlias and tuberous begonias in a frost-free place. ▪ Cut back ornamental grasses from the end of the month onwards.

Ponds and water features

- Ice forming over the pond traps gasses from decaying vegetation, which harm fish. Install a pond de-icer, or float a ball in water.

- If ice forms, place a pan of boiling water on the ice, keeping hold of the handle until the ice melts. Cover hole with a sack.

- Do not pour boiling water all over the ice as this will harm fish.

- Remove net coverings so that maximum light can reach the water.

- If pond freezes over, create an ice-free hole, as above.

- Try not to disturb pond water. Do not break any ice. It will cause shock waves that could harm any creatures over-wintering below.

- If pond freezes over, create an ice-free hole, as above.

Fruit and vegetables

- Prune apple trees; pruning of fruit bushes, such as gooseberries, red, white, and blackcurrants are pruned from Nov–March.

- Harvest winter vegetables and check on those you have stored.

- Pick Brussels sprouts.

- Grow herbs, such as cress and parsley, on the windowsill.

- Harvest winter cabbage, leeks and Jerusalem artichokes.

- Dig over new vegetable beds and leave the clods of earth to be broken up by frost.

- Over-winter vegetables and salad crops, (leeks, sprouts, green cabbage, rocket and endives) under a poly tunnel or horticultural fleece if necessary. Ventilate occasionally.

- Cover any beds to be used for early sowings with black mulch sheeting to warm up the soil and prevent weeds.

- Sow early carrots, cress and spinach outdoors under cloches.

- Sow tomatoes, cucumbers, courgettes and aubergines in seed compost and place on a windowsill or in a heated greenhouse to germinate.

Tubs and containers

- Group tubs and containers closely together outdoors, standing on blocks of wood so that they do not become frozen to the ground and pack well with protective material such as straw or horticultural fleece.

- Prune container-grown vines.

- Deadhead flowers from winter-flowering plants.

- Get tubs and containers ready for next season and plan spring planting.

Tools and installations

- If you have not already done so, have the mower serviced and secateurs and shears sharpened.

- Remove dirty sand from the sand-pit, keeping it to sprinkle onto icy paths.

- Repair fences and supports for espaliers.

- Clean and service the pond pump.

- Get estimates for any planned conversion work and order building materials for delivery in the spring.

- Ventilate greenhouses and glass propagators on sunny days.

- Clear paths and terraces of algae and moss.

Planting solutions for all situations

Low-maintenance plants, the correct tools and tried and tested gardening methods will all help you get your garden in top condition with minimum effort.

Make your garden reflect the house

Careful planning of all the **areas that adjoin** your house ensures that the outdoor and indoor **living spaces** complement each other. A good design will incorporate **visual appeal** with a layout that is **easy** to keep clear and tidy.

Introducing your home

The front garden is your link with the street; the bridge between the outside world and your house. As such it should be welcoming and an appropriate reflection of your home. It may also be a place to park bicycles and cars and store rubbish bins. At the design stage, you should balance the sometimes conflicting requirements of visual appeal and practical use. Choose a layout that is easy to keep tidy, saving you time and effort. Paths should be kept clear and should be solidly constructed. In planting schemes for front gardens, designs generally have low-growing plants in the foreground and taller varieties towards the rear, allowing easy access.

Paths and driveways

Paths leading from the front to the rear garden also need to be taken into account, along with driveways into the garage. Paved or blocked drives and paths are easy to keep neat and tidy and can be softened with colourfully planted tubs and containers, narrow flower beds or strategically positioned green plants.

View the house and garden as a whole

You can link the garden and the house effectively using climbing plants, which can rampage up the front of the house, or swathe ornamental pillars or pergolas. They can also cover a large expanse of bare wall or form the perfect camouflage for less appealing features.

Well planted borders, and paths and steps edged with brightly coloured, cushion-forming plants create an elegant harmony between house and garden. And don't forget that a distinctive tree in front of your house can provide an individual, decorative touch, as well as privacy and shade.

Finally, perhaps the quickest and easiest route to creating a positive impact at the front of the house is to plant up tubs of bright flowers. Placed on either side of the door, they give visitors a friendly welcome.

Welcome home Bushy climbers frame a door, flanked by tubs full of flowering plants. The overall effect is a charming and welcoming entrance for visitors.

Eye-catching features
A riot of flowering shrubs, combined with colourful autumn foliage and ornamental fruit, provide all-year-round interest.

Easy access
It is a good idea to make the main path up to the house about 1.5m wide so that two people can walk comfortably side by side or pass each other easily.

A perimeter hedge
A low hedge provides a clear definition to the boundary without cutting the garden off from its surroundings.

A distinctive tree
An attractively shaped tree supplies a natural link between the building and the garden area.

Flower-covered pergola
Use a climber with fragrant blooms to provide a canopy over a delightful seating area.

Ornamental arch
An archway covered with flowering climbers makes a picturesque alternative to a garden gate.

An inviting wild garden
A wild patch of plants has an unkempt beauty as well as providing a haven for beneficial insects and other wildlife.

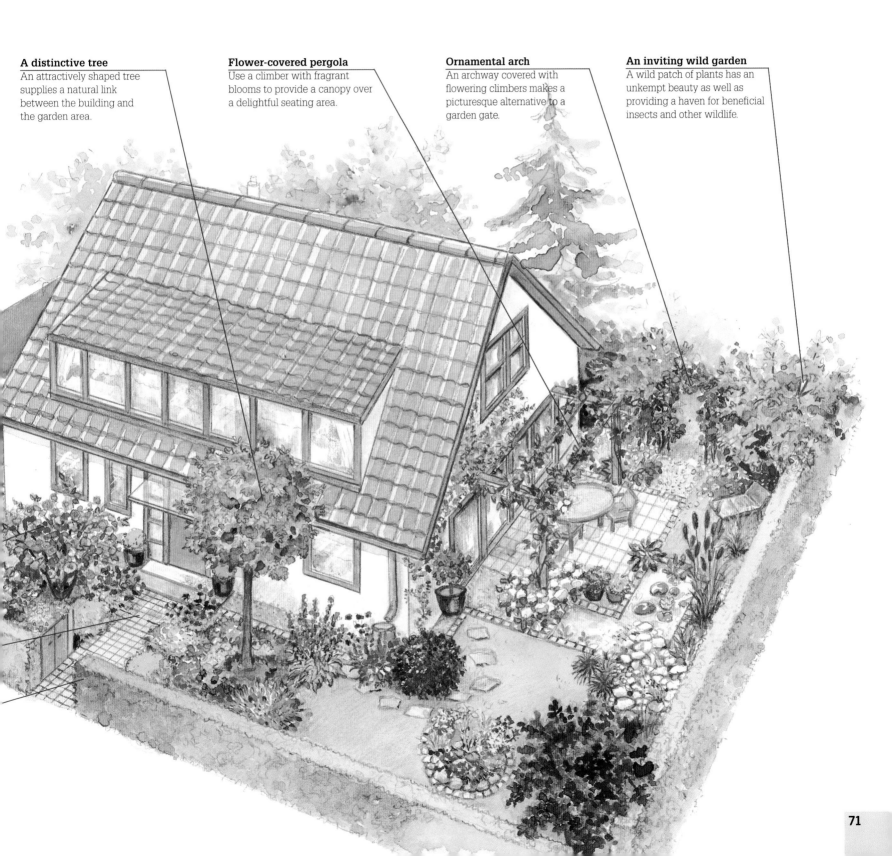

Creating an attractive entrance

The entrance area **should be a welcoming place** for visitors throughout the year. Plan the beds and borders so that they provide **eye-catching** interest whatever the season, yet are **easy to maintain**.

Curves and colour
Spheres of box provide year-round appeal .and interest, but are brightened by clumps of flowering ground cover plants, such as thyme, in the summer months.

Plan a year-round display

There are care-free plants for every season. All that is required to create year-round interest in the garden is a little planning. You don't need to rely on an endless succession of flowers; plants with striking foliage, such as heucheras and hostas, are just as attractive as any flower. Flowering shrubs, such as the ornamental cherries (*Prunus*) or serviceberries (*Amelanchier*), remain attractive all year, providing colourful spring blossom and a further splash of colour in the autumn when their leaves change colour. Trees and shrubs such as ornamental maple (*Acer*) or berberis also have spectacular autumn hues.

You can save time and effort by avoiding plants that die back quickly and have to be replaced. Instead choose species that have lasting value, such as lady's mantle (*Alchemilla*), which combines long-lasting attractive flowers with delightfully lush foliage.

Year-round border in spring Berberis and cotoneaster form the framework of this year-round border. Tulips and flowering cushion-forming plants add splashes of colour in spring.

Year-round border in autumn Later in the year, sedums, asters and grasses complement the cotoneaster's red and the burnished foliage of the berberis.

If your beds remain attractive with pretty foliage from spring until autumn, then all you need do in summer is fill in any gaps with some annuals. These are easy to grow and provide almost instant colour.

Think carefully about winter, too, and aim to bring in splashes of colour to enliven this cold, grey season. Plant glossy evergreens, such as box (*Buxus sempervirens*), mahonia and small conifers, and shrubs with colourful bark such as dogwood (*Cornus*).

Choosing your plants
Depending on the climate and location – sun or shade; dry or moist – first choose a framework of trees for your planting scheme. Next, select suitable companions, low-maintenance shrubs, grasses or ferns, or a variety of foliage plants in a range of colours. You can create a striking effect with tall ornamental grasses that give almost sculpture-like height when planted in a relatively low bed of ground-cover plants.

Decorative finishing touches
Complete your front garden by integrating elegant decorative features, such as tubs of roses, garden ornaments, shapely terracotta urns, pedestals, a sun dial or an ornamental watering can. Lighting features also provide an additional attraction.

Plants in tubs and containers can easily be changed according to the season, alternating between spring flowers, summer annuals, decorative fruit and Christmas arrangements.

Planting plan: a new flower bed The main feature here is the yucca palm, flanked by ornamental grasses and native shrubs. A strip of golden oregano threads its way between the different plants, leading the eye and tying the scheme together.

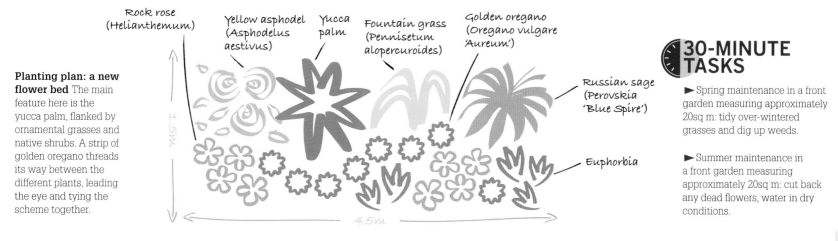

Rock rose (Helianthemum)

Yellow asphodel (Asphodelus aestivus)

Yucca palm

Fountain grass (Pennisetum alopercuroides)

Golden oregano (Oregano vulgare 'Aureum')

Russian sage (Perovskia 'Blue Spire')

Euphorbia

1.5m

4.5m

30-MINUTE TASKS

► Spring maintenance in a front garden measuring approximately 20sq m: tidy over-wintered grasses and dig up weeds.

► Summer maintenance in a front garden measuring approximately 20sq m: cut back any dead flowers, water in dry conditions.

73

An inviting front garden

Your front garden can be **open** to the street and still retain a **clear boundary**. An **enclosed** front garden provides a higher degree of **privacy**, but can seem smaller than it really is.

Make it colourful Brightly flowering shrubs dotted among the evergreens provide splashes of colour in this open-plan garden.

Two types of front garden

Your front garden may be open or enclosed – or even a combination of the two. Homes in quiet residential areas often have no boundary fences, creating an inviting appearance, while gardens in busy urban areas are likely to be surrounded by fences, hedges and walls to screen off busy roads, hide unpleasant views and form a barrier against dirt and noise.

If you have an open-plan garden, you can still define your private area by planting around the boundary or filling the entire front garden with a collection of densely growing plants, creating a carpet-like effect. Alternatively build raised beds that provide depth and interest as they rise in stages from the perimeter of the garden up towards the house itself.

Enclosed gardens can appear smaller than they actually are so it is important to use a planting scheme that creates a sense of space. Eye-catching ornamental features in the middle of a peaceful and simple basic planting scheme, such as a flowering shrub, a water feature or planted container, can help to distract attention from the limited space.

Seasonal chic A narrow border featuring easy-to-grow, short-lived varieties, such as violas and pansies, will add interest to your front garden and can change with the seasons.

Floral signposts Gate posts can be crowned with containers, spilling over with a colourful profusion of summer flowers.

Enclosing your garden with a low picket fence, a knee-high hedge or a border of scented shrubs will leave it open yet at the same time clearly defined. Passers-by will be able to see in, but access will be discouraged and you will still have an unrestricted view. A covered archway, a pair of pyramids made of box, two small standard trees or planted tubs on either side of the entrance will help to signpost the way in for visitors.

You should always check with your local planning authority before constructing or dismantling any walls and fences in your garden, as there are regulations governing their height and position (see page 103).

Trees and ground cover

If you feel that herbaceous perennials and summer annuals are simply too labour-intensive, you may wish to consider evergreens or deciduous trees as a useful low-maintenance alternative for the entrance area. Low-growing species, in particular, require virtually no maintenance. After planting they will flourish in almost any soil and need no watering, except in extended periods of drought. Go one step further and add ground-covering species such as cotoneaster and periwinkle (*Vinca*), for example, and you can almost leave the leafy entrance area to its own devices.

Colourful branches, colourful foliage

To create a strong planting scheme that provides year-round interest yet requires minimum maintenance, ideal candidates are conifers and deciduous trees, which are both very undemanding.

These can be combined with each other in a variety of ways. Low, ground-covering species of creeping juniper, for example, grown beside miniature varieties of cypress, such as 'Minima Glauca' or the almost spherical balsam fir (*Abies balsamea*) 'Nana', keep the area lively even during winter months. Interspersing these conifers with deciduous shrubs adds colourful accents when they bloom or fruit, as in the case of the Siberian pea tree (*Caragana arborescens*), weigela or firethorn (*Pyracantha*).

30-MINUTE TASKS

► Plant five shrubs in a front garden bed that has been prepared.

► Add seasonal plants to a low-maintenance tree or shrub bed.

Planting plan: an enclosed front garden The front gate opens straight onto a shady garden, which provides an inviting entrance area. A neatly trimmed box sphere or an elegant sculpture in the centre adds interest. The ample, wide path is flanked by blue and white perennials, whose colours will make the garden appear larger than it is.

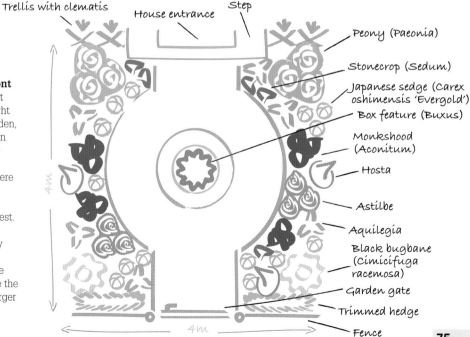

Trellis with clematis

House entrance

Step

Peony (Paeonia)

Stonecrop (Sedum)

Japanese sedge (Carex oshimensis 'Evergold')

Box feature (Buxus)

Monkshood (Aconitum)

Hosta

Astilbe

Aquilegia

Black bugbane (Cimicifuga racemosa)

Garden gate

Trimmed hedge

Fence

4m

4m

75

Add interest to a bare area at the base of the house walls

The **strip of ground** directly beneath the eaves and next to the house can be **transformed** into an **attractive** narrow border. The plants help to hide expanses of bare brickwork.

From mini to maxi
Dwarf succulents, such as houseleeks (*Sempervivum*), above, are ideal for planting in gravel as well as a variety of shrubs (main photo, far right) or even climbing plants (illustration, right).

Create a gravel bed within a gravel strip

At the base of some house walls there is a narrow strip of gravel, about 50cm wide. It is directly beneath the eaves of the roof and allows water to drain away even during long spells of persistent rain, diverting moisture away from the house walls. The same area is often dry and sheltered by being next to the house and beneath the overhang of the roof. For most plants, this is not an ideal location but a handful of survival experts thrive in such conditions. Use them to turn this narrow strip into an attractive gravel bed.

The gravel layer

A gravel strip normally consists of a top layer of coarse gravel covering a bed of hard-core and very likely some building debris too, all of which will allow water to drain through freely. The stones are not large enough to leave gaps in which fallen leaves or other debris can

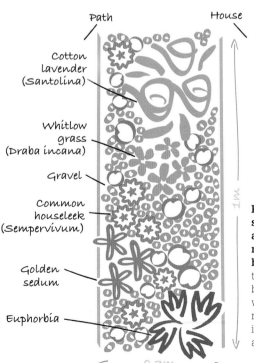

Path   House

Cotton lavender (Santolina)

Whitlow grass (Draba incana)

Gravel

Common houseleek (Sempervivum)

Golden sedum

Euphorbia

1m

0.3m

Planting suggestion: a decorative narrow border Widen this narrow border if you wish to by mirroring it or adding another row.

Flowers between the stones Many cushion-forming perennials, such as campanula or dianthus, more commonly seen in alpine gardens, cope very well with the sparse conditions beneath the eaves.

accumulate but they are heavy enough to allow dead leaves to be raked off the surface. You can either plant in the existing gravel or replace it with something more to your taste. A natural mixture of different sized pebbles can prove very attractive.

Suitable plants for the site

Choose specialist varieties that thrive in very dry conditions with a limited nutrient supply. Fortunately, there is a wealth of delightful perennials and grasses, even small dwarf trees, that can cope with and even thrive in such adverse conditions. Foremost among these are succulents, such as sedums or houseleeks (*Sempervivum*), which store up moisture in their thick leaves. Cushion-forming plants, such as rock alyssum (*Alyssum montanum*), stonecress (*Aethionema warleyense*), dianthus and varieties of spurge (such as *Euphorbia polychroma* and *E. myrsinites*) will also do well here. Plants that originated in dry climates such as the tough Mediterranean shrubs will also thrive, including rosemary (*Rosmarinus officinalis*), thyme (*Thymus*) or lavender (*Lavendula*). You can also try growing grasses and vivid summer flowers that flourish in full sun (such as species of *Dorotheanthus*) – all of which are extremely undemanding and easy to grow.

Planting in gravel

Prepare the ground by pushing the gravel to one side before digging large holes in the porous layer beneath in which to place the plants. Place each plant in a large pot, filled with soil, then bury the pots in the holes. Finish off by covering over the rim of the pot and topsoil with gravel. Give the plants a little water to start with but once the roots have become established no further watering will be necessary. The only maintenance required from then on is to pull up weeds from time to time and to cut back old growth in the spring.

Never allow soil, gravel or any other material to pile up against the wall above the level of the damp-proof course. It could form a bridge that would transmit moisture to the walls and could eventually lead to rising damp.

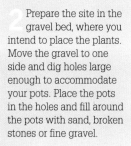

WATCH OUT!

Be careful not to over-water these plants. With their preference for dry conditions, too much moisture can cause them to rot and die.

PLANTING IN GRAVEL

1 Place each plant in a large clay pot filled with suitable soil (equal parts of compost, sand and loose gravel, or cactus compost).

2 Prepare the site in the gravel bed, where you intend to place the plants. Move the gravel to one side and dig holes large enough to accommodate your pots. Place the pots in the holes and fill around the pots with sand, broken stones or fine gravel.

3 Finally, cover the rim of the pots with gravel. The advantage of this method of planting is that by containing the growing medium within a compact area, it is easier to tend individual plants than if soil were spread throughout the gravel bed, encouraging the growth of weeds.

30-MINUTE TASKS

- Pot up five plants
- Dig five holes and sink the plants, complete with pots, into the gravel bed.

Make your house stand out with a distinctive tree

Not only does an **attractive tree** add a touch of distinction to your house but it is also a source of shade. It requires relatively **little upkeep** and, once it has reached maturity, it makes an **eye-catching feature**.

TIME-SAVING TIPS

☐ Choose a tree that grows naturally into a rounded shape. This will save you approximately five hours a year in pruning.

☐ A tree next to a garden seat provides natural shade, saving you the tedious business of moving sun umbrellas around.

Time for a tree Long-lived and easy to care for, trees are excellent value in the garden. Shade-loving plants will thrive in the cool shadows found beneath a small tree.

Choosing your tree

A garden tree does not need to be positioned directly by the front door, as though it is on guard. It can be sited elsewhere, serving both as a decorative feature and a welcome source of shade.

When it comes to choosing a suitable species, it is important to take into account the eventual size and shape as well as its appearance over the changing seasons. Deciduous trees are a popular choice for garden locations, with foliage that attractively changes colour with the seasons.

Some of the most stylish trees are those with a classic, clearly defined crown and trunk. Try the globe or mop-head robinia (*Robinia pseudoacacia* 'Umbraculifera'), globe Norway maple (*Acer platanoides* 'Globosum'), dwarf southern catalpa (*Catalpa bignonioides* 'Nana') or dwarf ash (*Fraxinus excelsior* 'Nana'). None of these trees grows much above 5m in height and all form a neat, rounded 'lollipop' of foliage without the need for pruning.

Attractive alternatives include tall trees with an upright habit, such as the ornamental cherry *Prunus serrulata* 'Amanogawa', which has the bonus of delightful blossom in spring. Small fruit trees can be equally appealing, especially half standard flowering cherries or crab apples (*Malus sylvestris*). Magnolias, with their showy flowers, or trees that bear spectacularly coloured

Restful glade A large tree with a spreading canopy is an ideal way to provide shady shelter above a seating area.

30-MINUTE TASK

▶ Dig a suitable hole to plant a tree.

▶ Plant the tree, secure it with a stake and water in well.

foliage in autumn, such as red-leaved maples, are other eye-catching options.

If you are lucky enough to own a sizable garden, you can afford to plant a large, majestic species of tree, such as a lime, a traditional favourite, or a fragrant birch. Always site large trees at an appropriate distance from the house to ensure that their roots have enough room to develop without interfering with the drains or foundations, and to prevent the foliage from making adjacent rooms too dark.

Right tree, right place

When selecting a tree from the nursery, make sure that you choose one that is healthy. Its trunk should not be damaged, its crown should be symmetrically rounded and its root ball round and firm. Where you site the tree depends both on the type of conditions it requires as well as structural considerations: underground cables and pipelines running too close to the root system, for example, can easily be damaged by roots as they spread. The tree should be planted far enough away from the house to accommodate its ultimate size. A good rule of thumb is to plant a tree at a distance equivalent to about half its predicted mature height (which should be

stated on the plant label). Dig a hole wide and deep enough to accommodate its roots comfortably and plant the tree at the same depth that it was planted at the nursery. Enrich the soil with well-rotted compost before filling in the hole.

The first few years of maintenance

Keep the area around the roots free of weeds after planting. A covering of bark chippings can help with this. Ideally, you should keep the ground weed-free for years to come, enriching it on a regular basis with mulch and compost, preferably in spring. During the first two years after planting, young trees also need regular watering. Adding compost in the spring does away with the need to add a mineral fertiliser. In any case, you need to be careful in this respect since mineral salts may have a corrosive effect on the tender roots of newly planted trees. Give the young tree support for at least the first 4–5 years until it has become firmly established. The trunk should be tied – not too tightly – to a solid post, which will support it during heavy rain and windy weather. Loosen the tie annually.

PLANTING A TREE

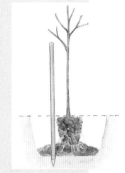
1 Dig a hole for planting. It should be at least twice as wide as the root ball and one-and-a-half times as deep. Place the tree in the hole and fix a support to one side of the root ball.

2 With the tree in position, fill in the hole with a mixture of compost and soil, pressing down firmly as you work. Water the tree slowly and thoroughly using at least 20 litres of water.

3 Tie the tree trunk to the stake, ensuring that the ties are firm, but not cutting into the trunk. Finally, cover the area around the base of the tree with a layer of bark mulch or other mulching material.

Keep the base clear The area around the foot of a young tree should be kept clear of weeds, plants and lawn, and covered with a layer of compost and mulch.

The easy charm of a rose-covered archway

An **archway covered** in roses is an entrancing feature for any house. It is not difficult to **train roses** to grow up a suitable support and to have them produce an impressive and **long-lasting** display of magnificent flowers.

30-MINUTE TASKS

► Erect an arch from a kit.

► Plant roses around the arch and tie in stems to the support.

► Prune established climbing roses on an existing arch.

Flowers beckon you through

A rose-covered archway enhances the entrance to any garden or pathway, inviting you to wander through to enjoy its delightful fragrance. It takes a few years to establish, but then requires little more than a yearly tidy. Arches suitable for training climbing plants are available in a wide variety of materials: wood, decorative wrought iron or plastic-coated steel. When making your choice, check that it is stable and strong enough to bear the weight of the climbing plants and make sure that it is set in solid concrete footings.

Climbing roses are often used to clothe arches, although clematis and honeysuckle are other trouble-free options. It is best to avoid vigorous climbers, such

Roses for arches There are a number of roses that will happily grow up an arch. Climbers such as 'Santana' are repeat-flowering, whereas ramblers tend to bloom only once, although often dramatically, in mid June.

as Japanese knotweed (*Fallopia japonica*), wisteria or pipevine (*Aristolochia elegans*), because they will require frequent pruning to keep them in check.

All climbing plants grow straight up towards the light – even after they have reached the top of the arch. The flowers form mainly in the upper sections of the plant, but with proper care and pruning, you can achieve an even distribution of flowers, and cover the lower parts of the support as well as the top with a marvellous display.

Train roses for maximum flowering

To ensure climbing roses give an abundant and evenly distributed display of flowers, they should only be allowed to grow in height slowly. It is the horizontal growth that produces the most buds. Bend new soft and springy side shoots in and around the arch framework before they mature and stiffen. Leave firm, upright shoots to flower in the gaps between the latticework of the arch. Tie the shoots in gently with twine or rose ties at the end of February or early March.

Climbers and ramblers

There are two different types of climbing rose: climbers and ramblers. Climbers have long, firm, upright shoots ending in large single flowers or clusters of flowers, and most flower from summer to autumn. Ramblers have long flexible shoots with clusters of small flowers and usually flower only once in early summer.

Prune climbers in late autumn to early spring, before growth resumes. In the first two years cut back only dead, diseased and damaged growth, unless they have grown vigorously. Do not cut back climbing bush roses within the first two years or they could revert back to bushes.

In the third year cut back main shoots so that they can be trained to fill any gaps and reduce side shoots to about 15cm or 3–4 buds, to a vigorous shoot, which should be tied to the support. In subsequent years cut back one or two older shoots to 30–40cm.

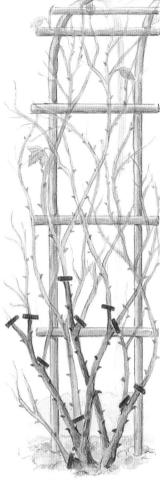

Pruning an old climbing rose
Old roses, which are producing flowers only on their uppermost stems and are bare at the base, can be coaxed back to health and vigour by cutting any weak growth right back to the base and pruning strong shoots hard. Take the opportunity to repaint or repair the arch if it needs it at the same time.

Fairytale entrance An archway bearing an abundance of roses in full bloom is a magical and enticing sight. Two vigorous roses planted either side of an arch will cover the framework within just a few years.

Prune ramblers in summer, after flowering. In the first two years train the main shoots onto a support, cutting back to about 40cm. Cut back side shoots by 7–8cm or to 2–4 buds, to a vigorous shoot; fan them out and tie them to the support. In subsequent years cut back side shoots as before and cut out one in three of the oldest main shoots at the base. This prevents the plant from becoming congested, which leaves the foliage vulnerable to fungal disease.

Renewal pruning for old climbing roses
Old or neglected climbing roses can be coaxed back to life with hard pruning (see illustration, top). Be careful with old and fragile specimens as hard pruning can sometimes stop growth completely. To avoid this, rejuvenate climbers in stages over two or three years, removing a third of the old stems each year. In the case of old ramblers, reduce to five or six young and vigorous shoots and reduce side shoots by two thirds. Prune the leading shoots to encourage growth lower down. Feed rejuvenated roses with a rose fertiliser and lay a mulch of compost around the base in spring.

Winter protection for roses
Although most roses grown in a temperate climate do not need winter protection, they can die in harsh winters if left exposed. If you live in an area where there are severe winters or bouts of prolonged frost, protect your roses by piling up earth or packing straw (loosely tied in place) around the base of the plant. It may also be necessary to loosely wrap the top of the plant in horticultural fleece. Remove any protection in spring, before the plant starts to grow again.

PLANTING A ROSE-COVERED ARCH

1 Soak bare-rooted or pot-grown climbing roses for 1–2 hours in a bucket or basin filled with water so that their roots can absorb a maximum amount of water.

2 Dig a planting hole at the base of the arch, large enough to accommodate the rose comfortably. Loosen the soil at the base of the hole.

3 Place the rose in the hole, tilting it slightly towards the arch so that all its shoots can reach the support.

Clever camouflage for unsightly garden essentials

Rubbish bins or drainpipes can spoil the **appearance** of your house. Fortunately there are plenty of vigorous and easy-to-grow plants that will **conceal anything unsightly** in next to no time.

Using a hedge as a screen

Recycling boxes and rubbish bins are often kept in the front garden near the entrance so that recyclable materials and rubbish can be disposed of efficiently. The bins and boxes themselves are generally far from attractive, so turn the area where they are kept into a

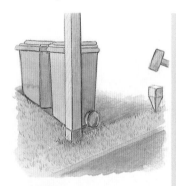

CREATING A SCREEN

1 Sections of trellis can easily be turned into a screen to camouflage rubbish bins. Drive metal post holders into the ground where the posts are going to be sited and secure the posts in place.

2 Screw the trellis to the posts. For a 1.8m post allow three screw fixings per post. Most trellis kits come with the screws and fittings provided.

3 Finally, dig holes alongside the posts for the plants that will cover the trellis. Lean the plants slightly in towards the trellis. Tie the shoots to the trellis with twine or string to create a screen of greenery as quickly as possible.

A camouflage curtain A climbing vine quickly produces a dense curtain of leaves around unsightly storage areas. Evergreen climbing plants, such as ivy, provide a robust and dense screen, even in winter.

pleasant corner that blends in with the rest of the garden. It is quick and easy to achieve and need not require much expense.

A simple, long-term solution for concealing bins is to site them in a leafy corner where there is a mature hedge or evergreen conifers such as Japanese cypress (*Chamaecyparis plumosa*). These can easily be trimmed into shape and retain their foliage all year round, whereas deciduous trees and shrubs are bare in winter. A bin area concealed by a hedge requires quite a lot of room: you will need 5 square metres for a hedge to screen an area large enough for two dustbins. If your front garden is small, you may need a different solution.

Climbing plants as camouflage

A space-saving way of disguising rubbish bins is to train climbing plants along a wire mesh. Drive posts into the ground at the corners of the bin area and string wire

30-MINUTE TASKS

► Erect a trellis between two posts and plant climbers.

► Spread suitable soil on the roof of a rubbish bin storage house and fill with suitable plants.

between the posts, using tension screws so that the tension is easier to regulate. Climbing plants can now be trained along these wires and should develop quickly into a dense curtain of foliage and seasonal flowers.

Alternatively, instead of stretching wire between the posts, you can erect trellis between them (see steps, far left). You can buy ready-made trellis in most DIY stores. Or, you could make one yourself fairly easily, using slats of wood. Plant ivy (*Hedera*) or a fast-growing Russian vine (*Fallopia baldschuanica*) against it and it will soon be covered in green.

Dustbins beneath a canopy of green

You may store your rubbish bins in a concrete or wooden shelter, which is almost as unattractive as the bin itself, but even this can be transformed into a planting possibility.

QUICK CLIMBERS TO COVER A TRELLIS

PLANT	QUALITIES
Ivy (*Hedera helix* 'Buttercup')	Year-round coverage with bright yellow foliage.
Morning glory (*Ipomoea tricolor*)	A fast-growing annual with bright sky-blue flowers in summer.
Black-eyed Susan (*Thunbergia alata*)	A vigorous plant with cream to orange flowers in summer.
Clematis montana var. *rubens*	A rampant climber with abundant, scented, pale violet flowers.
Purple bell vine (*Rhodochiton atrosanguineus*)	Rapid climber. Purple flowers from summer into autumn.
Sweet pea (*Lathyrus odoratus*)	Rampant climber. Pink, white or purple flowers in summer.
Woodbine *Lonicera periclymenum*	Vigorous scrambling plant with sweetly scented cream flowers.
Crimson glory vine (*Vitis coignetiae*)	Good leafy covering providing spectacular autumn colour.
Russian vine (*Fallopia baldschuanica*)	Rampant climber with delicate flowers.

Attractive camouflage A profusion of colourful flowering plants covering its roof turns a rubbish bin shelter into an ornamental feature.

Planting plan: a bin shelter in bloom Cover the roof with low clumps of free-flowering plants, interspersed with sedum to ensure greenery all year round.

Orange hawkweed (*Hieracium*)
Dianthus
Golden flax (*Linum flavum*)
Thyme (*Thymus*)
Evergreen stonecrop (*Sedum*)
Soapwort (*Saponaria*)
0.8m
1.6m

You will need to build a wooden framework that can be mounted on top of the roof of such a shelter in order to be able to plant on top of it. The roof of the shelter may be at a slight angle so leave a gap along the lower edge to allow rainwater to run off. Ask a local firm to build a metal planting box with drainage holes to fit into the wooden frame you have constructed or drop in one or more plastic trays to fill the space. Make sure that your planting boxes have drainage holes drilled in the base.

Alternatively, you can line the framework with pond liner. Spread a layer of porous clay over the base for drainage then place a layer of fleece on top of this to separate the clay from the soil. Next, fill the box with a free-draining layer of soil, 5–10cm deep, consisting of a mixture of equal parts of garden soil, sand and porous clay or gravel.

Fill the box with plants that can tolerate a wide variety of conditions. Cover any exposed areas of soil between the plants with fine gravel. Water sparingly, at first, and only in dry conditions, after which you can leave the planted roof to its own devices.

Concealing a drainpipe Climbing plants can be trained up a collar of plastic-coated open mesh placed around a drainpipe, quickly making the drainpipe itself invisible.

Around the house
Covering a facade in greenery

Cloaking the front of your house in plants is a quick and efficient way to **add charm** to your property. After initial training and tying in, the plants do the rest, draping the house in **living colour**.

WATCH OUT!

■ Do not grow climbing plants with rigid shoots, such as climbing roses, against a hinged trellis or the stems may snap when you fold back the trellis.

■ Vigorous climbers, such as wisteria, should not be planted anywhere near drainpipes or gutters. They are strong enough to damage the pipework.

Clinging on If you need to move a Virginia creeper to paint the house wall behind, moisten the suckers with a little water then leave them to soak for a while. This makes their powerful grip easier to release.

Different climbing habits
With a wide range of colours, flowers and growing habits to choose from, you will find a plant to suit your purpose, whether you want to cover the entire house or just soften a few sections with greenery.

Ivy (*Hedera*), Virginia creeper (*Parthenocissus quinquefolia*) or climbing hortensias are self-clinging. They don't require supports, as they attach themselves to walls with their own suckers. Climbing roses and jasmine have a spreading habit, thrusting their stiff shoots between the struts of a trellis, while clematis species wind themselves around thin supports with their leaf stalks. Other climbers, such as wisteria, wind their shoots upwards through vertical supports such as taut wires.

When planning your display, choose the right type of support for the plant in question, or choose the right kind of climber for a support already in position.

A curtain of mauve A single wisteria will climb a surprising distance, reaching up to and around this balcony (right), its flowers hanging down in purple cascades.

84

30-MINUTE TASKS

► Fix wires or trellis supports to the house wall.

► Plant a climbing plant and tie in shoots to the support, if appropriate.

Growing tips next to a house wall

The ground is usually dry at the base of a house wall since little rain reaches this area. Plant climbers around 50cm away from the wall, where their roots will be watered by rainfall. Ensure that no soil is allowed to pile up above the level of the house's damp-proof course, which should be visible as a line of slate, damp-proof membrane or a wide course of concrete in between rows of bricks. To help the shoots make contact with the base of the trellis as quickly as possible, settle plants in at an angle, leaning towards the wall.

The soil is often poor in this area, so make the planting hole at least one-and-a-half times as wide and as deep as the root ball and backfill with some organic material. If planting roses or wisteria, ensure that the graft union, visible on the main stem, is at least 5cm below the surface. Train the shoots onto the trellis, fanning them out and securing with twine. Self-clinging climbers do not need trellis, but secure the shoots with adhesive tape until they start to cling on their own.

Before planting, check the condition of the wall and its rendering, particularly if you intend planting ivy or other self-clinging varieties. The wall should be

Growing through the wires A plastic-covered metal framework makes an ideal support for climbing plants. Use spacers to mount it several centimetres away from the wall so that air can circulate freely.

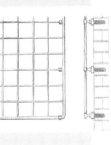

Easy access Hinged trellis is a wise precaution if you know you will need access to paint the wall behind. The trellis is attached to the wall by means of hinges at its base and hooks at the top. This allows you simply to unhook it at the top and fold it down to reach the wall behind.

completely free of cracks and damp patches and the surface should be finished in a durable, weatherproof material. Walls painted with emulsion or emulsion silicate finishes tend to develop cracks over the years, which can collect moisture and provide a foothold for shoots to penetrate. If the façade is damaged in any way do not plant any climbers against it. Plants with a twining habit or those with aerial roots or tendrils can force their way into cracks or gaps in the masonry, widening them and causing more serious defects.

Climbers will not damage a wall whose surface is intact. They could even provide a form of insulation and protection against the weather, with rain sliding off their leaves and away from the wall. Do not allow climbers to reach guttering, window ledges or roofs as they could soon cause considerable damage.

1 Diagonal trellis is ideal for climbing plants that spread out in a fan shape. Garden centres normally stock a wide range of different types and sizes.

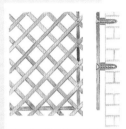

2 Lengths of wire, usually plastic covered, attached either vertically or horizontally, make good supports for wisteria-type twining plants.

3 Wire or plastic mesh is good for plants that attach themselves with tendrils, allowing the plants ample opportunity to get a good grip.

■ If you opt for self-clingers, such as ivy or Virginia creeper (*Parthenocissus quinquefolia*), you will not need to erect any trellis and save yourself the two hours it would take to install it.

■ Ivy grows fast and can get out of control. Don't waste hours up a ladder pruning and pulling down shoots; identify the stems that are heading for the roof and cut them off at the base. Once they have withered, they are easy to pull down from below.

Creating a paradise for useful wildlife

Leaving a corner of your garden for **wildlife** is the ultimate in care-free gardening. Allow the plants to **naturalise**, with a few wildflowers and even nettles. It will not take long for wildlife to move in.

Insatiable appetite Ladybirds are the gardener's friends, consuming up to 150 aphids a day.

Busy pollinators Honey bees are among the main pollinators of the fruit trees in the garden.

Helpful hunters Frogs and toads help to rid the garden of slugs, snails, beetles and other small insects.

Nocturnal scavenger Beetles, grubs, wireworms and snails are among the hedgehog's favourite foods.

Energetic feeders Earwigs keep down the numbers of woolly aphids, leaf aphids, mites and other pests.

30-MINUTE TASKS

► Build a pile of stones for frogs and toads.

► Fill a pot with straw and hang it upside down on a cane as an earwig refuge.

A little untidiness can be a good thing

All gardens produce plant material that does not biodegrade easily, for example, hedge cuttings, tree branches or even stumps. Do not be too quick to get rid of this, but use it to attract lacewings, ladybirds, hoverflies, hedgehogs and birds into your garden and they will help you to combat pests such as snails, aphids and caterpillars. Allow a small patch of nettles to grow and they will provide food for butterfly larvae; red admiral, peacock and small tortoiseshell butterflies all love a sunny nettle patch.

Creating a wildlife refuge

Dead wood, stones and leaves provide a refuge for many animals and predatory insects. During the day ground beetles hide in the dark recesses, emerging by night to feast on snails, worms and other small insects.

Frogs and toads also hide under woodpiles and stones. A mound of natural stones in varying sizes adds a creative touch to the rock garden and makes an attractive feature beside the gravel edges of a garden pond. Any visiting frogs and toads will soon make use of your rocky retreat and while they are in your garden they will be feasting on slugs and snails. They also like to hide among tall grass, so watch out for them when mowing or strimming at the edges of the lawn.

In autumn, ladybirds seek shelter among fallen leaves or in cracks in the bark of trees. Both adult insects and larvae are voracious consumers of aphids, while some species feed on woolly aphids and scale insects. Fertilised hoverfly females also need branches, leaves, cracks in walls or other tiny openings in which to overwinter. Early in the spring they lay their eggs among colonies of aphids, which serve as food for the emerging larvae.

A pile of old wood is best left undisturbed, especially through the winter. As well as harbouring beneficial insects it may be home to a hibernating hedgehog or a nest site for native garden birds, such as wrens and robins.

BUILDING AN INSECT 'HOTEL'

1 Drill some small holes into bricks, blocks of wood or sections of tree stump. Insects will overwinter in these holes or lay their eggs in them.

2 Build a wooden framework with an overlapping roof to keep nesting areas dry. Divide it into several sections to accommodate the different nesting materials that you have.

3 Finally, place nesting materials in the box. Slot in the bricks and blocks you drilled and fill other compartments with thin twigs, bamboo canes, straw or other dry natural materials.

Insect hotel If you do not have room for a designated wildlife corner in your garden, you could build an insect 'hotel' – a high-rise nesting site for a wide variety of beneficial garden visitors.

Patios and seating areas

A comfortable, low-maintenance place to relax

No garden should be without a **secluded corner** where you can sit and admire the view. Pots and containers are quick and easy to plant, making the **patio** the most **labour-free** area of the garden. All the time saved in the rest of your easy-care garden can be spent here **relaxing**.

An idyllic seating area beside the house

If you have only just moved into your house, the patio will probably be the starting point for your redesign project. You will want to transform it as quickly as possible into a pleasant, family space – an outdoor living area where you can all relax and unwind.

The size of the patio will depend on how you intend to use it, but it is better to be generous and create one that is too big rather than too small. For a family of four, allow at least 10 square metres and for a family of six, 15 square metres. If you want to include a barbecue area add another 5 square metres to the total.

When choosing furniture weigh up comfort with portability. Some materials may need to be moved under cover during winter or when it rains. Alternatively, opt for furniture that can be left outside in all weathers such as plastic chairs or rustic-looking slatted benches.

Sheltered but not confined

Hedges and tall herbaceous plants or bushes create a sense of intimacy, but don't plant them too close to the patio or you will feel hemmed in by plants. If your garden is over-looked, wooden screens and latticework trellis will give some privacy and act as windbreaks. Climbing plants can quickly envelop trellis in green foliage and colourful flowers.

Pots and tubs will add all-year-round life and colour to the patio area. Planting a different combination of plants each season will keep them interesting. If you have a very sunny south-facing patio, you may need to incorporate some form of sun protection. Awnings and parasols allow you to sit out on the patio even at the height of summer. A pergola covered with climbers, however, makes a delightful alternative.

Large picture windows or sliding doors
A wide opening will seem to extend the living room out onto the patio.

Comfortable furniture
Choose with comfort in mind to make your patio a pleasant place for relaxing.

A profusion of flowers in tubs
An easy way to add almost instant colour is to surround your seating area with plants in pots.

The need for privacy
When designing a garden seating area it is important to incorporate some form of screen that prevents outsiders from peering in and yet does not spoil the view. You can do this with screens fronted by flower beds (left) or shrubs and herbaceous plants (below).

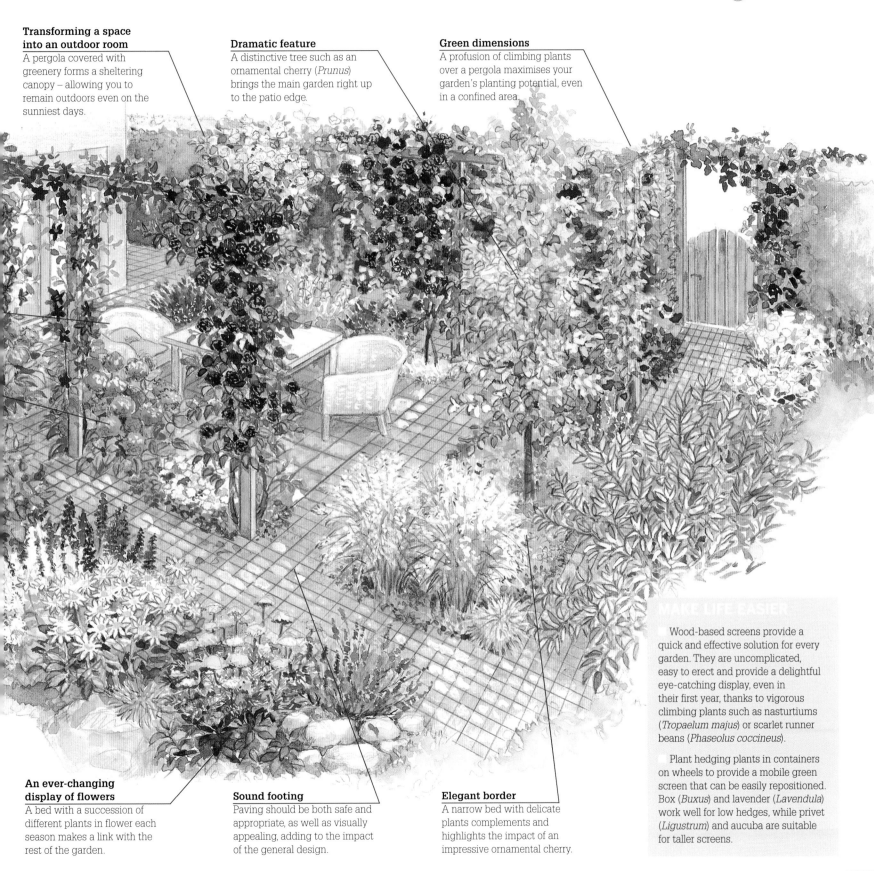

Transforming a space into an outdoor room
A pergola covered with greenery forms a sheltering canopy – allowing you to remain outdoors even on the sunniest days.

Dramatic feature
A distinctive tree such as an ornamental cherry (*Prunus*) brings the main garden right up to the patio edge.

Green dimensions
A profusion of climbing plants over a pergola maximises your garden's planting potential, even in a confined area.

An ever-changing display of flowers
A bed with a succession of different plants in flower each season makes a link with the rest of the garden.

Sound footing
Paving should be both safe and appropriate, as well as visually appealing, adding to the impact of the general design.

Elegant border
A narrow bed with delicate plants complements and highlights the impact of an impressive ornamental cherry.

MAKE LIFE EASIER

Wood-based screens provide a quick and effective solution for every garden. They are uncomplicated, easy to erect and provide a delightful eye-catching display, even in their first year, thanks to vigorous climbing plants such as nasturtiums (*Tropaelum majus*) or scarlet runner beans (*Phaseolus coccineus*).

Plant hedging plants in containers on wheels to provide a mobile green screen that can be easily repositioned. Box (*Buxus*) and lavender (*Lavendula*) work well for low hedges, while privet (*Ligustrum*) and aucuba are suitable for taller screens.

Roses surround a patio with scent

Enclose your patio in a cloud of **sweet-smelling** petals. At first glance it may seem like a demanding project, but the rose, **queen of flowers**, demands little maintenance in the long term.

Enjoy an abundance of flowers with the minimum of effort

Hybrid tea, floribunda and patio roses are ideal for creating a low-maintenance rose bed next to the patio. The crucial thing to remember is to choose vigorous, healthy varieties. The Royal National Rose Society conducts trials for new breeds of roses and has lists of the best cultivars. Also look out for the RHS Award of Garden Merit (AGM), which is given to plants of a particularly high standard. Plant robust specimens a suitable distance apart in well-prepared soil, and your rose bed should soon become a magnificent spectacle

Rose-tinted dreams Roses are perennial garden favourites – either as climbing roses tumbling around a pergola (above) or a colourful mixture of shrub and bush roses (left). The patio is the perfect place to really appreciate these magical flowers.

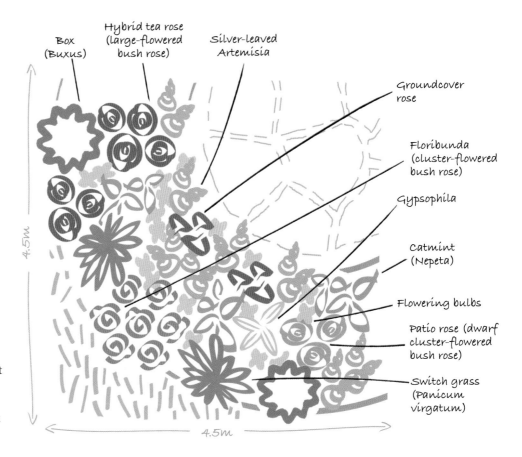

Box (Buxus)

Hybrid tea rose (large-flowered bush rose)

Silver-leaved Artemisia

Groundcover rose

Floribunda (cluster-flowered bush rose)

Gypsophila

Catmint (Nepeta)

Flowering bulbs

Patio rose (dwarf cluster-flowered bush rose)

Switch grass (Panicum virgatum)

4.5m

4.5m

for years to come. Choose your own favourite colours and make a note of each plant's flowering season and individual habit.

Single-flowering species will only produce one flush of blooms each year, yet this single display will produce a profusion of flowers. Repeat-flowering roses will keep blooming throughout the season. Hybrid tea and patio roses are best planted in groups of three. The former will soon merge into a thick bush, disguising any weak shoots. Plant them approximately 50cm apart in individual groups. For tall varieties, provide some support at the time of planting, such as a pyramid-shaped climbing frame or obelisk. For more variety mix in one of the wild or species roses.

Roses and their companions

Roses need not be planted in isolation. Tall delphiniums make excellent companions for large hybrid tea roses, while sage (*Salvia officinalis*) goes well with small roses. Lady's mantle (*Alchemilla mollis*) or catmint (*Nepeta*) make good foreground fillers. Any

How roses are sold
Bare-rooted roses are sold with no soil around their roots or with a root ball with soil around their roots and normally wrapped in polythene. The roots need trimming by a third before planting to encourage vigorous growth. Container-grown roses should already have a well-developed root system within the pot.

additional plants you use should favour the same conditions as roses, namely heavy soil, enriched with well-rotted compost or specially mixed rose soil.

A good start leads to healthy growth

When planting individual roses, ensure that the graft union (the thick nodule between the roots and shoots above ground) is approximately 5cm below the surface, where it will be protected from frosts. Water thoroughly and cover the ground with a layer of bark mulch to keep the ground moist and friable while at the same time discouraging weeds.

Roses should be fed with a specially formulated rose feed in the spring after pruning and again in late June or when developing a second flush of flowers. Water newly planted roses regularly during their first season. Established roses can tolerate dry conditions but should be watered during extended dry periods. Deadhead regularly to encourage speedy repeat flowering. Most newly planted roses should be pruned hard to about 10cm from ground level to encourage the development of shoots and roots, while patio roses should be cut back by half in the first season after planting. Each type of rose has its own pruning requirements (see page 123).

Planting plan: a rose bed next to a patio Add to the sensory appeal of a semi-circular patio with a border of roses. Two evergreen box bushes, trimmed into globes or pyramid shapes, provide a restful focus for the eye. Spring-flowering bulbs could be planted in the gaps to provide interest early in the year.

 **30-MINUTE TASKS**

▶ Dig two planting holes and enrich the soil that has been excavated with compost.

▶ Plant two roses and water in thoroughly.

91

A pergola provides shelter

A pergola planted with some **attractive climbers** is an ideal way of providing your seating area with protection from the sun and wind. Follow **a few simple rules** at the construction stage and you will reap the **rewards** from its lovely, scented curtain of foliage.

Under a cloud of mauve blossom
This free-standing pergola, entwined with wisteria, is visually stunning and provides a pleasant seating area with some dappled shade.

30-MINUTE TASKS

► Make concrete footings, incorporating a metal post spike for a pergola support.

► Mount the pergola supports in their concrete bases.

A leafy roof A climbing plant such as Russian vine (*Fallopia baldschuanica*) will quickly cover a pergola with a thick layer of foliage that keeps out bright sun, wind and light rain.

Winter colour The bright fruit of *Celastrus scandens* (below) adds colour to the garden until deep winter.

Building a pergola

For a quick and easily constructed pergola you can buy ready-made kits from any good DIY store. In general, pergolas consist of uprights supporting horizontal beams and cross-beams. They can either be free-standing or anchored to a wall. Most are built of wood, although the uprights may be stone or metal. Wood is the easiest option if you plan to build the pergola yourself. A pergola should be at least 2.2m high to accommodate people standing up beneath it and you will need a gap of about 1.5m between posts to allow two people to walk through side by side.

Concrete and wood

The size of the wood and the amount required depends on the size of the pergola. A medium-sized pergola, measuring 4m x 2m and 2.2m high, would require six upright posts 2.2m long, two bearers 4m long, and five cross-beams 2.2m long. All the timber should be 10cm x 10cm. The larger the pergola, the thicker the timber needs to be. To ensure the structure's stability, the uprights are held in metal post spikes, which are driven into the ground. (Larger structures will need concrete

footings for the posts.) Once each upright is slotted into its metal holder it is bolted in place. Check that the posts are vertical.

Once the uprights are in place, the two horizontal bearers can be added. The most common way to fix the beams is by full or partial cross-joints, cutting slots into the beams so they interlock. Secure the beams with screws, but check that the bearers are level before fixing. Lastly add the cross-beams in the same way, allowing an overhang of 10cm at either side.

Depending on the type and finish of the wood used, the pergola should now be given a weatherproof coating to ensure durability against the elements. Choose a wood stain or paint that is not harmful to plants that may twine around it. Read the instructions on the packaging or ask an expert.

Covering the pergola with vigorous climbing plants

You can soon cover a pergola with greenery using low-maintenance climbers and twiners such as honeysuckle (*Lonicera*), Virginia creeper (*Parthenocissus quinquefolia*) or wisteria. Plant the new climbers leaning towards the supports so that they can quickly find their way upwards. Silver vine (*Actinidia polygama*) is a good choice for fast coverage as is grows at a tremendous rate.

If you choose a clematis or climbing rose, it is a good idea to install additional supports, such as lengths of strong wire, around the sides of the pergola to achieve a more dense coverage. You can, of course, attach anything you want to your pergola, including hanging baskets, lanterns or birdfeeders.

TIME-SAVING TIP

☐ Use pre-treated timber for the structure, saving you time by not having to weatherproof it.

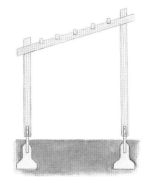

A comfortable height The height of the pergola should be at least 2.2m to enable an adult to move around freely underneath. The cross-beams (struts) should be of the same strength as the uprights.

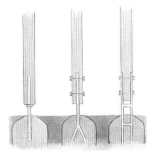

Concrete footings Larger constructions need concrete footings to hold the uprights securely in place. There are several types of bracket for fixing the upright to the concrete (above), but all prevent the wood from rotting below ground.

Choose hard-wearing plants to fill gaps in paving

Do not waste time replacing **old paving stones** on your patio. Make a feature of the weathered look by placing **robust,** clump-forming plants **between the gaps**.

Make a feature of careworn paving

Time leaves its mark on every patio. The stones become weathered and are often covered in a layer of moss and lichen. There may be cracks and gaps or broken slabs, which are an open invitation for weeds. Yet you can avoid the time (and cost) of laying a new patio simply by filling the gaps between slabs with undemanding, low-maintenance clump-forming plants. Choose varieties that do not mind being stepped on, such as thyme (*Thymus vulgaris*) which gives off a lovely smell. Before long your old patio will have a charming rustic look that requires minimal maintenance.

MAKE LIFE EASIER

■ If you don't mind the gradual weathering of the stones, you can dispense with the time-consuming job of regular cleaning. Be aware that the stones may become slippery and clean them before they grow unsafe.

■ Filling the gaps between paving with cement prevents weeds from taking hold, eliminating the need for regular weeding.

Planted paving
An interesting paving layout can be created by removing some of the slabs altogether. Fill the gaps with clump-forming shrubs that will crowd out weeds.

Containers as camouflage
An attractively planted container strategically placed can conceal cracks or damaged areas.

Secure footing
A large slab spanning the mini pond allows safe and easy access across the patio.

Colourful filling material
Use gravel and stones of various sizes and colours as an interesting way to fill in the cracks and gaps.

Cushions of flowers
You can transform an uninteresting paved area into a colourful mosaic of clumps of flowers, grasses and sparkling water quite easily. Lift individual paving slabs and fill the gaps with plants, create a mini pond and soften the paved area with patches of gravel.

PLANTS FOR PAVED AREAS

PLANT	BOTANICAL NAME
Biting stonecrop	*Sedum acre*
White rock rose	*Helianthemum appenninum*
New Zealand burr	*Acaena microphylla*
Saxifrage	*Saxifraga callosa*
Corsican mint	*Mentha requienii*
Bugle	*Ajuga reptans*
Irish moss or pearlwort	*Sagina subulata*
Thyme	*Thymus (various species and forms)*
Linaria	*Chaenorhinum glareosum*
Variegated ground ivy	*Glechoma hederacea 'Variegata'*
Gentian	*Gentiana species*
Chamomile	*Chamaemelum nobile*

Start by removing any weeds that have found their way into the cracks between the paving slabs using a patio weeder. Then fill the cracks with sand, fine chippings or gravel by brushing the material in with a broom. Rinse down with lots of water.

Plant low-growing perennials in the cracks and self-seeding species such as dwarf snapdragons (*Antirrhinum*), ground ivy (*Glechoma hederacea*) and rupturewort (*Herniaria*), all of which can survive being stepped on. Also try thyme (*Thymus vulgaris*) and chamomile (*Chamaemelum nobile*) for fragrance and the slow-growing pearlwort (*Sagina*).

Flowering 'islands' soften paved areas

In larger areas of paving the occasional slab can be removed and the gaps filled with plants. These plant 'islands' add interest and soften the expanse of stone. Dig over the soil in the gap and add a mixture of sand and fine gravel. The site is now ready for planting with carpet-forming varieties, cushion-style rock garden plants or low-growing grasses or shrubs. A small ornamental pool gives scope for water plants.

CLEARING WEEDS

Use a patio weeder to make light work of clearing the weeds out of cracks between stones and paving slabs.

A gas or petrol-powered flame weeder will burn any weeds that have managed to propagate in the cracks. These are also ideal for eliminating moss and algae growth from paved surfaces, paths, steps and walls.

30-MINUTE TASKS

► Weed between the cracks in a patio of 15 square metres using a patio weeder.

► Lift two slabs to create flowering 'islands' within the patio paving.

Creating a secluded spot

In a **newly planted** garden any hedge surrounding a patio will naturally be **quite small**, so that the patio can remain overlooked. Fortunately there are **short cuts** you can take to create some privacy.

A world apart
Create an intimate atmosphere by enclosing a seating area with planted containers equipped with an integrated trellis framework. Add fast-growing climbers to make a secluded garden hideaway.

A plant-covered wall
Build a sturdy wooden frame and add brackets to hold planted window boxes to make an attractive divider that screens off an area, while still allowing you to see through to the rest of the garden. Fill the troughs with annuals, climbing and trailing plants and they should give you pleasure well into the autumn with a succession of colourful flowers.

Easy solutions for instant privacy

If your terrace is overlooked you can make it a more relaxing space by creating some privacy with screening. An easy way to do this is to mark out an area with containers that have an integral trellis. Fill the containers with fast-growing climbers that will quickly transform the trellis into green windbreaks. Perennial climbing plants such as clematis or honeysuckle (*Lonicera*) are ideal for this purpose, as are annual climbers such as scarlet runner beans (*Phaseolus coccineus*) or morning glory (*Ipomoea*) vines. Tall grasses such as bamboo or perennial sunflowers, create atmospheric Spanish-style screens. Large containers can also be planted with mature shrubs, such as privet (*Ligustrum*), thuja or cherry laurel (*Prunus laurocerasus*), to create an instant hedge.

Many garden centres sell containers complete with various types of trellis built-in, but it is easy to make your own climbing support for containers and boxes. Wooden containers mounted on wheels are ideal for this purpose, or stand the containers on a base that has been mounted on casters. This enables the screen to be moved easily, even when the container is heavy and full of soil. Make sure that there are sufficient drainage holes in the bottom of any container before you plant into it.

Space-saving wooden screens

A wall provides the most effective form of privacy. Painted white and with a framework covered with climbing plants in front of it, it can make a delightful eye-catching feature. If you don't have a wall around your terrace, a quick solution is to erect wooden screens, trellis or a simple lattice framework that you can make yourself or buy as panels ready constructed from a DIY store or garden centre.

Screens made from hazel twigs are an attractive alternative. Be sure to choose good quality panels that have been solidly constructed and ensure that they are fixed firmly in place: they will be exposed to considerable stress in high winds.

Plant climbers at the base of the screen or hang pots or troughs planted with colourful annuals or herbaceous plants from a sturdy wooden frame (above) to add a living element to your garden room divider.

30-MINUTE TASKS

► Mount one section of a screen onto a wall or between two posts.

► Fill a container that has a section of trellis built-in with compost and plant it up.

► Fill containers, each 1.5m long, with loam-based compost and plant with hedging shrubs.

Moving screens for versatility Fixing furniture casters to the base of a container (see main picture, opposite) or placing it on a ready-made pot trolley (left) available from garden centres enables you to move your screen or heavy pot as required, creating a flexible private space.

Extend your garden's welcome into the evening

If you do not have **time** to sit in the garden during the day, create a terrace that you can **enjoy in the evening**. There are easy-to-grow plants that bring **colour** and **fragrance** to an evening in the garden.

Flowers to light up the dark

Creating an outdoor seating area that can be enjoyed in the evening is not difficult; simply choose plants that will enhance the experience. Vibrant reds and oranges, together with dusky purples and blues, are easily lost in the twilight and fade to a uniform grey. But light colours – whites, creams, pale pinks, light blues or yellows – reflect even the faintest rays of light and become almost luminous at dusk, with moonlight showing them off to their best advantage. White lilies (*Lilium*), angel's trumpet (*Brugmansia arborea*), tobacco plants (*Nicotiana*) and pale shades of petunias all shine in twilight conditions.

Many flowers have a much stronger scent in the evening, while some, such as evening primrose (*Oenothera*) or sweet rocket (*Hesperis matronalis*), only open up at night. Planted around the edge of the patio, they will fill the evening air with a sweet fragrance. If the seating area is in a sheltered corner, one or two fragrant flowering plants or a single prolific honeysuckle (*Lonicera*) will probably be sufficient. If the perfume is too intense or the variety of scents too great, the result can easily become overpowering and even unpleasant.

NIGHT-SCENTED FLOWERS

PLANT	LOCATION	COMMENT
Angel's trumpet (*Brugmansia arborea*)	Sun; damp, fertile, clay soil	Spectacular blooms; all parts highly poisonous
Jasmine (*Jasminum officinale*)	Sun; fertile, porous soil	Vigorous, hardy; profuse flowers
Honeysuckle (*Lonicera*)	Sun to semi-shade; light soil	Vigorous climber
Regal lily (*Lilium regale*)	Sun; light, sandy soil	Base should be in shade
Night jasmine (*J. grandiflorum*)	Sun to semi-shade; light, sandy soil	Whitish, heavily scented flowers
Evening primrose (*Oenothera*)	Sun; poor soil	Flowers for weeks on end
Sweet rocket (*Hesperis matronalis*)	Sun/semi-shade; light, sandy soil	Profuse flowerer, but short-lived
Tuberose (*Polianthes tuberosa*)	Sun; light, rich soil	Heavy honey fragrance; tender
Four o'clock flower (*Mirabilis jalapa*)	Sun; dry, light soil	Not hardy

Clever lighting needs careful planning

Subtle lighting adds the final touch for an enjoyable evening on the patio. Large candles or small tea lights can be romantic, and strings of lights will bathe the patio in a warm glow on a summer's evening. Indirect lighting is generally more attractive than direct lighting, but is not as effective at illuminating the area – choose appropriate lighting for your needs.

Think carefully about the distribution of any electric lights you intend to install. The trick is to create a pleasant atmosphere without dangerous cables or wires running all over the place. Try to run the cables where they will be hidden from view and will not be a trip hazard. Ideally, use an electric light source to provide the basic background lighting and candles or lanterns to create additional atmosphere.

30-MINUTE TASKS

► Plant two strongly scented plants in containers.

► Install a set of outdoor string lights.

Intense perfume
The flowers of angel's trumpet (*Brugmansia arborea*), right, and honeysuckle (*Lonicera*), far right, give off a heady scent in the evening.

1 Special scented candles and tea lights containing citronella oil give off a scent that acts as a mosquito repellent. Always place them in a candle holder before lighting.

2 Slow-burning citronella coils positioned around your seating area will keep you mosquito free all evening long. They also repel other flying insects.

3 Place scented geraniums, tomatoes or incense plants around the seating area. Rubbing the leaves releases a scent that is disliked by mosquitoes.

Twilight garden
Carefully placed lamps and candles will create a magical evening atmosphere.

Comfortable warmth
The heat radiating from a small stove or chiminea enables you to enjoy the patio on cool evenings.

You may wish to install lights along the edge of the patio to highlight specific plants or decorative features. These are especially effective when the light is angled upwards. Wand lights radiate light at a low level and are ideal for illuminating paths and beds, as are solar-powered spike lights, which can be repositioned easily without depending on a fixed electricity supply. Lanterns are another way to add interesting lighting and can also be repositioned easily.

The lure of the flame

Outdoor evenings need not be confined to the warm summer months if you install some form of heating. Fire and flames, such as a barbecue, outdoor stove or chiminea make an attractive focal point as well as providing heat. A small cast-iron or terracotta chiminea is easy to use even in strong winds.

Gas-powered patio heaters heat a seating area so efficiently that you can be warm enough even in the winter. But they can be expensive to buy and run, are a very inefficient use of fuel and are often criticised for their polluting emissions so use them sparingly, if at all.

Create a restful, leafy corner

The main seating area of a garden is generally the focus of family life; if you need a corner where you can enjoy complete privacy, create an alternative retreat in a quiet part of the garden.

A quiet corner for contemplation
The main seating area in your garden is likely to be close to the house, so create your alternative retreat under a tree or near a distant garden wall. From this remote hideaway you will be able to enjoy a fresh perspective on your garden. This will be a special place for you alone, a quiet corner for contemplation.

If you plan to use your retreat frequently, it is a good idea to remove the grass underfoot and lay a hard surface. A leafy corner for one is quick and easy to create if you have an area 3m x 2m available that already has a gravelled surface. A small circular or semi-circular area of paving stones can also be made to blend unobtrusively into the garden.

A reflective mood A floral bower and small, still pool of water turn this simple bench into a haven of peace and quiet.

The type of paving surface you choose depends largely on your style of garden. Loosely laid natural stones or rustic wooden decking will look good in an informal garden, whereas paving with a clearly defined pattern is more appropriate in a formal situation.

Seating wall Warmed by the sun and retaining a bed of fragrant plants, a low, deep wall can shore up a sloping bank, create an individual garden area and also provide you with occasional seating.

Surrounded by a variety of scents

Make your seating area even more relaxing by surrounding it with flowering plants that have stimulating or relaxing scents. The sweet fragrances of roses or mock orange (*Philadelphus*) are at their most intense in full sunshine. Added to the aromatic perfumes of Mediterranean herbs such as rosemary (*Rosmarinus officinalis*), sage (*Salvia officinalis*) and lavender (*Lavendula*), they evoke a holiday mood.

Water can be extremely relaxing, particularly when it is gently trickling or bubbling. The simplest way to include a water feature in your personal corner is with a bird bath or a planted water trough. If you also have access to a power point, you can install a small fountain or create a simple waterfall.

A scented sofa

If you are looking for something a little different for your personal corner, you could try making a scented seat. This garden feature, much loved by Victorians, is where a raised bed is planted with fragrant plants that form a comfortable cushion upon which to sit.

To make the aromatic seat you will need to construct a conventional raised bed retained by a wall built to a comfortable seating height. The seat itself is formed from robust and springy carpet-forming plants that release their scent as soon as you sit down on them. Chamomile (*Chamaemelum nobile*), lemon thyme (*Thymus × citriodorus*) and alpine calamint (*Acinos alpinus*) are all good choices.

Restful corner
A quiet, leafy corner of the garden, backed by a hedge or group of shrubs, can become a private oasis in which to relax and think, bury your head in a book, snooze or even sunbathe – with the help of a screen for privacy and a comfortable chair.

Build a solid retaining wall to surround the seat bed. Make the long side 1–2m long, depending on how many people it is to accommodate, and build to 50–60cm in depth and height. Fill the bed with coarse gravel and chippings, topped with a layer of sand, fine gravel and soil 10–20cm deep. Plant with closely spaced cushion-forming plants, allowing them to become established before you start to use the seat.

30-MINUTE TASKS

► Install the framework for a small garden seat.

► Assemble the seat.

Stylish solutions for defining your boundaries

Walls, fences and hedges **enclose your garden**, giving instant visual definition and a clear framework. **Choose your style**, from country cottage to a formal city look to **set the scene** for the rest of the garden.

Setting clear boundaries

To limit casual access to your garden and ensure privacy, you must make sure its boundaries are clearly marked. The method you choose, whether hedge, wall or fence, can determine the look of the whole garden.

If you decide to erect a fence, you have a choice between one that is designed to be on show and one that is designed to be less obvious. Chain-link fences are inconspicuous, but utilitarian and seldom attractive. They are ideal for smaller gardens because their openness can give the illusion of space. For additional screening, plant sweet peas (*Lathyrus odorata*) or other annual climbers along the mesh fence or conceal it behind an arrangement of tiered planting beds.

You can draw attention to the outer boundaries of a property, from both within the garden and from the road, by choosing decorative fences of wood or wrought-iron, possibly in combination with a stone or rendered and painted wall. This kind of boundary fence can be an attractive feature in its own right. Wrought-iron is traditionally found in urban areas, whereas wooden fencing lends a more rural feel to the garden.

Fencing as a feature
The white paint of these simple wooden palings is the perfect foil for the bold pink flowers and silvery-grey foliage of the plants growing beside it.

Light-coloured, solid or heavy fences can dominate the garden and make it look smaller. Dark-coloured fences or those with a more open spacing of uprights blend into the background, making less dominating visual boundaries.

The choice: walls or hedges?

Walls of brick, natural stone or concrete form a barrier against noise and exhaust fumes. However, in a small space they can have a claustrophobic effect and create too much shade, limiting choices for planting. A dry stone wall makes an attractive, naturalistic alternative and can feature a variety of colourful plants.

Hedges often take years to grow and become thick enough to form a dense boundary. Once mature, they can be as effective as walls at creating privacy and providing a barrier against noise. They also help to improve the air quality of their immediate surroundings, actively filtering out pollutants and they provide shelter for a wide variety of wildlife.

Some restrictions may apply

When deciding on which type of boundary to install around your property, check with your local authority first regarding any restrictions concerning position, height and materials. You will need planning permission to erect a wall or fence more than 1m high along a boundary adjoining a highway, or more than 2m high along any other boundary.

Hedges are exempt from planning control, but the local authority has the right to cut back any that obscure the view of traffic or overhang the pavement. In addition, local authorities have the power to consider applications from neighbours to reduce the height of evergreen hedges that are deemed to be causing a nuisance. It means that they can take action on complaints made about hedges that consist of two or more evergreen or semi-evergreen trees or shrubs in a line which are more than 2m high, and can force the homeowner to cut them back or remove them.

Fragrant boundary
Scented sweet peas (*Lathyrus odorata*), left, trained up a simple wire fence, make an eye-catching feature along a boundary.

Flowering wall A dry stone wall (above), filled with colourful plants, forms a solid barrier that is truly part of the garden itself.

MAKE LIFE EASIER

■ Fences are easy to erect if you use ready-made fencing panels, particularly if you use metal post supports.

■ As with turf for lawns, hedges can also be bought by the metre, allowing you to create an almost instant green boundary.

Plant a natural flowering hedge

Choosing to grow a **flowering hedge** will save you a considerable amount of trimming time over its more formal clipped cousins. Its flowers can be just as **impressive** as a bed of herbaceous perennials, but for much less effort. It also **provides a haven** for many useful garden creatures.

A wreath to welcome visitors Bridal wreath spiraeas (*Spiraea* 'Arguta' and *Spiraea × vanhouttei*) bear a profusion of blooms. These easy-to-grow shrubs require almost no maintenance and, here, create an inviting floral entrance to the garden.

TIME-SAVING TIP

☐ If you prune the individual shrubs in a hedge radically every five to six years (right down to the base), you can save two to three hours of hedge cutting per metre a year.

Just let it grow!

A flowering hedge makes a truly easy-care boundary, as it can be left to grow naturally with little trimming, but you need to be sure that you have enough room for it. You should allow for a width of at least 2m, if not more. Anything less will limit the hedge's potential for producing lots of flowers and for providing garden creatures with sufficient food and living space. Create an informal look by planting a hedge of mixed shrubs, including plants that have different flowering seasons and which produce various colours of foliage and ornamental fruit. This will give your hedge year-round interest. On the other hand, an informal hedge consisting of a single variety of shrub, such as dog rose (*Rosa canina*), can be just as attractive.

Spring climax If left unpruned, these flowering currant bushes (*Ribes sanguineum*) will produce an abundance of blossom from April to May, and will form a simple screen of foliage throughout the rest of the year.

► Dig a trench 1m in length.

► Plant five or six dog roses (*Rosa canina*) in the trench.

PLANTING A HEDGE

1 Before planting a hedge mark out its proposed length with a piece of string. Dig a trench along this line, twice the width of the root ball of the shrubs, but the same depth.

2 Place the shrubs at evenly spaced intervals along the trench, using a tape measure for accuracy. Dig in the shrubs, refilling the trench with the excavated soil. Press the soil down firmly around the base of each plant.

3 Prune back any long, non-sprouting branches immediately after planting in order to encourage vigorous new growth. Water the new shrubs well and cover the ground between the plants with a layer of mulch or bark chippings.

Less pruning means more blooming

Spring-flowering shrubs, including forsythia, bridal wreath spiraea (*Spiraea* 'Arguta' and *Spiraea* × *vanhouttei*), ornamental currant bushes (*Ribes sanguineum*) and weigela, begin forming flower buds in the autumn on one or two-year-old growth. They will actually reward you if they are neglected. If pruned too hard, they produce fewer blooms the following spring. To help shrubs retain as many flowering stems as possible, just cut back the oldest and most vigorous new growth every two or three years. Slow-growing shrubs, such as viburnum or flowering dogwood (*Cornus florida*) do best if left unpruned altogether.

Hedges made of summer-flowering species and wild roses need only their dead wood pruned. Although cultivated roses may benefit from occasional deadheading, easy-going wild roses should be left well alone. Their flowers will eventually be replaced by brightly coloured hips that are decorative in their own right – a delight to the gardener for being both low maintenance and visually appealing.

Wall of flowers A flowering hedge, such as this magnificent spiraea, can turn a boundary into a sea of blossom and need not cost a fortune. Spiraea does particularly well in open, sunny positions.

Plant in autumn for good root growth

Early autumn is the ideal time to plant hedging shrubs – plant them in spring only if you have no alternative. Planting in autumn ensures that root systems have time to establish themselves before the first winter frosts, after which the plants will enter their dormant period. Hedges planted in spring will develop quickly

above ground, leaving their roots unable to keep pace. Whether you plant them in autumn or spring, hedges should be watered thoroughly during any dry periods in the first year to prevent damage from drought.

The distance you should leave between each plant varies according to the variety, from 30–45cm for ornamental currants (*Ribes sanguineum*) to 60cm for firethorn (*Pyracantha*). Most of these shrubs require little attention after planting. They flourish in almost any garden soil and are rarely affected by garden pests. Give them a spring treat of well-rotted compost to encourage growth and bud formation and they should remain healthy for years.

Make more of your garden fence

Fences are commonly used by gardeners to create clearly defined boundaries. You can make these **more attractive** by disguising them with a **border of flowering plants** or smothering them with **climbers**.

Plants and fence in harmony

Fences should be a friendly indicator of where your private property begins. The secret of unobtrusive fencing lies in the plants you choose to disguise it. The style of fence and the adjacent plants should complement each other. Elegant ornamental fences, often considered features in their own right, can be made even more attractive by planting distinctive, specimen shrubs, such as roses or rhododendrons. In contrast, a simple, carefully trimmed hedge highlights the visual impact of individual plants by providing them with an unobtrusive background.

This side and that
A simple picket fence has almost disappeared behind a wall of brightly coloured summer flowers, sown both within the garden and on the other side of the boundary fence.

30-MINUTE TASK

► Prepare a flowerbed along a 5m strip of fence and sow it with summer flowers.

Natural willow green
An informal garden is the ideal setting for a woven willow fence. The living branches are pushed into the soil and entwined around posts and horizontals.

Use vigorous climbing plants to soften the effect of particularly high fences or to screen boundary walls. Intrusive fencing panels can soon be covered by a curtain of leafy foliage and flowers. You may find you don't like some of the walls or fencing inherited from previous owners. Planting different types of climbers can transform an eyesore into something far more visually appealing.

One of the most natural types of fence is one made of living willow. You can buy the whips from specialist gardening firms towards the end of autumn. Insert them into the ground along the boundary line and they will soon start sprouting; when loosely intertwined, they form a delightful living fence.

Flower beds adjacent to a fence

A colourful bed of herbaceous perennials or roses planted along a fence will bring the perimeter of your garden alive. Tall bushes and summer-flowering plants are particularly good for planting along a fence. Wire fences soon disappear from view beneath the foliage and palisade-style fences look much more appealing if the heads of sunflowers, for example, are peeping over the top. A fence can also act as a useful support for tall shrubs, dispensing with the need for stakes and other types of support.

COMPLEMENT YOUR FENCE

A wide bed filled with flowering bulbs will ensure that your garden fence looks at its best in spring.

Patio roses and herbaceous perennials will soon fill out to become an impressive, fragrant hedge of flowers in front of an open iron railing fence.

Old and new
Swags of foliage from a burnished Virginia creeper (*Parthenocissus quinquefolia*) complement the faded old wood of the fence beneath it.

Plant fast-growing climbers such as sweet peas (*Lathyrus odorata*), nasturtiums (*Tropaeolum majus*) or honeysuckle (*Lonicera*) against fencing made of wire-mesh or trellis and you should soon have a dense, colourful curtain of leaves and flowers.

Maintaining a formal hedge

Formal hedges make **excellent** garden boundaries. They take up a limited amount of space and **protect you** from nosy neighbours, exhaust fumes and noise. Hedges are easy to grow but require **regular trimming**.

Evergreen or deciduous

Formal hedges normally consist of just one species of shrub, which helps to give a uniform structure and makes caring for them easier. The choice of suitable shrubs is more limited than for its free-growing informal counterpart, but you will still have to choose between deciduous or evergreen varieties. If you opt for a deciduous species, such as hornbeam (*Carpinus betulus*) or copper beech (*Fagus sylvatica*), remember that they lose their leaves in winter, reducing their ability to provide privacy at that time. On the positive side, a deciduous hedge provides changing interest, often with

Care tips for a tip-top hedge Keeping a box hedge looking thick and neat requires regular trimming. Use lengths of string to guide your hedge cutters as you work and to keep the cut edges level.

TIME-SAVING TIPS

■ Choose slow-growing shrubs for hedging. A hedge that needs to be cut just once a year will save you around two to three hours of trimming time per metre of hedge.

■ Before you start, spread a large piece of sheeting beneath the hedge to catch the clippings, moving it with you as you work your way along the hedge. This will save time as you will not have to rake up the cuttings afterwards; you can just bundle up the clippings and dispose of them.

attractively coloured foliage in autumn, and does not block out light in the darkest months of the year.

Evergreen hedges remain thick and green all year round. Two favourites are common privet (*Ligustrum vulgare*) and spotted laurel (*Aucuba japonica*), both of which are extremely robust and able to withstand drastic pruning. Evergreen conifers, such as *Thuja* or cypress, need only limited amounts of space, which makes them ideal for creating narrow hedges, next to a driveway, for example. Regular pruning is a must with these varieties because, unlike deciduous alternatives, they can often fail to produce new growth if they are pruned back to old wood too late or too severely.

Plant close together for thick hedges

If you are aiming for a thick hedge, make sure the individual plants are placed at the correct distance apart. Larger species, such as hornbeam (*Carpinus betulus*), copper beech (*Fagus sylvatica*), *Thuja* or yew (*Taxus baccata*), should be spaced at intervals of

Safety first It is much easier to cut tall hedges if you stand on a solid platform. Make sure you choose a good make with a reliable safety rating. Look for a British Standard (BS) number or kite mark.

Choose the right tools
The job of regular trimming is unavoidable with a formal hedge, but is made much easier when you use the right tools. Electric hedge cutters, equipped with a long blade, are vital for wide hedges. Invest in a model with a powerful rechargeable battery and a spare so that you do not have the nuisance of managing cables.

Small hedges can be trimmed with a good pair of shears. Choose a lightweight pair that you find easy to handle. Compact battery-powered shears are ideal for small box hedges.

approximately 60cm, while smaller varieties, such as box (*Buxus*) or privet (*Ligustrum*), need to be planted closer together, ideally around 30cm apart.

Regular trimming is crucial during the first few years after planting in order to encourage the plants to form a solid, bushy hedge. Never allow hedges to grow too high; keep trimming them back and you will end up with a dense, even hedge.

Cut hedges at least once a year

The best time to cut a hedge is the middle to end of June, when deciduous woody species have come to the end of their first annual growth spurt. By this time, any birds that have been nesting in the hedge will have usually raised their first broods and the nests will have been abandoned. Hedges that grow vigorously, like beech, may also need cutting in autumn.

Low hedges are easy to trim with shears, but you will need electric hedge-cutters for long, tall or wide hedges. Larger areas are easier cut with a longer blade, which will need a more powerful motor to drive them. Hand-held shears are best for hedges of large-leafed plants, such as laurel or holly. Start with the front and back of the hedge, cutting evenly and starting at the bottom and moving upwards. Then cut the top. Finally, neaten the edges. If you are pruning a very tall hedge, use a step ladder or some other form of solid, stable support to help you to reach the tallest parts.

Box-shaped: The hedge is trimmed flat on all sides, creating a rectangular profile; ideal for beech, yew or box hedges.

Trapezium-shaped: The hedge is narrower at the top, which permits sunlight to reach the base; suitable for most hedging plants.

Rounded: Like the trapezium, this hedge allows sunlight to reach the base; a good shape for bushy shrubs.

30-MINUTE TASKS

► Trim a hedge of 5m in length.

► Clear up and dispose of the clippings.

Garden boundaries

Growing a screen of bamboo

Bamboos grow quickly and are **excellent** for **screens**. They need little attention, although they are so **vigorous** you will need to take precautions when you plant them to keep them **under control**.

An Oriental environment

These ornamental grasses look their best when grown against a wall or façade, which acts as a windbreak. A wall also restricts root growth, at least in one direction, leaving just the front edge of the bed to be contained.

Bamboos are tropical plants and many will not tolerate our winters. Several varieties are hardy enough, but even they are susceptible to wind damage. They need plenty of space as they can grow to 4m in height and spread quickly, reaching maturity after three years.

Although bamboos do not flower frequently – some species flower only once every 100 years – all varieties do produce flowers eventually and afterwards they usually die. In order to avoid the inconvenient and difficult task of digging up the roots of dead bamboo, always check with staff at the nursery or garden centre when you buy a bamboo that your chosen plant is not expected to bloom within the next few years.

Preventing an invasion

Many varieties of bamboo send out runners and are very invasive. Aggressive new shoots can even

PLANTING BAMBOO

1 Begin by watering the bamboo thoroughly: remove it from its pot and soak the roots for about 30 minutes in a large tub of rainwater. Remove any damaged roots.

2 Stand the bamboo in its planting hole. Bamboo roots need to be contained so place heavy duty liner or metal sheeting around the sides of the hole to a depth of 50–75cm to form a barrier. Make sure you allow the roots enough room to become established.

3 After filling in the hole, make sure the root barrier protrudes a few centimetres above the surface. This will help you to spot any runners that are beginning to push their way over the edge of the barrier, so that you can remove them before they become established.

A graceful wall of green
Bamboo generally stays green throughout the winter if it is not overexposed to the sun or wind. Cut back any unsightly older canes in spring, and this will help to promote fresh shoots and dense growth.

30-MINUTE TASKS

► Dig planting holes or a trench for a line of bamboo and line it with a sturdy root barrier.

penetrate drains and pond lining. When planting bamboo, you will need to install a barrier around the roots to prevent the bamboo from growing out of control.

Use a root-proof liner around the inside of the planting hole. The membrane should extend to a depth of at least 50cm, or ideally 75cm. Once the bamboo is planted, the liner should protrude 4–5cm above soil level. If planting a bamboo hedge in front of a wall, dig a trench at least 1.5m wide to accommodate a single row of plants. Then plant the bamboo, spacing the plants at intervals of at least 60cm.

Blocking the spread of rhizomes
Insert a barrier around the roots of vigorous, spreading varieties of bamboo, regularly pruning back runners as necessary.

Caring for bamboo

Water bamboo during the first summer, until it develops a good root system. Once established, it will need minimal attention: it must just be watered in dry conditions and treated to a good dose of organic manure or compost in spring. Any leaves that fall can be left among the canes; they will serve as a useful mulch layer. Bamboo canes can be cut down after new shoots have formed in spring. Remove dead culms after flowering.

BAMBOO PLANTS FOR SCREENING

PLANT	GROWTH/HEIGHT	LOCATION
Bisset bamboo (*Phyllostachys bissetii*)	Bushy, dense foliage/ 3–7m	Sun to semi-shade; wind tolerant
Bronze bamboo (*Phyllostachys humilis*)	Upright, bushy/ 2–5m	Sun to semi-shade
Umbrella bamboo (*Fargesia murieliae* 'Simba')	Weeping habit, very dense/ 1.5–2m	Semi-shade
Yellow-groove bamboo (*Phyllostachys aureosulcata* 'Spectabilis')	Upright, loose/ 3–5m	Sun to semi-shade
Umbrella bamboo (*Fargesia murieliae* 'Dragon')	Compact growth drooping tips/ 3–4m	Semi-shade
Umbrella bamboo (*Fargesia murieliae* 'Jumbo')	Light and bushy/ 2–3m	Sun or shade
Zigzag bamboo (*Phyllostachys flexuosa*)	Upright with occasional kinks; drooping tips/ 3–5m	Sun to semi-shade

TIME-SAVING TIPS

■ Compared to a formal hedge that is kept trimmed, a bamboo hedge of 10m in length will save you 20–30 hours of work in spring and summer.

Enclosing your front garden

A front garden should be attractive, easy to maintain and **suited to its situation**. A wall or fence may be the best choice as a **boundary**, although a suitable hedge can be more **interesting and adaptable**. Whatever your choice, it should make a positive statement about the **property** inside.

Don't block out the light
Keep boundaries low around small front gardens so that they do not feel dark and enclosed. Choose slow-growing hedges and trim them regularly to keep them neat.

Assessing your options

Your choice of boundary material at the front of the house will depend mainly on its setting. If you live on a busy road you may find a wall or fence a less troublesome option than a living boundary that is susceptible to the effects of the traffic fumes. A town house would suit an elegant wrought iron fence, while a country cottage would look more at home behind an informal hedge or painted picket fence. You may wish to discourage wandering dogs, intruders or vandals or simply mark the edge of your property with a low wall.

Planning regulations govern the height of a wall or fence that adjoins a highway (see page 103), so if you want privacy, you may need to plant a hedge. But the taller the hedge, the more difficult it will be to trim, and remember that screening the property too effectively can be a burglar's blessing. Hedges must be trimmed to prevent them overhanging a pavement or road. A small front garden should always have low boundaries to prevent it feeling too enclosed and shaded.

A brick or stone wall will last indefinitely, and is more vandal-proof than a fence; with a little practical knowledge it is not difficult to build this kind of wall

✗ WATCH OUT!
Never trim a hedge when birds may be nesting.

High style, low maintenance A combination of brick and iron railings is a classically stylish option for a period town property and requires minimal upkeep.

HEDGES FOR PROBLEM AREAS

VARIETY	EVERGREEN OR DECIDUOUS/ PRUNING REQUIREMENTS
TOUGH HEDGES TO WITHSTAND DAMAGE	
Spotted laurel (*Aucuba japonica*)	Evergreen, height to 2m. Prune annually with secateurs in late summer.
Portugal laurel (*Prunus lusitanica*)	Evergreen, height to 2m. Clip or prune in late summer.
Box (*Buxus sempervirens*)	Evergreen, can be kept to low or medium height. Clip in late summer.
Forsythia	Deciduous, low or medium height. Clip after flowering (late spring).
Hypericum	Semi-evergreen, low or medium depending on variety. Flowers all summer. Prune to keep in shape in spring.
Laurustinus (*Viburnum tinus*)	Evergreen, medium height. Flowers all winter if clipped in early spring.
HEDGES TOLERANT OF POLLUTION, SALT AND DOG URINE	
Sea buckthorn (*Hippophae rhamnoides*)	Deciduous, height to 1.5m. Clip in early spring.
Shrubby mallow (*Lavatera thuringiaca*)	Semi-evergreen, height to 2m. Cut back fairly hard in spring. Flowers all summer.
Quickthorn (*Crataegus monogyna*)	Deciduous, can be clipped to any height. Trim at any time when birds are not nesting.
Japanese spindle (*Euonymus japonicus*)	Evergreen, can be pruned or clipped to any height. Clip in spring.
Hornbeam (*Carpinus*)	Deciduous, but retains brown leaves all winter. Makes a good medium or high hedge. Clip in late summer.
PRICKLY HEDGES TO KEEP OUT INTRUDERS	
Pyracantha	Evergreen, with white flowers followed by red, orange or yellow berries. Can be trained to any height up to 2m. Clip new growths in summer to keep tidy.
Rosa rugosa	White or cerise flowers followed by red hips. Up to 1.5m according to variety. Prune back from late autumn to early spring.
Barberry (*Berberis*)	Evergreen or deciduous, and low, medium or tall according to variety. Clip in late summer.
Holly (*Ilex*)	Evergreen, medium or tall. Clip in early spring.
Quickthorn/ blackthorn mixture (*Crataegus monogyna/ Prunus spinosa*)	Deciduous, can be clipped to any height. Trim at any time when birds are not nesting.

yourself. A low fence is even easier to erect, although you may need another person to help. Use metal post spikes embedded in concrete for the greatest stability: never embed wooden fence posts directly in concrete as they will quickly rot off near ground level.

Hedges for front gardens

If you opt for a hedge, it is tempting to choose a fast-growing type, but this will soon outgrow its situation and give you a lot of work in regular trimming. Avoid green privet (*Ligustrum ovalifolium*) and shrubby honeysuckle (*Lonicera nitida*) for this reason. For quick effect, it is better to spend more money on larger plants of a slower variety, such as common laurel (*Prunus laurocerasus*), copper beech (*Fagus* Purpurea group), holly (*Ilex*) or laurustinus (*Viburnum tinus*). Remember that a hedge bordering a public footpath or pavement must not block it in any way (page 103).

A hedge along a main road will have to cope with pollution, winter salt spray, possible dog urine, and maybe even vehicle damage. It needs to be tough, chemical tolerant and quick to recover from damage. Avoid conifers, which soon turn brown with salt spray and the attention of male dogs and try pollution-tolerant *Aucuba japonica* or *Euonymus japonicus* instead.

In areas where vandalism is a problem, prickly hedges are an effective deterrent. A mature spiny hedge will also discourage burglars from entering the property from a lonely footpath along a side boundary. In less problematic areas, a flowering front hedge can make an eye-catching feature. Choose species with a long flowering season, such as repeat-flowering shrub roses, lavatera, escallonia or potentilla.

Keep out A prickly hedge of pyracantha is an effective deterrent to intruders, but a glorious sight in autumn and winter when it is covered with bright, glossy berries. For prickles without the berries, choose a deep purple berberis.

30-MINUTE TASK

► Wire brush a fence of iron railings ready for repainting.

► Trim 5m of hedge.

► Treat a 3m length of wooden fence panels with wood preservative.

Trees and shrubs

Make a focal point of large plants

Trees provide a garden with a **long-term living framework**. Think about **crucial aspects** such as the shadows they will cast – and how big they will eventually grow – **at the design stage**.

Low-maintenance garden features

Trees and shrubs can divide a garden into different areas and provide interesting focal points. They offer a range of options for long-lasting, easy-care ornamental garden structure. Evergreens provide year-round interest together with welcome splashes of greenery in the winter garden. Deciduous trees mark the seasons as they change and, even in winter, their distinctive silhouettes are attractive – particularly when a tracery of branches is sprinkled with frost.

In spring and summer, blossom and foliage provide interest and colour, while in autumn fruits and berries introduce vibrant new hues. Trees provide shelter and food for birds and other creatures, and privacy and natural shade for you.

Long-term garden residents

You may opt for a tree or a group of shrubs rather than a flowerbed; you may decide on evergreens rather than deciduous trees and shrubs. Whatever your choice, one thing is certain: your final selection will have a long-lasting impact on the future development of your garden.

The successful integration of trees and shrubs into the rest of the garden depends upon them being compatible in both size and style. You should also consider the spread of their roots (see page 79), making sure that they are planted at a safe distance from your house and neighbouring properties and will not pose a future risk to the foundations.

Remember, too, the changes trees undergo during the year: their flowering season, when they come into leaf and the colour of the leaves in both summer and autumn, and whether or not they bear fruit.

Seasonal colour
Brightly coloured fruit, such as rosehips, provide a splash of autumn colour.

Dominant features Trees
help to establish structure in a
garden. When planted along the
perimeter, they form a natural,
living wall. Their dense canopy
of leaves creates a restful
background for flower beds and
borders (main photo). Many
species, such as acers (above)
produce a spectacular autumn
display of colour.

MAKE LIFE EASIER

Choose trees and shrubs that are
compatible with the size of your
garden. Trees that reach heights in
excess of 10 metres are generally too
large for most gardens and need too
much maintenance.

Container-grown shrubs and trees
can be planted at any time of the year,
providing the ground is not frozen.

Buy a taller, more mature specimen
with a ready-formed crown rather
than a young sapling to avoid having
to prune it into shape.

Trees and shrubs

Plant a colourful stand of shrubs

A mixed group of deciduous and evergreen shrubs involves little work but remains attractive **all year round**. The plants' spring blossom is **often fragrant**; later in the year they will **add interest** to your garden with their variously **textured** and coloured foliage and decorative fruit.

Versatile, low-maintenance shrubs

Once established, shrubs don't require special attention. Plant several attractive trees and shrubs in a cohesive group and they will soon develop into a feature that is just as appealing as a herbaceous bed but demanding much less care. A shrub bed has uses other than decorative – its dense growth makes it as good as any hedge as a windbreak or as a screen for privacy.

Colour palette Shrubs can provide bright splashes of colour, such as the deep pink foliage of a Japanese maple (*Acer japonicum*) (below) or the striking, brightly coloured fruits of the spindle (*Euonymus europaeus*) (right).

30-MINUTE TASKS

► Mark out the planting area for a group of five to six shrubs.

► Prepare the soil for planting.

► Plant two or three shrubs.

116

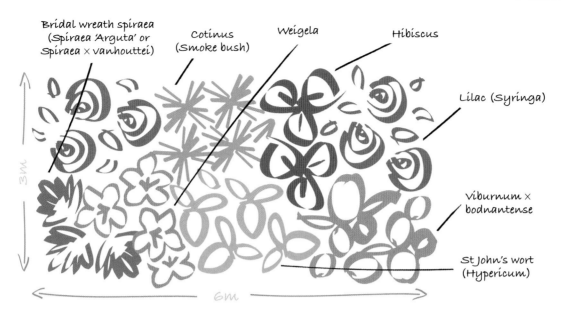

Planting plan for a bed of flowering shrubs
Maintain fresh visual interest in your shrub bed by combining varieties that flower at different times. *Viburnum*, for example, flowers very early in the year, followed by bridal wreath spiraea (*Spiraea 'Arguta'* or *Spiraea × vanhouttei*), then lilac (*Syringa*) and *Weigela*. Summer colour is provided by smoke bush (*Cotinus*) and St John's wort (*Hypericum*), while *Hibiscus* marks the close of the season.

Labels on plan:
Bridal wreath spiraea (Spiraea 'Arguta' or Spiraea × vanhouttei)
Cotinus (Smoke bush)
Weigela
Hibiscus
Lilac (Syringa)
Viburnum × bodnantense
St John's wort (Hypericum)
3m
6m

Ring the changes

To create an interesting and varied bed, combine shrubs of different shapes and varying heights, remembering to plant taller species at the back and lower-growing varieties towards the front. Tall, slender species should alternate with bushy, spreading varieties and ones with a vigorous, sprawling habit.

Apart from their distinctive shapes, shrubs have other qualities that complement the garden through the seasons. Some can brighten winter days with the striking colours of their bark. Red-barked dogwood (*Cornus alba* 'Sibirica') with its vivid red stems or white-stemmed bramble (*Rubus*), such as *R. cockburnianus* make striking additions to any winter border. Others bear flowers: *Viburnum × bodnantense* produces a mass of sweetly fragrant pale pink flowers in late winter, making a surprising and delightful feature of the garden at this often rather bleak time of year.

Spring is heralded with a profusion of flowering *Forsythia* and lilac (*Syringa*), followed by summer foliage – including several variegated varieties. Fruit and berries add splashes of colour to the autumn garden, including firethorn (*Pyracantha*) and *Viburnum*. These decorative fruits will often persist well into the winter, outlasting the spectacularly colourful display of the autumn foliage, which ends in late autumn.

The stars of your shrub bed are at their most spectacular when surrounded by a few less showy companions. Good foils for their splendour include evergreens such as cherry laurel (*Prunus laurocerasus*), or modest standards such as *Forsythia* – after a riotous burst of yellow blooms in spring, this retires discreetly into the background with its plain green foliage.

Care-free plants

To give your shrubs a healthy start and minimise later intervention, dig over the ground before planting and enrich it with compost or humus. Plants need watering regularly for the first few weeks after planting but, thereafter most shrubs require little attention. Some varieties thrive on neglect and flower profusely with no pruning at all.

Most flowering shrubs need only occasional pruning: cut off spring flowers once flowering has finished and prune summer flowerers in late winter or spring.

PREPARING A PLANTING AREA

1 Mark out the planting area for your shrub bed, using sand, chalk or sawdust. Create smooth curves with a makeshift compass, made from a piece of string tied to two wooden pegs.

2 Using a sharp spade or half-moon cutter, slice into the ground along the marked line, then remove the grass from the planting area. The turf can be re-used elsewhere, perhaps to repair damaged patches on the lawn.

3 Before planting your shrubs, remove any weeds, thoroughly dig and loosen the soil, working in some well-rotted compost or manure. The bed can be bordered with edging stones.

TIME-SAVING TIP

☐ Choose slow-growing shrubs or varieties that do not need pruning, such as Japanese maple (*Acer japonicum*), serviceberry (*Amelanchier*) or witch hazel (*Hamamelis*), as well as dogwood (*Cornus*) species and *Viburnum*.

Bringing new life to an old tree

Instead of uprooting old trees, give them a speedy makeover. Transform an ageing apple or give an old cherry tree a new lease of life by training climbing plants, such as clematis or roses, to grow up the trunk, covering the old tree in a profusion of flowers.

Two trees in one

Encouraging flowering climbers to scramble up into old, failing trees gives ageing fruit trees two 'flowering seasons' each year. Vigorous, fast-growing climbers, such as rambler roses, are ideal for the task. They quickly scramble up to the crown of a tree and will flower week after week – for although most rambling roses have just one flowering period each year, it lasts for four to six weeks. For the remainder of the year, the old trees are festooned with dense foliage.

The perfect host

A climber should complement its host tree. Never select small, weak trees as support. They could easily collapse under the weight of a vigorous climber. Instead, look for a good, solid trunk. Trees with a relatively open canopy make ideal supports for roses, which prefer light and sunny conditions. If the canopy is too dense, lighten it by cutting out any old or unwanted branches to allow the roses sufficient air and light.

After planting the roses at the base of the tree, tie any long shoots to the supporting trunk. This will help them to find their way up into the top of the tree more quickly.

Blooming sculpture An ageing tree is rejuvenated by a climbing rose. The alternative would be to fell the tree and remove its roots – a major job.

Rope, canes or wire can be used to give shoots extra length, and you can tie them into the top branches of the tree. Once the runners have become firmly anchored in the crown of the tree, you can dispense with these supports.

Climbing species planted at the foot of a tree will obviously compete with their host for nourishment and water. The fact that the tree is already established gives it an advantage and its roots may deprive its new neighbour of water and nutrients. A good tip for helping roses to thrive is to place a large container, such as a bucket, with its base removed in the prepared planting hole and plant the rose in it. This will help to keep the rose and tree roots separate and allow you to target the roots of the rose when feeding and watering.

Good companions

Many varieties of clematis enjoy winding their way up through old trees and can also weave through shrubs and conifer hedges. They are frequently combined with roses, which like similar growing conditions. Clematis in its natural state grows on the fringes of woodland; although it climbs up towards the light, it prefers to have its roots in shade. Early flowering clematis (such as *C.* 'Montana') require little or no pruning – though if the plant is scrambling through a tree you may need to cut it back from time to time to prevent it stifling its host. It makes an ideal companion for vigorous rambling roses, which likewise need no pruning. Give your roses a headstart of a few years before introducing any clematis.

Climbing frame
Stretch a length of rope between one of the thicker lower branches and a peg in the ground and train shoots upwards along it into the crown of the tree.

REMOVING A BRANCH

1 Reduce the weight of the branch you are going to remove by sawing through a quarter of its width, from below. Make the cut 10–20cm from where the branch joins the main trunk.

2 The main cut is made from above. Placing the saw at a point 2–3cm further along the branch, saw through it entirely. The undercut will be pressed together in the process, preventing the branch from breaking under its own weight.

3 Saw the remaining stump off as close as possible to the trunk, starting from below, and take care not to damage the bark on the trunk itself. Then remove the stump completely by sawing it off cleanly from above, as close as possible to its base.

4 Neaten the edges with a sharp knife (preferably curved), leaving all the cut surfaces smooth and clean. Finish by applying a specialised wound paint to the entire exposed surface.

30-MINUTE TASKS

► Thin out a crowded tree by sawing off a branch (above).

► Plant a climbing plant next to a tree and tie in any long shoots to encourage them to climb up into the tree.

Trained to the highest standards

With their graceful shapes, standard trees and shrubs **make ideal features** for smaller gardens. They look impressive and are **much easier** to grow and care for than they look.

Trees in miniature

Standards are trees or shrubs that have been trained to have a clear length of stem below the first branches. Their distinctive shape, together with their slow growing habit, makes standards particularly attractive for small gardens. Use two to flank the entrance in a front garden or plant one in a flower bed to draw the eye upwards. And because they cast little shadow, you can cultivate a show of flowers beneath them.

Most nurseries offer a range of hardy evergreen and deciduous species trained as standards, as well as some flowering standards, such as cluster-flowering,

Perfect specimen The long arching branches of this dwarf weeping willow, *Salix caprea* 'Kilmarnock', are covered with silvery, furry catkins from early February. This standard will not grow any taller as its rootstock – the stem – is no longer growing vertically.

A crown for the queen of the garden Not only can the prolific blooms of standard roses be admired at eye-level, but maintenance tasks, such as pruning, can also be carried out from a comfortable standing position.

STANDARD TREES AND SHRUBS

PLANT	CHARACTERISTICS
Guelder rose (*Viburnum opulus*)	Deciduous; white, lace-cap style flowers in May/June; red berries in autumn.
Japanese holly (*Ilex crenata*)	Evergreen; small, shiny leaves.
Cherry laurel (*Prunus laurocerasus*)	Evergreen; shiny leaves; white flower spikes in early summer.
Privet (*Ligustrum*)	Evergreen; small, shiny leaves.
Photinia × *fraseri* 'Red Robin'	Dark green, glossy leaves, red when young; flowers in spring.
Rose (*Rosa*)	Deciduous; flowers abundantly; rounded crown or arching depending on variety.
Willow (*Salix*)	Deciduous; arching branches with catkins in the spring.
Strawberry tree (*Arbutus unedo*)	Hardy evergreen; rich brown/red bark; cream flowers; bright-red fruits.
Dwarf variety of medlar (*Mespilus germanica*)	Semi-evergreen; leaves remain on the branches for long periods; tiny white flowers; decorative red-brown fruits.

shrub or dwarf roses grafted onto an upright stem. Many Mediterranean herbs with woody stems such as bay (*Laurus nobilis*) are also available as standards; these are particularly suitable for cultivation in pots.

Standards with long, arching branches, known as 'weeping', are produced by grafting a shoot or bud from a weeping variety onto the rootstock of another, upright variety. Weeping varieties of willow are available, for example, such as dwarf weeping willow (*Salix caprea* 'Kilmarnock'), as well as weeping versions of climbing and ground-covering roses.

All they need is a little attention

Standards make just the same demands on soil as other plants. Loosen the soil before planting and dig in some compost. Their slender stems need to be supported by a stake, which should extend the length of the stem up to the crown. If it is not pre-treated, treat the stake with a preservative that is not harmful to plants. When it is dry, drive the stake firmly into the ground close to the centre of the planting hole. It is important to do this before you position the plant, so that hammering it in does not damage the roots.

Container-grown, tender standards, such as Chinese Hibiscus (*Hibiscus rosa-sinensis*), should be brought indoors in winter; if planted in a bed they may need protection from frost. Pile leaves or soil around the stem to protect the base and wrap the crown in horticultural fleece. Container-grown standard evergreens left outside to overwinter may need to be shaded from direct sunlight on bright sunny days, to prevent them from losing water and drying out.

30-MINUTE TASKS

► Plant and stake a standard.

► Prune the crown of a standard to shape it.

► Wrap a tender standard ready for winter.

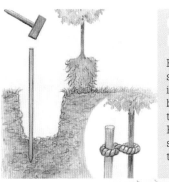

CORRECT MAINTENANCE

Every standard needs good support. Hammer a stake into the planting hole before planting and secure the stem with tree ties. Position the tree on the side of the prevailing wind to prevent rubbing.

Prune branch tips regularly throughout spring and summer to maintain shape. Cut back all branches by a third to a half in late winter or early spring, just before new growth resumes. Pinch out tips of evergreen standards before growth resumes in spring to make them grow thicker.

TIME-SAVING TIPS

☐ Plant standards, especially tender varieties, in large containers, which are then sunk into the ground. This means you can lift them easily in autumn and take them indoors for the winter, avoiding the job of swaddling them with winter protection.

To protect a tender variety left outside during winter, wrap the crown and stem in hessian packed with dry leaves or straw, or horticultural fleece, taking particular care to protect the crown and the vulnerable graft at the top of the stem.

Trees and shrubs

A riot of richly rewarding roses

The rich blooms and **heady scent** of roses make them the stars of the garden in summer. If you choose the right varieties and give them good growing conditions, they are also **easy to maintain**.

A mass of flowers
Choose the right varieties to ensure an abundance of flowers over a long period and to minimise hard work.

Sun, space and soil

Wild roses and varieties approved by associations such as the Royal National Rose Society are normally almost trouble-free. Plant a rose in suitable soil, in a good position with enough space and sunlight, and it will require little attention and give pleasure for years. So it's worth spending some time giving it a good start.

Prepare a planting hole large enough to take the roots or root ball comfortably; the graft union (the thick nodule at the base of the stem between roots and shoots) needs to sit 5cm below ground level. If the soil has a high clay content, loosen it with a fork and improve it by adding sand and compost or well-rotted manure. Carefully firm the soil around the newly planted rose with your foot

⏱ 30-MINUTE TASKS

▶ Feed roses in spring with a suitable fertiliser.

▶ Check roses for suckers and pull to tear them off the rootstock.

and water it in well. Ensure good flowers and healthy growth by feeding the plants twice a year with a compound fertiliser or organic fertiliser – once in spring and again in June after the first flush of flowers.

Simple pruning guidelines

Pruning improves flowering; it is a simple, quick and satisfying job. Large-flowering bushes (hybrid tea) and cluster-flowering bushes (floribunda) flower on the current year's growth. Prune these when they are dormant before new growth starts again in spring, but not during frosty conditions. Remove weak, diseased, dead, damaged and crossing stems so that strong new stems can grow from the base of the plant. Cut the main stems of large-flowering bushes to 20–25cm from ground level and cluster-flowering bushes to 25–45cm.

Prune shrub roses (including species and old-fashioned roses) after flowering, unless you wish to preserve their hips in which case prune between winter and early spring. These need little pruning in the first few years, and may require only a little light pruning as they age. In addition to removing dead, diseased, weak and crossing stems, cut back older wood to encourage new growth and avoid congestion, keeping the plant light and airy. Ground-cover roses require little pruning other than to remove any upright stems since their purpose is to provide a thick, colourful spread. Patio roses also require little pruning, apart from to keep their shape and remove dead and diseased stems. (For ramblers and climbers, see page 80.)

Hard pruning encourages growth, so naturally vigorous varieties, such as shrub roses, need only gentle pruning to prevent them growing too fast. Hybrid tea roses and bush roses, which grow more

slowly, will benefit from vigorous pruning. Always use sharp secateurs. Cut back to healthy wood to an outward facing bud, using a slanting cut.

Sometimes, suckers may grow from the original rootstock and should be removed. They can usually be recognised easily as their foliage will be different from the hybrid – for example, the sucker's leaves might have seven matt green leaflets whereas the hybrid's leaves have five glossy leaflets. Uncover the neck of the rootstock and tear off the sucker; if you cut it off it is more likely to regrow.

Protect from pests and diseases

Feeding roses in spring and in June will strengthen their resistance, but check them regularly. Many pests can be treated with derris dust or a solution of soft soap or household detergent. Aphids can be sprayed off with a jet of water or picked off and crushed with your fingers. Remove diseased leaves from the bush and from the soil – don't leave them lying on the ground. Try to resist planting new roses in an old rose bed, as this can result in stunted plants due to 'rose sickness' caused by viruses and fungi in the soil, and nutrient depletion.

Naked roots Plant bare rooted roses in late autumn. Soak them thoroughly beforehand so that they will quickly become established.

Large-flowering bush rose   Shrub rose

Pruning roses
▶ Cut back the stems of large-flowering bush roses (hybrid tea) to 20–25cm before new growth starts in early spring and remove dead, damaged and diseased wood at the same time (far left).
▶ Prune shrub roses lightly – at the most back to a third – and remove dead, damaged and diseased wood and any crossing stems (near left).

YEAR-ROUND ROSE CARE

SPRING

Complete pruning before new growth starts, but not in frosty conditions. Apply a fertiliser. An 8cm layer of mulch applied after pruning helps to suppress weeds and maintain high moisture levels.

SUMMER

Inspect roses regularly for pests and diseases, remove suckers, regularly deadhead faded flowers, water newly planted roses in dry weather. Water established roses in extended dry periods. Give a second feed of fertiliser in June.

AUTUMN

Plant bare rooted roses. Prepare and dig over the ground beforehand. Cut back growth on large and cluster-flowering bushes by about one third to prevent wind-rock, cutting all shoots to above a bud. Provide winter protection if prolonged cold and harsh weather is forecast.

WINTER

A light fall of snow can act as an insulator, but heavy snow can break rose branches, so shake the snow off before it gets too heavy. Check to see that any winter protection provided at the base of the plant is intact. If severe weather is forecast, heap earth around the base of the plant. Prune now that the plants are dormant, but not in frosty conditions.

Tricks with topiary

A shrub clipped into a **novel shape** gives a garden character and creates a **focal point**. Plants with small leaves or needles are surprisingly **low maintenance**.

Green globes Neatly clipped box balls make a striking group on a mat of weed-supressing ivy.

Living sculpture

Gardeners have shaped trees and bushes to create a focal point since Roman times. Spheres, pyramids and cones were favourite shapes during the Baroque period and there was scarcely a single stately home garden that did not contain examples of bushes clipped carefully into different forms. Since then, topiary has become popular in even the most ordinary houses. The art has progressed beyond pure geometric shapes and today you may see anything from chess pieces to aeroplanes.

Not every plant is suitable

The most common plants for topiary are box (*Buxus*), yew (*Taxus baccata*), or evergreen privet (*Ligustrum*). They all bear

Any shape you like Chicken wire guides can be used to create elaborate shapes. Place the frame over the bush and wait for it to grow and fill out. At regular intervals, simply trim off any shoots that protrude beyond the frame.

30-MINUTE TASKS

► Clip and tidy up an established piece of topiary.

SHRUBS FOR A NATURAL TOPIARY EFFECT

PLANT	GROWTH PATTERN/HEIGHT
Weeping Norway spruce (*Picea abies* 'Inversa')	Columnar conifer, medium growth, overhanging, height 2–3 metres
Berberis thunbergii	Compact-growing rounded bush, height approximately 50cm
Rocky mountain juniper (*Juniperus scopulorum*)	Columnar conifer, height 3–4 metres
Columnar yew (*Taxus baccata* 'Fastigiata')	Columnar conifer, height 4–6 metres
False cypress, such as *Chamaecyparis lawsoniana* 'Chilworth Silver'	Dwarf conical growth, maximum height 1.5 metres
Dwarf Alberta spruce such as *Picea glauca albertiana* 'Conica'	Spherical conifer, height 2–3 metres
Dwarf balsam fir such as *Albies balsamea* 'Nana'	Hemispherical dwarf form, height up to 1 metre

a dense covering of small leaves or needles that are easy to clip into a decorative shape and grow back quickly after cutting. Other options include laurel (*Laurus*), holly (*Ilex*), *Forsythia* and hornbeam (*Carpinus betulus*), all of which have larger leaves but are happy to be shaped into topiary forms.

Using templates and guides

To minimise fussy maintenance choose a simple shape, such as a sphere, which can be judged by eye. If you don't feel confident enough to trim freehand, cut a semicircle template out of strong card or plywood and move it around the shrub as a cutting guide. If the shape is more ambitious – an animal or bird, for example – or is geometric with flat surfaces and angles, a guide can be essential in helping you to get a neat, professional result.

For most basic shapes a young plant can first be clipped freehand and the shape judged by eye. Then a guide made from bamboo canes and wire may be used in the following year. Garden centres also sell topiary frames made of wire or metal, which are placed over the shrub whilst it is still young. The shrub then grows inside the frame and all you need to do is to cut off the growth that appears outside it.

Keeping in shape

Topiary may not seem a good choice for a time-saving garden – but for slow growing shrubs, such as yew, only one shaping per year is needed. Other shrubs will look perfectly trim with just one or two clips a year. Aim to

Shaping aids Make a guide for a box topiary cone by using wooden poles or bamboo canes and wire. Position three poles together in the shape of a wigwam, fastening the tops together with wire. Circles of wire hold the canes in place and define the conical shape.

prevent uneven growth becoming noticeable – which will happen more quickly in the case of fast-growing plants. And avoid clipping too late in the year and not beyond the end of September – any young shoots produced after clipping need time to mature to be able to withstand winter cold and frosts.

Weed and water

Box, yews and privet shaped into topiary will do best if watered, fed regularly with organic fertiliser and kept free from weeds – a carpet of ground cover is a good way to stop unwanted weeds.

If heavy snowfall is forecast, protect weaker parts of a clipped shape with netting and knock snow off flat surfaces to avoid damage. If the plant is damaged by frost, the shape of the plant will inevitably be affected. Cut out the dead wood and the gap will eventually be filled by new growth.

Reaching for the sky
Rocky mountain juniper (*Juniperus scopulorum*) forms a slender column.

Bright and easy rhododendrons

Rhododendrons steal the show in spring with a burst of bright colour after the drabness of winter. They are remarkably trouble-free shrubs, provided they are grown in a position that suits them and in an acid soil.

Flowering hedges

Rhododendrons make a splendid informal hedge: many keep their attractive foliage all year round and their large clusters of flowers light up the garden with radiant colours in spring. Most rhododendrons prefer lightly shaded positions sheltered from the wind, such as under tall trees whose canopies allow light to filter through – although some will tolerate full sun. Many varieties of rhododendron are accustomed to British weather from the damp snowy winters and wet rainy summers of their native Asia, including China, Tibet and the Himalayas, but they can be sensitive to cold winds.

Tree of roses The word rhododendron comes from the Greek (*rhodon*, rose and *dendron*, tree). The genus *Rhododendron* also includes *Azaleas*, which are generally smaller, growing to around 90cm in height.

Encourage healthy growth Cut off dead flowers (left) and spread a thick mulch of bark on the ground beneath the plants (below).

Only plant in acid soils

Most rhododendrons are sold as container-grown plants, which you can plant out at any time of year providing the ground is not frozen. If planted between May and August they will need regular watering.

Before planting rhododendrons, use a kit (cheaply available from DIY stores and garden centres) to test your soil – it should be lime-free and acid, with a pH-value of 4.5–5.5. If the soil is too alkaline the leaves will turn yellowish and growth will be stunted.

The soil should also be quite loose and open. If it is too heavy or compacted, loosen it and dig in some organic matter such as leaf mould and pine needles (these also help with the acidity). Dig in a generous amount of ericaceous compost, which is specially formulated for acid-loving plants. Ensure that the rootball is not planted too deep – it should be just below the surface – and when firming up the soil after planting, take care not to stamp on it.

A little care

Being shallow rooted, the plants do not relish having the ground beneath them being raked or dug over too much. Feed them – preferably in spring – with an acidifying fertiliser or use a 5cm layer of half-rotted compost, taking care not to disturb the roots just below the surface.

In prolonged dry periods water rhododendrons thoroughly and add a mulch of bark humus or pine needles to the ground under the shrubs. Water thoroughly once again in late autumn if there has not been much rain. This will enable the plants to withstand the winter more easily; they generally do not freeze, but will dry out if their leaves lose water through evaporation and the roots are unable to replenish supplies from the frozen ground.

If you love rhododendrons but have alkaline soil, try making a raised bed, which will help to prevent groundwater containing lime seeping in from the surrounding soil. Fill it with ericaceous compost.

Another option is to dig a planting hole twice as large as usual, put a layer of drainage at the bottom and line the sides with a strong membrane to prevent limey groundwater seeping in from the surrounding soil. Then fill in around the plant with ericaceous compost.

⏱ 30-MINUTE TASKS

► Dig a trench large enough for two shrubs.

► Improve the soil and put in two rhododendrons

Colourful shrubs attract birds

Choose shrubs and trees that provide food, shelter and **nesting sites** for birds in your garden. They will **return the favour** by eating harmful insects, caterpillars and other pests.

Garden feast Migratory birds that spend the winter in this country, and residents such as the blackbird, really appreciate the berries of *Rowan* and other trees and shrubs. In return, they prey on many pests and delight us with their song.

A natural larder

You don't have to spend a fortune on nuts, seeds and squirrel-proof bird-feeders to attract birds into the garden. Shrubs and trees that bear fruit or berries will do the job very well. And it is not only the birds that make use of natural, informal hedges and shrubs to feed from, sleep, nest and take shelter in – many other common garden creatures do too.

Trees and shrubs such as elder (*Sambucus*), *Berberis*, cornelian cherry (*Cornus mas*), rowan or mountain ash (*Sorbus aucuparia*), quince (*Chaenomeles japonica*) and dog rose (*Rosa canina*) attract a variety of wildlife – many

are home to various beetle species and therefore to the birds and other wildlife that feed on them. Informal wildlife hedges formed of dog rose, sloe (*Prunus spinosa*) and other spiny plants offer shelter and food at the same time. Planted close together, their dense, tangled branches provide ideal nest sites while the prickles and thorns deter cats and other predators. In spring, the blossom attracts insects, which in turn provide a source

30-MINUTE TASKS

► Plant a shrub that will offer shelter or food for birds.

► Fix a nesting box in a suitable site in the garden or on a house wall.

Eating the leftovers
The seedheads of flowers such as alliums and poppies (right) and of grasses are also a good food source for birds, so don't be in too much of a hurry to deadhead flowers once they fade.

of food for birds. During the breeding season even habitual seed-eaters such as chaffinches feed on insects, so they and their young benefit from a protein-rich diet. Many shrubs, such as wild pear (*Pyrus communis*), elder, quince, cornelian cherry and medlar (*Mespilus germanica*), provide food in the form of nutritious fruits from autumn until well into the winter.

Turning shrubs into nesting sites

With a little pruning you can model a shrub so that it grows with a group of branches radiating out from a central trunk, and this provides an ideal support for nest building. To prune large bushes or shrubby trees such as hawthorn (*Crataegus monogyna*) and cornelian cherry in this way, cut back all the upper branches on a vertical stem or trunk to within 15–20cm. New side shoots will emerge in the spring, which you should cut back again the following winter. These will, in turn, result in

SHRUBS THAT OFFER SHELTER AND FOOD FOR BIRDS

PLANT	SITE	SPECIAL FEATURES
Rowan (*Sorbus acucuparia*)	No special requirements	Provides nesting sites in its branches and fruit.
Cornelian Cherry (*Cornus mas*)	Sunny site; dry limey soil	Provides nesting sites and fruit.
Spindle (*Euonymus europaeus*)	Sunny site; moist soil	The berries are poisonous, but robins love them.
Elder (*Sambucus*)	Sunny site; dry soil	Food and shelter for birds; blossom attracts insects.
Hawthorn (*Crataegus monogyna*)	Sunny site; dry soil	Ideal nesting sites and fruit.
Dog rose (*Rosa canina*)	No special requirements; tolerates shade	Ideal nesting sites and rosehips are good source of food.

further shoots. A small platform will soon form, providing good support for a nest that can be used by blackbirds or chaffinches.

Plant them and forget them

Most native shrubs like sunny, well-drained, limey soil and, once they have become established, make very few demands. When planting an informal wildlife hedge, leave a distance of 50cm or so between plants so they have room to fill out and grow naturally. If space is at a premium, plant a formal hedge of native shrubs such as hawthorn and sloe, placing them about 30cm apart. Hornbeams (*Carpinus betulus*) are particularly amenable to being kept neat and tidy. While a formal, trimmed hedge will not flower as much as an informal one, it will still attract birds and other garden wildlife.

Siting a nesting box

Birds such as tits, nuthatches, starlings and tree sparrows nest in holes, raising their young in hollow tree trunks, abandoned woodpecker holes and other nooks and crannies. Manmade nesting boxes can help replace the ever decreasing number of natural nesting sites. Nesting boxes are available from garden centres, or you can make a simple wooden box yourself. Position it in a relatively undisturbed spot, out of strong midday sun and sheltered from prevailing winds and rain. Make sure that it is safe from predators, particularly cats. Try planting something thorny, such as a rose, beneath the box. Clean the nesting boxes thoroughly in winter before the breeding season begins.

NESTING BOXES

Tits and sparrows will use nesting boxes with a small, round hole – 25mm is suitable for blue tits, marsh tits and coal tits, but it needs to be 28mm for great tits and 32mm for sparrows.

Wagtails, spotted flycatchers and robins prefer to build their nests in niches or holes in walls. They may also use open-fronted nesting boxes and robins sometimes nest in the most unusual places, including old boots.

Starling boxes are similar to tit boxes but the entrance hole needs to be larger. Position them around 5 metres above the ground. Woodpeckers and nuthatches will also use these nesting boxes quite happily.

Wrens prefer enclosed, round nesting boxes, that mimic the nests they build themselves, positioned fairly low down, in a bush or tucked into a sheltered part of a wall.

Pruning flowering shrubs

For the best display of colourful and often **sweetly scented blossom**, most flowering shrubs need pruning. But you need do this only every **two or three years** to maintain their shape.

Free-flowering
Some simple pruning will ensure that flowering shrubs, such as *Forsythia*, remain vigorous and spectacular (main picture, far right).

No holding back
To reinvigorate a neglected and overgrown shrub, prune hard between autumn and early spring when it is dormant. Cut back up to half the oldest stems close to ground level and shorten the remaining ones by half.

30-MINUTE TASKS

► Thin out a spring-flowering shrub such as *Deutzia* after the flowering period, removing dead stems, and cutting back thick branches.

► Prune a summer-flowering shrub by cutting back some old shoots to ground level.

Spring-flowering shrub   Summer-flowering shrub

The importance of pruning

Many flowering shrubs provide colour and fragrance over a period of many weeks. Because they need little looking after, shrubs are suitable for planting at the back of a herbaceous border, where access is restricted.

Pruning controls both the growth and flowering potential of your shrubs, as it encourages new shoots. Always angle the cut slightly above an outward facing bud and ensure that the bud is not damaged. Take care not to leave any branch stumps projecting.

If you need to remove a branch completely, cut it off cleanly at the base. If you want to shorten it to encourage the shrub to spread out, make a cut immediately above an outward facing bud, which will produce strong growth. If the bud points inwards, the centre of the shrub may become congested, so choose outward pointing buds to encourage an airy shape.

Some simple guidelines

As a rule, evergreen shrubs need little formative pruning to shape them and remove dead, diseased or crossing branches. Deciduous flowering shrubs need more attention, and any that are left unattended can soon become straggly.

Prune deciduous shrubs that flower on the previous season's growth such as *Forsythia* (spring-flowering) and *Deutzia* (summer-flowering) straight after flowering. Prune deciduous shrubs that flower on the current season's growth, such as *Spiraea*, in spring to promote the growth of flowers. Prune fairly lightly in spring, but be more vigorous when pruning after summer flowering. In either case, the shrub will benefit from having some stems cut to the base to retain an open framework, while dead, diseased and damaged wood should be removed.

It is a good idea to prune deciduous shrubs annually to keep them tidy, although they can be left for two to three years between pruning. One exception is *Buddleja*, which grows vigorously and needs to be pruned hard to keep it under control. Cut back some of

the new growth to the base to ease congestion and cut back the previous season's growth to two or three buds above the old wood. Finally, remove any suckers (shoots that arise from part of the plant below ground level) from your shrubs. Tear them off rather than cutting, as this is more likely to discourage regrowth.

Reviving untidy hedges

Untended informal hedges can become so dense that light is blocked out, so they lose their leaves from the centre outwards and flower only sparsely. To revive them, cut each individual shrub right back to just above ground level – but do this one side at a time so that you retain part of the hedge during this renewal process.

Pruning flowering shrubs
► Prune spring-flowering shrubs (left) lightly after flowering, cutting a few stems to base.
► Prune summer-flowering shrubs (right) more vigorously after flowering.
► Prune both types annually, or every two to three years to keep them tidy and promote flowering.

TIME-SAVING TIPS

■ Use the correct secateurs for the type of pruning you are doing – for example bypass secateurs with rounded points are best for softer stems. They must be sharp otherwise they will crush the stems.

■ Choose specially coated blades – these are less likely to stick together when covered in sap and reduce the need for cleaning as you work.

■ Planting slow-growing flowering shrubs such as *Magnolia* or flowering dogwood (*Cornus florida*) will save around five hours pruning time a year.

A clean cut Whatever kind of pruning job you need to do, there is a tool that is specially suited for it.

Trees and shrubs

Weeding beneath shrubs

Pulling out weeds in between shrubs by hand is **tedious and time-consuming**. Fortunately there are other ways to **get rid** of at least some of these **unwanted plants**.

Fighting persistent weeds

Persistent weeds with roots that spread rapidly, such as ground elder (*Aegopodium podagraria*) and couch grass (*Elymus repens*) in particular, but also deep-rooted weeds such as stinging nettles (*Urtica dioica*) and brambles (*Rubus fruticosus*), are often widespread under shrubs and trees. They become tangled up in the root systems of shrubs, making them very difficult to get rid of. The best preventative measure is to painstakingly remove every weed and every little root segment from the soil before planting, but even this cannot guarantee complete success.

Defeatist as it may seem, weeding is still the best way to deal with weeds – preferably on a dry sunny day in spring, when any weed remains left lying around will wilt quickly. Work the ground beneath the shrubs thoroughly but carefully with a hoe. If possible, remove all the roots from as deep as possible in the ground

30-MINUTE TASKS

► Weed beneath a small group of shrubs.

► Spread a thick layer of mulch under a group of shrubs or a hedge.

Fight or tolerate Ground elder was cultivated in the Middle Ages as a medicinal herb for treating gout. Today this most pernicious of weeds is every gardener's nightmare, resisting even the most conscientious weeding.

Not desirable, but useful
Stinging nettles (*Urtica dioica*) steeped in water make a useful liquid manure. They also attract many different butterflies.

Pretty, but a nuisance
Ground ivy (*Glechoma hederacea*) has beautiful flowers, but its creeping stems spread rapidly under shrubs.

SUFFOCATING WEEDS

Lack of light and air kills off weeds. Cover the ground between the shrubs with black polythene sheeting, weigh it down with stones and hide it with a layer of mulch.

Placing several layers of newspaper around the base of shrubs fulfils the same purpose. Cover the paper with a thin layer of soil or grass cuttings – the weeds cannot grow without light and air.

using a fork. After a few weeks, remove any weeds that have reappeared, along with any new weeds.

Annoying though they may be in a flowerbed, plants we now consider to be weeds were once hedgerow delicacies. It is best not to put weeds onto your compost heap, as they can come back when you spread the compost on your beds, but ground elder, nettles, chickweed and dandelion leaves all make tasty additions to soups and salads, so don't just throw them away.

Suppress weed growth with mulch

Persistent weeds are difficult to eradicate just by digging and shallow-rooted shrubs do not like the ground beneath them being disturbed, but applying a layer of mulch in spring is a good eco-friendly way of tackling weeds. It is a particularly useful method if the roots of the weeds have become entwined with the shrub's root system, so that weeding would damage the shrub.

Use organic materials such as bark mulch or wood chips, which decompose slowly. Spread them in a layer several centimetres thick, making sure the mulch does not touch the stems of the shrub. Bark mulch draws nitrogen out of the ground and deposits tannic acid, so is unsuitable for newly planted shrubs, but it will not harm established shrubs. If a nitrogen deficiency occurs (noticeable yellowing of the leaves and stagnating growth) the imbalance can be corrected with fertiliser.

Mulch with grass cuttings only if you are sure they are weed-free, and leave them to wilt first or they will attract snails.

An organic mulch will decompose eventually and need replenishing, and it does not always completely suppress weeds. But there are other materials that can be used. A layer of newspaper or black polythene sheeting is one alternative; the unattractive appearance can be masked with a layer of bark mulch. Special mulch matting made of hemp or flax is also available, or gravel can be used. They all work in the same way. Any weeds that have already grown that are covered by the mulch are deprived of both light and air and eventually die, while weed seeds do not have the chance to germinate.

Alternatively, plant shade-loving ground-cover plants with decorative foliage beneath shrubs – such as purple-leaved varieties of bugle (*Ajuga reptans*) or various types of variegated white dead-nettle (*Lamium album*). Weeds will no longer be able to thrive once these plants have carpeted the ground between the shrubs.

Manageable solutions for autumn leaves

Planting deciduous shrubs at the back of a border is one way to avoid raking up **piles of leaves** each autumn. But it's worth **collecting and storing** fallen leaves and turning them into **precious leaf mould.**

Fallen leaves – too precious to waste

At the end of the gardening year, deciduous shrubs make an attractive display with their brightly coloured foliage. The warm colours of their leaves create a spectacular show at a time when little else is in flower. Sadly though, the leaves finally fall to the ground and have to be cleared. The garden leaf bin is overflowing and there is no more room on the compost heap. So where can you put the leaves?

As a natural raw material, leaves are much too valuable simply to throw away – so depriving the garden of the nutrients

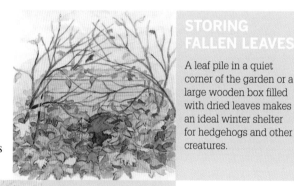

stored within them. It is quite safe to leave them lying on the ground beneath trees and shrubs. They will form a natural mulch, which decomposes slowly, turning into a humus-rich layer and returning valuable nutrients back to the soil. But leaves left lying on the lawn, on paths or in and around a pond are unsightly and damaging (they can kill the grass in a lawn), and also dangerous as they are a slipping hazard.

STORING FALLEN LEAVES

A leaf pile in a quiet corner of the garden or a large wooden box filled with dried leaves makes an ideal winter shelter for hedgehogs and other creatures.

Leaves rot down more rapidly when combined with other garden waste in a rapid composter with a lid. Fill it with dead shredded leaves and other compostable material and sprinkle on compost powder to accelerate decomposition.

The benefits of a pile of leaves

It can take leaves up to three years to break down into humus because of their high tannic acid content. So if you have a lot of leaves in your garden, make your own leaf mould rather than adding them to normal mixed compost, as their addition will slow down the normal composting process unless you have a rapid composter.

The leaves of oak (*Quercus*), walnut (*Juglans*) and sweet chestnut (*Castanea*) trees, in particular, decompose slowly. Shredding them and adding nitrogen or powdered compost accelerator to the heap will reduce the time it takes.

A good container for leaf mould is a square one made from timber and fine wire mesh. It keeps the leaves together and prevents the wind from blowing them around. Half-rotted leaves make an excellent mulch, while fully rotted leaf compost with no added lime makes ideal compost for acid-loving plants.

If you have enough room in your garden, you can simply rake the leaves into a heap and leave them. In winter, hedgehogs may use the pile for hibernation and other creatures, such as frogs and toads, also appreciate piles of leaves. Remember to leave the pile alone for the whole of the winter so as not to risk disturbing any wildlife. Over the years the leaves will break down,

Use leaves as a mulch on vegetable beds, the ground under soft fruit bushes or strawberry beds. Spread the dried leaves loosely in a layer 4–6cm deep. A few twigs on top will stop the leaves from blowing away in the wind.

30-MINUTE TASKS

▶ Rake up the leaves from an area of lawn.

▶ Put the leaves through a shredder.

▶ Compost the leaves.

Vanishing act A blanket of fallen leaves will not harm ground cover plants (top). Leaves also provide a warm bed for hedgehogs (above).

Autumn fireworks Once the display ends, collect fallen leaves for leaf mould or compost.

producing valuable leaf humus that can be used to improve the soil in all parts of the garden. It is usually dark in colour and smells sweetly of the forest floor. You can use it in tubs and containers, to fill raised beds and mound up high borders.

Add bulk to the compost heap

If you only have a small quantity of leaves, you can mix them with other garden waste and shredded branches in the normal compost heap. Intersperse layers of leaves with alternate layers of coarse loose material (such as shredded branches and twigs) and finer material (such as uncooked vegetable waste from the kitchen) in between thin layers of grass cuttings and the leaves and stalks of flowering plants (not the flowers as they may contain seeds). This ensures good drainage and aeration through the compost. Small quantities of leaves will decompose quickly when mixed with these materials and help to make good quality compost that will be invaluable in improving the soil in your garden.

TIME-SAVING TIPS

■ Mowing the lawn (with the grass box on) in autumn shreds and collects fallen leaves. This can save hours of raking.

■ If you put autumn leaves through a shredder, they will decompose much more quickly.

Herbaceous borders
Use perennials for a spectacular, easy-care bed

Perennials provide **colour for every season** in the garden. Provided that their growing conditions are suitable, these plants do not require much attention and will reward you with **years of pleasure**.

MAKE LIFE EASIER

Clear the soil thoroughly of all weed roots and root segments when creating a herbaceous border. Once the bed is established it becomes difficult to get rid of these troublesome weeds without damaging the perennials.

A fiery backdrop
Golden yellow and vermillion *Helenium* brazen it out alongside summer bedding plants, such as scented *Nicotiana* and leggy larkspur (*Consolida ajacis*).

Long-lasting colourful borders

A well planned herbaceous border will give long-term structure to your garden. Perennial flowering plants come in many different shapes and sizes. They die back to ground level each autumn, growing back vigorously the following spring and flowering once again. As well as varieties that flower for only a relatively short period each year there are perennials that flower repeatedly throughout the whole summer – the perfect choice for low-maintenance gardening.

Christmas roses (*Helleborus niger*) unfurl their flowers while it is still winter and in spring primulas follow them. In spring, too, flowering bulbs such as snowdrops (*Galanthus*), crocuses, scilla and daffodils enhance any herbaceous border. The diverse varieties of phlox, bellflower (*Campanula*) and day lily (*Hemerocallis*) provide accents of colour from July until autumn, when the numerous varieties of yellow-flowering *Rudbeckia* grace the border for a rewardingly long period. And it is then that asters, sedums and chrysanthemums also come into their own.

Some early flowering perennials, such as bleeding heart (*Dicentra*), die back soon after flowering, leaving gaps in the border that can then be filled with summer bedding. Others, such as hostas and *Heuchera*, remain decorative after flowering, thanks to their foliage.

Herbaceous displays for every garden

There are perennials suitable for every type of garden, whether dry, sunny, shady or damp. Plant them together in borders according to flowering period, colour and size, so that they produce a pleasing show of blooms throughout the whole year, whether against dry walls in full sun or in shade under trees or around shrubs. When designing a planting plan for a border, take into account the different requirements of each individual plant. Shade lovers will not thrive alongside sun worshippers, and plants preferring a dry situation will be susceptible to fungal diseases if planted in a damp location.

Mix and match A cottage-style garden combines annuals and perennials. Here, pot marigolds (*Calendula officinalis*), phlox, snapdragons (*Antirrhinum*), *Echinacea* and sweet peas (*Lathyrus odoratus*) create an informal riot of colour.

The end of winter Year after year, clumps of vivid crocuses herald the advent of spring.

Remember, too, to include a variety of different flower shapes in a border as well as contrasting colours or combinations of similar tones.

A good supply of nutrients

Spring or autumn are the best times to plant a herbaceous border. Work compost or a slow-release fertiliser into the soil to provide vital nutrients before you start planting. Divide the bed into smaller sections and choose plants for each area according to size, colour and flower shape. Combining too many different varieties will make the border seem muddled, so restrict yourself to a handful of different plants, placing several of the same variety together. Position plants by height, with smaller ones in the foreground and taller ones at the back to ensure that the different varieties will be fully visible.

Creating a showy border

Taking time to devise **a good planting plan** will help you to achieve an impressive display, and minimise work later on. Combine shape and colour carefully for **dramatic effect**.

A well planned bed
You can achieve a striking effect by planting drifts of perennials interspersed with splashes of annual colour.

30-MINUTE TASKS

► Begin to plant a pre-prepared bed of 6 square metres. Put three tall perennials at the back to provide structure.

► Plant ten medium-height perennials in the central area.

► Fill the foreground with eight smaller plants.

Small plants towards the front

One of the secrets of creating an attractive herbaceous border is to position the plants so that they appear natural and, at the same time, to make sure that each plant has enough light and space in which to develop. Tall plants such as delphiniums, phlox and foxgloves (*Digitalis*) create focal points and form the framework. Their long-stemmed flowers tower over medium-height varieties such as *Erigeron*, loosestrife (*Lysimachia*) and cranesbill (*Geranium*), which should be planted further forward. Lower growing plants such as lady's mantle (*Alchemilla mollis*), or ground-cover plants such as creeping phlox (*Phlox stolonifera*) and aubretia are suitable for planting along the front of the border, where they also act as edging to a path or lawn.

From plan to finished border

Take into account the light and wind conditions when planning your border, and the type of soil as well as the visual aspect. These determine which perennials will thrive in the long term. Only plants with compatible requirements will thrive together in a border. Prepare a

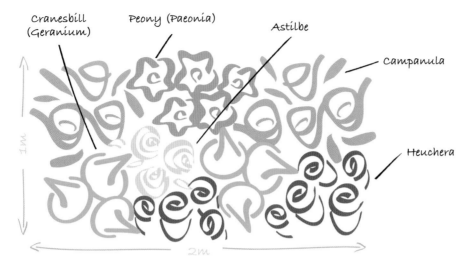

Cranesbill (Geranium)
Peony (Paeonia)
Astilbe
Campanula
Heuchera

1m

2m

Planting plan: short at the front, tall at the back
A peony (*Paeonia*) flanked by two *Campanula* give height at the back. Next in line are cranesbills (*Geranium*) and *Astilbe*, while *Heuchera* show off their foliage along the front of the border.

plan on paper first, checking planting requirements against a plant encyclopedia or the directory at the back of this book before you buy any plants.

Once you are happy with your plan, mark the outline of the different planting groups on the bed itself using a trickle of sand; use curved lines to make the arrangements of the plants look more natural. Then place the plants onto the bed in their pots. Vary the distances between the plants according to their height. Depending upon the variety, tall perennials such as delphiniums and foxgloves should be planted about 50–80cm apart; medium height plants should be around 40–60cm apart and small ones 20–30cm apart.

Buy healthy plants
Check that plants are free from pests and have strong healthy leaves and roots. It's best to plant spring and early summer flowering varieties in autumn and late summer and autumn flowering varieties in spring – though pot-grown plants can be planted at any time of year provided that the ground is not frozen and they are watered in.

Encourage root growth
Water plants thoroughly after planting and firm them in well. Do not apply any fertiliser in the first few weeks, as too many

nutrients will inhibit root development and the plants will be slow to become established. At 6–8 weeks, a slow-release fertiliser will ensure good growth and abundant flower formation. Borders need regular watering during hot dry summers, and a layer of mulch will help to prevent the ground from drying out.

Deadhead for a second flowering
Catmint (*Nepeta*), tickseed (*Coreopsis*) and feverfew (*Tanacetum parthenium*) have particularly long flowering periods. You can prolong the flowering of many other plants by deadheading as soon as the flowers fade. Lady's mantle and cranesbills, for example, will flower again if cut back by about 10cm after their first flowering.

Supporting plants
Tall plants are often damaged by wind and heavy rain and need good support. When planting, place a ring (far left) supported on sticks around the plant, or tie the stems to a framework made from bamboo canes or sticks. Protect your eyes by placing small pots or plastic caps over the tops of tall canes. Systems of interlocking plastic-coated wire supports (left) can be placed around individual or groups of plants.

Herbaceous borders

Planting a natural looking border in a dry, sunny position

In dry situations in full sun the leaves and flowers of many plants wilt quickly. Instead of worrying about watering, **exploit the conditions,** and create a natural border with tough **drought resistant plants.**

Alongside a path A strip of gravel winds like a dry stream bed through a prairie garden planting of sage (*Salvia*), lamb's tongue (*Stachys byzantina*) and several other varieties.

✗ WATCH OUT!

Never dig up wild flowers from the woods and meadows and take them home. Many species are protected by law. Garden centres and nurseries stock an excellent choice of native perennials to suit any situation.

Drought resistant, sun-loving plants

On hot, dry summer days it is easy to see which plants need little attention and which will wilt all too quickly unless you provide them with extra water. Many plants actually prefer a position in full sun, but few can withstand extreme drought.

With summer hosepipe bans becoming an annual occurrence in parts of the country, consider creating a border that needs little watering. The best way to do this is to choose a planting scheme that imitates nature. There are many flowering native or naturalised wild flowers that are attractive enough to earn a place in a garden border and that will even flourish on dry and infertile ground. Many species such as red valerian (*Centranthus ruber*), golden marguerite (*Anthemis tinctoria*) and sea holly (*Eryngium*) flower tirelessly throughout the entire summer and into autumn, attracting bees and butterflies into the garden with their rich supply of nectar. In addition, these plants are often resistant to pests and diseases, unlike the more highly bred and showy cultivated perennials.

140

PLANTS FOR A SUNNY BORDER

PLANTS	FLOWERING PERIOD AND COLOUR OF FLOWERS
Golden marguerite (*Anthemis tinctoria*)	Flowering period June to September; yellow flowers.
Verbascum, different varieties	Flowering period July to September; yellow, pink or violet flowers.
Globe thistle (*Echinops*)	Flowering period July to September; spherical blue flowers.
Evening primrose (*Oenothera*), different varieties	Flowering period June to September; flowers usually yellow.
Yarrow (*Achillea millefolium*), different varieties	Flowering period June to September; red, yellow and white flowers.
Gypsophila, different varieties	Flowering period May to September depending on variety; white or pink, double or single flowers.
Red valerian (*Centranthus ruber*)	Flowering period May to July, often lasting into autumn; red or pink flowers.
Woodland sage (*Salvia* × *sylvestris*)	Flowering period May to October; pinkish violet flowers.

Creating a prairie bed

Ensure you create ideal conditions for the plants when preparing the ground. Most of the sun lovers, such as marguerites (*Chrysanthemum frutescens*) and the sweetly scented evening primrose (*Oenothera*), are naturally opportunistic plants, which successfully colonise waste ground on embankments or tips. They love infertile ground and dry places. Mimic these conditions by incorporating sand and gravel into your garden soil to increase its permeability and reduce its fertility. If the pH value of the soil is too acidic, you can add a little lime to compensate.

A prairie bed effect can be achieved in a border by positioning plants along a gravel path or in front of a dry stone wall. Laying gravel or stone chippings between the individual plants also adds to the illusion that they are growing out of dry and barren ground. The effect will be most successful if you plant in groups of a few, but not too many different varieties, creating drifts of each different flower. Break up the planting with a few clumps of wafting grasses and include a few tall bulbs, such as *Allium*, to create striking highlights and to prolong the flowering season of the bed.

30-MINUTE TASKS

▶ Begin spring-cleaning a 12 square metre border. First remove old dried stems, then loosen the soil and get rid of obvious weeds.

Too much water can cause damage

Their strong, deep root systems allow sun-worshipping, drought-tolerant plants to withstand prolonged dry periods. They find moisture deep in the ground and can easily be overwatered if you add more yourself. Regular watering is only necessary during the first year after planting, to enable the plants to set down strong roots in their new position. Once the plants are established only water on the rare occasions when drooping leaves and flowers indicate that the plant has dried out.

TIME-SAVING TIPS

▢ Lay pebbles or gravel to give the impression of the dried-up bed of a stream running through the border. The material is natural in appearance and requires no maintenance. The artificial stream-bed also makes it easier to tend the border, as it allows you to reach the plants.

▢ Mineral material, such as stone chippings, fine gravel or coarse sand, sets off plants that grow naturally on barren ground particularly well, and restricts the growth of weeds.

Colours to warm and cool *Rudbeckia*, marigolds and foxtail barley (*Hordeum jubatum*) soak up the sun (left), while the blue stems of sea holly create a cooling effect on a hot, sunny day.

Herbaceous borders

Fill gaps in borders with bright summer bedding

When **gaps appear in beds and borders**, as they do in most gardens from time to time, look to fast-growing annuals – grown from **seed** or bought as **summer bedding** – for invaluable infilling.

30-MINUTE TASKS

► Fill gaps in a border with ready-grown summer bedding plants.

► Sow seeds for fast-growing summer flowers in empty areas of a border.

Quick and colourful
Nasturtiums (*Tropaeolum majus*) grow quickly and bear a profusion of bright flowers. They are ideal for filling large gaps in borders.

Golden candles
Robust yellow loosestrife
(*Lysimachia vulgaris*)
(far left) will colonise
ground that other plants
find inhospitable.

Cover a bald patch
Stand a flower-filled wooden
tub where absolutely
nothing will grow (centre).

Bridging the gap For a
stop-gap in a newly created
or rejuvenated herbaceous
border, sow seeds for
summer flowering annuals.
You should soon have a
carpet of flowers that will
then make way for the
planned permanent planting
in autumn.

Bare patches between perennials

Positioning plants too close to one
another can lead to overcrowding
and create a fertile environment for
pests and diseases. Correct planting
often means that a new border
contains bare areas between the
perennials, grasses and shrubs.
Not only are these bare patches unattractive; being
exposed to the weather, they can lose moisture rapidly
on a hot or windy day.

The best way to fill gaps is with summer bedding
plants. Choose unfussy varieties that grow quickly, such
as nasturtiums (*Tropaeolum majus*), pot marigolds
(*Calendula officinalis*), *Alyssum* or *Verbena*. You can sow
these directly into the ground or, preferably, plant them
out as growing plants. Make sure that they will be
compatible with existing plants – that the colours are in
harmony and that they won't crowd out their
neighbours as they grow. Plants with decorative foliage,
such as burning bush (*Dictamnus albus*), foxtail barley
(*Hordeum jubatum*) or love lies bleeding (*Amaranthus
caudatus*) will also blend in attractively.

Early flowering plants that die back quickly, such
as tulips or bleeding hearts (*Dicentra*), often leave gaps
in established beds and borders. Rigorous pruning can
also lead to gaps here and there. Summer bedding
plants again come to the rescue. Simply plant them
between the perennials. If you want to prevent bedding
plants from spreading too much, leave them in their
pots and sink them, pots and all, into the ground. In
autumn you simply take out the filler plants, or leave
them in situ over winter and dig the remains into the
ground in spring. The following year the gaps will be
smaller because the permanent plants will have grown.
You can then choose other colour combinations to
create a new visual effect.

Dealing with problem areas

In many gardens there are places that drive the gardener
to despair, because in spite of every effort nothing will
flourish. Either the ground is too heavy and is
constantly waterlogged, or it is much too dry and stony.
A simpler solution than undertaking costly and time-
consuming measures to improve the soil is to put a large
container full of colourful flowers in the problem spot.
Alternatively you could construct a raised bed that can
be filled with soil and compost that is better suited to
growing, so that you are not reliant on the poor quality
ground underneath.

MAKE LIFE EASIER

■ Cut off faded flowers from weeds
that self-seed easily before seed heads
develop. This will save you around
five hours weeding each year for every
10 square metres of border.

■ Instead of summer bedding, fill gaps
with decorative vegetables and annual
herbs, such as parsley (*Petroselinum
crispum*) and dill (*Anethum
graveolens*) – this is easier than having
to prepare a special bed for them.

■ In summer, place plants in pots,
such as azaleas, myrtle (*Myrtus
communis*), cyclamen or hydrangeas,
in the gaps in shady or partly-shaded
borders.

Herbaceous borders

Many herbaceous plants like a semi-shaded position

Herbaceous perennials that like semi-shaded positions, are among the most undemanding of plants. Create an easy-care border for them under a large tree or perhaps next to the house.

Dappled delight Places where the sun does not burn all day or is filtered through a light canopy of leaves are perfect sites for hostas, which provide interest with their plain and variegated leaves in a range of greens. The bright yellow flowers of black-stemmed ligularia and the plumes of an astilbe add light and colour.

Fabulous foliage
Hostas (above) prefer semi-shaded positions. Grown for their luxuriant foliage, there is a leaf colour and shape for every situation.

Nodding stars The delicate flowers of *Aquilegia* (right) come in myriad hues.

Blue and gold Tall spikes of delphinium and ligularia make a striking show (below).

A low-maintenance herbaceous border

In semi-shaded corners of the garden, such as under large bushes, conditions are similar to those on the edges of woodland. It is easy and quick to create an attractive, low-maintenance border with plants that are at home in these conditions. The results are particularly effective if you put several of the same plant together. They will spread rapidly via runners, or by layering or seeding, quickly filling neglected shady areas and flowering after a short time.

Once a semi-shaded border has been planted you can leave it to look after itself – more or less – except for a bit of basic maintenance: mulching now and again, thinning out slightly any plants that are growing too vigorously, and occasionally watering in dry years.

30-MINUTE TASKS

► Mulch the ground in a semi-shaded flower border 5 metres long.

► Remove faded flowers and cut off any dead leaves from the plants in a border.

Brighten up dark corners

Brightly coloured flowers bring light and colour to shady corners. The slim, radiant white flower spikes of bugbane (*Cimicifuga*) are made up of many tiny flowers. Depending on the species they flower at varying times from June until October. Just like goatsbeard (*Aruncus dioicus*) with its bright flower panicles, they brighten up the shady margins of a woodland area, as do blue monkshood (*Aconitum*), *Campanula* or sky blue Jacob's ladder (*Polemonium caeruleum*). The flowers of small plants such as aubretia are happiest left undisturbed and need little deadheading. Plants with decorative foliage, such as hostas or the early-spring-flowering barrenwort (*Epimedium*), are also ideal for semi-shaded borders. In moist ground, lungwort (*Pulmonaria*) will flourish. It flowers in March and bears attractive white-flecked leaves until autumn.

There are many easy-care creeping groundcover plants suitable for semi-shaded positions, such as creeping Jenny (*Lysimachia nummularia* 'Aurea') or bugle (*Ajuga reptans*). They flourish in any ground, provided it is moist. The white-flecked leaves of yellow archangel (*Lamiastrum galeobdolon*) will also spread quickly and cover the ground.

Dry ground conditions are a problem for many plants growing under shallow-rooted shrubs. You can help by mulching occasionally with leaves, wilted grass cuttings or mushroom compost. You should also water regularly. Plants such as wood cranesbill (*Geranium sylvaticum*) and Welsh poppies (*Meconopsis cambrica*), can usually grow even here without extra watering. A drip hose irrigation system hidden between the plants can be useful on inhospitable ground that has a tendency to dry out.

PLANTS FOR SEMI-SHADED SITES

PLANTS	FLOWERS/GROWTH HABIT/HEIGHT
Common aquilegia	Violet, blue, pink, white; upright; 50–70cm
Monkshood (*Aconitum*)	Blue; erect; 1–1.5 metres
Jacob's ladder (*Polemonium caeruleum*)	Skyblue; upright; 30–60cm
Clustered bellflower (*Campanula glomerata*)	Violet to lavender, blue or white; bushy; 50–60cm
Lungwort (*Pulmonaria*)	Pink, red, violet, purple, blue or white; bushy; 20–30cm
Common foxglove (*Digitalis purpurea*)	Purple, pink, white; upright; 1–2m
Bugbane (*Cimicifuga*)	White, cream; upright; 60–90cm
Goat's beard (*Aruncus dioicus*)	Creamy-white; spreading; 1–1.2m
Wood cranesbill (*Geranium sylvaticum*)	Blue to purple, pinkish purple, pink or white; bushy and upright; 50–70cm
Delphinium	White, blue, violet; upright; 60cm

TIME-SAVING TIPS

■ One benefit of a wild flower border is its natural appearance, which allows you to cut down on the time-consuming job of deadheading.

Light touches in deep shadow

Few flowering garden plants do well in **deep shade** – but you can create a cool, verdant herbaceous border using **grasses and ferns**. Once established, this border will have the advantage of demanding **little attention**.

A woodland feel

Some plants shun bright sunlight and flourish in gloomy half-darkness under thick tree canopies or in the shadows cast by buildings and walls.

Species ideal for turning shady places in the garden into romantic, permanent, low-maintenance borders include ferns, woodland grasses, such as wood sedge (*Carex sylvatica*) or melick (*Melica*), along with plants such as bugbane (*Cimicifuga*), meadow rue (*Thalictrum*), monkshood (*Aconitum*), hostas, *Astrantia* and Solomon's seal (*Polygonatum*).

Most of these plants prefer moist ground rich in humus, although a few of them will tolerate long dry periods and some do better in lime-rich soil. For the majority, loosen the soil with a spade or garden fork to a depth of about 30cm and work in leaf compost or a commercial composted bark until the earth has become dark and humus-rich. In the dry shade of a wall, plants may need additional watering.

Allow plenty of room when planting

Before planting the border, position plants on the area of ground that you have prepared. Allow enough distance between ferns and grasses, so that their shapes can be fully appreciated. A tree fern (*Dicksonia antarctica*) – which can grow up to 6 metres tall, though usually considerably less – looks particularly effective set against a carpet of low-growing ground-cover plants. Its crown may require some protection in winter.

Winter hardy ferns, such as species of hard shield fern (*Polystichum aculeatum*), are good in a shady border. These keep their fronds until the spring and provide a

WATCH OUT!

Do not plant any rampant ferns such as ostrich fern (*Matteuccia struthiopteris*). They will spread rapidly and can create more work keeping them under control.

A fairytale corner Softly lit by a few slender rays of sun, woodland grasses sway elegantly and ferns appear as if by magic, unfurling their fronds in hypnotic fashion.

Light show Variegated hostas and lime green fern fronds brighten up a shady corner.

30-MINUTE TASKS

► Plant a group of ferns in an area of prepared ground.

► Maintain a shaded border by cutting out dead flower stems and fern leaves.

splendid contrast to many spring flowering bulbs like snowdrops (*Galanthus*) and crocuses.

Allow plenty of space for flowering plants like *Astrantia* and Solomon's seal. These take up a lot of room when fully grown, but achieve their full potential only when allowed to grow freely – so resist thinning them out too soon.

Low maintenance

Water in thoroughly after planting and during the first few weeks to encourage root development. Once plants have become established, watering will be necessary only during long dry spells. If there are no ground-cover plants, a layer of mulch will protect the soil from drying out, retain warmth and prevent weeds from growing. Otherwise, all you need to do is to remove dead stems or faded flowers from time to time.

Over the years, clumps of offshoots from grasses and the spread of flowering plants should fill any gaps to cover the ground completely. There will then be no need to mulch, and the border will more or less look after itself.

Planting plan: colour in the shadows Pastel coloured flowers look particularly delicate in the half-light, while large leaves provide an attractive contrast.

PLANTING FERNS

1 Water the fern thoroughly before planting. Leave the root ball submersed in water until no more air bubbles rise to the surface.

2 The planting hole should be twice as deep and twice as wide as the root ball. Mix compost with the soil that you have removed from the hole.

3 Position the fern in the hole so that the crown is slightly above ground level. Fill the hole with earth.

TIME-SAVING TIPS

☐ Mulch with bark chippings. This avoids the need for soil improvement.

☐ If you are planting in the autumn, dig a large hole and plant a selection of bulbs and tubers at the same time. This will save about 30 minutes work for every square metre.

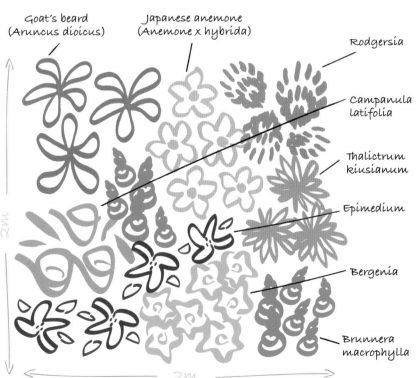

Goat's beard (*Aruncus dioicus*)

Japanese anemone (*Anemone x hybrida*)

Rodgersia

Campanula latifolia

Thalictrum kiusianum

Epimedium

Bergenia

Brunnera macrophylla

2m

2m

Herbaceous borders

A shady border conceals dead leaves

Areas under large bushes **where sunlight rarely penetrates** are ideal for plants with **interesting foliage**. These not only suppress weeds but, as a bonus, **hide fallen leaves** in autumn – so you don't have to rake them up.

30-MINUTE TASKS

► In autumn, remove dead flower stems and faded flowers from a border of up to 15 square metres.

► Divide a spreading perennial in an overcrowded area for planting elsewhere.

Green is never boring

Add interest to problem areas in deep shade, such as those found under shrubs, with lively foliage plants. Many of these specialist plants display their decorative leaves long before and after any flowers have faded. For maximum visual appeal, group a number of plants with leaves of different shapes and colours together.

Large wide leaves such as those of Chinese rhubarb (*Rheum palmatum*), giant *Gunnera* or *Ligularia*, will soon enliven large areas and contrast well with tall grasses. The broad, strikingly veined and, depending on variety, white or yellow-patterned leaves of hostas

Going for green A flourishing shady border features a striking variegated hosta, acid green ferns and pretty lady's mantle. Fallen autumn leaves can be left to lie under the plants' foliage, where they will decompose and fertilise the ground.

provide a contrast to the feathery leaves of *Astilbe* and ferns. Fill the foreground with *Bergenia* and lady's mantle (*Alchemilla mollis*), or low-growing ground-cover plants such as barrenwort (*Epimedium*) and perennial forget-me-not (*Myosotis*).

Most shade-loving plants require open humus-rich moist soil. If the soil is light, loosen the top with a garden fork or a hoe. If you need to improve the soil,

PLANTS TO HIDE DEAD LEAVES

PLANTS	LEAVES	HEIGHT
Bergenia, hybrids and species	Large, rich green, turning bronze or reddish in autumn.	20–60cm
Yellow archangel (*Lamiastrum galeobdolon*)	Serrated yellow leaves with creamy white centres.	30–60cm
Hosta, varieties and species	Strikingly veined; many different shades of blue and green with various leaf markings in white or yellow.	40–60cm
Spotted dead-nettle (*Lamium maculatum*)	Serrated, mid-green leaves with different and beautiful silver markings.	30–60cm
Heuchera, varieties and species	Varying from smooth to wavy; various shades of red, purple and brown according to species; also light green or orange; occasionally finely ruffled.	30–60cm
Rodgersia, varieties	Deeply veined large leaves; often bronze or red tinged with contrasting coloured veins.	60–180cm

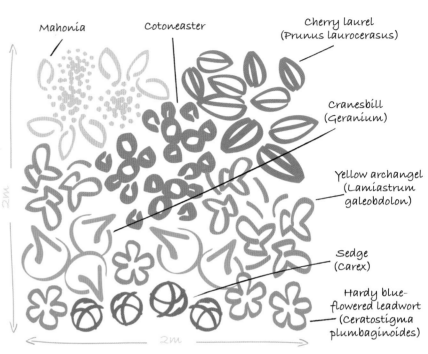

Planting plan: a border to hide dead leaves
Shrubs, perennials and short grasses grouped in light shade soon hide the fallen leaves of autumn. Alongside the brightly flecked leaves of yellow archangel (*Lamiastrum galeobdolon*), the evergreen foliage of *Mahonia* and cherry laurel (*Prunus laurocerasus*) provide colour in winter. Cranesbill (*Geranium*) and hardy blue-flowered leadwort (*Ceratostigma plumbaginoides*) add colourful flowers to the picture.

work in compost or manure. If the ground is heavy, dig it over and loosen it by adding sand. If possible, plant on cool, cloudy days: newly planted perennials will soon begin to suffer from lack of water in hot weather.

Lots of free time for the gardener

After planting, you will need to ensure that the soil is kept slightly moist, but once the border has become established you can more or less leave it alone. Leave any dead leaves from the surrounding shrubs on the ground in autumn to form a layer of natural mulch. This helps with water retention, provides a cover to retain warmth in winter and over time the leaves break down to form humus, so that the plants will need neither fertiliser nor compost. Just thin out any plants that have spread too much after a few years.

Creating a shady border

Rodgersia, foxgloves (*Digitalis*) and bugbane (*Cimicifuga*) are tall, upright, undemanding plants that give structure to a shady border. They brighten up shadows with their flowers and their leaves provide striking structural highlights. Position them at the back of the border so that they do not obscure other plants.

Use smaller plants such as *Astilbe* or hostas alongside the tall specimens at the back. They form an ideal foil for more statuesque, structural plants.

Finally, fill the gaps in the border with ferns, shade-loving grasses and smaller foliage plants. The varied colours and shapes of their leaves will help to bring the whole planting scheme to life.

Blue clouds Cranesbills (*Geranium*) and *Rodgersia* cover the ground with gossamer-light flowers and striking leaves.

149

Protecting flowers from slugs and snails

Slugs and snails are among the most destructive **enemies of flowers**. They can decimate your carefully nurtured shoots and newly germinated seedlings – but some of this damage **can be prevented**.

A wall of flowers
Begonias planted as a barrier at the front of a herbaceous border will help to protect other flowers in the border from the ravages of snails.

Likes and dislikes Snails steer clear of snapdragons (*Antirrhinum*), but normally make straight for cosmos and French marigolds.

TIME-SAVING TIPS

■ Rather than picking off the culprits one by one, drown snails in a beer trap or attract and trap them in old cabbage leaves or empty grapefruit halves. Collect them and dispose of them by putting them in your lidded green recycling bin or tipping them into a distant hedgerow or some non-cultivated ground.

First, select your plants

Experience has taught gardeners that certain plants are less susceptible to attack by slugs and snails than others. While delphiniums, dahlias and French marigolds (*Tagetes patula*) are all favourite foods, snails do not like hairy-leaved and strongly aromatic plants such as lavender (*Lavendula*), sage (*Salvia officinalis*), catmint (*Nepeta*) or cranesbill (*Geranium*).

For a sunny, snail-free bed, plant these and other varieties that snails dislike, including lady's mantle (*Alchemilla mollis*), yarrow (*Achillea millefolium*), rock rose (*Helianthemum*), Gaillardia, golden rod (*Solidago*), phlox, day lilies (*Hemerocallis*), speedwell (*Veronica*),

Slug and snail patrol
Welcome wildlife into your garden as a natural pest control army. Thrushes (left) and other birds will pick out and devour your snails; and toads (below) relish snail eggs, slugs and young snails.

sedums and obedient plant (*Physostegia*). Summer flowering nasturtiums (*Tropoaeleum majus*), Portulaca and some varieties of carnations (*Dianthus*) are also given a wide berth by hungry snails.

Snail-resistant perennials and summer bedding plants specifically aimed at the snail-plagued gardener are available from nurseries and garden centres, although you may have to ask for them.

Many perennials, such as the poisonous monkshood (*Aconitum*), are eaten by snails only as young seedlings, but not when they are mature plants. Try using a cut-down plastic bottle as a collar around young plants to protect them.

An edging of flowers to keep snails away

Edge your bed with begonias (*Begonia semperflorens*), snapdragons (*Antirrhinum*) or forget-me-nots (*Myosotis*). These plants will help to keep snails away. Snails may also be deterred by a mulch of straw, sawdust, gravel or coffee grounds as they find these surfaces unpleasant to move across. If rain softens the straw or sawdust, or washes the coffee grounds away, you will need to replace them. Special snail barriers made from zinc-coated steel (see page 239) can be used to isolate particularly susceptible plants – but make sure that no part of the plant extends or droops over the barrier as it could serve as a bridge, enabling the snails to breach it.

Slug pellets are the most effective way of combating slugs and snails. When choosing which type to buy, check that they are harmless to other garden creatures. Sprinkle the pellets evenly but sparingly between the plants you wish to protect; do not pile them up. Follow the manufacturer's instructions carefully to ensure you

apply the right amount. Slugs can also be controlled biologically with nematodes (thread worms), which bore into the bodies of the slugs and kill them after about a week. Nematodes are available from specialist suppliers; put them in water and pour it between the affected plants.

PROTECTIVE COLLARS

Cut off the top third or half and the base of a plastic bottle. Place the body of the bottle over the plant needing protection and push it firmly into the ground.

BEER TRAPS

Beer attracts snails from far and wide, so not only will the beer trap the snails that are already in your garden, but it may well attract armies of snails from further afield.

MAKE LIFE EASIER

Loosen the earth in beds regularly, so that the surface dries out quickly, making it harder for snails to move about. Look for snail eggs while you are doing this, especially in autumn and spring. They look like small white pearls.

On dry days, slugs shelter under pieces of wood and stones, and also under shady and bushy herbaceous plants; take the opportunity to hunt them down and collect the pests and dispose of them.

Easy grasses give year-round pleasure

Forget confining grass to the lawn. **Ornamental grasses** can add a subtle and **graceful touch** to a flowerbed or border. Planted in the right position, all that most grasses need is a good trim in spring.

Blue grass *Festuca glauca* is tough, easy to grow and lasts for years. Its steely blue stalks and coppery-brown flower buds make an impact at the front of any border.

WATCH OUT!

Do not remove the leaves and flower stems from grasses in the winter. They protect against moisture-induced rot and look attractive when covered in frost.

Gently eye-catching

Grasses lend a garden natural flair and enhance it with eye-catching detail all year round as they change with the seasons. The soft green of spring deepens to a lush, rich dark green in summer, when delicate flower clusters sway in the breeze. In autumn grasses glow in a multitude of brown and red hues. Move into winter and they cast a spell over the garden, their dry fruit clusters and tufts lightly dusted in snow or a sprinkling of hoarfrost.

Grasses are surprisingly versatile. They work well whether grown as a group of several varieties, planted alone as a specimen plant or used to loosen up a formal flower bed or to brighten a dull area.

30-MINUTE TASKS

► Pick out dead or unsightly material from three to five ornamental grasses.

► Cut back a large clump of ornamental grass with hedge clippers.

Stand alone or grouped?

The tallest species, such as pampas grass (*Cortaderia selloana*), *Miscanthus*, reed grass (*Calamagrostis*) or giant feather grass (*Stipa gigantea*), are particularly effective as stand-alone plants. Clumps of the slightly shorter fountain grass (*Pennisetum alopecuroides* 'Hameln'), with its charming flower clusters, also need plenty of space to show off their beauty to best advantage. By contrast, low-growing grasses like the various types of fescue look harmonious planted in groups.

There are grasses for all situations. Native to the prairies, blue oat grass (*Helictotrichon sempervirens*) or switch grass (*Panicum virgatum*) are best suited to dry, sunny positions. Sedges and woodrushes, on the other hand, require extremely moist, humus-rich soil and shade if they are to thrive.

Easy-care grasses

Most grasses are extremely undemanding providing they are grown in a suitable site. The best time for planting is in spring, when the soil is warming up and drier weather is approaching. Grasses planted in autumn often suffer with the onset of damper winter weather and come back only sparsely in spring.

Most grasses are perfectly happy without being fed with supplementary nutrients. Only tall species such as pampas grass appreciate a little compost every few years.

Most grasses need cutting back vigorously in spring. Use hand shears or hedge clippers and cut back all the old stems as low as possible, taking care to avoid young shoots. Low-growing, evergreen grasses such as the hardy *Carex comans* 'frosted curls' need no pruning at all. Just pick or cut out dead sections.

Dusted with icing sugar
Don't clip grasses in autumn, or you will miss out on a magical scene when frost visits the garden

As soft as a feather It's hard to resist brushing a hand over the tactile flowers of grasses such as fountain grass.

From time to time you will need to curb the growth of particularly vigorous grasses, such as *Miscanthus*, which quickly spread beyond the space earmarked for them. The easiest way is to trim back the roots with a spade. Rhizome barriers (see page 111) are also useful, but must be put in the ground when first planting the grass. An old container or tub with the base removed makes a good rhizome barrier.

DIVIDING GRASSES

1 For grasses that produce new rooted plants around the edges of the parent plant: carefully remove the new growth complete with roots. Plant in pots or replant elsewhere.

2 If the centre of a clump of grass has died and the plant is growing only around the outer edges, lift it and divide in two with two garden forks.

3 You can also slice up large clumps of grass in the ground with a sharp spade. Then simply lift and replant elsewhere.

TIME-SAVING TIPS

■ Avoid vigorous varieties or put in a root barrier when planting; this will save you around three hours control and cutting back a year.

■ Protect grasses in severe conditions in winter so they do not rot, saving you time in buying and planting replacements. Take hold of the grass and gather it together, twisting it rather like hair and tying with twine to prevent cold and wet penetrating the crown of the plant.

Bulbs and tubers delight with colour

Plant bulbs for the **promise of beauty** year after year. These perennial plants gladden the heart as winter ends, or bridge gaps in flowering whatever the season. Many bulbs can be **planted and forgotten** – until new shoots remind you of their presence.

The launch of the flowering season

Bulbs are ideal for making an early start to the gardener's year. Crocuses, daffodils and tulips create a blaze of colour in borders when other plants are only just beginning to make an appearance. Then at the height of summer, the lilies (*Lilium*), montbretias (*Crocosmia*) and dahlias add their colours to the show. Once the flowering season is over, just remove the dead flowerheads but leave the foliage in place to allow the bulbs to regain their strength for renewed growth the following year.

Only plant healthy bulbs

To get the best out of your plants, take special care when choosing bulbs and tubers. They must be undamaged, firm when you squeeze them and the roots should not have begun to grow.

PLANTING BULBS

Make sure that you plant bulbs and tubers at the right time and to the right depth. Large bulbs, which are planted singly, are easiest to plant with a bulb planter.

It is a good idea to use a special planting basket to plant a number of small bulbs. Place the basket in the hole and fill it about half full with the soil that you have dug out. Arrange the bulbs on this base and cover completely with soil, remembering to plant to the right depth.

PLANTING GUIDELINES FOR BULBS

PLANT	PLANTING DATE	DEPTH
Scilla	End of April–early June	5–10cm
Dahlia	September–October	10–30cm
Spring crocus	September–October	3–8cm
Tulip	September–October	10–15cm
Hyacinth	September–October	10–15cm
Lily	August–September	15–25cm
Montbretia	Mid-May–early June	5–10cm
Daffodil	September–October	10–20cm
Snowdrop	August–September	4–8cm
Grape hyacinth	September–October	4–10cm
Winter aconite	September–October	2–5cm

Reject bulbs with soft or damaged areas – these are signs of disease and insect damage. Plant bulbs and tubers promptly after buying them. Spring-flowering bulbs and tubers should be planted in autumn; summer-flowering ones in spring; and autumn-flowering ones in summer. Pot-grown bulbous plants can be planted at any time but be gentle with their fragile roots.

Many tuberous plants, such as gladioli and dahlias, are not hardy and, apart from in the mildest parts of southern England, can only be planted out after the danger of frost has passed. Once they have finished flowering and the first frosts have blackened the foliage, cut the stems down to about 15cm, lift the tubers and store them upside down in a dry, frost-free place for around three weeks until they dry out. Then store (the right way up) with the tubers buried in sand or sawdust in a cool, dark, frost-free place.

Correct planting depth is vital

Make sure that bulbs are positioned in their planting holes with the tips of the shoots pointing upwards. The rule of thumb for planting depth is to plant two to three

30-MINUTE TASKS

► Plant 20 bulbs in a flowerbed.

► Lift and store six tuberous plants in autumn.

Splashes of brilliance Many spring-flowering bulbs produce boldly coloured and patterned blooms and foliage, such as these striped dwarf tulips growing in a colourful rockery (left).

Flashes of fire The elegant flower spikes of montbretias (*Crocosmia*) add a striking splash of colour to any summer flower bed. The sooner they are planted, the sooner they come into full bloom.

times as deep as the height of the bulb. Plant them a bit deeper in light sandy soil and less deep in heavy clay. If you plant bulbs too deeply, they will sprout very late; too shallow and they may suffer in winter – and you may damage them when weeding or hoeing. Small bulbs such as crocuses, scilla and grape hyacinths (*Muscari*) should be planted at a depth of around 5cm, dwarf tulips at around 10cm and large bulbs such as daffodils, lilies or crown imperials (*Fritillaria imperialis*) at 25cm – with each bulb in its own hole. The ideal distance between bulbs is half the mature height, in other words 3–5cm for small species and 30–50cm for large ones.

Planting in baskets

Bulbs are most effective when planted in groups. The lower-growing the species, the more plants are needed to create a good effect. You can use planting baskets to plant groups containing different species very close together. Simply bury the planted baskets up to the rim in the flower bed and cover with soil. If you need to lift the bulbs in autumn, you can remove the baskets without damaging any surrounding plants.

In the wild, bulbs and tuberous plants grow naturally especially in areas that experience long spells of dry weather. This explains why they rot quickly if exposed to moisture for any length of time. To protect them, line the planting hole with a layer of sand, grit or fine gravel, then place the bulbs or tubers on top.

MAKE LIFE EASIER

■ Use a bulb planter with a scale marked on the side to help you plant individual bulbs at the right depth.

■ Voles and squirrels like to dig up and eat most kinds of bulbs. Protect them with an inverted wire basket or sheet of wire mesh placed over them.

Rockery plants brighten up stony ground

Create a **miniature landscape** in your garden by combining rocks and perennial plants. With careful landscaping and planting, a rock garden can be a particularly **easy-care option**.

A patchwork of colour
Tough ground-cover plants are easy to care for and produce masses of flowers.

Mountains in miniature

Rock gardens can take many forms. If you use uniform geometrically shaped stones, the effect can be quite architectural, but if you prefer a more natural look, you can create a mountainous landscape in miniature with a variety of shapes and sizes. Make use of an existing slope to build a rock garden or build up your own mound, or combine stones and perennial plants on flatter ground to create an area with an alpine feel.

Rocks of all kinds and in many shapes and sizes can be sourced from local quarries, and garden centres also stock suitable material. The choice includes sandstone, limestone or tufa – a porous limestone that absorbs and retains moisture so that plants can be grown in cavities on the rock as well as between stones. Tufa makes a good base for alpine plants that are difficult to grow in garden soil.

Stick to a single type of rock for a convincing effect, but vary the sizes for a natural look. Choose rocks that will suit the scale of your garden: massive boulders will look ridiculous in the small garden of a terraced house but will be a dramatic addition to a large garden. Remember that larger rocks are very heavy and difficult to manoeuvre.

Honey coloured slope
Rough blocks of warm sandstone and shrubby evergreens give this gentle slope a Mediterranean feel; tough, low-maintenance plants find a foothold in between the rocks.

Building a rock garden

Choose a sunny, open position with good drainage, preferably facing south or south-west to west. If you are building a mound from scratch, use rough chunks of rock, pebbles and rubble to form the basis, but take care not to make it too steep (the height should be no more than one third of the diameter). Then place a 10–20cm layer of soil on top. Keep the most interestingly shaped rocks to use on the outside where they will be seen.

A more level rock garden will need good drainage. Dig out the soil to a depth of around 40–50cm and add a 20–30cm layer of rubble or gravel. Then spread a layer of soil 30–40cm thick on top of this, and embed rocks or stones in it to create a landscape. It is better to use fewer stones rather than too many.

When building a mound, take care to arrange the stones so that they are secure and cannot roll away or slip out of place after heavy rainfall. Lay them flat on their broadest side or – better still – embed roughly a third of their volume in the slope. Tipping the rocks back slightly will make them more stable.

The best time to construct a rock garden is in autumn with a view to planting it up in spring. If you wish to plant in autumn, try to do so by the end of September, to give the plants time to take root before the first frosts. If you plant during construction, be careful to avoid crushing the plants or their roots as you position the rocks.

All in the mix

Small perennials that grow little more than 10–20cm in height are particularly effective in a rock garden. Check the flowering season when choosing your plants to make sure that there is always something in bloom. Plant bulbs such as wild tulips (*Tulipa sylvestris*) or miniature daffodils to flower in the early spring.

Planting suggestion: sloping rockery
A colourful mix of alpines nestles between rough hewn rocks on a sloping bed.

Many ground-cover plants, like creeping phlox (*Phlox stolonifera*) are spring flowering. Varieties of bellflower (*Campanula*) and carnations (*Dianthus*) flower in summer, whilst *Edelweiss* and gentians (*Gentiana*) bloom well into autumn. Low-growing grasses will enhance the natural character of a rock garden and, depending on the garden's size, dwarf conifers may fit in well. Even ferns will feel at home in the shade of a taller rock.

A bed of slate Miniature plants grow happily between slabs of rock; the open bed area is covered with a complementary weed-suppressing mulch of flat blue-grey slate chippings.

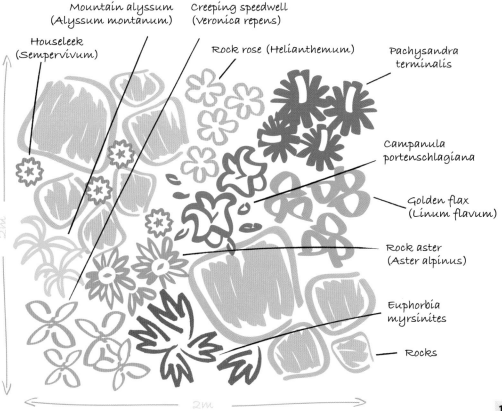

Mountain alyssum (*Alyssum montanum*)
Creeping speedwell (*Veronica repens*)
Houseleek (*Sempervivum*)
Rock rose (*Helianthemum*)
Pachysandra terminalis
Campanula portenschlagiana
Golden flax (*Linum flavum*)
Rock aster (*Aster alpinus*)
Euphorbia myrsinites
Rocks

Herbaceous borders
Using planted walls to landscape a slope

A sunny slope is the perfect site for a rock garden. Terracing and retaining walls will help to transform it into a low-maintenance focal point for your garden.

30-MINUTE TASKS

► Create two or three planting crevices between stones in the rockery, using a chisel if necessary.

► Fill crevices with tiny plants, using a mixture of soil and grit to pack round their roots.

A slope full of flowers
Retaining walls used to create terraces can give a sloping garden formal structure. In south or south-west facing situations, they are an ideal basis for a rock garden. Generous planting, primarily with ground cover or carpet-forming plants, will grow to conceal any harsh angles. Your choice of plants will determine the rock garden's style, transforming a geometric structure into a mountainous Alpine or Mediterranean style landscape featuring fragrant herbs and delicate flowers.

A dry stone retaining wall
The foot of a slope is the perfect place to build a dry stone wall. This type of wall, constructed without mortar, looks like part of the landscape and provides a habitat for plants and animals in its many cracks and crevices. Building a dry stone wall requires skill and it is best to enlist the help of a professional.

The wall will need to lean in towards the slope slightly for stability at an angle of around 15 degrees – so a wall 1 metre high will slope backwards by a total of 15cm over the full height. (It is not advisable to build a dry stone wall any higher than 1 metre.) It should have

Tumbling colour Flowering ground-cover plants such as aubretia and alyssum spill out over the top of this retaining dry stone wall.

sturdy foundations or 'footings' of hardcore or concrete, wider than the width of the wall, and laid in a trench 20–30cm deep. Ideally the footings should stop 5–10cm below the surface so that the first layer of stones can be set partly below ground level.

The stones should be large, with some the full thickness of the wall being used at intervals as bonding stones, especially at the base. The first course of stones should be set on the footings at a slight angle towards the slope; embedding some stones part way into the bank will increase stability. Stagger the stones so they overlap each other, using slightly smaller and narrower stones towards the top. Backfill between the wall and slope with hardcore to allow water to drain away freely.

Planting in crevices
To squeeze plants such as alyssum, saxifrage (*Saxifraga*), houseleek (*Sempervivum*), rock soapwort (*Saponaria ocymoides*) or rock rose (*Helianthemum nummularium*) into the crevices between the stones you may need to widen the gaps slightly with a chisel (wear safety goggles to protect your eyes from flying stone chips). Seedlings or small root cuttings are ideal for planting in

Two ways to retain a slope A wall built with mortar (right) is erected at right angles to the ground. A dry stone wall (far right) is built with natural stones, without mortar, and leans gently into the slope. Both walls need to be backfilled with hardcore for drainage.

Mini rock garden
A stone trough can be transformed into a miniature alpine garden with just a few plants. An effective drainage layer and free-draining soil formulated for alpines are indispensable (left).

Using gravel
Delicate grasses look even more fragile between heavy chunks of stone. Fine gravel has been used to level uneven rock surfaces, creating a rocky stairway.

crevices in a wall as their roots are still small. Even so, you may need to squeeze them a little to ease them into the gaps, but take care not to crush the roots by applying too much pressure.

Once you have guided the roots into the gaps, add a little soil and grit and firm in gently. Then spray with plenty of water. If you wish to plant an existing dry stone wall with rockery and alpine plants, first scrape any existing old soil out of the gaps in the wall.

An alpine garden in a trough

Even if you do not want to devote an area of your garden to a rockery, you can still enjoy the pleasures of rockery plants by creating a miniature alpine landscape in an old stone trough or sink. Genuine stone troughs are costly and hard to come by, but you can buy replicas made from reconstituted stone. Place pieces of broken pot over any drainage holes and add a layer of gravel or sand. Fill the trough with a compost specially formulated for alpines and plant it up.

Alternatively, choose a striking large stone and put it in the trough. Tufa is a good choice as it will provide an ideal home for small plants such as houseleeks. Fill the trough with alpine compost so that some of the main rock is still exposed, and arrange smaller stones around it. Position your chosen plants between the stones and cover any bare compost with a layer of gravel or grit.

Linking levels If your garden is on a slope, you may need some steps to link one terraced area to another. Building stone steps and retaining walls from the same material creates a satisfying uniform effect.

Herbaceous borders
Keep your flowerbeds looking fresh

After a few years, perennials may **get out of hand**, obscuring most of your original design. To restore your flowerbed to perfection, treat it to a **makeover**. This takes time but will give you lots of free plants and a healthy **rejuvenated border**.

✕ WATCH OUT!

Do not plant too closely together; set plants at least half their mature height apart. Never dig out and return perennials to the flowerbed without dividing them first.

Still blooming To keep beds flowering year after year, give perennials a regular tonic by dividing them every few years.

Ever-evolving herbaceous borders
The appearance of herbaceous borders varies every year, partly because the weather conditions suit different varieties in different years. In time, some plants spread, while others disappear. Likewise, some stop flowering as they get older and need dividing to revive them. You can intervene by curbing vigorously growing plants and creating space for less robust ones.

Sometimes, though, a flowerbed just does not turn out the way you had imagined, despite all the careful planning. It may be that the light conditions have altered because of a tree planted nearby or a neighbour's extension, or because weeds have got the upper hand. When this happens, it is time to consider a general overhaul. The best times to do this are in spring or autumn.

Giving borders a major overhaul
Unfortunately, there's no short cut when it comes to sorting out a bed or border that is overrun with pernicious weeds, such as ground-elder (*Aegopodium podagraria*) and couch grass (*Elymus repens*). But be assured – this time-consuming job will save you hours of tedious, repetitive weeding and frustration in the long run.

Fountain of youth
Dividing not only encourages plants such as phlox to produce more flowers, but also keeps them healthy.

The first thing to do is cut back all perennials radically. This gives you a better view of the whole border. Then lift the individual plants with a spade or garden fork and carefully tease out and remove any weeds tangled in the roots. A good way to do this is to plunge the whole rootball in a large tub of water and let it soak before giving it a good rinse. You'll then be able to identify and remove all the unwanted invading roots from the tangle much more easily.

Next, clear all the weeds from the bed, taking care not to leave any pieces of rhizome or root behind – otherwise the weeds will be back in no time. Weed on dry days if possible, when weed debris left on the surface quickly withers and perishes. Finally, dig the bed over or loosen the topsoil, level out any rough areas and work in some compost for a good supply of nutrients.

Rejuvenating plants by division
Whether or not you are overhauling the entire herbaceous bed, you should still aim to divide plants every three to five years, especially if they have become thin in the centre or too dense. Dividing plants keeps them healthy, and is an easy way to propagate them. But a word of warning: some plants hate the treatment – peonies and Christmas roses (*Helleborus niger*) do not flower for several years after being divided, so are best left alone. Most plants cope best if you divide and replant them in autumn.

Propagate the right plants
Choose only the strongest and best established plants for dividing and they will reward you with many new, healthy specimens. Plant the divided plants in drifts or dot them throughout the flower bed. When overhauling a bed, take the opportunity to move any plant that is being smothered by others or is not doing well to a position where it will not be outstripped by more vigorous neighbours. As you replant the bed, make sure you leave plenty of space between plants for them to fill out again.

DIVIDING PERENNIALS
1 Lift the plant with a garden fork. If the root stock is too hard and compact, first trim it with a spade.

2 You can divide hard and compact rootstock best if you use the sharp blade of the spade or a strong knife.

3 Lift plants with a loose root system out of the ground and pull the roots apart with your hands.

TIME-SAVING TIPS
- Only propagate by division those plants in your garden that are healthy and growing well.
- Instead of buying new plants to fill newly created gaps, sow robust, self-seeding summer flowers, which your rejuvenated perennials will replace within a few years.

Options for lawns and wild-flower meadows

A lawn may be a contrast to colourful beds and borders, an extension to a patio or a play area for the children. All lawns need some looking after, but there are options that require minimal maintenance.

Choosing between grass and flowers

An expanse of lawn gives even the smallest garden a spacious feel. How you design this part of your garden depends entirely on your personal preferences and how much time you have to spare for looking after it.

A tough, hard-wearing play area of utilitarian lawn takes little maintenance. You can have parties and let your children run around on it without worrying. During the growing season the grass will need cutting once a week and you should feed the lawn two or three times a year, depending on the soil and the type of fertiliser you use.

Another easy option is to grow an informal lawn. This is a good choice if you are aiming for a well-tended lawn that is in average use. The maintenance is the same as for a lawn used for sport, except it will not need to be cut quite so often. You may find that wild flowers such as daisies and speedwell (*Veronica*) begin to invade your lawn. Instead of weeding them out, allow them to grow. Your lush green carpet dotted with small flowers may not look perfect but it will tolerate a break from mowing once in a while.

An even less time-consuming choice is to grow a wild-flower meadow, which needs mowing just once or twice a year and does not need to be fed. It will not tolerate heavy use so is best for areas not in frequent use.

A formal lawn is much more work and needs cutting closely at least twice a week during the growing season. It has to be watered copiously during dry spells and to be fed several times a year, but the reward is a rich carpet of green.

A carpet of stars In sunny, dry positions, stonecrop (*Sedum*) forms a pretty carpet that is studded with countless brilliant flowers in the height of summer.

Let the flowers grow
While some gardeners wage war on dandelions and daisies, others welcome them in. Left unchecked, they will get out of hand, but a few of these charming wild invaders will not harm a lawn and can even make a pretty addition to the green sward.

A lawn to live with
Although a bowling-green finish is hard to achieve, lawns need not be high maintenance if you are relaxed about the result.

Shady cover Grass is hard to grow in shade so opt for ground-cover plants like Japanese spurge (*Pachysandra terminalis*). They give much more pleasure in shady areas, particularly as they do not need regular pruning.

Carpets of green
Laying a low-maintenance lawn

With a little thought at the planning stage and **good preparation** of the soil, you can create a lawn that is easy to look after and will **still look good** for many years to come.

Is your lawn ornamental or functional?

In order to enjoy your lawn to the full and for as long as possible, think of what uses it will serve. A formal, ornamental lawn is impressive to look at, but is not suitable for heavy use. If you want to use a lawn for family games and parties, however, you will need to grow grass that is robust enough to withstand regular and fairly heavy traffic.

The first tip is to lay a lawn in a simple geometric shape such as a square, rectangle or circle. This makes subsequent upkeep much easier. The minimum width for strips of lawn, such as those found between flowerbeds, should be the width of your lawnmower.

There are special lawn seed mixtures for almost every purpose, so once you have decided what kind of use your lawn will have, you can choose from a wide

Swathes of green A lawn with straight sides will make maintenance much easier. Sink any paving to or just below the surface of the lawn to make mowing the edges simple.

TIME-SAVING TIPS

- ◻ Sowing lawns in the spring or autumn, when conditions are moist, saves up to 30 hours' watering per 100 square metres.

- ◻ Use lawn seed mixtures containing slow-growing grasses.

1 Before you sow lawn seed, make sure the soil has been properly prepared. Take the time to work it thoroughly with a rotavator.

Rolls of turf allow you to create a neat, green lawn from a bare patch of earth in next to no time. Simply prepare the soil as for sowing a lawn and roll out the turf sections one by one, laying them flush with one another and tamping them down with the back of a rake, water thoroughly and regularly until well established.

range. For the most effective result, look for lawn seed that contains at least four different species of grass.

Common bentgrass (*Agrostis capillaris*) or red fescue (*Festuca rubra*) produce a fine-bladed, elegant lawn. Extremely resilient grasses, such as smooth-stalked meadow grass (*Poa pratensis*), perennial rye grass (*Lolium perenne*), crested dogtail (*Cynosurus cristatus*) and timothy (*Phleum pratensis* subs. *bertolinii*), should be chosen for hard-wearing lawns to be used for sports and games. In addition, if you also opt for quality seed, which results in slower-growing grass, you will be spared more frequent mowing later on. When you do mow the lawn there will be far fewer grass cuttings to rake up and dispose of.

2 Next, level it off as finely as possible with a rake, removing larger clods, stones and root remains. Then tamp down the surface carefully using the back of the rake.

Good preparation pays off

A robust, low-maintenance, hard-wearing lawn thrives on most normal soils, but the secret to a lawn to be proud of is soil that has been carefully prepared. Taking the time to do the jobs that initially seem to be onerous and time-consuming will save you plenty of trouble in subsequent years.

The first task is to loosen the soil well. The best and easiest way to do this is with a rotavator – you can hire petrol-driven machines or use a manual one – or you could dig it over with a spade. The top layer of soil should be fine and crumbly, yet firm. Water must be able to seep down through the soil properly, and air must be able to penetrate deeply enough. Loosen soils that are compact and heavy by working in sand, while soils that are too light and sparse can be enriched with compost. Bumpy ground could make mowing more difficult, so be sure to level out mounds and hollows, smoothing the soil with a rake. Remove all stones, rhizomes and weeds from the soil – it will pay off later – and let the soil rest for a month, then rake out any weeds that have grown in the intervening time.

Lawns need nutrients for healthy growth. Apply a special lawn fertiliser to the prepared ground then you can set to work sowing the lawn seed or laying the turf.

3 Using a seed spreader and keeping to the recommended quantity, distribute the lawn seed evenly, first lengthways, then crossways. Rake over the surface lightly.

4 Tamp the seed down with boards or a roller to ensure it is making good contact with the soil and to seal the surface. This should ensure a high germination rate.

30-MINUTE TASKS

► Dig over 15 square metres of earth and prepare for sowing a lawn.

► Sow 100 square metres of lawn using a seed spreader, rake in, and water.

► Lay 25 square metres of turf.

5 Water well. The seed should germinate within one to two weeks. Don't allow the ground to dry out and protect it from birds if necessary with netting. When shoots reach 5cm, give the lawn a light cut to around 2.5cm.

Mowing the lawn to keep it in trim

Done regularly, and **with the right equipment**, mowing need not be time-consuming, but it is an essential part of keeping your lawn in **peak condition**.

30-MINUTE TASKS

► Mow 100 square metres of lawn with a manual cylinder mower.

► Mow 200 square metres of lawn with a power rotary mower.

► Strim 20 square metres of lawn with a strimmer.

Mowing for healthy growth

Mowing is essential to achieve a dense, healthy and even lawn. Cutting the grass encourages it to spread and form offshoots, creating a rich, green swathe. There are a few tips that will help you to make the job as quick and simple as possible. Firstly, if the grass is wet, it is best not to mow it. Wet grass forms clumps and sticks to

Large lawns need large mowers The bigger your lawn, the wider your mower's cutting width should be, to minimise the number of passes. Motorised mowers speed up the job further.

the blades of the mower, clogging it up. Instead of being collected by the mower's grass box or bag, it falls back onto the ground, and you are left with the tedious job of raking it up. Secondly, lawnmowers cannot cut grass

Weighing power against noise Petrol-driven mowers and strimmers are noisier than their electric equivalents (above), but are more powerful and a better choice for a large area. When buying a battery-powered machine, consider the area of your lawn and check that the battery will be adequate for a complete cut.

Automatic mowers
Robot mowers do all the hard work for you. They use battery-operated motors: just program them, sit back and relax.

effectively when it is over 8cm high, so regular cutting is a must. Set the cutting height to maximum for the first cut of the year, then lower the cutting height and mow the area again. Do not mow too low or you will expose the roots, which may then die and leave unsightly bald patches that become colonised quickly by weeds. The ideal length of grass for an informal lawn is 2.5–3.5cm although formal lawns can be mown shorter (to a height of about 0.5–2.5cm). In spring and summer, and especially in warm, wet weather, it is advisable to mow an informal lawn once a week. In autumn, once a fortnight should be sufficient.

Sharp lawnmower blades are vital. Blunt blades rip instead of cut and risk tearing up the roots of the grass. The time of day at which you mow is also important. Mowing at midday in sweltering heat is particularly hard on the lawn, especially at the height of summer,

when the tips of the freshly cut grass are likely to scorch. It is better to mow in the morning or afternoon, when the atmosphere is a little cooler. In periods of drought your lawn will cope with the dryness better if you let the grass grow a bit longer.

Lawnmowers with boxes or bags that collect the grass cuttings make the job much easier. If using a simple manual mower without a collection bag, allow the cut grass to wither slightly, then rake it up. Removing grass clippings lessens the spread of annual meadow grass and weeds such as white clover (*Trifolium repens*). The grass cuttings can be added in thin layers to the compost heap.

Cylinder or rotary mower?

Cylinder mowers, available as manual or powered models (electric, battery or petrol), operate by cutting the grass between a spiral of blades mounted on a cylinder and a fixed lower blade. They produce an extremely fine cut, and are therefore particularly suited for formal, ornamental lawns. Rotary mowers, which are only available as powered models (petrol or electric), cut with a horizontally rotating blade, fraying the cut grass slightly in the process.

Your choice of mower depends on the size and type of your lawn. For small lawns of about 100 square metres, a manual mower with a 35cm cutting width is adequate. It has no awkward cable, and is virtually maintenance-free. For larger areas, petrol or electrically-powered lawnmowers with cutting widths of 40–50cm make the job easier. Note that power-driven cylinder mowers are harder to manoeuvre than rotary mowers, especially on uneven surfaces. Another option is a hover mower powered by electricity. These are particularly smooth-running and easy to handle.

If you have an enormous lawn, it may be worth investing in one of the large self-drive lawnmowers, more often seen on country estates and parkland. There are even robot mowers on the market, which will mow the lawn for you.

MAKE LIFE EASIER

■ As a rule of thumb, avoid cutting off more than one-third of the length of the grass at any one time; otherwise the grass will be slow to recover and the lawn will suffer.

■ With an irregular-shaped patch of lawn, mow the edges first, then the centre in parallel strips.

■ Cut edges and less accessible spots afterwards with edging shears or a strimmer.

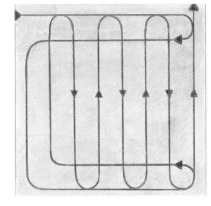

Strip by strip Begin mowing a strip at each end of the lawn, then mow up and down in slightly overlapping rows from one side to the other.

Easy-care solutions for neat lawn edges

Even the finest of lawns looks unkempt if its edges become **straggly** and the **grass spreads** unchecked into borders and onto paths. But there are various ways to **tackle** this common problem **quickly and easily**.

Neat lawn edges enhance the garden

When grass grows it tends to spread outwards horizontally along the ground. Save yourself the time-consuming job of weeding out grass that has encroached into borders, paths and patios by giving the edges of the lawn a quick trim every time you mow it. Careful maintenance of lawn edges also ensures that they stay green and in good condition and do not become straggly, or infested with weeds.

It is difficult to obtain a neat edge with a lawnmower because of the machine's design. Mowing grass at the edges of walls or fences is also tricky. Lawnmowers can slip on loose edges, while straggly bits of grass that lie close to the ground can easily escape the mower's blades. But all of these problems can be solved with some specially designed edging tools.

You can use ordinary garden shears on lawn edges, but special long-handled lawn or edging shears make life a lot easier. They have blades and handles set at a 90° angle to each other, which saves you from having to make awkward movements and because they have long handles you can work with them comfortably while standing, so avoiding bending over.

Work is even easier if you have a rolling lawn edger, which cuts with a rotating circular blade (a bit like a pizza cutter) or battery-operated grass shears. Both of these are available with telescopic handles. A strimmer is also excellent for tackling edges, slopes and other hard-to-reach places. It cuts the grass with a rotating nylon cord and is powered by battery, electricity or petrol. Some have height-adjustable handles and twistable heads for extra flexibility.

Keep your borders separate

As well as regular trimming, you should cut the lawn edges neatly at least twice a year to mark them out from any adjacent planted areas. Use a spade or preferably a half-moon-shaped lawn-edger to do this. Neatening the edges in this way clearly defines the borders against the lawn and increases the visual appeal of the garden.

Strimming The strimmer's fast-rotating nylon cord slices through the grass. Strimmers, which may be electrically powered or petrol- or battery-driven, give you easy access into any corner.

Small-scale mowing With battery-driven shears you can not only keep your lawn edges short, you can also cut small areas of grass too. Look out for powerful batteries, for which you can also buy replacements if need be.

Clever design Lawn edges with an integrated verge to accommodate the mower are simple to install and ensure that mowing right up to the edge is easy.

At ground level To make sure that it not only looks attractive but is practical too, lawn edging should be laid flush with the lawn surface.

Fixed lawn edging keeps the grass in check

Although there are special tools and techniques that help to make the upkeep of lawn edges much easier, it is simpler still if you can avoid having to trim them in the first place. You can do this by installing fixed lawn edging (left) or laying a strip of bricks or stone blocks around the perimeter of the lawn. These allow you to mow right up to and over the edges of the grass without encroaching upon the neighbouring flower borders. The time you spend installing the edging will be well worth the effort in future time saved neatening edges.

Long cut Lawn edging shears with long handles tame wild growth along borders without giving you back strain.

You can buy many different types of edging in both real and artificial stone or plastic. It should be laid at ground level, flush with the lawn. Special easy-to-install edging stones with an integral flat section that lies flush with the grass and along which the lawnmower wheels can run are available from garden centres and DIY stores. This kind of edging is available in stone or plastic and often as an interlocking system in sections of various lengths, straight or curved, so that you can position them according to your requirements.

To install this type of edging, dig a shallow trench along the edge of the lawn and lay a bed of sand in the trench. The sections of edging can then be laid on top of the sand. Some plastic interlocking systems come complete with a groove cut into them. This allows you to lay a cable or irrigation pipe at the same time. Galvanised metal lawn edging, which you drive into the earth with a plastic hammer, offers a very smart-looking alternative.

Installing a raised border such as one made from log rolls, concrete shapes, bricks or tiles, is not a very practical solution for the problem of cutting lawn edges. The lawnmower will not be able to cut right up to the edge of the raised border and you will still need to use a strimmer or an edger to keep the grass trimmed neatly. Whichever edging you install you need to trim up to it regularly for a neat finish.

■ Straight edges are simpler to maintain than round or curved ones, easily saving you 30 minutes every time you mow.

■ Place a board along the lawn edge and use it as a guide for trimming straight edges.

■ Fixed vertical edges stop grass from encroaching into borders, saving you around 2 hours of edge neatening twice a year.

■ For a lawn without fixed edges, a power edge-cutter that can be pushed along the edge makes the job easier.

■ Fixed edging with integral flat sections allows you to mow right up to lawn edges and saves you 3–4 hours of upkeep over a summer. Interlocking systems are easy to install.

■ Sink stepping-stones at ground level so that you can drive over them with the lawnmower, rather than having to go round.

30-MINUTE TASKS

► Cut 10m of lawn edge with shears.

► Cut 20m of lawn edge with a battery-operated cutter.

► Cut 30m of lawn edge with a strimmer.

Watering and fertilising the lawn

Is your lawn growing unevenly? Is it pale or yellowish in colour and does it look sickly? A lack of water and nutrients could be the cause. Careful watering and the selective application of fertiliser will help your lawn to thrive.

Establishing a lush, green lawn

Once the seed has taken root and the grass is showing well above the surface, a lawn will generally tolerate the odd passing dry spell. But if the dry spell is prolonged and accompanied by scorching sunshine, the grass will begin to wither and unsightly brown patches will start appearing. That is why – especially at the height of summer – a newly laid or seeded lawn must be watered regularly. The threat of drought is a good reason for not laying or seeding a new lawn in summer, especially if there is a hosepipe ban in your area. It is safer to wait until the spring to sow seed or lay turf, though you can also lay turf in autumn.

An established lawn can survive most ordinary summer droughts. If a hosepipe ban precludes watering, the best you can do for your lawn is to avoid mowing it altogether for a while – the longer shoots help to shade the roots and catch the morning dew.

Do not be tempted to cover the lawn in plastic sheeting to trap moisture as this will kill the grass. During a drought the lawn may appear to be dead, but it will quickly recover when the rain comes.

When you do water your lawn there are a few ways in which you can make the job quicker and more effective. The first rule is not to water little and often, but to water less frequently but thoroughly. The time of day is important too – either in the early morning or in the evening. At these times, the water will not evaporate immediately, but will soak into the ground and benefit the roots.

As a rule, a lawn needs 15–20 litres of water per week per square metre in order to remain in good condition. This should be enough to soak the ground down to a depth of 10–15cm, which reaches the roots of most grasses. If you only wet the surface of the soil, not only does most of the water evaporate and so is wasted, the roots, in search of water, do not grow deep enough and the grass becomes vulnerable in dry conditions.

If the lawn is on heavy soil, you will need to be careful with watering, or the mineral and oxygen uptake

Automatic sprinklers Permanently installed sprinkler systems may be worth while for extensive areas of grass. When the system is switched on, water pressure causes the sprinkler heads to pop up automatically. A computer-controlled timer switches the sprinklers on and off.

30-MINUTE TASKS

► Apply fertiliser to 100 square metres of lawn using a spreader.

► Water 100 square metres of lawn with a hosepipe.

An even application Watering or feeding a lawn by hand using a watering can may seem laborious, but it is an infrequent task and this method makes it easy to do the job consistently. Pace back and forth at a steady rate, watering evenly as you go.

DON'T WASTE WATER

Install a rain gauge in or at the edge of the lawn to measure the amount of water delivered by a sprinkler. 10 litres of water per square metre corresponds to 10mm on the rain gauge.

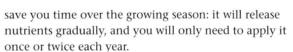

HOSE REEL

Mount a hose reel on a wall next to your outside tap to simplify the job of watering the garden. A reel equipped with automatic rewind will save you time rewinding the hose after use.

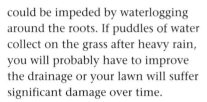

EASY FEEDING

A spreader allows you to apply fertilisers evenly. Push it backwards and forwards in parallel lines over the area being treated, then do a second pass, working crossways from the first.

could be impeded by waterlogging around the roots. If puddles of water collect on the grass after heavy rain, you will probably have to improve the drainage or your lawn will suffer significant damage over time.

Fertilise well for a rich, green lawn

Most garden soils are generally well supplied with nutrients. By contrast, lawns often suffer from an acute lack of nutrients. This is because grass is constantly drawing nutrients from the soil and losing them every time the grass is cut, meaning that they need to be continually replaced. Nitrogen deficiency, in particular, is easy to identify, since it slows the growth of the grass and causes it to fade to a light green or yellowish colour.

To provide your lawn with an optimum supply of nutrients, apply a special lawn fertiliser. This contains all the necessary nutrients – including the important trace elements – in a balanced mixture that has been specially formulated for the grass. A good feed is especially important at the beginning of the growth period in spring. Applying a slow-release fertiliser will

save you time over the growing season: it will release nutrients gradually, and you will only need to apply it once or twice each year.

Towards the end of the gardening year get the lawn ready for winter with a second application of lawn feed, which should contain less nitrogen than the first. Some suppliers offer special spring or autumn fertiliser mixtures. Never exceed the quantities stated on the packet. Too much fertiliser burns the grass and causes bald patches on the lawn. Spread the fertiliser evenly. An uneven application results in uneven growth and colour. Water generously after applying fertiliser to wash the nutrients into the soil.

TIME-SAVING TIPS

■ Slow-release fertilisers will often last for the whole gardening season from spring to autumn, and will save you over three hours' application time.

■ Water your lawn only when absolutely necessary, but make sure you water it thoroughly. Use the touch test: if the grass doesn't spring back when trodden on and a footprint is left behind, it urgently needs a good soaking.

Easy ways to beat moss and weeds

Over time **moss and weeds invade** most lawns. You can prevent this, and the time spent weeding, by keeping the lawn **aerated** and well fed. A healthy lawn **will grow well** and be able to hold its own against the weeds.

De-thatching the lawn At least once and ideally twice a year, run a de-thatcher over the lawn to remove old, congested grass and to encourage more luxuriant grass growth. You can also use a spring-tined rake to do this but it will take longer.

Weeding A daisy grubber gets right down to the roots of weeds.

![30-minute tasks icon] **30-MINUTE TASKS**

► De-thatch or aerate 100 square metres of lawn using a motorised de-thatcher.

► Weed 50 square metres of lawn.

► Spread lawn sand over 100 square metres of lawn.

Prevention is better than a cure

A modest sprinkling of daisies in a lawn looks attractive, but when they spread too freely along with plantain (*Plantago*), dandelions and other weeds, most gardeners will want to take action. Weeds are easy enough to remove with a hand fork or a 'daisy grubber', but it is a tedious time-consuming job that any gardener could do without. Fortunately lawn

weeding is one task that can be kept to a minimum by taking a few preventive measures.

Weeds are most likely to spread in a neglected and under-fertilised lawn, growing opportunistically between the undernourished grass, which they steadily squeeze out. Your main aim should therefore be to provide the optimum growing conditions for the grass. Proper aeration of the soil is the main requirement, along with thorough watering when necessary (see page 170) and correct feeding. In a well-nourished lawn, both grasses and weeds shoot up and can easily be cut back with the lawnmower. Since weeds are far less tolerant of regular cutting than grass, over time the grass out competes the weeds, which diminish drastically, if not completely. The odd stalwart can be dealt with individually. Before mowing the lawn, go over it with a broom or rake to raise any low-lying shoots of creeping weeds such as speedwell (*Veronica*) so that they won't escape the mower blades.

You may need to start from scratch

If parts of the lawn are particularly overrun with weeds, to the extent that the grass has been taken over by

RE-SOWING AND
REPAIR SEEDING

1 Long-lasting repairs for very mossy or damaged lawns are best dealt with by re-sowing. To do this, first remove the thatch from the affected area systematically and thoroughly.

them, it makes sense to clear the weeds, dig out all the roots and re-sow the patches with seed.

De-thatching and aerating

If the remains of dead plants and lawn cuttings are not gathered up routinely, a layer of thatch forms on the surface of the lawn, eventually becoming so dense that it stops water from penetrating the soil. If, in addition, the soil is compacted as a result of the lawn being used a great deal, it will be difficult for air and water to reach the roots and the grass will grow poorly and be at risk of being crowded out by moss.

To solve this, the lawn should be de-thatched and aerated at least once a year to stimulate root and grass growth. De-thatching involves cutting and removing

2 Next, rake over the patch to be re-sown. This removes moss and the remains of any grass on the affected patch, as well as any pernicious creeping weeds. Pull up individual deep-rooted weeds by hand.

the thatch of dead matter using a spring-tined rake or a powered lawn rake. The tool blades must not penetrate the soil any deeper than 1–2mm, or they will damage the roots of the grass.

Aerating involves punching vertical channels into the soil so that air can penetrate deep down. The simplest way of doing this is by using a garden fork or a hollow-tined aerator specially designed for the job. Spring or autumn is the best time for de-thatching and aerating – in damp weather conditions whenever possible, to allow the grass to recover more quickly from the stress – and you should always mow your lawn before de-thatching. Afterwards, apply a layer of lawn sand – on a dry day, if possible. This will improve drainage and help to break up the soil. If your lawn is small, just shovel some sand over it and spread it out with a rake or broom. You will need about half a bucket (about 5 litres) of sand per square metre. For larger lawns, a spreader does the job well.

3 Now scatter a fine layer of compost and spread a lawn seed mixture evenly over the ground. Press down firmly with a board to prevent the seeds washing away, then water with a fine spray.

✗ WATCH OUT!

Never remove thatch from your lawn if the grass is longer than 3cm or is wet from rain – in both cases, you could easily rip the grass out of the soil, roots and all.

TIME-SAVING
TIPS

■ A motorised lawn rake, which collects the grass and weeds in a basket, will save two or three hours of raking at the end of the job.

■ Lawn seed mixes for shady areas are available, but a more practical solution in dense shade would be to plant shade-tolerant shrubs and ground-cover plants, rather than run the risk of having a lawn that grows poorly and soon succumbs to weeds.

Sand for breaking up the soil Applications of sand make the soil loose, fine and crumbly, so that the grass grows better.

Create a wild-flower meadow

Transforming your garden into a **wild-flower meadow** is easy and once established it **requires far less upkeep** than a lawn. All you need is a mixed packet of seeds and some patience.

A pretty meadow
Wild-flower meadows suit natural and rural-style gardens very well.

30-MINUTE TASKS

► Scatter a layer of sand over 100 square metres of garden soil that has been prepared for sowing and raked to a fine tilth.

► Sow thinly with wild-flower meadow seed mix.

Wild flowers thrive on poor soil

A wild-flower meadow makes quite different demands on the soil compared to a lawn. Whereas grass grows best on a well-fertilised, nutrient-rich soil, many wild flowers make do with less and actually prefer nutrient-poor soils. Even a lawn that has been previously well-maintained can develop into a wild-flower meadow over time if it is never fed and left to its own devices. It is difficult to create a flower meadow on garden soil that is naturally rich, such as clay or loamy soils. These contain so many nutrients that they will remain fertile even without additional feeding. You can reduce the fertility of the soil by mixing it with plenty of sand, but it is less effort to work with the conditions you have and be grateful for a garden in which a traditional grassy lawn will thrive.

Less grass, more flowers

Wild-flower meadows either flower in spring (February–May) or summer (July–August). Unfortunately you cannot combine the two because they require different mowing regimes. Special seed mixes are widely available and you should follow the maintenance and mowing instructions recommended by the manufacturer. Wild-flower seed mixes contain a high proportion of flowers to 'flower-friendly' grass types such as common bent

1 Remove the area of lawn to be transformed by cutting out sections of turf. These can be composted, or used to repair bald patches of lawn elsewhere.

2 Dig over the exposed earth thoroughly. Since the meadow area will require poor soil in order to thrive, scatter 2–3cm of sand over the top and work this into the soil well.

grass (*Agrostis capillaris*) and crested dog's-tail (*Anthoxanthum odoratum*), rather than perennial ryegrass (*Lolium perenne*), which would soon crowd out the delicate flowers. Typical spring flowers include cowslips (*Primula veris*), sweet cicely (*Myrrhis odorata*) and meadow buttercups (*Ranunculus acris*), while a summer-flowering meadow may include flowers such as field poppies (*Papaver rhoeas*), field scabious (*Knautia arvensis*) and cornflowers (*Centaurea cyanus*). It is not easy to predict how your wild-flower meadow will develop. Many seeds will only germinate in an dry summer; others need plenty of rain. Birds and insects or even the wind will also introduce seeds from elsewhere.

3 Sow a special flower-rich meadow seed mixture into the gap. Alternatively, lay some flower-rich hay from an existing meadow in the bare patch of soil and wait for the seed that falls out to germinate.

Mowing a meadow

A newly sown meadow may not flower in its first year, but it will still need to be cut (mown or scythed) to help it establish. Keep it to a height of 5–8cm, and remove unwanted weeds such as docks (*Rumex*) individually. If the meadow is spring-flowering, cut in late June (after the flowers have bloomed and scattered their seed) and then again in late summer. For summer-flowering meadows, cut once in March and again in September or October down to about 8cm. Remove the clippings after each cut in order to maintain low soil fertility.

A herb lawn

Wild-flower meadows are not suitable for areas that are used a great deal, the flowers and grasses soon become flattened. A herb lawn is a colourful but resilient alternative, although not as robust as regular grass. Plant lawn chamomile such as *Chamaemelum nobile* 'Treneague' or a creeping thyme such as *Thymus caespititius*, which will release a scent when walked upon. When the plants have become established and merged to form a mat, they can be cut lightly with shears or a strimmer.

TIME-SAVING TIPS

■ Stop feeding your lawn and mow it less frequently; over time it will run to seed and could be transformed into a colourful meadow.

■ Speed up the transition from lawn to meadow by sowing seed or planting wild flowers in several smaller areas of your lawn that have been dug over and prepared.

■ Let your lawn turn into a wild-flower meadow naturally by cutting it less often and allowing weeds such as creeping cinquefoil (*Potentilla reptans*), bugle (*Ajuga reptans*) or daisies (*Bellis perennis*) to grow.

A mini meadow You can create even just a small patch of meadow within an otherwise well-tended garden, simply by allowing an area of grass to grow and flowers to develop freely.

A meadow path
Mow a path for access through the meadow so that you do not damage other areas by walking on them.

175

Carpets of green
Brighten a lawn with flowers

A few herbaceous perennials or bulbs will add interest and **a vibrant touch** to your lawn. The colour of the flowers is set off well against **the green of the grass** and the plants require **little upkeep**.

Plants for lawns that are mown regularly

If you mow your lawn regularly, plant species that flower in early spring or in autumn, which is outside the mowing season. Snowdrops (*Galanthus*), crocuses or Siberian squill (*Scilla siberica*) will add colour with their flowers at the end of winter and early spring. By the time your lawn is ready for the first cut of the year, the flowers should have died back and be gathering strength for next year. For wild herbaceous perennials, which flower from early May – such as oxeye daisies (*Leucanthemum vulgare*) and native bluebells (*Hyacinthoides non-scripta*) – delay mowing until after they have flowered.

Autumn is the time for planting

Winter-hardy bulbs that flower in spring can be planted from August onwards. Plant large bulbs such as daffodils (*Narcissus*) with a bulb-planter, but to ensure that the distribution of the plants looks natural when they start to come up, scatter them at random over the lawn, and plant them where they fall. The minimum distance

Clumps of daffodils Elegant daffodils (above) become more and more prolific every year, if left to naturalise. Let the leaves die back to yellow before tidying up because they feed strength back into the plants as they fade.

Siberian squill
With their charming blue flowers (above), scillas are reliable little plants that grow well in most places, even under trees.

A lawn of crocus
A mass of crocuses (right) push up bravely through the grass, heralding the spring.

30-MINUTE TASKS

► Scatter 20–30 bulbs at random over the lawn; dig holes with a bulb-planter, insert bulbs and cover with earth then replace the turf.

► Cut out patches of lawn turf with a spade and loosen the soil; insert bulbs and replace the turf.

between two bulbs should always be one bulb width. The ideal planting depth is two to three times the height of the bulb.

Using a bulb planter, remove a patch of grass and the earth beneath it from the lawn. Mix a little of the soil that has been removed with some fertiliser, and put this back into the hole at the bottom. Place the bulb in the hole on top of this and cover it with the remaining soil. Put the patch of grass back on top and firm it in so that the hole can no longer be seen.

Smaller bulbs are best planted in groups. You can do this with a garden fork by sticking the prongs of the fork into the grass and moving them back and forth until the holes are large enough to take the bulbs. Mix a little soil with some fertiliser and spoon the mixture into the planting holes. Insert the bulbs and cover them loosely with earth.

Naturalising in the lawn

Once planted, most bulbs will multiply and spread quite happily on their own, often forming fairly large groups after one or two years. Bear in mind just a few points and the bulbs you plant should provide splashes of colour for years to come.

Tulips and daffodils (*Narcissus*) must be deadheaded on a regular basis as the flowers fade; cut their stalks off below the flower head. Because they flower from February to May daffodils, tulips and grape hyacinths (*Muscari*) are only suitable for planting in lawns where you can afford to put off the first mowing of the season until they have finished flowering and have begun to die back. You may wish to allocate a section of lawn, such as under a tree, that can be left unmown. With daffodils in particular, the lawn must not be mown until their foliage begins to yellow, at the earliest usually six weeks after they flower.

If you want your bulbs to self-propagate, you must wait until the seeds have ripened and scattered from the capsules. Cut the stems to the ground after the seeds have been released.

BULBS THAT WILL NATURALISE IN A LAWN

PLANT	COLOUR/HEIGHT	FLOWERING PERIOD	SPECIAL FEATURES
Siberian squill (*Scilla sibirica*)	Blue/10–20cm	Mar–Apr	Loves humus-rich, shady spots.
Autumn crocus (*Colchicum autumnale*)	Pink-to-purple; rarely, white/10–25cm	Aug–Oct	Caution: the autumn crocus is highly toxic.
Crocus	Blue, yellow and white/10–15cm	Feb–Apr	Does best in sparse lawns.
Daffodils (*Narcissus*)	Yellow, white/10–30cm	Mar–Apr	Small varieties are particularly charming.
Snowdrops (*Galanthus*)	White/10–20cm	Feb–Mar	Prefers less vigorous grass.
Grape hyacinth (*Muscari*)	Blue/10–40cm	Apr–May	Plant in large groups.
Tulips	Various colours/20–45cm	Mar–Apr	Suitable only for bald patches of lawn.
Dog's tooth violet (*Erythronium dens-canis*)	Pink, white, violet/10–20cm	Mar–Apr	Thrives better in rockeries and at the edges of woodland.

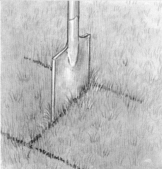

BULBS IN THE LAWN

It is easiest to plant large bulbs such as daffodils or tulips individually with a bulb-planter: Make a hole, place the bulb in it and refill with the soil and grass that was removed.

Smaller bulbs such as crocus and Siberian squill (*Scilla sibirica*) are usually planted in groups. Cut an H-shape into the turf with your spade, then cut horizontally underneath the turf and peel back the sides.

TIME-SAVING TIP

■ Plant bulbs in areas close to the edge of your lawn, to make it easy to skirt around them when you are mowing.

Now loosen the earth in the exposed patch with a garden fork. Scatter the bulbs over the area and press them in firmly with the growing tip pointing upwards. Replace the turf and press it gently back in place.

Easy repairs for damaged lawns

Most lawns **suffer damage** at some time or other. Paths that are worn into them, molehills and **compacted soil** are the kinds of problem that often occur. With a few simple tricks you can soon have your lawn back in **great shape**.

Turning bare spots green again

Areas of the lawn that are heavily used soon become flattened or even develop into bald patches, spoiling the overall look. Bare patches can be re-sown quickly with a little lawn seed. If possible, use the same seed mixture with which the original lawn was sown, or a special lawn-repair seed mix.

Prepare the area by loosening the soil with a rake, garden fork or cultivator, and scattering a mixture of soil and sand on top, if necessary, to even out any bumps. Sow seed by hand, pressing it in firmly with your feet or using a board, and scatter a very thin layer of soil or compost on top, just to cover the seed lightly.

Cut back to rescue the grass Where mature shrubs overhang and flop onto the lawn, the grass will die. Cut back spreading border plants to keep them in check then reseed the bare patches of lawn or repair them with turf.

Water with a light sprinkler and do not allow the area to dry out. The new grass should have begun to take hold after about a fortnight.

Using turf is quicker

If the areas that need to be replaced are fairly small, up to about a quarter of a square metre, it's quicker to cut out and remove the damaged area and fit a

Molehills Just remove the fine, crumbly earth of the molehill (which makes an excellent compost for container plants) and sow the bare patch underneath with seed.

Bare patches These often occur if fertiliser has not been applied evenly. If too much fertiliser has been applied in one spot and the grass is burnt, wash out the excess nutrients with plenty of water, then repair the lawn.

Unavoidable wear Where a lawn is subject to a lot of wear and tear – such as beneath a swing – bald patches are inevitable. Try to move the play equipment from time to time and repair the damaged lawn

section of healthy turf in its place. You can buy new turf for this or take it from another part of the lawn.

Cut out and remove a sufficiently large section of healthy turf with a spade. Loosen the soil of the damaged patch slightly and add a little fertiliser. You will probably have to cover the area with some soil in order to ensure a level surface. Fit the piece of healthy turf in position and press it down firmly with a board to ensure it knits well with the subsoil. Lawn edges can also easily be repaired in the same way.

Coping with water-logging

If the soil is so compacted in places that water collects in puddles after it rains, the roots won't be able to breathe and the grass will turn yellow over time and eventually die. Piercing the lawn with a garden fork or an aerator not only ensures that air can penetrate the soil, it also enables rainwater to drain into it. Fill the holes afterwards with sand, so that they remain permeable.

If the problem is serious, you may need to install a drainage system or soakaway, but this is a job for a professional.

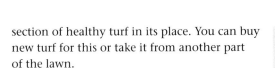

30-MINUTE TASKS

► Repair an area of damaged lawn edge (see box).

DEALING WITH DAMAGED PATCHES

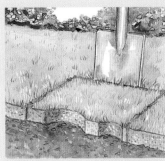

Edges of the lawn are ragged

1 Cut out the piece of lawn to be repaired in a rectangular section, using a spade or a half-moon lawn-edger.

2 Slide the turf section forwards, until you can trim off the damaged piece with the spade. Use a board to achieve a clean edge. Press down firmly.

3 The edge is smooth and straight again. Fill the gap left behind the patch with soil and sow with seed.

SMOOTHING OUT UNEVENNESS

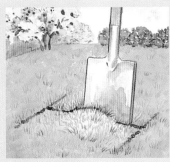

Even out irregularities in the surface

1 Whether hollows or bumps, cut an 'H' into the affected part of lawn with your spade. Carefully loosen the turf from the subsoil, and fold it back on both sides.

2 Fill hollows with soil and sand and level out bumps by removing the excess earth.

3 Fold the turf back down again and press in place firmly. Carefully fill the cut marks with soil and sand.

Carpets of green

Ground-cover plants are an attractive, easy-care alternative

Many **ground-cover plants** will grow where grass fails to thrive. Plant them in place of a lawn that is taking **too much time and effort** to maintain, particularly in the **shade under trees**.

A patchwork of colour Japanese spurge (*Pachysandra terminalis*), with its dark-green leaves and creamy-white flower spikes, spreads quickly, even in the shade of trees. In spring, daffodils will also push up through this dense carpet.

Creeping shrubs and groves of trees

As well as looking attractive, ground-cover plants suppress the growth of weeds and are therefore ideal for a low-maintenance garden. Site them in hard to reach places such as beneath trees and on slopes and banks, where they can be left to their own devices.

In autumn the ground-cover plants conceal the fallen leaves from deciduous trees and shrubs beneath their own foliage. The fallen leaves act as a natural compost and insulating blanket. As well as saving you the time that it takes to rake them up, they also make the spreading of fertiliser unnecessary.

Botanically, ground-cover plants are varied: some are annuals and others herbaceous perennials or creeping shrubs. What they all have in common is the ability to form dense plant cover in a relatively short space of time by sending out runners or long shoots.

With the quick-growing annual nasturtium (*Tropaeolum majus*), for example, it's easy to keep the ground under trees weed-free. Shade-loving plants such as creeping bugle (*Ajuga reptans*) – whose purple-leafed varieties such as 'Catlin's Giant' are especially popular – or different sorts of the variegated *Solenostemon scutellarioides* (previously known as *Coleus blumei*) are also very well suited for planting beneath trees and bushes, as are a range of cranesbill (*Geranium*). On steep

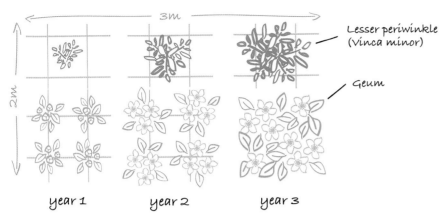

Lesser periwinkle
(Vinca minor)

Geum

year 1   year 2   year 3

Quick work This illustration shows how quickly a shrub (top row) and four perennials (bottom row) can develop over three years to cover an area of ground (from left to right).

banks particularly at risk of erosion, the roots of ground-cover plants such as the *Cotoneaster horizontalis* or singleseed juniper (*Juniperus squamata* 'Blue Carpet') will help to prevent the soil from being washed away. Honeysuckle (*Lonicera*) or the shade-tolerant Japanese spurge (*Pachysandra terminalis*), with its deep-green leaves, are also suitable.

Be cautious with vigorous sprawling plants such as periwinkle (*Vinca*). Only plant prolific species like these where you can allow them to spread unchecked – otherwise you will need to keep cutting them back to keep them under control.

Billowing flowers
Instead of weeds, there are geraniums growing here at the foot of an old tree. Ground-cover plants cope well in competition with tree roots, making it much easier to care for such problematic areas in the garden.

Good soil preparation pays big dividends

Once it has become established, a border planted with bushy ground-cover plants needs very little attention. But before it reaches this stage, it is worth taking the trouble to prepare the soil carefully. Segments of the roots of stubborn weeds such as ground elder (*Aegopodium podagraria*) or couch grass (*Elymus repens*) in particular can quickly choke the young ground-cover plants, so dig over the earth deep down and clear it of all weeds and root remains. This should spare you some time-consuming weeding while the ground-cover plants are becoming established.

In addition, improve the soil before you begin planting by working in compost thoroughly, or by mixing in blood, fish and bone or another organic slow-release fertiliser.

How far apart you position the plants depends on how prolifically each will grow, as well as on your patience and the amount of money you are prepared to spend. The closer together you plant them, the more quickly you will have dense cover; the greater the distance between the plants, the cheaper the initial outlay. Fix the long shoots or runners to the ground with pieces of wire bent in a 'U' to help them spread more quickly.

For each plant, dig a hole about twice the size of the root ball, then insert the plant ensuring that it is planted to the same depth as it was in its original container. Fill in earth all around the plant, and press down firmly but carefully.

⏱ **30-MINUTE TASKS**

► Prepare around 5 square metres of ground, dig holes for and insert ground-cover plants, water them in and apply a mulch.

MAKE LIFE EASIER

■ Plant specimens close together to achieve dense cover quickly.

■ Plant ground-cover plants on bare areas so that they cover the area with leafy foliage quickly.

■ Water thoroughly and ensure they continue to receive sufficient water, especially in the early days. Watch out for weeds; remove them immediately, so they don't crowd out the young ground-cover plants.

■ Prune back ground-cover plants hard every spring so that they remain short and compact if required, but also to remove deadwood and promote new growth.

■ For ground-cover plants that you intend to plant under shrubs and trees, the best time to plant is in autumn after the leaves have fallen.

Moving in the right direction Support ground-cover plants by spreading their shoots out over the ground as much as possible and holding them in place with pieces of wire bent into a 'U'.

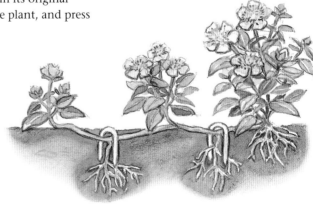

Laying a path across a lawn

A path **protects your feet** from the grass and the grass from your feet. Laying a path **need not be expensive** – a simple arrangement of stepping stones does the job and **looks attractive.**

A neat path rather than a worn track

If a part of your lawn is looking a little thin or, worse still, a track has been worn across it, it is time to take remedial action. Replacing the turf or reseeding the lawn is a temporary solution but in the long run you will save yourself time by installing a path of stone slabs. If this is too expensive, opt for the compromise of a series of stepping stones. This solution is particularly effective in smaller gardens where a solid path could carve up a lawn needlessly.

Lay stones at intervals of 60–65cm, roughly the length of an average adult stride, but make sure they are laid flush with ground level for ease when mowing. Most garden centres stock a range of natural stones as well as reconstituted slabs (ground up stone mixed with cement). Make sure that the surface provides a good

grip to reduce the risk of people slipping. Moss and algae soon develop on wood so this is only suitable for certain types of path and situation; it needs to be able to dry off quickly and should only be used for paths that are used infrequently and are in sunny, open areas.

Bark chippings and gravel – a quick fix

You can quickly create a path using bark chippings or gravel. This gives a natural look, particularly suitable for a path across a wild-flower meadow, and sets off lawns and planted areas well. Bark chippings cushion your step and give off an aromatic, spicy fragrance when you walk on them, while gravel paths crunch satisfyingly underfoot.

Paths with a loose surface do not require deep footings. Dig out the path area to a depth of

Every step of the way
Stepping stones, paving stones or slabs – the choice is up to you.

Grid work For areas that are used heavily, such as a driveway, reinforced cellular paving is recommended – it is the best of both worlds, supporting heavy loads but also allowing grass to grow between the cells (above).

approximately 12–20cm and, to keep weeds at bay, lay a geotextile membrane at the bottom. A retaining edge of wooden boards can be inserted to help stop the gravel spreading beyond the path edges. Fill with a layer of compacted hardcore to 1.5–2cm below ground level. Then add the surface layer of gravel.

If the path is across or beside a lawn, loose bits of gravel in the grass can cause a nuisance when mowing. In this case bark chippings are a better solution and can suppress the growth of weeds on their own, but you need to top them up from time to time.

Access paths that are used frequently may need a more permanent and robust surface and there are several materials available. Cellular paving consisting of pre-cast interlocking paving sections (in concrete or plastic), pierced concrete pavers and 'grass-crete' are easy to put down. They allow grass to grow through them yet still provide a hard-wearing surface.

Think about rainwater drainage

One of the advantages of reinforced cellular paving and stepping stones is that rainwater can drain away easily. This is not the case with paths of closely laid slabs, so you will need to slope the surface slightly to encourage water to run off into the grass.

Walking on air A path of bark chippings (above) can blend in with the rest of the garden more sympathetically than one made of stone and is particularly suitable for a woodland area. It also cushions your step as you walk.

2 Next, lift the turf for each stone, scoop out the earth below, and level the surface. The depth of the hole should be twice the depth of the slab, to accommodate a base of gravel and allow the surface of the slab to sit just below the level of the lawn.

3 Half-fill the hole with fine gravel and place the slab in position. Check that it is level and build up or scoop out more earth as necessary. Hammer it firmly into place using a rubber mallet.

A container garden

Containers of plants and flowers are a **quick solution** for problematic parts of the **garden**. They can be used to brighten up interior **courtyards, balconies** and **patios**, too occasionally.

Plants for a container garden

Most plants, whether bulbs, summer flowers, trees or shrubs, will happily grow in containers as long as they have enough room for their roots. Even climbers can be grown in a container and trained to climb up trellis, walls or fences. For early spring colour plant containers with crocuses and daffodils (*Narcissus*) and other early-flowering plants such as pansies (*Viola × wittrockiana*), violets, primroses (*Primula vulgaris*) or forget-me-nots (*Myosotis*). Replanting the containers with summer bedding plants will carry on the show until autumn, while hardy evergreen trees and shrubs can remain outside in their containers throughout the year.

Suitable containers and the right soil

Once you have chosen an appropriately sized container for the plant you wish to grow, the next step is to add a layer of stones or broken crockery in the base for good drainage and then to fill it with soil. Plants grown in containers need to be well watered and fed and the right soil is of vital importance. Specially formulated compost for container plants is available from garden centres. It should be loose, fine and crumbly, and should be able to hold water and nutrients while at the same time being sufficiently permeable to allow excess water to filter through. The compost should remain loose and not form clumps. You can buy slow-release fertilisers and water-retaining additives such as vermiculite, perlite and gels to keep the growing medium moist and fertile.

Have fun with containers The pot can be as attractive as the plants you put in it. Look beyond the traditional terracotta and ceramic options to more imaginative planters. This old fruit crate makes a charming home for grasses, *Leucojum*, thrift and thyme, which all like dry conditions.

30-MINUTE TASKS

► Fill two planters with compost, sow seed in them, and cover with horticultural fleece.

► Pre-soak 10 nutrient-rich seed pellets (see below), sow seeds in them, place them in a propagator and cover with lid.

► Thin out overcrowded seedlings in two 80cm planters.

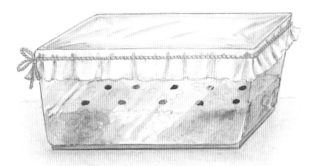

Home made propagator It is quite easy to build your own propagator. All you need is a box filled with soil and some perforated film, a plastic lid, or a sheet of glass to make a transparent cover.

surface a few times to settle the soil then press it down gently but firmly using a small board and smooth the surface.

Sow the seeds in an even layer, then sieve a layer of compost approximately 1cm thick over the top and press down again with the board. (Some seeds need to be surface sown – follow the instructions on the packet.) Water the seeds after sowing, using a watering can with a fine rose. Water slowly and carefully to avoid washing the seeds away. Finally, stretch some horticultural fleece over the planter or bowl and secure it at the edges with wooden clothes pegs or string.

Place the containers in their chosen locations immediately. The fleece will protect the seedlings from late frosts and prevent the soil from drying out too quickly. Alternatively, you can stretch some clear cling film over the top of the container, punched with plenty of holes for ventilation. Water sparingly, making sure that the soil does not dry out – but do not drench.

In rank and file Always group reconstituted pots or pellets close together in a propagating tray. This helps to prevent them from drying out quickly and so helps the seedlings to grow.

Make sure there is no mould present and that the seeds have enough air to grow when they have germinated. Once the first true leaves appear, after the cotyledons (seed leaves), the seedlings can get tangled up with one another as they compete for space. If they grow too closely, you will have to thin them out. You can plant the thinned out seedlings elsewhere in the garden, or in their own little pots.

Germinating on a windowsill

Many favourite container plants are not normally sown directly into their pots; they have to be raised from seed in a propagator. This is a cheaper option than buying ready grown plants, but it requires some planning. Busy lizzie (*Impatiens*), dwarf French marigolds (*Tagates patula*), godetia, yellow cosmos (*Cosmos sulphureus*) or even zinnia are just some of the many suitable, low-maintenance choices that germinate readily.

Sow the seeds in small biodegradable pots filled with seed compost. The seedlings remain in their pots when they are planted out into their permanent locations. The pots gradually break down, releasing nutrients as they do so. Do not let the pots dry out, even after planting them out, or they will harden and create an almost impenetrable barrier preventing the roots from growing through them into the surrounding soil. You can help the roots to penetrate into the soil around them by cutting or tearing the sides of the pots at planting out.

You can also buy dehydrated peat-free pellets that have been impregnated with all the nutrients needed for seedlings to grow; the compressed discs swell up when soaked in water and are held together by a plastic mesh. Once fully reconstituted, they are ready for sowing.

Put the biodegradable pots or reconstituted pellets close together in the propagator tray. Put one or two, and at most three, seeds in each pot. Keep them in light, warm conditions and the plants will germinate quickly.

Seed tapes, sheets and sticks avoid the need for pricking-out and thinning of the seedlings. The environmentally friendly base paper is biodegradable.

Seed tapes ensure that the seeds are evenly and correctly spaced. The strips are made of biodegradable paper that incorporates flower seeds at fixed intervals. Just place the seed strip on a layer of compost in a planter, then cover it with a thin layer of soil.

Circular sheets impregnated with seeds are suitable for pots. They are available in many sizes to fit different pot diameters.

Seed sticks also make the sowing process easier. Seeds are glued to small cardboard strips, which you insert into the soil at the correct distance and depth as indicated by a mark on the stick.

Rejuvenating pot-bound plants

If a container plant virtually **stops growing** and **refuses** to flower properly despite regular watering and feeding, it usually needs a **bigger container**.

Repotting gives a new lease of life

Container-grown plants are more dependent upon the gardener for their care than plants grown in open beds. If the compost is depleted of nutrients and the plant is root bound so that the compost holds little water, the plant will wilt very quickly, even with frequent watering. In this case the only solution is to repot the plant in a bigger container with fresh compost. Most plants need repotting every two or three years.

Use a container that is roughly 2–4cm larger in diameter than the old one. It is possible to reuse the old container if you prune the roots of the plant (see right).

Water the plant thoroughly a couple of hours before repotting, since a well-soaked root ball can be lifted out of the pot more easily than a dry one. Carefully remove the plant from the container. With large, heavy plants, the best way to do this is to lay the pot on its side, loosen the soil all around with the ball of your thumb, your fist or a rubber mallet, and pull the root ball out.

Remove as much of the old compost as possible, as well as rotten or damaged roots. If the root ball is heavily compacted, carefully loosen the edges with a hand fork to encourage the roots to start growing again.

For plants that are to be replaced in the same container, cut back the root ball as described below. Root pruning can often help to rejuvenate old plants that are flowering less profusely than before. Before you

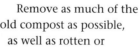

Well wrapped and well protected Wrap a mature plant loosely in horticultural fleece, hessian or an old blanket, and tie it loosely with twine. This will enable you to take hold of the plant much more easily to tug it out of its pot without damaging its shoots.

REJUVENATING A POT PLANT

1 Work a large knife along between the edge of the pot and the root ball so that the plant can be removed from the pot more easily.

2 Reduce the size of the root ball by cutting off a layer of 3-5cm from all around it. Alternatively, first scrape off the earth with a fork or small rake, then trim the roots with scissors.

3 Place the root-pruned plant back in its pot, and fill in the gaps with fresh compost. Tamp down hard around the root ball at the sides with a piece of wooden dowelling to ensure no air holes remain.

30-MINUTE TASKS

► Remove a plant from its pot, loosen the root ball, fill the new container with drainage material and fresh compost, replace the plant in the pot, firm down the soil and water.

► Top dress the soil in the container of an existing plant and cut it back.

Bid for freedom When plant roots grow out of the bottom of the pot or even destroy the container, as with this asparagus fern, it's high time to repot.

place the plants back in their pots, cover the drainage holes in the base with pieces of broken clay pot or brick, or with small stones.

Drainage to combat 'wet feet'

Though plants need water to grow, an excess of water can cause problems, too. Place a drainage layer of coarse sand, fine gravel or stone chippings in the base of the pot, so that the roots will not be left sitting in a pool of water. Next, put a layer of 5–10cm of fresh compost in the container. Position the plant in the pot and fill in around it with more compost. Make sure the plant is standing straight and is at the same depth as before.

Make sure that the level of the compost in the container is about 2cm below the rim, so that you can water it without compost spilling out over the top. Firm

down the compost and water thoroughly to create the closest possible seal between the root ball and the new compost; otherwise the roots could be in air pockets rather than the fresh soil and the plant will gradually wither despite the repotting. If the level of compost then sinks, add some more.

Top dressing

When you water a container-grown shrub or small tree, does the water run straight out the bottom of the container? If so, this means the plant's roots have spread throughout the whole pot, leaving too little soil to absorb the water. If you don't wish to repot immediately, you can buy some time by top dressing. Loosen and remove the top 5–10cm of soil. Replace it with fresh compost, ideally adding a slow-release fertiliser at the same time. The fresh compost will provide more nutrients but only for a limited time and the plant will then need to be repotted.

TIME-SAVING TIPS

☐ Make sure you have everything you need for repotting to hand before you begin. Cover your work area with a sheet so that if you spill any soil it can easily be gathered up and put back.

☐ Repotting large and heavy container plants is a two-person job. Enlist some help at the start to make the job quicker and easier.

☐ If you prune roots at the same time as you repot, you'll save about an hour's additional work. The rejuvenated plant should reward you with a host of new shoots in spring.

☐ Adding slow-release fertiliser to the compost when you repot will save you two or three hours' work over three to four months by making additional feeding unnecessary during this time.

Winter protection made easy

While tender plants grown in containers need to be **brought into the house** in winter, others are more hardy. **Effectively protected**, they can survive the cold season on the patio or balcony.

30-MINUTE TASKS

► Cover two containers loosely in horticultural fleece, insert dry straw between the plant and the fleece and tie to secure.

► Cover two large container-grown plants in horticultural fleece and secure it with sisal garden twine or colourful twigs (see below).

It's a wrap You can improve the look of plants wrapped in fleece for winter by binding them in an attractive pattern or by using colourful branches, such as cornus twigs, to hold the wrapping in place. Placing heavy pots on castors makes it easy to move them under shelter if bad weather is forecast.

Leave out or bring in?

Many popular container plants come from the Tropics or parts of the world where the weather is mild all year round. Plants that need warmth such as bougainvillea or the half hardy Chinese lantern (*Abutilon × hybridum*) must be moved indoors before the first frosts occur – a temperate greenhouse or moderately heated room in the house at around 7°C, should keep them happy. Agapanthus and brugmansia like to spend the winter in a cool, dark, frost-free place such as a garage or shed at a temperature of about 5°C. By contrast, bush daisies (*Euryops pectinatus*) and orange and lemon trees (*Citrus*

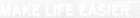

Help on wheels
A small trolley is invaluable in shifting heavy containers and plants.

Cure for cold feet
If containers stand directly on the ground, the plants' roots soon get cold, particularly in winter and especially if the container is on a cold stone patio, so raise your containers on terracotta pot feet (above left). Standing them on thick pieces of polystyrene (left) or sturdy pieces of square timber also provides good protection.

limon) need brighter conditions in winter and a temperature between 5–12°C.

Not all container plants need to be hustled indoors, though. Frost-resistant plants such as small conifers or deciduous trees, roses, rhododendron and box (*Buxus*) can spend the winter outside, provided their roots are kept warm and they are sheltered from the wind. In mild regions the olive (*Olea europaea*), *Euonymus* 'Ovatus Aureus' and *Convolvulus cneorum* can

overwinter quite well in sheltered spots but they can only tolerate harsh, frosty winters when their branches are wrapped in a thick protective layer of fleece.

It is important to insulate all outdoor containers because the soil in a container freezes much more quickly than that in a border or bed. If the soil freezes the plants' roots cannot draw any moisture and so the plants wither and die.

PLANTS THAT OVERWINTER OUTSIDE

PLANT	WINTER LOCATION/ADVICE
Grasses, e.g. maiden grass (*Miscanthus sinensis*)	Not too damp, if possible. Place pot on base.
Evergreens, such as box (*Buxus*) and rhododendron	Protected from bright sunlight. Wrap pot to protect roots; water occasionally.
Conifers	Shady spot. Wrap pot warmly; water occasionally.
Deciduous native trees and shrubs	If possible, do not allow to become too damp. Wrap pot well.
Herbaceous perennials such as phlox, delphinium and tickseed (*Coreopsis*)	Ideally under overhanging roof. Ensure there is a sufficient drainage layer.

PLANTS THAT TOLERATE SHORT FROSTS

PLANT	FROST TOLERANCE/ADVICE
Bay	Down to -5°C. Needs little light in winter.
Oleander (*Nerium oleander*)	Down to 0°C. Overwinter in light spot; water infrequently.
Olive (*Olea europaea*)	Down to -5°C, even below that for brief periods. Needs very light winter quarters in sheltered spot.
Dwarf palm (*Trachycarpus fortunei*)	Down to -5°C for short periods. Water sparingly.

Protecting outdoor container plants from the cold

Protect plant roots by wrapping the containers in insulating material such as hessian packed with straw or bubble wrap. Use garden string to hold it in place. Wrap the plants themselves in material such as hessian, horticultural fleece or rush matting. (Bubble wrap should only be used around the container, not the plant as it is not breathable.) Gather together the leaves of palms and cordyline and tie them to protect their crowns. Wrap the trunks and crowns of tree ferns (*Dicksonia antarctica*) with fleece or hessian stuffed with straw. Even in winter, evergreen plants such as dwarf pines, box (*Buxus*) or rhododendron lose water through their leaves, especially on mild, sunny days. Move the plants to a shady spot, which will also help to prevent the winter sun scorching their foliage. Water now and again on frost-free days.

For bulbous plants or winter-hardy shrubs that lose their foliage in winter, long-lasting wet or damp weather is the greatest danger, so they should be sheltered from the rain.

MAKE LIFE EASIER

- Use a trolley or similar piece of equipment to move container plants – many of which can be quite heavy – to where they will spend the winter.

- Place container plants in a simple coaster on wheels (see page 97) – they can then be moved around easily.

- If you have to do it by hand, remember to lift heavy container plants in the correct way to avoid damaging your back. Bend your knees, keep your back straight and lift by straightening your legs.

- Whenever possible, choose frost-hardy plants that do not need to be moved under shelter for the winter.

A tower of flowers in double quick time

If you want a feature in a hurry that is **eye-catching** and **colourful**, then you cannot go wrong with a climber. All you need is a **large** container, a **sturdy** support and a **vigorous** plant.

Rapid success with annuals

Vigorous annual climbers such as black-eyed Susan (*Thunbergia alata*), nasturtium (*Tropaeolum majus*), sweet pea (*Lathyrus odoratus*), morning glory (*Ipomoea purpurea*) and scarlet runner bean (*Phaseolus coccineus*) can create a pyramid of flowers quickly and easily. They must be sown or planted afresh every year, but they more than repay the effort with their rapid growth and abundant flowers. As annuals, they do not need overwintering – simply pull out withered stems and start again the following spring.

A charming effect can be achieved by planting different annuals in the same container. A mix of morning glory, black-eyed Susan and firecracker vine (*Manettia cordifolia*) will produce flowers from early summer right through into the autumn. To get the best from these climbers make sure their container is large enough and the compost has good water retention.

Clematis and rose – the perfect match

Perennial and shrubby climbers are also suitable for containers and tubs. If they are winter-hardy as well, they can remain outdoors all year round. Planting a climbing rose and clematis together produces a

CLIMBING DOUBLE ACTS

PLANT DUO	SPECIAL FEATURES
Clematis viticella 'Huldine' with a red rambling rose	The white-blooming 'Huldine' is one of the small-flowered cultivars.
Heavenly Blue morning glory (*Ipomoea tricolor* 'Heavenly Blue') with annual morning glory (*Ipomoea purpurea*)	The annual morning glory flowers from June to the beginning of October. The flowers of Heavenly Blue change from purplish-red to blue during flower opening. There are also red and white-flowered varieties of morning glory.
Black-eyed Susan (*Thunbergia alata*) with nasturtium (*Tropaeolum majus*)	Flowering from June to October, these intensely yellow and red-blooming climbers tolerate sun and half-shade.
Canary creeper (*Tropaeolum peregrinum*) with scarlet runner beans (*Phaseolus coccineus*)	Canary creeper produces masses of yellow flowers, while the runner beans produce edible beans after their scarlet flowers.
Climbing snapdragon (*Asarina scandens*) with balloon vine (*Cardiospermum halicacabum*)	Pink or purple climbing snapdragon flowers are an exciting foil for the light-green balloon-vine fruit.

MAKE LIFE EASIER

■ Use containers with inbuilt supports for your climbing plants.

■ Pre-shaped plastic-coated wire supports are suitable for containers of all sizes. Insert them firmly in the pot and train the climber's shoots along them.

■ Wicker baskets with long canes that can be tied together at the top – into a wigwam – look attractive even while you wait for the climber to grow.

The height of beauty
With a little imagination and a few different materials you can make a variety of climbing supports.

A tower of blossom Red nasturtium (*Tropaeolum majus*), morning glory (*Ipomoea violacea*) and yellow-red firecracker vine (*Manettia cordifolia*) race each other to the top of their support, all from the same large container.

spectacular display. The rose climbs up the pyramid support, while the clematis winds itself around the rose's shoots.

To thrive, these deep rooting plants need a large container – at least 50cm deep – and they will need to be repotted from time to time (roughly once every three of four years). Clematis is not a particularly demanding plant, but does like to keep its roots cool and in the shade. A ceramic tile or broken piece of terracotta placed over the roots can help. The late-flowering species such as *Clematis viticella* and *C. integrifolia* and their various

cultivars are the easiest to grow: they will not fall prey to clematis wilt, a fungal disease that attacks the stem base of early-flowering hybrids in particular, causing the shoots to wither and die quickly.

Stylish climbing supports

Many kinds of different climbing supports are available but they can also be made at home very successfully from different kinds of materials. Freshly cut willow canes are particularly suitable for shaping into original and attractive climbing supports as they are both strong and pliable.

The supports need to be sturdy for perennial climbers such as clematis or rambling roses. A wire or wooden trellis anchored firmly in the planter or tub is suitable or you can build a sturdy pyramid.

To make sure that the support won't be damaged by strong winds, it is a good idea to position the planter in front of a wall or against a fence, which will provide some shelter.

By contrast, annual climbers require a great deal less effort and expense. Supports do not have to be so robust for these short-lived plants and you can make them yourself from canes or unusually shaped branches tied together. Create a simple pyramid shape by using three bamboo canes or hazel sticks tied together at the top with twine.

There is really no limit to the kind of materials that can be used, just your imagination. Shoots can even be fixed in place with ordinary clothes pegs, ideally wooden ones, taking care not to squash them. Or you could choose special plant clips and ties available from garden centres.

30-MINUTE TASKS

► Fill two pots with soil and insert climbing supports.

► Plant two climbers and trail the shoots around the supports.

CREATING A PLANTED PYRAMID

1 Place a stone or a piece of broken clay pot over the drainage hole in the tub and fill the container with soil. Add the plant or plants.

2 Push several long, canes or sturdy hazel sticks deep into the soil at regular intervals around the edge of the pot.

3 Tie the sticks firmly together at the top with raffia or hemp twine, and carefully guide the climbing shoots up them.

Eye-catching hanging baskets

Colourfully planted hanging baskets attached to fences or walls, or suspended from pergolas, draw the eye upwards, giving height to your garden.

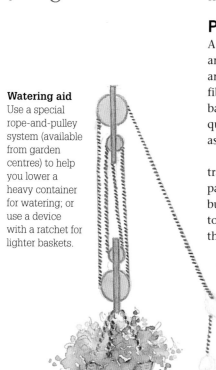

Watering aid
Use a special rope-and-pulley system (available from garden centres) to help you lower a heavy container for watering; or use a device with a ratchet for lighter baskets.

Planters for every taste

Hanging baskets festooned with colourful summer flowers such as calibrachoa, diascia, lobelia, bacopa, busy lizzie (*Impatiens*) or *Bidens ferulifolia* are a delightful welcoming feature by a front door, as well as on a balcony or patio. There are many different kinds of container available, including terracotta, wicker and rod and wire. There are also half-baskets for mounting directly to a wall and pots can be suspended with various kinds of brackets and supports. Choose plants to suit your container, creating an informal jumble of cottagey plants in a rustic wicker basket or a mass of a single pink fuchsia in galvanised metal.

Planting the whole basket

A liner is essential to retain the soil in a basket and there are many different kinds available, including hessian and moss and some, such as those made of coconut fibre, with holes pre-punched for planting. When a basket is suspended above eye level, the lining can look quite ugly. Avoid this by planting along the sides as well as in the top of the basket.

Insert plants through the holes: plants with a trailing habit such as lobelia, bacopa or *B. ferulifolia* are particularly suitable for basket sides. Choose upright, bushy species such as begonias pelargoniums or fuchsias to create a focal point in the top of the basket, although these species have trailing varieties, too.

Don't forget to water

Regular watering and a good supply of nutrients are essential for hanging baskets, even if they are planted with low-maintenance plants. The soil dries out particularly quickly in hanging baskets because there is no rigid container to hold in moisture, but you can buy containers with a water reservoir in the base, which allows water to be taken up by the absorbent liner gradually.

EASY-CARE PLANTS FOR HANGING BASKETS AND CONTAINERS

PLANT	SPECIAL FEATURES
Diascia Various shades of red and pink	Little or no deadheading; prolific bloomer even if not cut back.
Scaevola Purple	Vigorous grower; little or no deadheading.
Trailing petunia (Petunia hybrids) Red, yellow, blue, pink and white	Requires little or no deadheading.
Lobelia Various shades of blue, also pink varieties	Little or no deadheading; suitable for half-shade.
Bacopa White, also pink	Little or no deadheading; water carefully.
Variegated ground ivy *Glechoma hederacea* 'Variegata'	Heart-shaped leaves edged with white; vigorous grower.
Calibrachoa Red, yellow, blue, pink, white	Little or no deadheading required.
Bidens ferulifolia Yellow	Vigorous grower (one plant can fill a whole pot); little or no deadheading.

A living wall decoration A wicker basket lined with plastic film serves as a container for this lantana.

PLANTING A HANGING CONTAINER

1 Rest the rounded base of a container in a large bucket whilst planting to keep it stable. Putting a few large stones and/or some water in the bucket beforehand will make it even more stable.

2 Now fill the container about two-thirds full with fresh potting compost. Add a slow-release fertiliser to the soil at this stage, following the instructions on the pack. This will keep the plants well nourished for many weeks.

3 Insert the plants to the same depth as they were in their propagating pots. Fill in the gaps with compost and firm everything in place. Now water the newly planted container thoroughly and hang it in position. Don't forget to water regularly.

When watering, an extension attachment (a long pipe with a fine spout or rose that turns down at the end) that fits to a watering can or hose pipe allows you to water hanging containers without needing to fetch a ladder or to take them down. Alternatively, use a pulley device with a ratchet that will allow you to lower the basket easily to water it.

30-MINUTE TASKS

► Prepare two hanging containers, line them and fill with soil. Insert plants and hang containers in their intended positions.

Pink-and-purple cascade Trailing petunias bloom tirelessly from May to the first frosts, provided they are given plenty of water, fertiliser and light.

A harvest of fruit from decorative containers

Just because space is at a **premium** there is no reason to go without **home-grown** fresh fruit. Strawberries, blackcurrants, apples and other **delicious fruit** can be grown on a patio or balcony in tubs and pots with a **minimum** of effort.

Give fruit plenty of light

Berry bushes in particular are easy to grow in large containers. They are especially decorative as single-stem plants and even fruit-tree varieties grafted on to a slow-growing rootstock can be grown in containers. Heat-loving fruit trees such as peach (*Prunus persica*) and apricot (*Prunus armeniaca*) often do better on a balcony or patio than in the garden.

Set the containers in a sunny spot, or at the very least somewhere that receives a minimum of three hours of sunlight a day. Choose a container suited to the size of plant with ample room for growth. Use ready-made potting compost or a mixture of garden soil and compost. As with all pots, a drainage layer of pebbles or gravel at the base of the container is essential for preventing the accumulation of water.

Nurturing a good crop

Provided you care for them correctly, producing a bumper harvest from container-grown fruit trees could hardly be easier. If there is the chance of frost occurring after a fruit tree has blossomed, place some horticultural fleece over the crown to protect it. Regular watering and feeding are extremely important. Fruit trees need plenty of water particularly when they are flowering. From spring onwards, feed the plants with a suitable slow-release fertiliser, and top up with fertiliser once again in early summer if required.

Stop feeding after July so that the trees do not carry on forming new shoots well into the autumn and become susceptible to frost. Otherwise, they just need an occasional thinning out; remove shoots that are dead or damaged, or that have failed to fruit, provided the plant fruits on new not old wood.

30-MINUTE TASKS

▶ Remove 9–12 strong runners from established strawberry plants.

▶ Pot them up in fresh compost in three containers, firm in place and water well.

An abundant harvest is guaranteed
Dainty minarette or 'ballerina' columnar apple trees produce masses of blossom and fruit, even when just a few years old.

Berry delights The tayberry (*Rubus* hybrid), a cross between a raspberry and a blackberry, produces sweet fruit in late summer. Small berry bushes like this make attractive pot plants.

Minarettes and espalier fruit

Columnar fruit trees, sometimes called minarettes or ballerina trees, in which short side shoots bearing fruit grow around a strong vertical central trunk, are ideal for the balcony. Minarette apple trees, for example, rarely grow more than 30cm wide, and even after five years seldom exceed 2m in height.

Some nurseries offer duo or 'family' trees, a speciality in which two or more different varieties are grafted together to grow from the same trunk. This not only ensures variety in taste and colour of the fruit, but also mutual pollination – guaranteeing a plentiful harvest each autumn.

The minarette cherry 'Stella' , which bears ripe fruit from mid-July onwards, is suitable for a balcony or patio. If you prefer a small tree with a round crown, there are also numerous varieties of dwarf apple, cherry and pear trees grafted onto slow-growing rootstocks. These small specimens bear normal-sized fruit, but often grow no taller than 1.5m. You could also train a fruit tree into a narrow espalier form against a warm wall by tying and pruning its shoots as they develop. Plants can also be bought already trained.

No need to scrump cherries A white fence makes the perfect backdrop to a tempting crop of glossy cherries, grown in a pot on a patio.

Precautions for winter

Even grown in a container, hardy fruit trees usually have no problem surviving the winter out-of-doors. Cluster them together in groups or move single specimens into a sheltered spot, such as close to a wall, or even better beneath an overhang. If you are concerned about very harsh conditions with prolonged periods of frost, place a piece of polystyrene underneath the containers and wrap the containers in fleece to protect the roots. Make sure even in winter that the root ball is neither too wet nor too dry.

After two or three years, if the plant has outgrown its container and the soil is heavily compacted and depleted of nutrients, repot into a container that is only slightly larger (if the roots remain slightly restricted the plant will put more energy into producing fruit rather than growing roots), or renew the top layer of compost, preferably in the spring (see top dressing of pot-bound plants on page 191).

Many fruit trees – particularly apple – are not self-pollinating, and only produce fruit if another variety of the species is growing nearby. In order to ensure a good crop, two different varieties should be placed near each other if possible.

A strawberry harvest from containers Strawberries need little space for their roots, and are simplicity itself to grow in containers. These herbaceous perennials do especially well in a strawberry pot (far left), with 'pockets' in which the individual plants can be grown. Trailing strawberries are shown off to good advantage in hanging containers. So-called perpetual varieties such as 'Bolero' or 'Vivarosa' keep on producing new flowers, providing fruit from June to September. The runners can also be trained upwards along an espalier.

Small fruit from the wild Aromatic wild strawberries can also be grown in containers. To prevent grey mould, avoid wetting leaves and fruit when watering.

A bumper vegetable crop – in a pot

A variety of **herbs and vegetables** can be grown in troughs and containers. Lettuce, radishes, chives and others **taste so much better** when picked from your own garden.

Decorative leaves and colourful fruits

Most culinary herbs can be grown in planters and pots on your balcony or patio. Dill, parsley, chives, rosemary and thyme all grow well in containers and decorative varieties of basil and sage, with their attractive, aromatic leaves, provide pleasure for both the palate and the eye. Mint is especially well suited to growing in a container as it can be invasive in beds in the garden. A large pot keeps this vigorous herb in check. Herb towers, like strawberry pots (page 199) allow you to grow a range of common culinary herbs in a single container – an ideal solution for small spaces.

Plenty of sun for a good harvest

When choosing vegetables for pots and planters, select compact-growing early varieties. They need plenty of sunlight, and growing them successfully on balconies and patios depends on their position. Vegetables do best in south, south-west or south-east facing positions. Herbs that are Mediterranean in origin also need plenty of sun while others prefer moist, partial shade. If they are placed in a well-ventilated position, rainwater will not remain too long on leaves, reducing the risk of problems like mildew. You can even grow heat-loving plants such as aubergines (*Solanum melongena*) in an open and sunny position, provided it is also sheltered. From early April, you can start sowing vegetables and herbs that tolerate the cold, such as radishes, lettuce and chives, in window boxes on a balcony. More tender species, such as cucumber, tomatoes, sweet pepper or basil, should be raised from seed under cover and planted outside in May. Alternatively buy healthy young plants from a nursery.

A WOODEN BOX FOR LETTUCE

1 Line a wooden box carefully with plastic sheeting. Punch some small holes in the bottom for drainage.

2 Fill the box with compost and put in your seeds. You can buy ready-made seed tapes that contain the correct number of seeds, spaced appropriately. Press the seeds down carefully, cover with a thin layer of soil and then water.

3 You should soon be able to pick the first leaves of 'cut and come again' varieties. Cut or pick the outer leaves only of frilly types of lettuce such as Lollo Rosso, leaving the heart intact and the plants will keep on growing providing you with more leaves.

A plentiful supply of water A water-filled bottle with the base cut off placed upside-down in the compost allows water to seep out gradually and will keep containers or boxes moist for several days.

30-MINUTE TASKS

▶ Line a trough and fill with compost. Plant a row of young tomato plants. Add sticks for support, and water in.

Good enough to eat
Colourful plants, such
as aubergines and
tomatoes, supply
decorative touches.

CONTAINER VEGETABLES

PLANT	VARIETIES
Aubergine (*Solanum melongena*)	'Bambino', 'Black Beauty'
Basil (*Ocimum basilicum*)	'Horapha', 'Purple Ruffles'
Scarlet runner bean (*Phaseolus coccineus*)	'Scarlet Emperor'
Cucumber (*Cucumis sativus*)	'Marketmore', 'Boothby Blond'
Pumpkin (*Cucurbita maxima*)	'Baby Bear'
Swiss chard (*Beta vulgaris* Cicla Group)	'Vulkan', 'Feurio'
Sweet pepper (*Capsicum annuum*)	'Canape', 'Gypsy' 'Gold Star'
Lettuce (*Lactuca sativa*)	'Lollo Rossa', 'Lollo Bionda'
Tomato (*Lycopersicon esculentum*)	'Moneymaker', 'Tiny Tim'
Courgette (*Curcubita pepo*)	'Zucchini', 'Gold Rush'

Head to head
Varieties of lettuce
with differently
coloured leaves make
an interesting window
box display (above).

Handy herbs
Grow a small herb
garden in your window
box so that you'll have
colour, aroma and taste
within easy reach.

will do as a growing medium. Most of these are already nutrient-enriched. A special compost is also available for herbs, which do not thrive in rich soil.

Watering correctly

Leaves need to be able to dry off before nightfall in order to minimise the risk of disease. Water plants in the morning and take care to keep the leaves as dry as possible. With tomatoes, sweet peppers and other fruiting vegetables, it is important to water around the plant bases and not over the top of the leaves. Rather than little and often, water less frequently but using plenty of water. Feed your plants every three to four weeks for a plentiful harvest. Many gardeners prefer to use organic fertilisers when growing vegetables.

Vegetables and herbs are easy to grow in most containers. When choosing a container, ensure that it can accommodate the eventual size of the plant and that it has sufficient drainage. Any commercially available compost that retains both air and water well

Container planting for a roof garden

Lack of space often motivates people living in urban areas to create a roof garden. With the **right choice of plants** grown in spacious containers, you can create an oasis for the senses that is quick to grow and easy to look after.

Sturdy and stable Add stability to plants growing in small containers by placing them inside a larger 'cache pot'. Weigh down the large container with coarse gravel or a few heavy stones filled in with sand. Layer a piece of fleece or a filter mat on top of the stones before positioning the plant on top. This helps the plant to take up moisture from the outer pot.

Up on the roof

It is easy to create a luxuriant garden on a roof terrace. Before you get going, however, make sure that the construction of your roof area is sturdy enough to take all the extra weight your garden will involve. If you are in any doubt, ask an architect or engineer to take a look. When planning the layout, remember to consider some form of sun protection, such as an awning. You will need to consider the effect of high winds and ensure that it is fixed securely.

For plants to do well on the roof, they will need sufficient space for their roots to grow. Choose large containers filled with suitable compost, in a style that suits your rooftop garden. A rustic wooden planter has a rural feel, elegant terracotta gives a Mediterranean effect, or ceramic an Asian influence. Remember that stone and terracotta containers are heavy, so choose plastic containers where you can without ruining the effect to minimise the load on your roof.

Make sure your chosen containers are heavy enough to remain stable in high winds. If you want the design to be flexible, put tubs or containers on coasters (platforms on wheels) so that you can easily move the containers around. Good drainage is also important so that rainwater can drain away instead of accumulating in the containers.

Creating themed areas

Just as in a normal garden, a roof garden can have areas devoted to different types of plants. You may want to create colour-themed areas or planting combinations that evoke a particular style, but remember that roof gardens are often subject to extreme weather conditions, such as fierce winds and intense heat and sun and the plants you choose must be able to withstand this. Seed mixes such as those offered for wild-flower meadows, containing corn flowers (*Centaurea cyanus*), field poppies (*Papaver rhoeas*) and

A Mediterranean feel Despite its sparse planting, this roof garden contains a lot of variety and remains low-maintenance.

Babbling, bubbly and cool Since temperatures on a roof garden are often very high, water is a welcome feature.

Wild flower varieties
Robust, small perennials thrive in window boxes and ensure you have some colour throughout the year.

Roof meadow
In large wooden containers, colourful flowers can thrive and mature next to sturdy grasses.

Miniature pond
A range of aquatic plants can be grown around a bubbling stone in a water-tight container.

Flowering shrubs
Use small flowering shrubs as an attractive windbreak in exposed areas.

A kitchen garden
Herbs and fruit will do well in the most sheltered corner of your roof garden.

corn-cockle (*Agrostemma githago*), are particularly suitable. The latter are short-lived species that grow naturally in cornfields and are quick to self-seed. In conventional gardens they will not produce a long-lasting wild-flower meadow, but they perform well in rooftop situations. A hedge planted with viburnum, serviceberry (*Amelanchier*) or wild roses (*Rosa canina*) can help by screening against wind and creating a sheltered atmosphere.

Choose plants that are undemanding, such as the famous houseleek (*Sempervivum*): you can create an attractive display in a container with its many different cultivars. These can be accompanied by plants that cope well with drought conditions, such as saxifrages, thrift

(*Armeria maritima*), stonecrops (*Sedum*) and the many small grasses available that will bring movement to the garden as they sway in the breeze.

A refreshing touch

A water feature can be a welcome addition in such a potentially hot spot. As long as your roof can take the extra weight involved, a water feature can be made using large containers such as an old bathtub or half-barrel, but any watertight container will do.

Running water features, such as a bubbling stone or a fountain, will add extra sensory appeal. Place a water feature in a shaded, sheltered spot to minimise evaporation and disturbance from the wind.

TIME-SAVING TIPS

Cover the compost in your containers with a layer of mulch, using fine decorative chippings or gravel, for example. This will stop it drying out quickly and you will need to water less frequently.

Install an automatic watering system to take care of all your plants. This could save you up to five hours of watering time each week.

The water garden
Creating a cool oasis

A pond or water garden provides an attractive habitat for much plant and animal wildlife. You just need to choose a suitable location and then decide which plants you would like to grow.

Clouds and water The reflection of clouds in the water in a pond makes a garden seem larger.

WATCH OUT!

Children can drown in even very shallow water so always be alert and make sure that every pond or water-filled container in the garden is safe.

Water as a habitat

Plants need water to survive, making it a key factor in every garden. During the summer, water can have a cooling effect in your garden and its gentle sound can be a distraction from other more annoying noises. A well-lit water feature, babbling away in your garden, can create a very special atmosphere at night.

Plan a water garden carefully. Once installed, it could be difficult to move. Research and choose the design and type first: a mini pond in a container, a small natural basin, a larger pond lined with butyl rubber or PVC, a bubbling stone, a stream or a waterfall. Then choose a suitable location in your garden, taking into account your habits and lifestyle, the direction of the

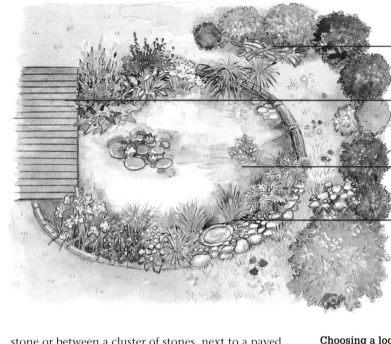

Dead wood
Winter accommodation
for toads, frogs and newts

Decking
A practical place on
which to relax and enjoy
the garden

Water margins
An important habitat for
plants and animals

Bog garden
A tranquil transition from
water to land

water (if there is a stream that already flows through or into your garden), the area surrounding the water garden and any existing plants.

Relaxing by a pond is particularly lovely during the evening, but a tree can provide welcome shade during the heat of the day. A bubbling stone, a small feature with water pumped up through a hole in a large

stone or between a cluster of stones, next to a paved sitting area is refreshing in the midday heat. A waterfall works best on a natural slope, feeding into a stream or basin. You can create an entire water landscape with little effort and space. If you are excavating a pond, plan a use in the garden for the soil you dig out so that you do not need to have it taken away. Are there any hollows that need to be filled, or do you want to create a terrace on a slope or a raised bed?

Harnessing technology

Beyond a certain size, a well-planned pond needs little maintenance but to make the most of clear, running water in fountains, streams, waterfalls and bubbling stones, some equipment is required. Pumps, filters and hosepipes are all readily available. You can buy the materials and equipment for building and maintaining a whole water garden scheme, or you can combine separate features for a more individual design.

Before building a pond, take into account water and electricity supply, any lighting you may need and how it can be controlled, as well as how to cope with water overflow and how to clean the filters. Remember that any electrical installations in the garden must comply with Part P of the Building Regulations (see page 43). You should also consider how plants will survive the winter and think about securing netting over the pond to protect against falling leaves in the autumn – this will save you much time and effort when it comes to cleaning the pond. Rocks and plants positioned around the edge of the pond will provide animals with refuges in which to hibernate over winter.

Choosing a location and the surroundings for your pond
Build your pond in a place where there is shade between 11am and 3pm during summer, so that you can spend time by the water in the middle of the day. Part of the edge of the pond should be next to an area of grass, a hedge or a bed of wild flowers to allow access into and out of the water for creatures. Piles of dead wood or stones can shelter newts, frogs and toads, and wild flowers attract insects which may lure in hungry dragonflies.

⏱ 30-MINUTE TASKS

▶ Clear the algae out of your pond using a net or insert a stick into the mass of weed and twist the algae around the stick so that it can be pulled out; alternatively lift it out with a garden rake.

▶ Sweep and treat the decking beside a pond.

Make room for a water garden on your patio

A water feature does not always have to be in the form of a pond. You could **convert** a couple of **attractive containers** into two small water gardens. Miniature ponds are **low-maintenance** alternatives for small gardens.

A pond in a tub

Wooden tubs or troughs are frost-resistant and relatively easy to transport. Many garden centres stock half beer barrels, which make ideal water garden containers. They must be watertight and clean inside – clean them thoroughly with an environmentally friendly detergent and plenty of water. Alternatively, you can line them with a plastic liner. If the tub has been treated with tar, which is harmful to any plant, line it with heavy duty liner – PVC or butyl are strong and last longer than polythene – ensuring there are as few creases as possible as you smooth it against the walls of the tub. Pour in gravel and soil (loam or pond compost) as required and top up with water so that the liner is flattened against the sides. Tack the liner to the top of the tub, around the rim, well above the water line, and cut off any excess with scissors or a knife. Wooden tubs supplied with rigid plastic liners are also available.

The right compost

Your choice of compost is crucial for healthy plant growth and easy maintenance. Do not use normal garden compost in a water garden – it contains far too many nutrients and would trigger an explosion in algae – use a special pond compost

instead. Alternatively, use loamy garden soil, which releases minerals into the water gradually.

The right plants

There are several types of aquatic plants. Bog and moisture-loving plants grow in very moist soil, the kind typically found at the edge of a pond in the wild, but you can create a bog zone beside your garden pond by

Babbling water If you place several smaller containers at different heights, you can build a very appealing and refreshing water cascade, even in a very small space.

TIME-SAVING TIPS

- Avoid cleaning or resealing an old or leaking barrel by placing a suitably sized plastic container inside it.

- Choose hardy, native plants that can happily spend the winter outside.

- Small containers are easier to move around if placed on wheels.

- Plant up containers of different heights with a variety of aquatic plants that grow at different depths.

WATCH OUT!

Never bury wooden containers in water since they will rot. Place them on a stone patio surface or on a waterproof saucer if you have decking. A layer of gravel under the container will give additional protection from rotting and drain off any surplus water.

Still life with tubs
Planted in attractive containers and cared for correctly, aquatic plants should thrive and look as if they are in their natural habitat.

digging out a bed to about 45cm depth, lining it with a heavy duty liner pierced with just a few small drainage holes and then filling with loam. Once planted and soaked with water, mulch with organic matter to keep the moisture in.

Marginal plants grow with their roots in soil in shallow water, around 8–15cm in depth, though some prefer around 30cm. They can be grown on ledges around the sides of ponds. Deep-water plants are grown in water around 30–90cm deep. They can be planted in soil or in baskets containing soil. Young deep-water plants such as water lilies (*Nymphaea*) can be positioned in the centre of a pond by planting them in a basket placed on a stack of bricks, which can be lowered as the plant grows. The roots of floating aquatics such as water hyacinth (*Eichornia crassipes*) are not anchored but hang in the water from which they draw nutrients. They help to discourage the growth of algae. Oxygenating plants such as spiked water milfoil (*Myriophyllum spicatum*), which help to clean and oxygenate the water, are planted in soil and are submerged.

The right position

Miniature ponds look attractive in a sheltered spot against an uncluttered background. Since they heat up quickly, smaller containers should not be exposed to direct sunlight for more than six hours a day to minimise rapid evaporation – a quiet corner that gets the evening sun is ideal. On sunny patios, a plant such as bamboo grown in an adjacent container may help by providing temporary shade for the water-filled tub. You could also put up a parasol at midday, but you will still need to check the level and top it up with rainwater (not fresh tap water) from time to time.

Planting and maintenance

Aquatics should be planted when they are in active growth, when the water is warm and light levels are good, ideally between late spring and mid summer. You also need to consider the size of the container – three or four plants are normally enough for one container measuring 50–60cm in width or diameter. One single species per container can be just as decorative as a mixed planting with different heights. Frost-resistant containers and plants are easiest to maintain, since they do not need to be cleaned out or protected during the winter. Remove dead plant parts by cutting them off carefully below the water surface. If your plants grow too quickly, remove part of them or divide them to ensure the right balance between plants and water is maintained, but only do this in late spring after the dormant winter period.

WATER PLANTS FOR A TUB

A pot for bog plants: 50–60cm diameter; moist, loamy soil; 5cm water.

Plants: Marsh marigold (*Caltha palustris*) or pennywort (*Hydrocotyle vulgaris*), candelabra primula, water avens.

Hardy marginals: 50–60cm diameter; loam or pond compost, depth of water 8–10cm.

Plants: Sedge (*Carex*), bog arum (*Calla palustris*), buckbean (*Menyanthes trifoliata*), arrowhead (*Sagittaria*). Keep a third of the water surface plant free.

Hardy deep marginals: 50–100cm diameter; loam or pond compost, depth of water 15–30cm.

Plants: Sweet sedge (*Acorus calamus*), flowering rush (*Butomus umbellatus*), sweet galingale (*Cyperus longus*). Cover soil with pebbles to keep in place.

30-MINUTE TASKS

► Fill a prepared container with about 10cm of pond compost, fill with water and plant with hardy marginal species.

The water garden

A bubbling stone generates a cool atmosphere

A small water feature area with one or two **bubbling stones** makes a peaceful water garden. You can buy small, ready-made water features made of **natural** or artificial stone, but it is also quite **easy to build** one yourself.

The trickle of water in a small space

Bubbling stone water features (below and right) need only a small reservoir of water, which can easily be hidden from view. Dig out a basin for the reservoir and then place the bubbling stone on a mesh over it, camouflaging the mesh with pebbles. Water features integrated into the ground always look more natural than those simply placed on the surface. Most garden centres sell complete kits that include the container, mesh, pump, bubbling stone, decorative gravel and pipes. If you prefer not to go for a ready-made concrete or natural stone option, ask a stonemason to drill a hole through a suitable stone or attractive boulder.

Japanese style
This small water feature is the perfect place for quiet meditation, with a boulder used as a bubbling stone sitting on gravel in front of a simple backdrop of upright grasses.

MAKE LIFE EASIER

■ Avoid drilling a hole through a stone by placing several stones close together and hiding the trickle water jet between them.

Natural sounds
Bubbling water features look good and serve a purpose – their quiet gurgling sounds are refreshing and calming.

PERENNIALS FOR EDGING A PATIO

PLANT	HEIGHT	FLOWERS
Bearded iris (*Iris germanica*)	20–70cm	Blue, yellow, multicoloured
Mountain sedge (*Carex montana*)	10–20cm	Reddish-brown (autumn)
Aubrieta	10–15cm	Light blue, dark blue, pink, purple
Blue fescue (*Festuca glauca*)	10–30cm	Feathered panicle
Globe flower (*Trollius*)	15–80cm	Yellow flowers
Acorus gramineus 'Variegatus'	15–30cm	Green and cream
Water forget-me-not (*Myosotis scorpiodes*)	30–50cm	Blue
Clustered bellflower (*Campanula glomerata*)	15–60cm	White, light blue, violet
Marsh pennywort (*Hydrocotyle vulgaris*)	2–5cm	Dark blue
Day lily (*Hemerocallis*)	20–120cm	Yellow, orange, red
Anemone rivularis	60–90cm	white

Bubbling stone
Refreshing sound of water

Pebbles
Give the impression of a stream

Wooden decking
Gives the illusion of a bridge over a dry river

First impressions
A wooden footbridge, bubbling stone and the right selection of plants create the illusion of a stream bed running through a garden.

One pump and trickle water jet is usually enough for a number of stones, but the power of the pump needed will depend on the number of trickle outlets it is to supply. It will also need to be pressure-regulated to ensure regular water flow.

Building a bubbling patio feature

Lift a few slabs or stones from your patio floor and dig a hole in the ground beneath to take the water reservoir. Insert the reservoir with several flat stones beneath it so that the rim projects up to 2–3cm above the level of the patio. Fill up the space around it with sand or gravel packed in firmly. Fill the reservoir with water and put the pump in it. Now balance the mesh on some flat stones placed around the edge of the reservoir. Place the bubbling stone or stones in position and look at the arrangement from all sides, including the view from the house. Once satisfied, install the jets, and the electricity cabling, then give the installation a trial run. If it works, lay a piece of fleece over the mesh to act as a filter and camouflage this with attractive stones. Place larger stones first followed by smaller ones.

Low-maintenance plantings

Although patios are normally quite dry places, you can create the impression of water with plantings of bearded Iris (*Iris germanica*) and day lilies (*Hemerocallis*). You can even give the impression of the bank of a stream with

miscanthus and bamboo. Bugle (*Ajuga reptans*), blue fescue (*Festuca glauca*), blue grama (*Bouteloua gracilis*) and blue-leaved hostas also look attractive. Plant these in groups of three or five. Place a layer of pebbles between the plants to create the illusion of a dried-up stream bed running through the garden.

Getting ready for winter

Clean out your water feature before the first frosts arrive. Connect a length of hosepipe to one of the jets and pump the water out of the reservoir. Disconnect the power supply and take the pump out to clean it. You should also empty out the reservoir and clean it.

Building a bubbling water feature You need only a few components to create a small water landscape with a bubbling stone: a bucket or tub sunk into the ground, power and a pump and a covering and stones to disguise the underground workings.

WATCH OUT!

When installing a water reservoir, or sump, make sure it has a lip around the rim or that its edge is above ground level. This will prevent rain water running into it from the patio and polluting it or washing in soil from the surrounding border.

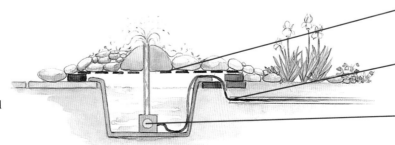

Mesh
Supports the bubbling stone and pebbles

Electrical cabling
Safely buried below the surface and well hidden

Underwater pump
To ensure the water keeps circulating

Installing a rigid pond liner and planting in and around it

Ready-made ponds come in all shapes and sizes, and even the smallest can be planted in an appealing way. Fountains and attractive lighting will add to their charm.

Simple steps to successful installation

Rigid, pre-formed pond liners are generally made from moulded plastic or glass fibre. They are quick and easy to install, creating an attractive feature with a minimum of work. Site a small pond in a partially shaded corner that is visible from the house. Nearby seating and lighting will enable you to enjoy the pond at any time.

INSTALLING THE POND

1 Dig a hole 30cm wider than the pond liner. Remove all sharp stones and rocks from the hole, level out the base and cover it with 2.5cm of sand.

2 Lay the liner in the hole and check that it is level by laying a spirit level on a straightedge across the pond. Run in 10cm of water and backfill the gap between the liner and hole with soil or sand. Carry on filling the pond slowly, backfilling as you go.

3 Pour pond compost or loam onto the planting ledges and plant some marginal species in the soil. Place gravel or pebbles over the soil in the planting zone for decoration, but also to keep the soil in place. Position the pump. Top up with water.

✗ WATCH OUT!

If siting a pond in a lawn, do not allow the grass to grow right up to the water's edge. Lay a strip of paving or gravel around the pond to protect the edge of the plastic liner during mowing and to prevent grass clippings from falling into the pond.

Place the pond liner in its planned position. Dig out a hole 30cm wider than the circumference of the liner, trying to make the depth and shape of the hole match that of the pond liner as closely as possible. Bear in mind that you will need to cover the base of the hole with a 2.5cm layer of sand. Lay a straightedge across the hole and use a tape measure placed at right angles to the straightedge to measure the depth of the hole at different points to check that it matches the depth of the pond liner.

Remove any sharp stones or roots and cover the base of the hole with a layer of sand. Lower the liner into the hole and check it is level and flush with the edge of the ground. Don't fill the pond with water in one go, but do it gradually, backfilling around the liner as the water level rises (see steps, far left) to prevent air pockets occurring.

PLANTS FOR PONDS WITH A FOUNTAIN

PLANT	FLOWER COLOUR	WATER DEPTH
Water speedwell (Veronica anagallis-aquatica)	Blue	up to 10cm
Arrowhead (Sagittaria)	White	up to 10cm
Common spikerush (Eleocharis palustris)	Brown	up to 50cm
Japanese water iris (Iris ensata)	Purple, blue, white	20–50cm
Narrow-leaved water plantain (Alisma gramineum)	Pink	up to 20cm
Flowering rush (Butomus umbellatus)	Rose pink	100cm
Water forget-me-not 'Icepearl' (Myosotis scorpiodes 'Icepearl')	Blue, white	up to 20cm
Marsh spurge (Euphorbia palustris)	Dark yellow	up to 50cm

Natural curves
Rigid liners come in geometric shapes or more natural, irregular forms (left). As the marginal plants mature, they will soften the hard edge of the liner.

30-MINUTE TASKS

► Fit the rigid liner for a small pond into a prepared hole.

► Plant up a bog zone around the edge of the pond.

A gentle glow In the evening, the soft light from floating light balls on a pond creates a special atmosphere.

If you are planting marginal plants directly in beds within the pond rather than in baskets, spread a layer of pond compost or loam on the ledge before the water level rises that far. Insert the plants and cover the soil around them with a layer of fine gravel. Finish filling the pond, then install the equipment for any fountains and lighting, taking care to conceal electrical cabling safely (see page 43).

Lights, pumps and fountains

Ensure that only approved electrical fittings are used and that a qualified electrician checks and certifies any wiring installations, in accordance with Part P of the Building Regulations (see page 43). Pumps for fountains can be run from the mains supply at 240 volts or via a transformer that reduces the voltage. If your fountain pump is submerged in the pond, raise it on a couple of bricks to avoid it clogging with the silt that collects at the bottom. Solar-powered fountains and lights are available, but are less powerful.

As well as powering a fountain, pumps circulate the water, helping to keep it oxygenated for plants and fish. The fountain and pond must be compatible in size to ensure that the water lands back in the pond even in windy weather, although plants at the edge of the pond will benefit from the higher humidity generated by the spray. When choosing plants, note that some, such as water lilies (*Nymphaea*), do not like being placed near moving water.

Make your pond to measure with a flexible liner

A pond lined with flexible material is **easy to build** and gives you the option of being able to **decide upon the shape** of it yourself.

Construct a pond any shape you like

Flexible pond liners allow you to build a pond of any shape and size. Large ponds more than a couple of metres wide can be time-consuming to construct and are probably best left to an expert. A small pond should be relatively easy to build yourself.

Mark the outline of the pond on the ground using rope or a garden hose. When you are happy with the size and shape, dig it out. Finishing the pond edging is sometimes considered the hardest part, but if you take into account the kind of edging you wish to fit (far right) in advance, you should avoid any problems.

To check the pond base and any ledges you have created for marginal plants are level, drive small wooden pegs into the soil at intervals, so that they protrude by about 2–3cm, and lay a spirit level across them on a straightedge. Lower or raise the pegs until the straightedge is level, then dig out or fill in with soil

MAKE LIFE EASIER

■ Give some thought as to how you can use the excavated soil from a pond elsewhere in the garden, so that, if possible, you can tip the soil directly where you need it. Remember to reserve some soil for backfilling between the liner and hole – sieve the soil first before backfilling.

■ Liner is more flexible and easier to fold in summer – spread it out in the sun to warm it before installing it. Getting one or two people to help you lift and arrange the liner in the hole will make the job much easier.

A firm edge Flat stones secure and hide the edge of the liner and prevent the soil or lawn around the pond from slipping into the water over time.

around the pegs to ensure a consistently level base. An ideal width and depth for ledges is 30cm, and the deep-water zone should be 80–100cm deep over an area of at least 1 square metre.

Remove the pegs and any sharp stones or roots from the base and walls of the hole and cover with a layer of sand around 2.5cm deep to protect the liner and allow it to slide more easily into place. A special pond liner underlay is also available for this purpose.

How much liner?
Lay a rope or hose pipe across the pond at the parts with the largest width and length, making sure it follows all the contours of the hole. Add at least 100cm to both measurements to allow for the edge.

Drape the liner over the hole following its contours as closely as possible leaving a generous overlap at the edges. The weight of the water will mould it to the sides. Carefully smooth out creases in the liner.

Fill the pond with water slowly using a hosepipe. Do not cut off the excess liner at the edges until you have established what kind of edging you will install. Insert soil and plants (see pages 210–11) and by the next summer, your pond should be well established and blend in naturally with your garden.

In perfect shape
Flexible pond liner allows you to create virtually any size and shape of pond.

Plan for heavy rain

A heavy downpour or prolonged period of wet weather can make a pond overflow. To lead the excess water into one part of a garden, such as a flower bed, rather than another, such as a lawn, make an overflow channel. When the pond is full, lower the edge slightly at one point and shape a piece of liner to form a small channel, leading excess water away. Make sure that water cannot get underneath the pond liner. You may need to dig a shallow trench to encourage the water to flow to where you want it.

✗ WATCH OUT!

Pond liner should not be exposed to prolonged sunlight, which could damage it. Once the pond is finished, ensure that any visible liner is fully covered with edging material.

EDGING THE POND

1 A shallow trench is useful if you want to plant around the pond edge with non-aquatic plants or to decorate it with gravel. Place a layer of horticultural fleece over the pond liner.

2 An edge made of paving stones is a clean, low-maintenance option. Cut out a shallow ledge around the pond edge. Make a firm, level stone or concrete shelf and lay the liner over it. Finish off with decorative paving stones to hold the liner in place.

3 The liner can be fastened on to walls or the uprights of an overhanging wooden deck by screwing through a wooden batten. Make sure the liner is far enough above the water line so that water does not seep down behind it.

⏱ 30-MINUTE TASKS

► Level up to 3m of pond edge with infill and trim off excess liner.

► Cover up to 3m of pond edge with horticultural fleece and slabs or pebbles.

► Cover up to 3m of pond edge with soil and plant.

The water garden

A cascade brings a slope to life

A **terraced** slope is the ideal spot for a small fast-flowing **stream** or **cascade** powered by a pump. Pre-formed units make this kind of water feature **quick** and **easy** to **build**.

A man-made stream

Ponds and pools are difficult to build on sloping sites, and they can end up looking unnatural. Small streams with water happily gurgling down over different levels look much more natural in this setting. Thanks to pre-formed cascade units, you don't need to be an expert to build this kind of feature. A pump will solve the problem of keeping the water circulating. The number of cascade units you will need will depend on the height and gradient of the slope. They are available in plastic and reconstituted stone, but glass fibre is a good choice because it is lightweight and strong. Moss also becomes established quickly on its rough surface, which makes the cascade lose its artificial look in no time at all.

Water is pumped up to the top of the cascade from a reservoir or pond at the base. The capacity of the pump depends upon the volume of water that is to flow down the cascade and the power depends upon the cascade's length. A large cascade may require an externally mounted pump but a submersible pump is adequate for most small-scale features. Most pre-formed cascade units are designed so that they can be angled

BUILDING THE CASCADE

1 Install the water reservoir and pump. Fill the reservoir, bury the hose for the water and the electric cable alongside the route the cascade will take, and connect the pump.

2 Create steps in the slope (avoiding where the hose and cabling are buried). Arrange the cascade basins on them, working from the base up. The edge at the top should be flush with the ground. Check the angle of the basins and the spilling edge position.

3 Introduce the end of the hose into the top basin, for example threaded into a piece of rigid piping sandwiched between two large stones. It should appear just above the first basin to stop the water spraying out to the sides when it strikes.

A cascade with a bubbling fountain at the head

The flow of the water corresponds to the capacity and power of output at the source, in this case a lively bubbling stone.

Lively flow
Creates an animated stream.

Cascade basins
Number depends on the gradient

Banks
Add plants for colour and life.

Like a woodland waterfall
A cascade made of flexible pond liner and stone steps (left) has a natural appearance, thanks to the choice of plants along its banks.

Plain framework
Artificial pre-formed units make it much easier to build a cascade, but the finished natural look depends on the right planting along the edges.

WATCH OUT!

To keep the feature looking as natural as possible, do not install pre-formed units at such an angle that there is no water left in each of the basins when the pump is switched off.

Decorate around the edges of the cascade with pebbles and stones and insert suitable plants to give the feature a natural look. Dwarf trees and shrubs, herbaceous plants and grasses are particularly well suited to slopes. Allow the plants to overhang the water so that they mimic the arrangement of plants found growing wild beside a natural stream.

The sound of water

While the volume of water and flow rate determine the sound level, the shape and type of materials the water flows across define how the water will sound when it falls. You can create an appealing babbling brook effect with stones of different sizes arranged in the individual cascade basins.

The rhythm of the falling water is important too, affected mainly by the form of the cascade units and the gradient of the slope. The more unevenly the water splashes down the cascade, the more natural the sound will be. You can prevent the rhythm becoming too regular by placing a few pebbles in the water basins and at the spillway. Stones also provide a habitat and refuge for plants and wildlife.

slightly at installation, which makes it possible to create a sweeping effect. Interlocking units are also available. A cascade is easy to install on a slope that is already terraced, but if the site is very steep, arrange the cascade to run diagonally to lessen the gradient.

Installation and planting

A cascade can be built to run down into an existing pool of water, or a container can be buried at the foot of the cascade to also act as a reservoir from which water is pumped back up to the top of the cascade. Place the pump on bricks to avoid silt at the bottom of the reservoir entering it. Start the pump and test the system before decorating with pebbles and stones. Always have any electrical installations wired in or checked and certified by a qualified electrician, in accordance with Part P of the Building Regulations (see page 43).

PLANTING ON THE SLOPE

PLANT	COLOUR	HEIGHT (CM)
Dwarf rhododendron	Light red or pink	40–60
Large selfheal (*Prunella grandiflora*)	Purple, pink or white	10–30
Lesser calamint (*Calamintha nepeta*)	Bluish purple	20–45
Dwarf sedge (*Carex humilis*)	Brown	15–25
Purple willow (*Salix purpurea*)	Yellow catkins	100–150
Meadowsweet (*Filipendula ulmaria*)	White	60–90
Cowslip (*Primula veris*)	Yellow	10–20
Remote sedge (*Carex remota*)	Brown	30–50
Dwarf bearded iris (*Iris pumila*)	Purple, white, yellow, blue	10–15
Dyer's broom (*Genista tinctoria*)	Yellow	30–60
Erica	White, pink, red	15–30
St John's wort	Yellow	20–40

MAKE LIFE EASIER

☐ To make sure that all the individual components are compatible, buy a cascade in kit form. The pre-formed units, pump and hose will be designed to work together. You will just need to establish the size of the water reservoir that you need to install.

A seasonal guide to looking after your garden pond

Planted and laid out correctly, the more closely a pond is **modelled on nature**, the **less maintenance** it will need.

Transparent protection
An elegant dome like this can be used to support netting in the autumn to shrug off fallen leaves. In winter it can be draped in fleece to stop the pond from freezing over.

Spring and summer pond care

Towards the end of spring, cut off any dead plant material protruding above the surface of the water and add it to the compost heap. From May onwards, when the water has warmed up slightly, divide and replant any bog plants and water lilies that have grown too large. You should take great care when doing this, as many frogs and toads will already have spawned in March and it is important not to disturb their eggs.

By early summer, algae have often colonised the water surface, which is now heating up rapidly. A sudden explosion of algae growth, known as an algal bloom, can turn the water's surface completely green, almost like a lawn. Aquatic plants in the deeper, cooler water may have trouble competing with algae for space and nutrients. If you are patient, you will find that microorganisms eat up the algae in just a few days – and the water will clear. Bog and water plants, which

Green menace
In the summer a glut of algae is a sign that your pond's nutrient levels are too high – perhaps due to leaves that fell in during the previous autumn.

⏱ **30-MINUTE TASKS**

► Take water lilies out of the pond, divide and replant them.

► Stretch netting over your pond to catch autumn leaves.

take up a lot of nutrients during the summer, may help to prevent an algal bloom occurring later on in the year, provided that nutrient levels in the pond are not too high. An occasional algal bloom is entirely natural and no cause for concern, so you do not need to keep disturbing the ecological balance of your pond by removing it. If you are using an air pump to aerate your pond, you should start to clean the filter more regularly.

Do not start feeding fish until the water reaches 10°C, or warmer. If aquatic plants are healthy and growing well, there is no need to give goldfish extra food. Overfeeding will encourage fish to breed more which, in turn, can affect the water quality.

Autumn and winter pond care

The leaves that fall from trees and shrubs into your pond will sink to the bottom and, together with dead plant material from any bog and water plants, will eventually form a layer of mulch. Drawing on the oxygen in the water, microorganisms feed on the decaying plants and convert them into mud. This natural process will eventually lead to your pond silting up, so that after a few years, you will have to clean it out. The fewer leaves that land in your pond, the longer you will be able to put off this onerous task. Avoid siting a pond where a lot of leaves can fall into it, and during autumn, when the leaves are falling, stretch some netting across the pond (see below) to catch those that would otherwise land in the water.

Before the first winter frosts, remove any electrical equipment such as pumps and lights from the water. Once winter has arrived, do not disturb the pond water or hack at the ice if the pond freezes over – the shock will disturb any hibernating wildlife.

If you want to keep part of the water free of ice, install a floating pool heater, or (for a lower tech and cheaper alternative) float a tennis ball or piece of polystyrene in the pond. This will keep the pond from freezing over completely and allow gases to escape. Aquatic plants will also help the pond not to freeze up and provide a habitat for any overwintering wildlife at the bottom of the pond.

DIVIDING WATER LILIES

1 If water lilies have grown too large, take them out of the pond in May and divide them using a knife or spade.

2 Remove all black, rotting roots and any dark, matted fibre using sharp scissors or secateurs.

3 Finally place the rejuvenated rhizome into a bucket of new soil and resubmerge it in the pond.

Tall wooden posts
Hammer these in under trees and shrubs.

Pegs
Use these to secure the netting in place.

Netting
This should not touch the water.

Leaf catcher
Supporting a leaf net on stakes means that you can raise it above the level of marginal plants, to avoid squashing their upper leaves.

✗ **WATCH OUT!**

Chemicals should never be introduced into a pond as they may harm the many types of wildlife that are attracted to ponds and water features.

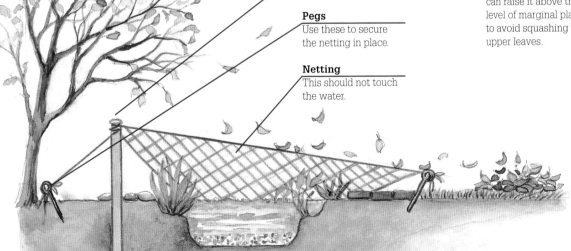

The kitchen garden

Grow your own fruit, vegetables and herbs

A well-tended kitchen garden **appeals to all the senses**. Fragrant herbs are just as **attractive** as tasty vegetables and **delicious** fruits. With thoughtful planning and carefully selected plants, you will be sure to **reap plentiful rewards**.

A sunny and open site

Locate your vegetable garden in a sunny, open site as far away as possible from the road. How much land you want to set aside for your kitchen garden depends on the conditions of your plot and on how much fruit and vegetables you need to grow. Some crops take up more room than others, but on average a 3m by 3m plot should be enough to provide vegetables for a family.

Most vegetables and many fruit trees and bushes will grow in any good garden soil provided it is loamy, rich in nutrients and has good drainage combined with good moisture retention. Applying compost in autumn will ensure that the soil has a good humus content, but if you are growing a herb garden there is no need for compost as most herbs prefer poor, dry soils.

When sowing seeds, always follow the recommended planting distances given on the packet. Plants do not like to be too close together and diseases thrive in cramped conditions. Many vegetables are now available in disease-resistant varieties that are immune to common problems such as mildew and wilt and they often produce higher yields.

Planned cultivation

Since different crops have different nutrient requirements, and to prevent pests and diseases specific to one type of crop accumulating in the soil, annual vegetables should be rotated from bed to bed each year, completing the circuit in three or four years. Plants with a high nutrient requirement can be followed the next year by a crop with a low one to ensure that the soil is not exhausted of any particular nutrient. Keep a garden diary so that you know which vegetables you have grown where and when.

You may also choose to incorporate companion planting principles into your plot, where specific plants and vegetables profit from beneficial effects that they have on one another. For example, French marigolds (*Tagetes patula*) planted next to broad beans will attract hoverflies which eat aphids that would infest the beans.

Mouth-wateringly red Apples that are grown on your own tree are impossible to resist. Low-maintenance varieties are available to suit every garden, region and climate.

MAKE LIFE EASIER

☐ When planning your vegetable garden, incorporate paths or boards so that every part of the bed is within easy reach.

☐ Locating your vegetable garden near an outdoor tap or water butt will save you lots of time and energy carrying heavy watering cans.

☐ Mulch the beds with wilted grass clippings to prevent the soil from drying out and to impede the growth of weeds.

☐ If your garden soil is poor, grow your vegetables in raised beds so that you can add good-quality topsoil – it will also save you bending down, so your back will appreciate it too.

A feast for the eyes and the taste buds
With careful planning and clever planting, a vegetable garden will yield bumper crops even with minimal effort.

Laying out a low-maintenance plot

Your own **vegetable** garden will supply you with **delicious** and **healthy** food. Provided it is well laid out, the plot should reward you with an **abundant** harvest of **quality** produce.

30 MINUTE TASKS

▶ Prepare a vegetable plot measuring 4m by 1.2m. Break up the soil, remove any weeds and level off with a rake.

▶ Cut back green manure plants on a vegetable plot measuring 4m by 1.2m and dig them back in to the soil.

Site and soil

Choose the sunniest site in the garden for your vegetable plot. Salad plants, cucumbers, peas and beans are not the only plants that require plenty of light to grow. Even vegetables that grow beneath the soil, such as carrots and potatoes, produce a good crop only when their foliage receives sufficient sunlight. Most vegetables grow only when the average daytime temperature rises above about 6°C between spring and autumn. It is worth remembering that temperatures in hollows and dips may be a few degrees lower than in

Easily accessible A paved pathway that is wide enough for a wheelbarrow will make working in your vegetable garden easier.

the surrounding area. Wind also affects growth – a windbreak such as a low hedge can provide much-needed shelter in a blustery site. In cold regions, a raised bed or a low wall around the vegetable plot provides extra warmth.

Start preparing the soil as early as autumn. A friable loam soil is ideal as it does not dry out too quickly and does not become waterlogged. Adding humus and clay

Animal shelter Attract earwigs, which gobble up aphids and fungal spores, by filling a clay plant pot with wood shavings or straw and hanging it so that it touches a branch. Alternatively hang it over a cane.

Non-stop temptation Once you have had your fill of strawberries, juicy redcurrants are next on the menu.

Easy pickings When sowing mange-tout peas, insert pea sticks between the seeds for the plants to climb over. Picking the pods will then be an easy task.

TIME-SAVING TIPS

▪ The fruit on a soft fruit small standard can be picked while standing, which is much quicker than picking from an ordinary bush.

▪ Apply a straw mulch between strawberry plants or fruit bushes to keep weeds away. The soil will not dry out so easily and will not require such frequent watering.

▪ Plant onions and garlic between strawberry plants and fruit bushes to help protect against fungal infections.

standards, they take up little space and provide rich pickings even in their first year. Raspberry (*Rubus idaeus*) canes too, especially the repeat-fruiting varieties, provide a source of tasty fruit. You can also try specialities that are less commonly found in the supermarket, such as tayberries, a blackberry and raspberry hybrid, or jostaberries (*Rubus* hybrid), which combine the best features of blackcurrants and gooseberries. Cultivated blueberries (*Vaccinium corymbosum*) or American cranberries (*V. macrocarpon*) are ideal choices for gardens with humus-rich, acid soils.

Strawberries into autumn

Even in the smallest of gardens, there is space for a delicious crop of low-maintenance strawberries. Most varieties form numerous runners and will spread to produce an abundant harvest: choose from 'Elvira' (an early cropper), 'Hapil' (mid-season fruit), 'Maxim' (late) and 'Bolero' (for perpetual fruit). Cut back the foliage after picking the fruit.

Alpine strawberries (*Fragaria vesca* 'Semperflorens'), which produce fruit from June until the autumn, do not form runners and therefore make excellent edging plants for a flower or vegetable bed.

Applying a straw mulch around and beneath your strawberry plants will help to prevent botrytis, a fungal disease that is common in strawberries, as well as deterring slugs from your precious crop.

30 MINUTE TASKS

► Lay out fruit garden (1.5m by 1.5m) and prepare soil.

► Plant out and water plants.

Getting the best from fruit trees

Fruit trees come in all **shapes** and **sizes**, so that there is one for every garden. Once **established**, they should provide a **plentiful crop** and need remarkably **little maintenance**.

30-MINUTE TASKS

► Inspect smaller fruit trees and remove lower sideshoots and suckers (vigorous, unproductive shoots).

► Cut away old and congested branches and shoots and clear away the cut branches.

Small varieties for small gardens

Low-growing fruit tree cultivars are best for most domestic gardens. With a crown not exceeding 2.5m in diameter, and a stem height of about 60cm, apples and pears sold as spindlebushes are easy to look after and to harvest. Half or full standards, on the other hand, have stem heights of 1–2m and mighty 10–12m wide crowns that would burst the boundaries of many gardens.

There are small cultivars of sour (*Prunus cerasus*) and sweet cherry trees (*Prunus avium*), plums (*Prunus domestica*) and damsons (*Prunus damascena*) with a stem height of 60cm and a 3m wide crown. The crowns of

Plum fruits The best plum cultivar for gardens is 'Mirabelle de Nancy' (above), with its exceptionally juicy fruit.

Easy pickings A telescopic apple picker (right) enables you to reach fruit in the higher branches.

Prune established trees lightly

Prune young trees hard

Never leave fruit trees unpruned. Columnar trees will remain in shape, but without corrective pruning all other varieties will deteriorate quickly and will soon cease to bear fruit and become susceptible to disease.

apricot (*Prunus armeniaca*) and peach trees (*Prunus persica*) usually measure about 5m across. They prefer warmer spots, but both can be trained as an espalier against a sheltered house wall.

Fruit trees are available as bare-root, root-ball or container-grown plants. Bare-root and root-ball trees are best planted in the cooler months of spring or autumn, while container-grown plants can be planted out all year round as long as the ground is not frozen. Whatever the root type, soak the roots in a bucket of water while you prepare the hole. It should be about 1m wide and 60cm deep so that there is plenty of room for the roots. Trim the roots of bare-root trees a little before planting. Always plant the tree so that the grafting site, which is visible as a thickening in the trunk, remains above ground. Tread down the soil around the trunk to firm it and tie the tree to a stake so that it will withstand strong winds.

Pruning fruit trees

Immediately after planting, remove competing branches, leaving only the central branch and a maximum of four strong leader branches. Over the next few years, prune formatively so that the numerous shoots coming from the leader branches do not get in each other's way and are not too congested. This will

Extended arm Pruners or loppers with control cables and telescopic handles do away with the need for a ladder when pruning, making it possible to prune fruit trees up to 7m tall.

also shape the crown nicely. In subsequent years, pruning keeps the crown in shape for a good yield and thins out branches that are too congested. Remove any stray shoots sprouting from the base of the trunk together with any long 'water' shoots on the branches that take nutrients from the tree without producing any fruit. If necessary, prune large branches right back to the trunk. To ensure that the crown gets sufficient light, regularly cut away congested growth that prevents stronger branches from developing. Cut old fruit branches back to the point where young shoots are growing, which will in turn set fruit.

Help with aphids

Creating a circular bed around a young fruit tree promotes healthy growth. Remove weeds, grass or other plant matter from an area measuring about 1.5m across around the tree. Mulch the bed with compost in autumn, then sow nasturtiums (*Tropaeolum majus*) in spring to provide shade for the soil and prevent it from drying out. Nasturtiums are a magnet for blackfly so will help keep the tree free of this pest. Put up nesting boxes to attract blue tits. The birds feed on insects living in the branches. Alternatively, hang a clay plant pot upside down in the branches (see page 225) and fill it with straw to attract earwigs, which prey on aphids.

Correct pruning Don't be timid when pruning fruit trees: ensure that plenty of light and air gets into the crown. A fruit tree will usually recover quickly from hard pruning, but will age prematurely if not pruned enough. Prune hard in the early years, removing branches close to the trunk: this will produce a well-balanced tree with a strong branch framework capable of carrying heavy crops of fruit. For mature trees, make the pruning lighter, trimming young wood around the edges of the crown: just enough to encourage fruiting.

■ Slow-growing cultivars (ask for them specifically) can reduce the time spent on pruning each year by more than half, while columnar fruit trees can get by without any pruning at all.

■ In severe winters, cover small trees with horticultural fleece to protect them from frost damage. This will also avoid the job of cutting out frost-damaged branches later.

■ Place sticky grease bands around the trunks in mid autumn to prevent wingless female moths climbing up to lay their eggs. It will save you from picking over the fruit to check for damage from the grubs.

Early cropping under glass and polythene

Growing **young plants** and vegetables under glass and polythene sheeting is a convenient way to **extend the growing season** and achieve a bumper yield.

Cold frames and polytunnels

If you want to raise a few plants for planting out into the garden later, then a simple cold frame covered with a pane of glass is ideal. For growing crops permanently under cover, ready-built greenhouses are available, some even fitted with heaters, automatic ventilation and lighting, so that you can carry on gardening even in the frosty depths of winter. When growing under cover, ventilation is important to avoid diseases, so be sure to open the vents in greenhouses, cloches and polytunnels from time to time to allow fresh air to circulate.

To grow tomatoes, sweet peppers or aubergines under protection, a polytunnel or polythene enclosure is ideal. You can make a simple polytunnel by pulling plastic sheeting over a series of arched metal rods secured in the ground or over a homemade framework of stakes. Stretch the sheeting over the frame until it is taut and attach it firmly to withstand wind. To make the structure more stable, weigh down the edges of the sheeting at the sides with planks or heavy stones or by digging them under the soil. You could also tether the structure to stakes or pegs using rope.

Easy to erect Constructing a polytunnel from a kit is easy – just insert the arched tubing into the framework and stretch the plastic sheeting over it.

Instant greenhouse Plastic sheeting is a quick and easy option for building a greenhouse (right). Make sure that the sheeting is made from a UV-resistant material and that it lets through as much light as possible.

30-MINUTE TASKS

► Prepare a bed to be protected by plastic sheeting.

► Plant six sweet pepper or tomato plants.

► Insert stakes beside the plants and tie the plants to them; firm down and water the soil.

CULTIVATION PLAN FOR THE GREENHOUSE

MONTH	SEEDS OR PLANTS	HARVEST
March	Lettuce, kohlrabi, radishes, early carrots	Spinach
April	Lettuce, kohlrabi, radishes	Lettuce, kohlrabi, radishes
May	Aubergines, tomatoes, sweet peppers, cucumbers, runner beans	Early carrots
June		Cucumbers, tomatoes, runner beans, sweet peppers
July	Kohlrabi, chicory	Cucumbers, tomatoes, runner beans, sweet peppers, aubergines
Aug	Butterhead lettuce, spinach, lamb's lettuce, radishes	Cucumbers, tomatoes, sweet peppers, aubergines
Sept		Kohlrabi, butterhead lettuce, radishes
Oct	Spinach	Chicory, lamb's lettuce
Nov		Chicory, lamb's lettuce

Low-growing, compact plants such as lettuce can also be started off and grown on under plastic sheeting. Remove the sheeting to water plants and when the weather is hot, replacing it in the evening.

A long cropping season

You can sow spinach or lamb's lettuce in an unheated greenhouse as early as February for harvesting in March. From March onwards, use the beds for lettuce, kohlrabi, radishes and other fast-growing vegetables. That way you can have your first fresh salad vegetables as early as April. In May at the latest, when the outdoor-grown season for these sorts of vegetables starts and you can

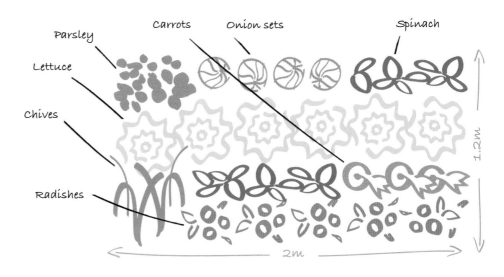

plant them out, you will have space in the greenhouse for heat-loving fruiting vegetables such as aubergines, sweet peppers and tomatoes, which will provide you with produce from July until the end of September.

Carrots grow slowly even in a greenhouse. Sow them in March for harvesting in June at the earliest. To have fresh vegetables in October and November, sow chicory and lamb's lettuce in August or September. August is also the month for sowing kohlrabi, butter head lettuce and radishes for a late harvest.

A good crop of tomatoes

Tomatoes need light, warmth, a moist soil and plenty of nutrients. Brown rot, particularly when the leaves get wet, can kill a plant. Choose resistant cultivars and protect tomatoes from the rain by growing them beneath the eaves of a roof, or under a plastic shelter. Always water the roots of tomatoes, never the leaves.

Planting plan: a polytunnel in spring There is space for a few herbs at two corners, with a row of fresh lettuces, flanked by spinach, onions and carrots. The radishes will be ready for harvesting first.

Watering tomatoes Sink clay plant pots or plastic bottles with the base removed into the ground next to the plants. Fill them with water, which will seep in slowly to the roots.

Under shelter A roof of plastic sheeting protects these tomatoes (left) from rain damage.

A productive plot without an aching back

If you have only a **small space** in which to grow vegetables, then packing them into a **raised bed** full of nutrient-rich soil is the answer. What's more, the vegetables will be **easy to maintain** and **pick**.

Off to a good start

The soil in a raised bed warms up quickly in spring because the sides catch the sun as well as the soil surface. Rotting matter such as manure that has been dug into the soil during preparation of the bed also gives off heat, which is why you can often sow and plant up a raised bed as much as two weeks earlier than an ordinary vegetable patch. Heat-loving plants thrive in a raised bed and, at a height of 75–90cm, many jobs can be carried out while standing.

Until about mid April, the first seeds for sowing are fast-growing radishes, spinach or lettuce. From May onwards you can plant out young cabbage, butterhead lettuce or tomato plants and cucumbers. To make the most of a raised bed, position taller plants in the centre, plants of medium-height at the sides and smaller ones at the very edges.

Easy maintenance for your crops

There are various ways of keeping unwanted insects away from a raised bed: fine-mesh wire netting at the base keeps out mice and voles, and strips of tin folded back and laid along the outer edges make an excellent snail barrier.

Be kind to your back If you have trouble bending down, a raised bed is a good solution, not just for routine maintenance but also for when you need to harvest the fruits of your labours.

Ready for planting
Vegetables thrive in the uppermost layer of topsoil enriched with compost.

For rapid growth
Shredded fresh garden waste, perhaps combined with dead leaves, forms the layer that stimulates growth in the first spring.

Keeping in heat and nutrients
An optional layer of manure provides warmth and a long-lasting supply of nutrients.

Ventilation at the base
The layers of coarsely broken branches and twigs, moistened paper and coarsely chopped garden waste provide ventilation at the base.

Raised beds dry out more quickly than conventional beds and need more frequent watering. Line the insides of the retaining walls with pond liner to prevent water from seeping out quickly when watering and to help retain moisture.

The ideal time to build a raised bed is autumn, when the garden has a plentiful supply of branches, twigs and other organic matter that you can use for the various layers. Another advantage is that the soil in the bed will have enough time to settle and compact over the winter.

In the first and second year plant the raised bed with plants that have a high nutrient requirement. From the third year onwards change to a more diverse planting of medium and low nutrient-requiring plants, followed by legumes, which will fix nitrogen back into the soil. Top up the bed each year with compost and fresh soil. Dig it over lightly in spring and cover it with a layer of mulch in autumn. After about six years the soil will be exhausted and you will need to replace it.

Making a raised bed

To make a raised bed, you will need fine-mesh wire netting for the base, pond liner, thick planks of wood (Douglas fir or larch wood) for the sides and sturdy posts for the corners. An area measuring about 1.5m by 4m is a good size and the finished bed should reach a working height of 75–90cm.

Dig out the soil to a depth of 25cm and put it to one side. Erect the retaining walls and posts and line the insides with pond liner. Cover the base of the bed with fine-mesh wire netting. Begin filling the bed with a bottom layer of twigs and branches. The next layer consists of lightly moistened paper, followed by coarsely shredded garden waste, then a layer of fresh garden waste and autumn leaves. Top off with a layer of compost mixed with the soil that was excavated.

MAKING GOOD USE OF SOIL NUTRIENTS

YEAR	CONDITIONS	PLANTING
1	The bed has a high nitrogen content	Plants with high nutrient requirements such as sweet peppers, tomatoes and leeks.
2	There is still plenty of nitrogen.	Plants with high nutrient requirements such as cucumbers, courgettes and fennel.
3	Nitrogen content is beginning to decline.	Plants with medium nutrient requirements such as kohlrabi, carrots, radishes, strawberries.
4	Even less nitrogen available.	Plants with medium to low nutrient needs such as mange-tout peas, radishes, lettuce.
5	The soil now has a comparatively low nitrogen content.	Plants with low nutrient requirements, such as onions, carrots, radishes and strawberries.
6	The raised bed rots down and nutrients are exhausted.	Plants with low nutrient requirements and nitrogen-fixing plants such as beans, peas, broad beans and potatoes.
7	Spread the filling elsewhere in the garden and refill the raised bed.	Plants with high nutrient requirements as in the first year.

30-MINUTE TASKS

► Fill a raised bed (0.75m by 2m) with layers of shredded branches, garden waste, garden soil and compost.

Plant a tempting, tasty hedge

Even the smallest of gardens has **room for fruit**. Make the most of your boundary by planting it with **fruit bushes** and low-growing fruit trees to create a hedge that will be **pretty and productive**.

Apple and soft fruit hedges

Low-growing apple spindlebushes are ideal for making a hedge or to train as a low-growing and attractive espalier against a house wall. Undemanding soft fruit bushes are another easy way to make an effective fruit hedge. Most soft fruit bushes thrive in almost any site, whether in full sun or partial shade, as long as the soil is rich in humus and nutrients. They will need a position in plenty of sun if you want them to produce their sweetest fruit.

Currants need light and air

Depending on the variety, currant bushes, which can reach a height of 2m, bear fruit from June to August. Autumn is the best planting season, so that the plants will have had time to become established by spring and will be able to set their first fruit. Give them plenty of space and encourage them to produce as many new roots as possible by planting them slightly deeper than they were at the nursery. Finally mulch the ground around them with straw, leaves or bark. After planting prune the bushes to stimulate growth (see box, right).

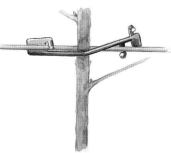
Quick clips An easy way to attach fruit canes to a wire frame is by using special clips (above).

Raspberry hedge Wires stretched between stakes make a framework to support arching raspberry canes (right).

1 Before planting the bushes, soak the roots for an hour in a container of water. This will help the bushes establish themselves more quickly.

2 The planting hole must be deep enough for the plant to sit at the same depth in the soil as it was in its container or at the nursery. Apply a layer of well-rotted compost to the base of the hole before planting.

3 Backfill the hole around the plant with soil and firm it down well. Mound up soil around the plant so that it forms a wall about 15cm from the stem and water well. The wall should retain the water, allowing it to seep into the soil around the plant.

4 Cut raspberry and blackberry canes to a bud 25–30cm from the base. Cut back all stems of blackcurrants to a bud 3–5cm above the base. Cut back all stems of red and white currants by a third and gooseberry branches by half.

Prune currants between November and March. Red and white currants set their fruit on two or three-year-old wood, whereas blackcurrants fruit on the previous season's growth. The bushes of red and white currants need to be airy, so prune the centres of established bushes, leaving between eight and 12 stems (just pruning the tips of these). Cut back side shoots to one bud. Blackcurrants also need light and air but need

30-MINUTE TASKS

► Maintain a 5m long raspberry hedge, cutting back canes that have already cropped. Remove up to five new canes per plant.

► Spread well-rotted manure on the ground beneath the plants, avoiding the stems.

They make your mouth water
Raspberries do not require much attention and are heavy croppers. To prevent the bushes from growing too dense and to keep them under control, check for fruited canes regularly and cut them down to ground level.

more vigorous pruning to achieve a good crop. Cut back a third to a quarter of all fruited branches on established bushes, leaving about eight healthy stems. For gooseberries, cut back the side shoots that were produced in summer to four or five leaves from the base and remove any dead, diseased or crossing stems from the heart of the bush.

Raspberries and blackberries

In the wild, raspberries and blackberries grow at the edges of woodland. In the garden these fruits love a sunny site (but can tolerate partial shade) and a loose soil with a high humus content. Train them as an espalier or along a wire frame.

Different varieties of raspberry produce fruit at different times. Some even produce two crops, one in the summer and another in autumn. Watch out for raspberry beetle infestation on the summer crop; this is not a problem for autumn-fruiting cultivars. Thornless cultivars of the vigorous blackberry make harvesting much easier. They are less hardy than the wild variety and need a sheltered spot as they can be damaged by frost. Blackberries and raspberries bear fruit on young wood, so cut back all shoots that have previously borne fruit right to the ground after the fruit has been picked. Tie in the new season's canes to the frame.

Growing a raspberry hedge

Plant a raspberry hedge in autumn, leaving a 50cm gap between each plant. To encourage growth, add plenty of well-rotted compost to the planting holes. Ensure that the leaf buds on the roots, which go on to produce new canes, are about 5cm beneath the soil. Water the planting site and mulch with well-rotted manure. Construct a simple wire framework and attach the canes to the wires.

TIME-SAVING TIPS

■ Choose cultivars that are less prone to pests and which have proved successful in your area to save time and money on pest control and nurturing struggling plants.

■ Container-grown plants are quicker and easier to plant out than bare-rooted plants, saving you about 15 minutes per plant.

Effective pest control for edible crops

The presence of **pests** in the vegetable patch is often due to simple cultivation errors. Making use of a few **tricks of the trade** during selection and planting will help you to keep your vegetables **healthy** and save you the trouble of subsequent **pest control**.

30-MINUTE TASKS

▶ Check over a 1.2m by 3m vegetable patch for pests; remove affected plant parts and spray remaining plants with an infusion of horsetail as a preventative measure.

Choose pest-resistant cultivars

Good soil conditions and a liberal supply of nutrients, water, light and air are important for healthy plant growth. But the choice of varieties also has a crucial influence on whether or not your vegetables will be attacked by pests.

Summer varieties planted outside in spring always do badly and have little resistance to attack. Likewise, outdoor varieties that are kept under glass often fall prey to pests and diseases. Always choose appropriate varieties for your situation and use cultivars that are resistant to fungal, bacterial or viral infections as well as to common garden pests.

Good company Companion planting of flowers and vegetable crops in the vegetable patch creates a colourful display and the plants are healthier too.

Plants to help one another

Companion planting makes the most of the beneficial effects that plants can have on each other and on pests. Aromatic compounds in roots, leaves and flowers or secretions from parts of some plants can act as effective deterrents to many common pests. Growing carrots with leeks, garlic or onions is a tried and tested combination, with the companions protecting each other in turn against carrot fly and onion fly. When

GOOD AND BAD NEIGHBOURS

VEGETABLES	GOOD NEIGHBOURS	BAD NEIGHBOURS
Peas	Carrots, cucumbers, kohlrabi, lettuce, courgettes, radishes	Beans, potatoes, tomatoes, onions, leeks
Cucumbers	Peas, kohlrabi, leeks, dill, caraway	Tomatoes, radishes, potatoes
Potatoes	Spinach	Tomatoes
Cabbages	Dill, coriander, caraway, butterhead lettuce, chicory, peas, beans, potatoes	Strawberries, onions, mustard, garlic
Butterhead lettuce	Dill, cress, radishes, leeks, carrots, tomatoes, cabbages, onions	Parsley, celery
Carrots	Onions, leeks, garlic, Swiss chard	Beetroot
Tomatoes	Parsley, lettuce, leeks, cabbages	Peas, potatoes, fennel, cucumbers
Onions	Carrots, winter savory, dill, strawberries, lettuce	Beans, peas, brassicas

Simple, but effective
Fine netting or horticultural fleece keeps flying pests away from vegetables (left), while a collar around the stem can protect cabbages from cabbage root fly (below).

grow alongside shallow-rooting plants, compact plants with broad leaves alongside thin-leafed plants. This means there is less room for weeds to take hold.

planted between strawberries and vegetables, onions and garlic also help to protect against fungal infections. Strong-smelling winter savory protects dwarf beans against blackfly, whereas nasturtiums help to protect tomatoes and fruit trees from greenfly and the woolly apple aphid. When planted among vegetables, secretions from the roots of pot marigolds (*Calendula officinalis*) and French marigolds (*Tagetes patula*) help to deter eelworms. Planting celery between cabbage plants drives away cabbage white butterflies, so that they look elsewhere for a place to lay their eggs. And the aromatic leaves of sage also deter cabbage white butterfly as well as being offputting to snails and ants.

As well as protecting against pests, companion planting results in fewer weeds as deep-rooting plants

More tips for eradicating pests

Use netting, horticultural fleece and collars to keep vegetable fly, leek moth and cabbage fly away from your vegetable patch. Spraying with an infusion of horsetail (*Equisetum arvense*) helps to prevent fungal infections. Just boil up two dessertspoons of the dried weed in two litres of water, leave to infuse for 15 minutes, cool, then strain. Every two or three weeks, on a sunny morning, spray the infusion over the plant and the soil.

If you grow vegetables in the same position year after year then certain pests and diseases will be quick to establish themselves, lying dormant in the soil between growing seasons. You can prevent this by rotating crops in the vegetable patch (see page 231).

(see page 231)

TIME-SAVING TIPS

■ Choose pest-resistant or pest-tolerant seed varieties. Butterhead lettuce cultivars such as 'Dynamite', 'Cassandra', 'Action' and 'Avon defiance' are largely unaffected by downy mildew. The same is true for the 'Saladin', 'Lakeland' and 'Malika' cultivars of crisphead lettuce. Lamb's lettuce 'Elan' is resistant to mildew. The 'Gourmet' tomato cultivar is resistant to most diseases including tomato wilt.

Companion planting for vegetables
This planting plan for a summer vegetable selection maximises the beneficial effects of companion planting. By choosing cultivars that are resistant to various pests and diseases, you should achieve a bountiful harvest.

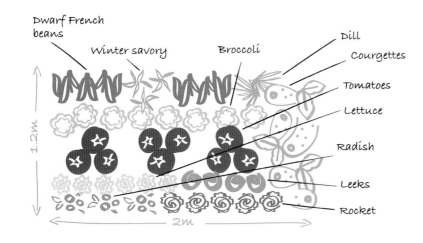

Dwarf French beans
Winter savory
Broccoli
Dill
Courgettes
Tomatoes
Lettuce
Radish
Leeks
Rocket
1.2m
2m

Immune to pests 'Fly Away' and 'Nandor' carrot varieties are resistant to carrot fly, which can decimate an entire crop.

The kitchen garden
A feast for the eyes

Many vegetables are **attractive** and **colourful**. Choose varieties carefully and your vegetable patch will **look** as good as the food in it **tastes**.

Bright and cheerful

Plant different types of vegetables and you can soon create a brightly coloured vegetable garden that will be a feast for the eyes as well as for the tastebuds from spring through to autumn. Combine tall-growing varieties with shorter ones and plants with different coloured leaves with green-leafed varieties to make your vegetable garden eye-catching and attractive. You'll have the best of both worlds as visual appeal will go hand in hand with practicality.

A work of art Arrange different types of vegetables together to create a living tapestry that's good enough to eat. Here, different varieties of lettuce cluster alongside chard, other brassicas and the feathery foliage of fennel.

Plant robust lettuce varieties with leaves of varying shape and colour, such as the red and green oak leaf lettuce, 'Lollo rossa' and 'Lollo bionda', to create an imaginative mosaic of colour in spring and autumn. As you pick a lettuce or two, simply fill in the gaps with subsequent sowings or new plants. Brassicas also come

Simply stunning With their towering stems and splendid flowerheads, globe artichokes are the crowning glory of any flower or vegetable bed.

30-MINUTE TASKS

► Plant three rows of 15 plants of different types of lettuce in a vegetable plot (about 1.2m by 4m) and water thoroughly.

Glowing brightly You don't have to wait for Hallowe'en to enjoy the impressive sight of majestic pumpkins (*Cucurbita maxima*). Their vibrant colours stand out against the green foliage as soon as they appear in the garden.

in different colours and can be used to attractive effect. Green or purple-headed cauliflower ('Romanesco' or 'Minaret'), red-leafed curly kale (*Brassica oleracea* Acephala Group) and even the unusual black Tuscan cabbage are tasty, rich in vitamins and extremely decorative. Provided there is not too much frost over winter, ornamental cabbages can make an attractive decoration for the vegetable garden right through into spring.

Swiss chard (*B. vulgaris* Cicla Group) works well in ornamental beds with its eye-catching leaves and stems, which may be brilliant red, yellow or orange depending on the variety. As you rarely need to pick more than a couple of its leaves and stems, it will add a decorative touch to the vegetable patch the whole summer long.

Ornamental plants

For a particularly bright and cheerful vegetable garden, plant herbs, herbaceous plants and annuals, such as sage, lavender, phlox and zinnias, in between lettuces and cabbages. Pot marigolds (*Calendula officinalis*) and nasturtiums (*Trolpaeolum majus*) not only liven up the

garden with their glowing flowers, but also do a useful job of keeping pests such as eelworms and blackfly away from your crops.

Vegetables in the flower garden

If you don't want a dedicated kitchen garden, you can easily grow vegetables in a flower bed. Tomatoes with their red fruits and courgettes with their silver-veined leaves and yellow flowers are not the only plants to hold their own in the ornamental garden. Imposing globe artichokes (*Cynara scolymus*) with their blue-grey leaves and thistle-like flowers look stunning. If left, they will burst open into large purple flowers in autumn.

Red-stemmed Swiss chard goes particularly well with yellow French marigolds (*Tagetes patula*) and all red-flowered plants. Soft fennel (*Foeniculum vulgare*) leaves waft around herbaceous plants and a butterhead lettuce produces an attractive rosette of leaves.

ATTRACTIVE VEGETABLES

PLANT	DECORATIVE PARTS
Artichoke	Leaves and flowers
Cauliflower 'Purple Graffiti'	Head
Crisphead lettuce 'Web's Wonderful'	Leaf edges
Kale 'Redbor' F1 hybrid	Flowerheads
Swiss chard 'Bright Lights'	Leaves
Black Tuscan cabbage 'Nero di Toscana'	Leaves
Leaf lettuce 'Lollo rossa'	Leaves
Scarlet runner bean 'Hestia'	Flowers
Red oak leaf lettuce	Stems
Spinach 'Reddy' F1 hybrid	Foliage
Savoy cabbage 'De Pointoise 2'	Head, leaves

TIME-SAVING TIPS

■ During summer, as soon as you create gaps in your vegetable garden by harvesting a crop, plant something new. Repeatedly 'topping up' your plot breaks down the time-consuming task of replanting the whole plot at once at the end of the season.

Pretty and practical: edging for beds

Edging in the kitchen garden offers some **protection** against wind and rain, keeps pests away and can **enhance** the appearance of your **vegetable garden**.

Protective and decorative hedges

Low fencing and hedging adds an attractive touch to the edges of the vegetable garden while at the same time creating an area with a favourable microclimate, more sheltered from the wind. It is also useful for keeping footballs out of your prized crops if you have children who play in the garden.

Low-growing common privet (*Ligustrum*) or box (*Buxus*) are popular choices for a green edging. If you decide to use box, choose a slow-growing cultivar, such as 'Suffruticosa' to prevent the hedge growing too tall too quickly. Globes of box planted at the corners of the bed will add to the decorative effect.

Neatly edged Even simple timber planks or boards make attractive edging for a vegetable patch and offer effective protection against crawling pests.

Another option is to plant culinary herbs or fragrant miniature and dwarf shrubs as a border around the vegetable plot. An edging of parsley and chives will serve two purposes: not only will they be useful in the kitchen, but the essential oils within them and in their scent will also deter pests such as caterpillars and grubs, aphids and even snails.

Southernwood (*Artemisia abrotanum*), cotton lavender (*Santonlina*), winter savory, hyssop and lavender can easily be pruned to an attractive shape in

30-MINUTE TASKS

► Erect snail deterrent fence using ready-made interlocking parts around a bed of 1.2m by 2m.

Stop, border control!
A snail barrier with the upper edge bent sharply back keeps them at a safe distance from your crops, as long as no plant overhangs the fence to provide a bridge for them to creep over.

spring. You can also use them as low-maintenance hedging that requires no clipping, although this option does require more space.

Space-saving hard edging

Living edging not only needs to be trimmed and tended regularly, but it also needs space in which to grow, reducing the area available for cultivation. Borders made of stone, wood or metal require considerably less space. Bricks inserted diagonally into the soil, woven willow, logs, hurdles or even aluminium strips are good, quick ways of creating a clear boundary. Just make sure they are inserted securely. Some may also serve as supports for taller plants.

Make clever use of the heat-retaining properties of stone and wood to improve the microclimate in your vegetable garden. Stone is especially good at storing the sun's heat during the day and slowly releasing it at night. Heat-loving plants thrive particularly well if planted close to brick edging, reducing the need to go out with additional protective measures as soon as there is the slightest threat of a night frost.

All edging serves the important purpose of retaining the soil in the bed. Even after torrential rain, heavy watering and a generous application of compost, the edging will keep the bed in good shape.

Combating snails

In wet summers, snails can be a menace in the vegetable garden, sometimes managing to gobble up every single plant in just one night. There are various means available to help you battle against these unloved garden creatures, including snail deterring barriers to keep them out of the vegetable plot (above). Normally made of plastic or metal, they come in sections that slot together and are hammered into the ground. The upper edge is bent back sharply to deter the snails from crawling over the top. Make sure that there are no plants overhanging the barrier in either direction as the snails will make use of even the most slender stems to gain access to the plot. Once you have installed your barrier, check the vegetable plot carefully to make sure that you have not left any snails inside.

A low-tech but effective way of ridding a plot of snails is to make regular checks after rain, simply picking off the sails and collecting them in a bucket. You can then drown them or release them in an area of waste ground.

TIME-SAVING TIPS

■ Ready-made, interlocking plastic sections of edging with an integral mowing edge are quick and easy to install. As well as providing a neat edge, they allow you to push the lawn mower over them, saving you about 10 minutes' of trimming for every 10m of lawn edge (see page 168).

Edging made of herbs
Thyme (far left), chives (centre), parsley, strawflower (*Helichrysum bracteatum*) (left), curry plant (*H. serotinum*) and cotton lavender (*Santolina*) make good edging plants for a vegetable patch. Apart from their decorative effect, these herbs also protect the vegetables from mildew, aphids and snails.

Redesign now to save time later

It may seem drastic, but a well-planned redesign will save time and effort on maintenance in the future. The keys to success are sensible, appropriate planting and a well thought-out division of the garden plot.

Choose gravel rather than grass for easy maintenance

A **gravel garden** is perfect for gardeners with a **limited amount of time**, who are too busy for regular garden maintenance, or who spend long periods away from home. Plants that **prefer dry conditions** will not need watering, even in the summer.

The starting point

This garden is well past its best. Large pine trees cast a shadow over much of the site. The south-facing patio is too small and too hot in summer. The pond and shed have been positioned without much thought and are accessible only by stepping stones across the lawn. Maintaining the hedge and the herbaceous border by the patio are labour-intensive tasks. The lawn is in poor condition, particularly in the shadow of the pines and in front of the hedge, where it is too dry. The plot will look unkempt as soon as it suffers the slightest neglect.

The low-maintenance alternative

A gravel garden demands minimal attention and can flourish without watering for several weeks, even during summer. The garden's informal design means that it can tolerate a little neglect, so it will always look welcoming even after you have been away on holiday. You can leave the drought-resistant flowerbed to its own devices, while the evergreen hedge does not have to be cut with precision. Low-maintenance grasses create a natural transition between shrubs and ground cover.

The garden has gained an east-facing patio and a cooler seating area next to the shed, linked by a railway sleeper-and-gravel pathway. With its adjoining bog garden and natural stone slabs, the pond looks more natural and complements the garden. One pine tree has been replaced with a plant-clad pergola, offering privacy and protection from the wind. Even this reasonably large garden will need only limited maintenance to keep it looking its best.

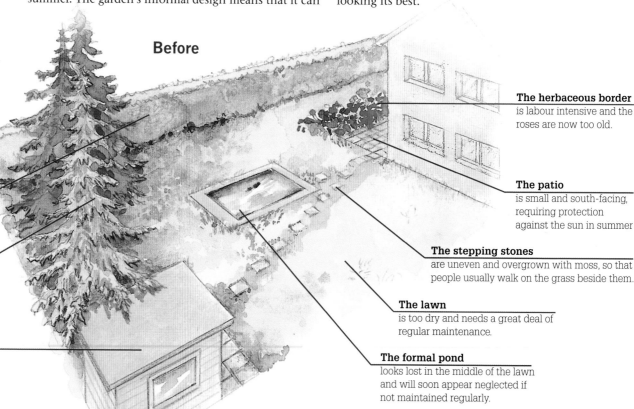

Before

The herbaceous border
is labour intensive and the roses are now too old.

The patio
is small and south-facing, requiring protection against the sun in summer

The stepping stones
are uneven and overgrown with moss, so that people usually walk on the grass beside them.

The lawn
is too dry and needs a great deal of regular maintenance.

The formal pond
looks lost in the middle of the lawn and will soon appear neglected if not maintained regularly.

The evergreen hedge
must be cut carefully and neatly to avoid appearing neglected.

A pine tree
casts shadow and is too close to the shed. The grass no longer grows in the area around the tree.

The shed
looks isolated and obtrusive and has to be repainted each year.

After

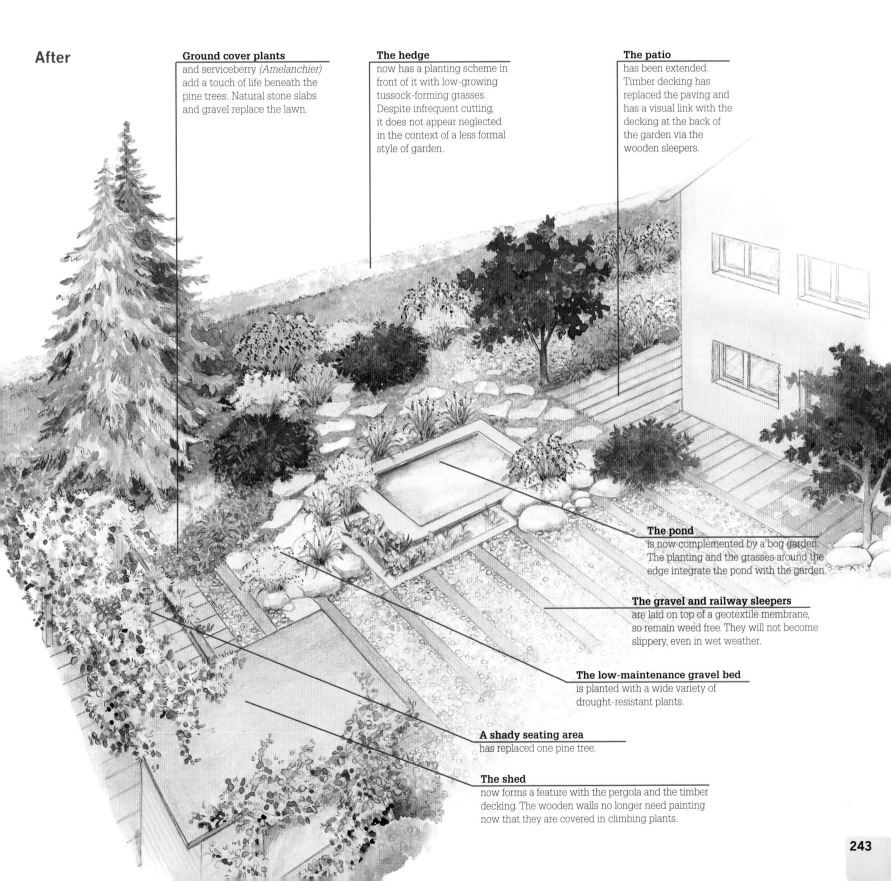

Ground cover plants
and serviceberry *(Amelanchier)* add a touch of life beneath the pine trees. Natural stone slabs and gravel replace the lawn.

The hedge
now has a planting scheme in front of it with low-growing tussock-forming grasses. Despite infrequent cutting, it does not appear neglected in the context of a less formal style of garden.

The patio
has been extended. Timber decking has replaced the paving and has a visual link with the decking at the back of the garden via the wooden sleepers.

The pond
is now complemented by a bog garden. The planting and the grasses around the edge integrate the pond with the garden.

The gravel and railway sleepers
are laid on top of a geotextile membrane, so remain weed free. They will not become slippery, even in wet weather.

The low-maintenance gravel bed
is planted with a wide variety of drought-resistant plants.

A shady seating area
has replaced one pine tree.

The shed
now forms a feature with the pergola and the timber decking. The wooden walls no longer need painting now that they are covered in climbing plants.

A stylish gravel garden

Order of work

The first task is to arrange for a tree surgeon to remove the pine tree that is growing too close to the shed. The next is to remove and dispose of the lawn – another job for a professional landscape gardener, who can then rotavate the soil and dig in plenty of sand, to a depth of about 20cm. This can be done during winter, when professionals tend to be less busy. If you don't mind a little DIY, you can erect the pergola and timber decking yourself on frost-free days in winter and create the base for the bog garden, again on frost-free days. You can also clear the herbaceous border yourself.

Two options for low-maintenance gravel beds
▶ In the top picture, the topsoil has been removed and replaced with soil mixed with sand or crushed stone to make it less fertile. This is spread over horticultural fleece or a geotextile membrane.
▶ In the lower picture, the existing poor subsoil is used as the growing medium, and is then covered with horticultural fleece or a membrane to keep weeds at bay.

Make a start on the foundations for the patio, gravel pathway and natural stone flagging. This, too, is a job for a professional landscape gardener, who can also lay the railway sleepers, the patio decking and the natural stone flags. It would also be wise to ask a professional to source and position the larger individual rocks.

Now it is your turn: plant the shrubs, climbing plants, herbaceous plants and grasses, spread gravel or crushed stone over pathways and between plants.

You might feel that such a radical redesign is rather drastic, but your courage will be rewarded as early as the following year, when you will find garden maintenance work has been dramatically reduced.

Two options for creating a low-maintenance gravel bed

Option 1: First remove the topsoil. Then line the base and sides of the bed with horticultural fleece or a geotextile membrane. Next, pour in a layer of prepared sterile growing medium such as gravel or coarse sand with a 20 per cent humus content. Plant shrubs and grasses in the newly prepared bed 20–30cm apart, and cover the bed with a 2–3cm deep layer of gravel or crushed stone. Depending on the species, the plants will propagate themselves by spreading their roots, creeping along the surface or dropping their seeds. You will have to thin out the plants after a few years. Although weed seeds will end up in the gravel, they rarely germinate.

Option 2: Remove the topsoil and then break up the subsoil to a depth of about 30cm, mixing it with sand or crushed stone to make it poorer and to improve drainage. Then cover it with a layer of horticultural fleece or a geotextile membrane. Cut X-shaped slits into the membrane and insert the plants and grasses through them. Then cover the bed with a 2–3cm deep layer of gravel. After a few years, you may need to replace old plants. Again, seeds from weeds will stand little chance of survival here.

- ☐ Lay a gravel bed and plant ground cover instead of a lawn.

- ☐ Plant drought-resistant species instead of high-maintenance roses and herbaceous plants.

- ☐ Cover a wall with climbing plants rather than paint it.

- ☐ Lay areas of gravel and paving.

- ☐ Use horticultural fleece or membrane to suppress weeds.

Gravel or crushed stone
acts as a mulch and reduces evaporation.

Sterile growing medium
such as horticultural sand, grit or gravel mixed with compost encourages moderate growth.

Horticultural fleece
or a geotextile membrane prevents weeds from growing around and through the plants' roots.

Gravel or crushed stone
conceals the liner beneath.

Horticultural fleece
or a geotextile membrane allows water to drain through and prevents weeds.

The existing soil
is adapted to suit drought-resistant plants.

Less work
A sunny gravel bed (left), laid over a layer of horticultural fleece or geotextile membrane and planted with drought-resistant plants, will be weed-free and easy to care for.

Flowers in the shade Ground cover plants, such as lesser periwinkle (*Vinca minor*) (above), provide a low-maintenance alternative to a lawn that becomes moss infested in the shade.

WATCH OUT!

Water sparingly; drought-resistant gravel plantings must not become waterlogged. They can survive hard winters, but persistently wet roots will rot.

LOW-GROWING PLANTS AND GRASSES FOR SUNNY GRAVEL BEDS

PLANT	HABIT/HEIGHT	FLOWERING PERIOD/CARE NOTES
Catmint (*Nepeta*)	grey-green leaves; 20–40cm	blue flowers (May-Sep); cut back after flowering if necessary
Lavender (*Lavandula angustifolia*)	narrow grey-green leaves; 20–40cm	purple flowers (Jul-Aug); cut back in spring if necessary
Sage (*Salvia officinalis* 'Icterina')	yellow variegated leaves; 30–80cm	upright blue flowerheads (May-Jul); prune in spring if required
Thrift (*Armeria maritima*)	cushion-forming; 5–15cm	bright pink, white, pink or red (May-Nov)
Rock rose (*Helianthemum nummularium*)	low-growing, loosely mat-forming; 10–30cm	single yellow flowers (Jun-Sep)
Hairy golden aster (*Heterotheca villosa*)	upright, graceful; 15–40cm	yellow flowerheads (Jul-Sep)
Green santolina (*Santolina rosmarinifolia*)	evergreen shrubby; 20–60cm	small bright yellow flowers (Jun-Sep); trim in spring if required
Dianthus carthusianorum	cushion-forming; 15–30cm	deep red-pink (Jun-Sep)
Mouse-ear hawkweed (*Pilosella officinarum*)	ground-covering; 5–25cm	yellow (May-Oct); pull up when too dense
Allium oreophilum	upright, graceful shrub; 20–30cm	pink clusters (Jun-Jul); deadhead if required
Biting stonecrop (*Sedum acre*)	ground-covering; 5–15cm	bright yellow (Jun-Jul)
Gypsophila repens 'Rosea'	ground-covering; 5–20cm	tiny pink flowers (May-Aug); good for flower arrangements
White stonecrop (*Sedum album*)	ground-covering; 5–20cm	white (Jun-Jul)
Cypress spurge (*Euphorbia cyparissias*)	small, linear leaves; 10–20cm	yellow flowerheads (Apr-Jun); cut back if necessary

30-MINUTE TASKS

► Lay horticultural fleece or a geotextile membrane covered with a suitable growing medium.

► Plant and water drought-resistant plants.

► Spread a decorative layer of crushed stone or gravel between the plants.

Creating a smart and welcoming front garden

A front garden has to **fulfil a number of practical functions**, but it should also look **welcoming all year round** – while being easy to maintain. First plan any **working areas** then move on to the planting.

An untidy patchwork

Several small paths criss-cross the front garden making plant care labour-intensive. Edging stones make it difficult to rake up dead leaves and uneven paving stones have become dangerous stumbling blocks. The parking space, with its paved tracks, is not suitable for any other use. The grassed areas have become overrun with moss and need serious attention. The gravel strips around the house look neglected, while the dustbins look ugly at the front of the house. The flowerbeds in front of the hedge make it difficult to trim. This garden needs a thorough makeover to give it both practicality and visual appeal.

The low-maintenance alternative

Combining large paving slabs with small stone blocks, or setts, and taking them right up to the front of the house makes the front garden look much larger. Strips of setts in contrasting colours edge the flowerbeds and paths. The plants are grown in two low-maintenance flowerbeds, both easily accessible on all sides. The dustbins are now hidden in a timber-framed structure, clad in easy-care climbers that complement the evergreen hedge on the other side of the garden gate. It is now no problem carrying shopping from the boot of the car straight to the front door. Benches in front of the house allow you to put shopping down or sit for a moment, while an outdoor tap and sink makes garden jobs easy – whether cleaning the car or washing muddy dogs and boots.

Before

The gravel strip
is dirty and mossy, while the gratings and dustbins are ugly. Concrete edging stones make maintenance difficult and there is no outside tap.

The bench
has to be moved out of the way to mow the grass. There is no path to walk around the house in rainy weather without getting wet feet.

The lawn
is covered in moss and is difficult to look after due to the edging stones and shady site. The paving stones are in the wrong place and are unstable.

The driveway
with its paved tracks cannot be used for any other purpose. Uneven slabs are a trip hazard.

The path to the front door
is too narrow, wide enough for only one person at a time to walk along it.

The container
placed over the manhole cover emphasises rather than conceals it and makes extra work as the container has to be looked after.

The flowerbed
makes it difficult to trim the hedge and is too wide to tend from the lawn without treading on the bed.

The paving
reaches right up to the front of the house, where two benches conceal the grilles where water drains away.

The driveway
is totally paved and now also doubles up as an excellent space in which to play, clean the car or do other work.

A dustbin store
is hidden by a dense layer of greenery, which clearly marks the boundary between the front garden and the street.

After

The front door
is now approached by a wide path, the contrasting strips of setts making it look shorter and broader.

The paving
in front of the hedge makes hedge trimming easier and integrates the inspection cover into the pattern of the setts.

The stone flowerbed borders
have no raised edges so dirt can be swept straight into the flowerbed. The centrally positioned beds are accessible from all sides and easy to maintain.

247

An impressive entrance

MAKE LIFE EASIER

- Fit an exterior electrical power point for garden and car-care appliances.

- Install an outside tap for connecting a garden hose.

- Consider fitting a sink beneath the outside tap for cleaning flowerpots, tools and muddy boots.

Order of work

The first task is to dig out any plants worth keeping from the flowerbeds. Store them in another shady flower bed or in shallow containers filled with soil and placed in the shade. Then carefully remove the soil from the beds and store it.

Next, remove the old hedge at the right of the entrance, together with its roots, to make room for the dustbin shed and the new climbing plants that will conceal it.

Remove all the old paving stones and ask a paving specialist to check the exposed subsoil. The expert can give you vital information that will help to ensure that the planned driveway and

Integrated manhole cover
Use a custom-made manhole cover, specially designed to take setts, or incorporate the lid into your overall design (right).

TIME-SAVING TIPS

- When laying paving, make sure that the stones run in such a way that you can easily sweep dirt into the adjoining flowerbeds.

A mixed surface Combining paving with gravel allows water to drain freely and also offers possibilities for planting low-growing species, such as violas, between the slabs (above).

Close up on the terraces Raised beds make it easy to plant and care for a wide variety of plants with different soil requirements. This closer view gives a more detailed look at the planting schemes in the three terraces on page 251.

✗ WATCH OUT!

Incorporate plenty of drainage material – hardcore rubble, for example – in the base of each terraced bed to prevent them from becoming waterlogged. Include some 'weep holes' in the retaining walls to allow excess water to drain through.

replace as much topsoil as he can salvage, rather than filling the terraced beds with subsoil. If necessary, buy some good topsoil for finishing off the beds.

Planning the planting

Prepare lists and plans of what will go in each bed and get the soil ready before you go shopping. The soil should be moist before planting and will benefit from the addition of well-rotted compost or manure. Work in a balanced fertiliser about a fortnight before planting.

If you want to grow herbs and vegetables in the terraces, put them in a sunny spot that is also easily accessible from the house. If you have a window that looks out directly onto the terraces, consider how the beds will look in each season and include a core arrangement of plants that will give interest to the beds all year round.

Level 3
Grasses at the edge of the patio and evergreen dwarf conifers are low maintenance and look good in winter too.

Level 2
A Mediterranean herb garden with lavender (*Lavandula angustifolia*), Sage (*Salvia officinalis*), lemon balm (*Melissa officinalis*), oregano (*Origanum vulgare*) and thyme (*Thymus vulgaris*). Mulch in between the plants with slate chippings.

Level 1
Pretty vegetables and fruit make an ornamental kitchen garden, planted with tomato 'Tumbler'; lettuce 'Lollo Rosso'; radish 'Cherry Belle'; carrot 'Amsterdam Forcing 3 – Sprint'; beetroot 'Mona Lisa'; Chard 'Bright Lights'; French bean 'Purple Teepee'; dwarf runner bean 'Hestia'; strawberry 'Flamenco'; aubergine 'F1 Calliope'; pepper 'Topgirl'; chives; garlic chives; parsley, moss curled; dill and basil. Keep a strip bare at the back of the bed for standing on when tending level 2.

Different terrace styles
On a gentle slope, sturdy hardwood planks or untreated railway sleepers make attractive terracing.

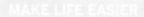
MAKE LIFE EASIER

☐ Install an automatic watering system at the time of construction. Kits are widely available, and can be operated manually or with a timer, which is worth considering if you are away from home a lot.

A new lease of life for an outgrown children's playground

Your children have grown up and what used to be their **play area** is now rather **forlorn**.

You can revitalise the corner by creating an **undemanding heather garden**, with a relaxing swing seat.

The starting point

An old sandpit occupies the now bare, former children's garden. Over the years, the sand has been spread out over the entire area. The ground under the swing is completely worn away, and compacted and dry around the silver birch tree in the corner. The frame of the swing is still intact and stable enough to be used for a new garden swing seat.

The low-maintenance alternative

A garden containing heathers and their typical companion plants is a particularly low-maintenance planting option for sunny and partially-shaded parts of the garden. Heaths and heathers need poor, sandy,

neutral to acid soil and grow particularly well with silver birch, so there is no need to remove the tree. Other suitable companion trees and shrubs are junipers, small pines and broom. Tussock-forming grasses and hardy herbaceous plants, such as the maiden pink (*Dianthus deltoides*), complete the planting.

The winding path with its log edging and scattering of large stones creates a naturalistic picture. Log slices and stone slabs, used as stepping stones, make access to plants easier. There is no need to feed a heather garden and it only needs to be watered during the first few weeks after planting. From then on, the only maintenance required is to cut back the heathers once they have finished flowering.

Before

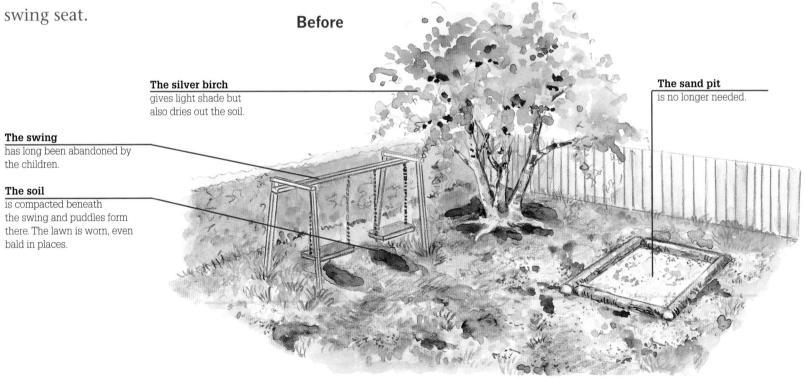

The silver birch gives light shade but also dries out the soil.

The sand pit is no longer needed.

The swing has long been abandoned by the children.

The soil is compacted beneath the swing and puddles form there. The lawn is worn, even bald in places.

Stone slabs
mark the start of the path of chipped bark mulch leading to the garden swing seat. Logs and grasses edge the path, and Dyer's broom *(Genista tinctoria)* and maiden pinks provide dashes of colour.

Around the silver birch
heathers grow alongside silver feather grass *(Stipa barbata* 'Silver Feather'). Stepping stones made of log slices allow easy access into the bed.

After

The swinging seat area
has been given a thick layer of chipped bark mulch to prevent weeds, while low-maintenance honeysuckle *(Lonicera)* provides greenery.

Dwarf and columnar juniper trees
provide a change in height, and are interspersed with groups of different coloured varieties of heather.

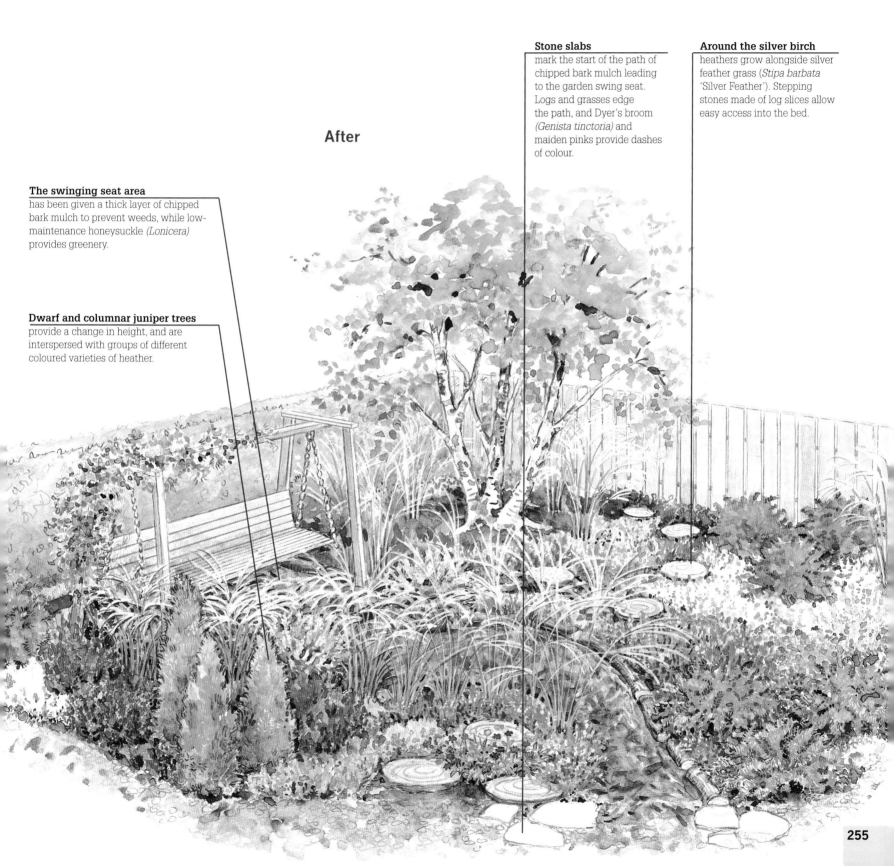

Changing needs

Order of work

Remove the sandpit edging and check if the wood can be reused. Then carefully remove the turf from areas planned as flowerbeds. This can be used to repair bald patches elsewhere in the lawn. Break up the soil with a garden fork or rotavator, taking care not to damage the silver birch roots. Next, focus on the path edging. Either use log sections laid horizontally – these can be screwed to short pointed stakes, which are hammered into the soil – or use sections of log roll or wood planks inserted vertically to keep the path and planting areas separate.

Once you have broken up the soil, adapt it to suit the plants you intend to grow by digging in compost and washed sand – use 40 litres of compost and 20–40 litres of sand per square metre of soil. Work it in thoroughly with a hoe, covering the area where the roots of the silver birch are close to the surface, but stopping short of the trunk. To prevent weeds growing up into the path, level off its base and then put down a layer of porous matting before filling with a layer of crushed stone, bark mulch or wood chips.

Next, position features such as rocks, stepping stones and old tree stumps. Look at the bed from all sides before setting out the plants – still in their pots for now. Move them around until you are happy with their positions. It's a good idea to arrange evergreen trees first and then position the dwarf conifers and heathers. For the best visual effect, plant heathers in groups of at least five plants of a single variety, 20–25cm apart.

Once you are satisfied with your arrangement, you can begin planting. Firm the soil and water each plant, using a watering can without a rose or a hose without a spray attachment so that the water can penetrate the roots effectively. Firm the soil again and apply a thick layer of wood chips or bark mulch.

A natural look An old tree stump is difficult to remove, but forms the focal point in the foreground for this heather planting, while junipers provide height to the rear.

PLANTING HEATHERS

1 A permeable, slightly acid and weed-free soil in a sunny to partially shaded site is a good start for a heather garden. Dig over and loosen the top layer of soil to improve the drainage.

2 Lay out larger design elements first, such as pieces of driftwood to give structure to the planting area. They look more natural if you bury them in soil to about a third of their height. Then position the plants.

3 Arrange smaller decorative items such as stones together with more plants. Then check the arrangement from all angles. It is easy at this stage to make changes to the arrangement. Make sure you view it from a window in the house, too.

4 Plant the heather, preferably in groups of at least five plants, with 20–25cm between each plant; water each plant with about 5 litres of water. Finally, apply a thick layer of chipped bark or wood chips as a mulch.

✗ WATCH OUT!

Heathers are robust but do not like to sit in waterlogged soil; ensure that the top 30cm of soil is broken up and dug over thoroughly, and check that it drains well before planting. Heathers do not thrive in limey soil, although some winter-flowering ones will tolerate it.

30-MINUTE TASKS

▶ In May to June cut back winter flowering heathers.

▶ Cut back summer flowering heathers in November to December.

ATTRACTIVE HEATHERS

PLANTS	APPEARANCE/FLOWERING TIME
Summer-flowering heathers (*Calluna vulgaris*)	
'Alba Plena'	Broad, upright habit; height up to about 40cm; green/grey leaves; pure white flowers, Aug-Oct.
'Aurea'	Compact; height up to 30cm; golden yellow shoots; pale purple flowers, Aug-Oct.
'Darkness'	Upright habit; height up to 50cm; grey-green leaves; evergreen; free-flowering, crimson flowers, Aug-Oct.
'Country Wicklow'	Particularly low-growing and semi-prostrate; height up to 20cm; bronze-coloured shoots and pale pink flowers, Aug-Sep.
'H.E. Beale'	Compact; semi-prostrate; height up to 25cm; salmon pink flowers, Aug-Sep.
Winter-flowering heathers (*Erica carnea*)	
'Myretoun Ruby'	Dark green leaves; height up to 20cm; wine red flowers, Mar-Apr.
'Ruby Glow'	Low-growing, compact habit; late flowering with profuse crimson flowers, Mar-May.
'Snow Queen'	Bright green leaves; upright habit; height up to 30cm; large white flowers, Jan-Mar.
'Vivellii'	Low-growing; height up to 20cm; leaves dark green in summer, bronze-red in winter; crimson flowers, Feb-Mar.
'Winter Beauty'	Very compact and short-sprigged shape with dark green leaves; long and free flowering; pink-red flowers, Nov-Mar.

Rejuvenating a wilderness
A breath of fresh air for an overgrown garden

If evergreen conifers planted 20 years ago have grown out of control it's time to **reintroduce some light** into the gloomy plot. There's no need to **redesign the garden from scratch** to do it.

The existing shady garden

Overgrown trees let little light onto the patio or into the house; the conifers have become far too tall and virtually nothing can grow beneath them. The roots protrude through the lawn – which is now made up almost entirely of moss.

Felling large trees becomes increasingly difficult and risky as they grow taller, so remove ones that are growing out of control before they get too big. Since there is no access to this garden for machinery, it will all have to be dealt with manually, leaving the tree stumps in the soil. If possible, use the felled timber somewhere else in the garden. Some of the logs and branches can be stacked up in a wood pile, while the rest can be shredded on site to form a mulch and path covering.

The low-maintenance alternative

The redesign has created a more diverse, naturalistic garden. Where the trees once stood, there are now tree stumps and some interesting plants. New flowerbeds have been edged with logs from the felled trees and filled with soil, beneath which the old tree roots can gradually rot away. The pond enhances the garden visually and creates a new environment for wildlife.

The planting scheme for the new flowerbeds focuses on the kind of robust, opportunistic plants that spring up naturally in forest clearings and after tree felling in woodland, such as foxgloves. Parts of the lawn have been rejuvenated with sand and fertiliser. Beside the patio is a small, easily-maintained, terraced bed with a low retaining wall built of logs, which makes the patio look larger. Some of the new paths have been covered with gravel, others with chipped bark. Light can now enter the garden again; it looks much larger overall and maintenance work has been reduced permanently.

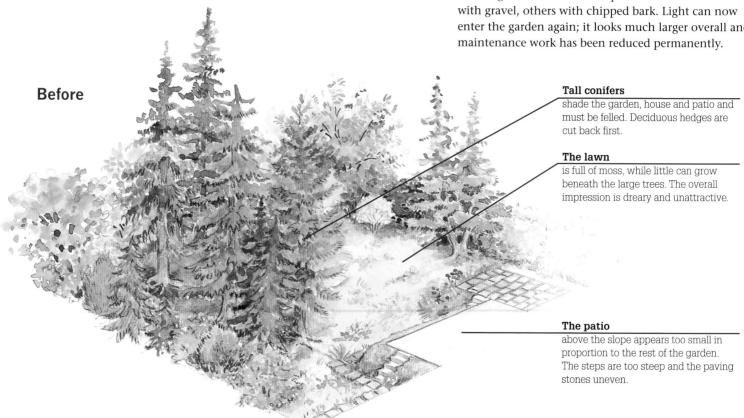

Before

Tall conifers shade the garden, house and patio and must be felled. Deciduous hedges are cut back first.

The lawn is full of moss, while little can grow beneath the large trees. The overall impression is dreary and unattractive.

The patio above the slope appears too small in proportion to the rest of the garden. The steps are too steep and the paving stones uneven.

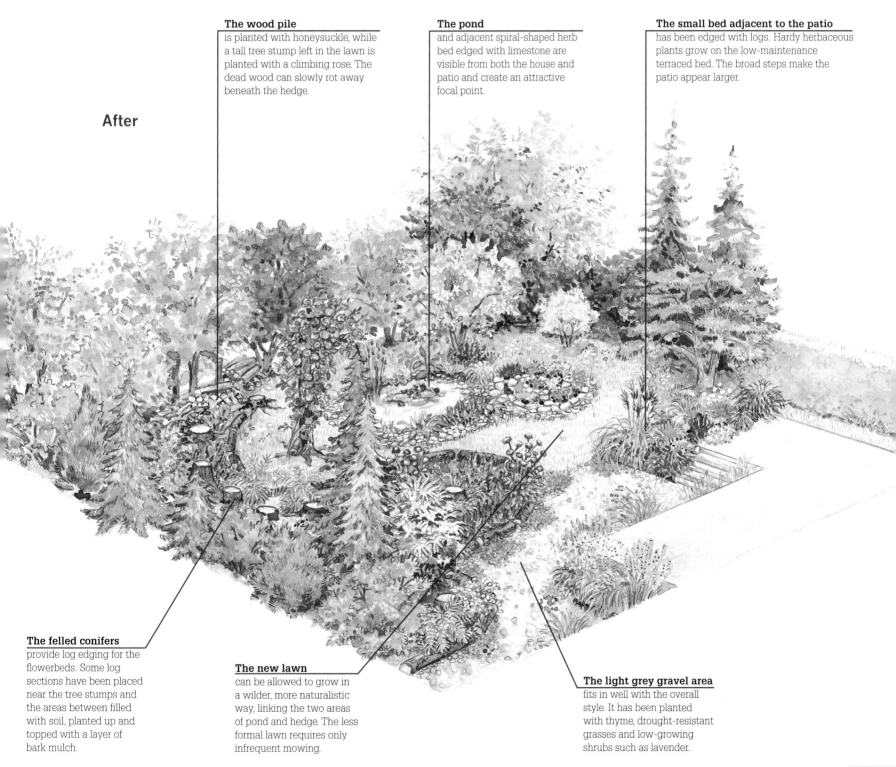

The wood pile
is planted with honeysuckle, while a tall tree stump left in the lawn is planted with a climbing rose. The dead wood can slowly rot away beneath the hedge.

The pond
and adjacent spiral-shaped herb bed edged with limestone are visible from both the house and patio and create an attractive focal point.

The small bed adjacent to the patio
has been edged with logs. Hardy herbaceous plants grow on the low-maintenance terraced bed. The broad steps make the patio appear larger.

After

The felled conifers
provide log edging for the flowerbeds. Some log sections have been placed near the tree stumps and the areas between filled with soil, planted up and topped with a layer of bark mulch.

The new lawn
can be allowed to grow in a wilder, more naturalistic way, linking the two areas of pond and hedge. The less formal lawn requires only infrequent mowing.

The light grey gravel area
fits in well with the overall style. It has been planted with thyme, drought-resistant grasses and low-growing shrubs such as lavender.

Rejuvenating a wilderness

Get trees felled by an expert

Before felling any trees, check first with your local authority to make sure there are no preservation orders in place and agree felling dates with a tree surgeon. You will also need to check that there are no animals living in them. Your local nature conservation society should be able to advise you. Decide beforehand which trees you want to keep. Tell the tree surgeon how you intend to use the felled timber before he starts work. He should then be able to cut the trunks to length for you on the spot.

As a rule, thinner branches are shredded on site and can be used to cover pathways and mulch flowerbeds. If this is not possible, cut them into manageable sections and pile them in a corner. Piles of wood make good nesting places for birds, hedgehogs

EDGING PATHS WITH LOGS

1 Dig out a hollow along the edge of the path. It should be between a third and a half as deep as the diameter of the branches or logs to be used and about twice as wide in order for them to settle into position.

2 When you have put the log in the hollow, backfill partially with the soil that has been dug out. Compact the soil next to the log sections to ensure they sit firmly in the hollow and don't roll. Dig the remaining soil that was excavated into an adjacent flowerbed.

WATCH OUT!

Don't attempt to fell large trees yourself; always employ a tree surgeon who will cut the tree down in sections working from the top. Professionals are also insured against any damage.

3 Fill the flower bed behind the edging with bark compost and enrich it with blood, fish and bone. Plant up and mulch the flowerbed, and then cover the path with a layer of wood chips 3–10cm deep.

Bring the slope to life Terraced flower beds, using logs as low retaining walls, lead up the slope to the patio. Wide steps make an area look larger.

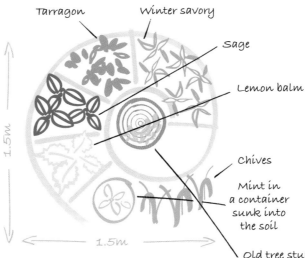

Tarragon
Winter savory
Sage
Lemon balm
Chives
Mint in a container sunk into the soil
Old tree stump covered with thyme or a container planted with thyme.

1.5m
1.5m

Suggested planting: herb spiral
The herb spiral with the tree stump at the centre is planted with (working from the outside in) chives (*Allium schoenoprasum*), mint (*Mentha spicata*), lemon balm (*Melissa officinalis*), sage (*Salvia officinalis*), French tarragon (*Artemisia dracunculus*), winter savory (*Satureja montana*) and thyme (*Thymus vulgaris*).

and habitats for other kinds of wildlife. If left alone they will rot down after a few years.

Short, thicker sections of trunk and branches can be piled out of the way beneath a tree or in another corner. They can provide an additional habitat for various creatures and have a viable place in any natural garden. Many types of wood are also suitable for burning in an open fireplace or woodburner or in a chimnaea or firepit on the patio. Cut them to size and stack them somewhere dry to season.

Concealing a tree stump

If a single tree has to be cleared to create a sunny spot in a lawn you can conceal the remaining stump by integrating it into a herb bed. Build a low dry-stone wall in the shape of a spiral radiating out from the stump. Then cover the bed you have created with plenty of sand or gravel for drainage. Next add a 20–30cm layer of poor, free-draining soil – such as a mix of sand, crushed stone and compost – to suit herbs. Depending on the height of the stump, you can also cover it with a layer of soil 10–20cm deep and sow it with thyme. Alternatively, put a shallow, frost-resistant container on the top and plant it with thyme, stonecrop or busy lizzies; or simply hollow it out and fill with water for a birdbath.

A stump in partial shade can be hidden by woodland-clearing style planting. Sprinkle 100g of blood, fish and bone over the soil around the stump and fork in plenty of chipped bark compost. Then plant out common and yellow foxglove (*Digitalis purpurea* and *Digitalis obscura*), campanula, Christmas roses (*Helleborus niger*), verbascum, creeping Jenny (*Lysimachia nummularia* 'Aurea'), wild strawberry (*Fragaria vesca*), and tussock-forming grasses and ferns.

MAKE LIFE EASIER

To kill a tree stump, make criss-cross cuts in the top and sprinkle a proprietary stump killer over it, cover with soil or a piece of polythene tied or nailed in place. To help a stump to rot down, cut deep grooves in the top; this will allow rain water to run in and speed the process up a little.

New life for an old tree When you fell a mature tree, ask the tree surgeon to cut the trunk and major branches into sections and you can make use of them around the garden as informal seats, stepping stones, border edging logs or – in this case – as a plinth for a pretty planted container.

30-MINUTE TASKS

► Spend 30 minutes shredding thin branches and twigs to produce a bag of woodchip mulch.

► Pile up a small stack of dead wood.

A relaxing water garden cuts down on maintenance

Would you like to stop having to mow the lawn or spending hours tending herbaceous borders? Consider this low-maintenance garden with a pond as its focal point.

A tired and out-dated garden

For many years, this small garden was used mainly by the children and had no recognisable design. Now that the children have grown up, it has outlived its purpose and the lawn could be renovated and more shrubs and trees planted around the boundary. The lawn would still have to be maintained on a regular basis, at least during the summer, so it is worth considering the alternative of laying less labour-intensive decking or paving and creating a large, stylish pond.

The low-maintenance option

The pond in the centre brightens up the garden and makes it look larger. The extensive area of timber decking provides plenty of places to sit or stretch out.

The decking projects out over the pond slightly, thus concealing the pond liner, and it also doubles as a path and edging for the flowerbeds. As a result, all the planting areas are clearly arranged and easily accessible.

A bamboo hedge and screens covered with plants ensure privacy. A good-sized summer house or greenhouse complements the small kitchen garden with its compost area, raised bed and soft fruit and vegetable bed. Low-maintenance shrubs or bamboo would also grow happily here. A straggly old conifer at the bottom of the plot have been replaced by small, low-maintenance, deciduous trees and shrubs and the remaining beds planted with ground-cover plants or covered with a layer of mulch.

The decking will need an annual clean and top-up coat of preservative, but the garden requires only a limited amount of attention each year, and can be left to its own devices for weeks in summer, providing it is watered as necessary.

Before

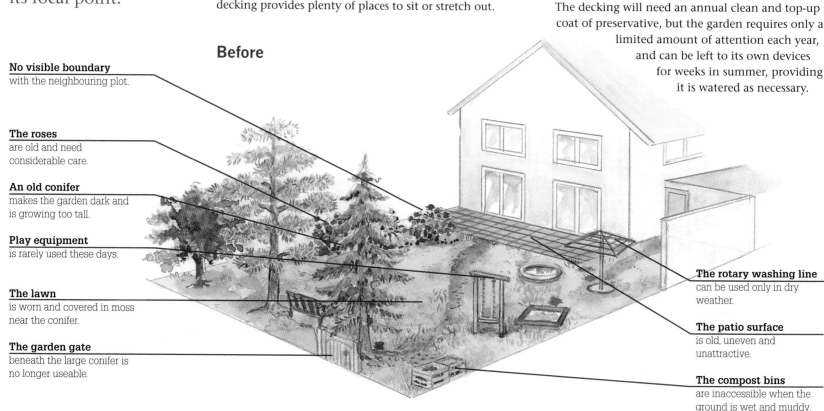

No visible boundary
with the neighbouring plot.

The roses
are old and need considerable care.

An old conifer
makes the garden dark and is growing too tall.

Play equipment
is rarely used these days.

The lawn
is worn and covered in moss near the conifer.

The garden gate
beneath the large conifer is no longer useable.

The rotary washing line
can be used only in dry weather.

The patio surface
is old, uneven and unattractive.

The compost bins
are inaccessible when the ground is wet and muddy.

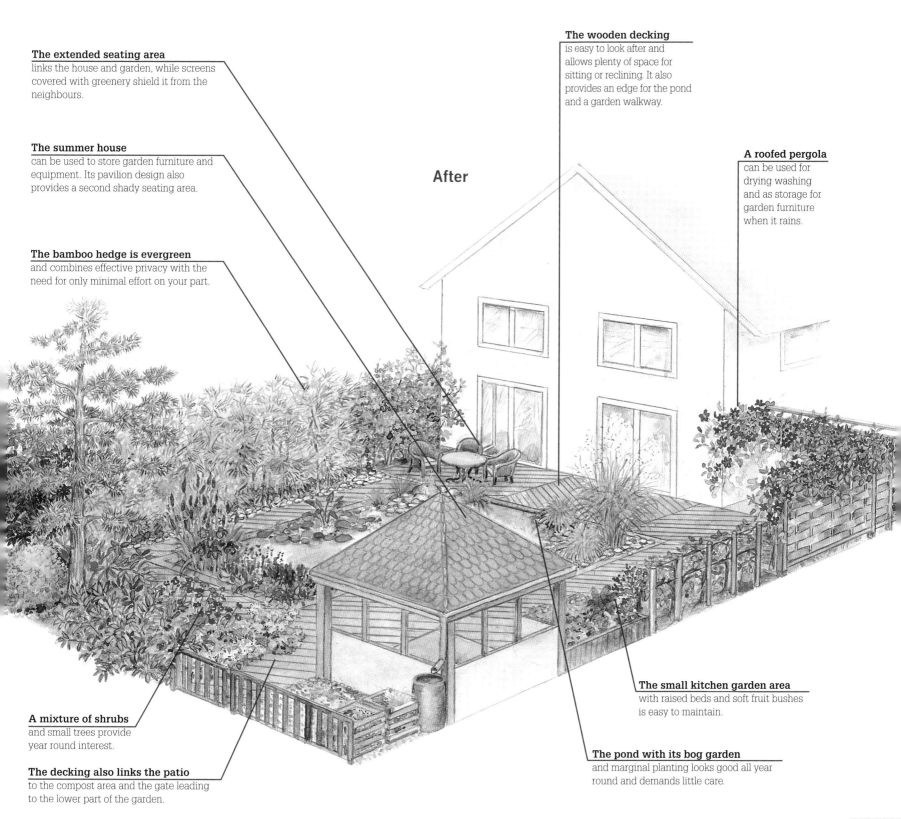

The wooden decking
is easy to look after and allows plenty of space for sitting or reclining. It also provides an edge for the pond and a garden walkway.

The extended seating area
links the house and garden, while screens covered with greenery shield it from the neighbours.

The summer house
can be used to store garden furniture and equipment. Its pavilion design also provides a second shady seating area.

After

A roofed pergola
can be used for drying washing and as storage for garden furniture when it rains.

The bamboo hedge is evergreen
and combines effective privacy with the need for only minimal effort on your part.

A mixture of shrubs
and small trees provide year round interest.

The decking also links the patio
to the compost area and the gate leading to the lower part of the garden.

The small kitchen garden area
with raised beds and soft fruit bushes is easy to maintain.

The pond with its bog garden
and marginal planting looks good all year round and demands little care.

Easy-care decking and water

MAKE LIFE EASIER

■ When laying grooved timber decking, make sure that the grain always runs in the same direction and towards a flowerbed. This makes cleaning easy as you can just sweep any dirt along the grooves and into the bed.

Planning the redesign

Remove the trees, the children's old play equipment and the patio paving; the paving can be re-used as the base for the posts for the wooden decking. Work out roughly how much soil will be dug out when the pond is excavated; you can use it to fill the holes created by the removal of old tree roots or to level the site. You can also use some of the topsoil to fill a raised bed by the summer house, but you will have to dispose of the rest.

Excavate the pond to the desired size and depth, creating terraced planting areas. If you make the pond a simple shape with straight sides it will be easier to finish the edges neatly. The bigger the pond, the less garden area there is to maintain – or use as seating areas. The base of the deep-water area (about 1 metre deep) must be level to give a solid base for containers of aquatic plants. A narrow bog garden, accessible from the decking, will be easy to maintain.

To work out how much flexible pond liner you need, lay a rope across the finished hole, allowing it to follow the contours, across the length and width, and add 100cm to each measurement. This will allow a 50cm overlap on all sides. If you intend to line the bog

Close to both water and land A bridge makes the centre of the pond easy to reach and to maintain.

Stylish and practical
An area of wooden decking borders the pond next to the patio providing people indoors and out with a good view of visiting wildlife.

The bog garden An area of lush bog garden within the rectangular frame of the pond helps to soften its otherwise geometric outline.

garden, add this area to your total. Choose a high quality liner – the length of guarantee is a good guide to quality; the best will be guaranteed for at least 20 years.

Line the cavity with protective underlay; a piece of old carpet is ideal. Lay the liner loosely over the cavity – this is a job best done by two people with plenty of time to get things right. Begin filling the pond with water. As the liner settles, fold it neatly around the shelves and corners. Don't finish the pond edge until the pond is almost full, then pack soil beneath the lining around the edge to get it perfectly level.

30-MINUTE TASKS

► In spring, clean an area of timber decking with water using a long-handled scrubbing brush or stiff broom.

► Treat a 5–10 square-metre area of clean, dry decking with wood preservative in summer.

► In spring, cut back and remove dead plants from the bog garden, working from the pond edge outwards.

► Take a water lily in its planting basket out of the water, divide it and replace in the pond.

USING DECKING TO EDGE A POND

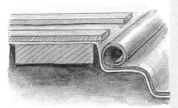

1 Lay hardwood deck joists on the soil parallel to the pond edge. Lay the excess carpet or fleece liner over the joists and fix in place using wooden battens set right angles to the pond edge.

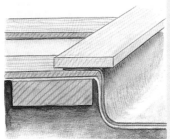

2 Lay the excess pond liner over the battens and hold it in place beneath a deck board. The pond must be almost full before you do this. Make sure that the edge of the board overlaps beyond the ends of the battens by its own thickness.

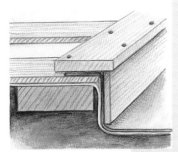

3 Fit a second plank beneath the overlap of the first, rather like the upstand of a step. Drill through the horizontal plank into the edge of the upright one and right through the battens and into the deck joist. Fix in place with zinc-plated countersunk screws.

4 Cover the battens with further decking planks. Then use steps around the pond edges for marginal planting at different depths. The upstand above the top step will hide the pond liner and protect it from UV rays if the water level drops.

The very best easy-care plants

Choose from these 220 carefully selected plants, plant them in the right position and you can save yourself both time and money.

LIGHT REQUIREMENTS

○ **Sunny:** the whole day in sun

◑ **Partial sun:** sunny but no full midday sun

◗ **Partial shade:** half the day in sun or beneath a light tree canopy

● **Shade:** the whole day without direct sun

PLANT SIZE

► **Average spread** when grown in isolation

▲ **Average height** including flowers

WATER REQUIREMENTS

◆ **Thirsty:** do not allow to dry out, must be watered a lot

◑ **Average:** Can be dry for a short time, water moderately

◇ **Little:** can withstand drought at times, must not be watered too much

The 10 best easy-care trees

Due to their large size, trees form distinctive **focal points** in gardens. Fresh and **shady oases** develop beneath their canopies in spring and summer, and in the autumn and winter their foliage may provide **welcome colour**. Some species also brighten up the garden with **decorative** flowers and fruits.

Japanese maple
Acer japonicum

◐ – ◗   ▲ 2–5m   ▶ 2–5m   ◌

The finely cut foliage of Japanese maple is attractive in spring and summer and in autumn produces a spectacular fiery display. These slow-growing deciduous trees need little attention and make an ideal focal point for a small garden.
Flower/Fruit Pale yellow or green flower clusters in spring. Red or green winged seeds in autumn.
Maintenance No pruning is necessary.
Tip Autumnal foliage ranges from fiery yellows and oranges to crimson.

Hawthorn
Crataegus laevigata 'Paul's Scarlet'

◐ – ◑   ▲ to 5m   ▶ to 5m   ◌

More often seen as a hedging plant, hawthorn can be grown as a tree. This variety has attractive double red flowers and glossy green foliage. Exceptionally care-free, it requires no pruning and is generally free of pests and diseases.
Flower/Fruit Showy display of large red flowers in spring, followed by red berries in autumn.
Maintenance None necessary.
Tip Make sure you have allowed your specimen enough space.

Manna ash
Fraxinus ornus var. *ornus*

◐ – ◑   ▲ to 10m   ▶ to 6m   ◌

The Manna ash is a tall, round-headed tree that needs plenty of space. Its main attraction is its large, white, scented flowers. It will tolerate exposed sites and urban pollution.
Flower/Fruit Panicles of fluffy, scented, creamy white flowers in early summer. Seeds have a single wing and hang in bunches.
Maintenance Pruning is not generally necessary.
Tip These trees are mature at 80 years but may live for 300 years.

Maidenhair tree
Ginko biloba

◐ – ◑   ▲ to 30m   ▶ to 9m   ◌

The distinctive fan-shaped leaves of this deciduous conifer turn an attractive golden colour in autumn. Slow-growing, it needs no pruning, tolerates urban pollution and is untroubled by pests and diseases.
Flower/Fruit The tiny flowers are insignificant. Female flowers give way to foul-smelling fruits.
Maintenance No pruning required.
Tip To avoid the fruits, plant male ginko trees.

Chinese witch hazel
Hamamelis mollis

◐ – ◑   ▲ to 4m   ▶ to 4m   ◌

When the rest of the garden is bare, the witch hazel can be relied upon to bring a burst of colour. Clusters of spidery flowers appear in profusion during mid winter, surviving the harshest frosts. The trees also have colourful autumn foliage.
Flower Small golden yellow flowers with a strong, sweet scent appear in mid winter.

Maintenance Remove any dead wood in autumn and winter.
Tip Although they are slow growing, witch hazels become as broad as they are tall and deserve to be given ample space in the garden.

Flowering plum
Prunus cerasifera

The flowering plum is grown for its dazzling spring display, with clouds of exquisite blossom. It is easy to grow, requiring just a trim in late summer after flowering.
Flower/Fruit Small pinkish white flowers appear in early spring, followed by yellow or red fruits.
Maintenance Give it a light trim to shape in late summer.
Tip Allow for its spreading habit.

Magnolia
Magnolia × soulangeana

Among the first plants to bloom in spring are the elegant magnolias, whose abundant, large and often deliciously scented flowers usually open before the leaves. They are easy to care for, requiring merely a tidy in late summer.

Flower Goblet-shaped flowers are seen in mid spring; there may be a second flush in late summer.
Maintenance Tidy up in late summer. Hard prune only mature specimens in spring.
Tip Does not flower until five years old, so buy a mature specimen.

Pine
Pinus heldreichii var. *leucodermis*

With evergreen needles and a tall, conical habit, a pine tree can add stature to a garden, provided there is plenty of space for it. Pairs of deep-blue, egg-shaped cones add interest in autumn.

Flower/Fruit Female flowers are purple-red and the male flowers open yellow. The deep blue cones turn yellow-brown with age.
Maintenance Pruning is seldom necessary.
Tip Do not mow beneath the tree as it may damage the shallow roots.

Pagoda tree
Sophora japonica

The handsome pinnate leaves of this round-headed tree lend an airy grace to the garden. Its dark green foliage contrasts with the creamy

white tubular flowers that appear on mature specimens in late summer.
Flower/Fruit Only mature trees of 30 years or more bear flowers. These are followed by long seedpods that resemble a string of beads.
Maintenance Pruning is not required.

Mountain ash, rowan
Sorbus aucuparia

Autumn berries and graceful foliage earn the easily grown deciduous rowan a place in most gardens. The pinnate leaves give rich coppery tones in autumn and the brilliant red berries are always plentiful. When grown as trees they require no pruning and are generally free of pests and diseases.
Flower Clusters of white, scented flowers borne in late spring followed by bright red berries.
Maintenance No pruning needed.
Tip The autumn berries are adored by birds and will attract them into your garden.

The 10 best easy-care shrubs

Shrubs give the garden **structure** all year round. Some produce **edible or decorative fruits,** others delicate flowers and charming foliage. Many will give great **pleasure** for little attention.

Pea tree
Caragana arborescens

The hardy pea tree, which is actually a shrub, makes a useful windbreak at the edge of a border. Delicate foliage and sweet-pea shaped flowers give it decorative appeal.
Flower/Fruit Yellow flowers are held in drooping clusters in late spring, followed by narrow cylindrical seedpods.
Maintenance Remove any dead wood in spring.
Tip The plant's upright habit becomes rounded with age.

Goat willow
Salix caprea

Like all the willows, the goat willow is undemanding and hardy. It grows quite rapidly into a giant and if given enough space at the back of a garden, will form a good windbreak.
Flower Silvery green female catkins or fluffy, bright-yellow male catkins appear before the leaves in spring.

Goat willow
Salix caprea

Maintenance No pruning needed.
Tip Small weeping cultivars such as 'Kilmarnock' are available for smaller gardens.

Bladder senna
Colutea arborescens

A pretty, fast-growing deciduous shrub that flowers from early summer through to mid autumn. Its small sweet-pea shaped flowers are held in clusters and followed by attractive bladder-like seedpods.

Flower/Fruit The yellow flowers begin in early summer and are followed by decorative seedpods flushed with red.
Maintenance Hard prune in early spring to give plants a better shape or to keep them under control.
Tip For best results plant in full sun.

Red-barked dogwood
Cornus alba

Grown for its flowers, foliage and brilliant winter stem colour, the red-barked dogwood has year-round

appeal. It is a vigorous plant and regular pruning encourages the production of numerous crimson stems. The foliage turns crimson and purple in autumn.

Flower/Fruit Flattened clusters of small yellow-white flowers in early summer, followed by pale blue-white berries.
Maintenance To maintain good colour, cut back to the ground every two or three years in late spring.
Tip For maximum effect, plant in large groups.

Common hazel
Corylus avellana

Favoured for its early spring catkins, attractive leaf shape and autumn colour, hazel is perhaps best known for its edible nuts. This hardy shrub is easy to grow in a wide range of conditions including shade. It will grow into a small tree, or it can be pruned and used for hedging.
Flower/Fruit Clusters of pendulous yellow male catkins can be seen in late winter before the leaves. The tiny, but brilliant scarlet

Buffalo currant
Ribes odoratum

female flowers develop into edible nuts surrounded by green bracts.
Maintenance Trees do not normally need pruning, but hedges should be trimmed between late autumn and early spring.

Smoke bush
Cotinus coggygria

 ○ – ◑ ▲ to 5m ▶ to 4m ◊

Plant the hardy deciduous smoke bush among green plants where its red and yellow autumn foliage will create an attractive contrast. The shrubs also make striking free-standing specimens with their rounded, spreading habit.
Flower/Fruit Profuse plumes of tiny fawn flowers are displayed in mid summer, turning grey later.

Maintenance Pruning not needed except to clear dead wood in spring.
Tip The leaves do not colour as well on rich, manured soils.

Common hawthorn
Crataegus monogyna

○ – ◑ ▲ to 7m ▶ to 4m ◊

Hedging is the main use for the hawthorn, since it forms a densely branched structure covered in sharp thorns. It also offers an abundance of flowers in spring and shiny red berries in autumn. In autumn its foliage turns orange and red.

Flower/Fruit Clusters of white, scented flowers appear in late spring followed by bright red berries.
Maintenance Trim hedges when the leaves have fallen.
Tip Birds feed on the berries.

Sea buckthorn
Hippophaë rhamnoides

○ – ◑ ▲ to 5m ▶ to 4m ◊

Tangles of sharp, spiny branches form an impenetrable screen that makes an excellent windbreak. The plant is salt tolerant which means

that it is especially useful for exposed coastal areas. Thick clusters of golden orange berries make an attractive display in autumn and winter.

Flower/Fruit Inconspicuous yellow-green flowers in early spring are followed by sumptuous displays of golden orange berries.
Maintenance Trim in mid or late summer.
Tip For a good show of berries grow a male specimen with several females to allow for pollination by wind.

Buffalo currant
Ribes odoratum

○ – ● ▲ to 2m ▶ to 2m ◑

Ornamental currants add colour and interest to mixed borders. This small, spreading shrub tolerates a range of conditions, producing an attractive show of yellow flowers that stand out among its pale green leaves. In autumn the foliage turns to various shades of red and purple.
Flower Bright yellow clove-scented flowers appear in mid to late spring.

Maintenance The flowers are carried on the previous season's growth, so trim immediately after flowering to maintain a good shape.

Fly honeysuckle
Lonicera xylosteum

○ – ● ▲ to 4m ▶ to 3m ◊

A shrub honeysuckle is ideal for use in a border. Like other species of honeysuckle, it encourages wildlife into the garden. The flowers attract flying insects while its berries are eaten by hedgehogs, mice and birds.
Flower/Fruit Yellowish white tubular flowers, often tinted red, appear in summer; these are followed by red berries.
Maintenance Thin and cut back after flowering to encourage bushiness.

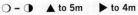

The 10 best easy-care flowering shrubs

Their lovely flowers turn these shrubs into real show pieces, which can easily take the place of a colourful bed of more labour-intensive bedding plants. Many also produce fruits and have very colourful autumn foliage.

Rose mallow
Hibiscus syriacus

The large showy flowers of hibiscus add an exotic touch to the garden. This species has an upright habit and is slow growing, so requires little in the way of pruning. Give it a sunny, sheltered site and it will prove hardy and easy to grow. The flowers are good value, appearing late into the season when many other flowers are over.
Flower Large lilac-blue flowers are freely produced from late summer to early autumn.
Maintenance Very slow-growing so pruning is not necessary.
Tip Deadhead regularly to prolong the flowering display.

Serviceberry
Amelanchier laevis

White spring blossom and spectacular bright red and orange autumn foliage make the serviceberry an outstanding plant for most of the year. Upright in habit, it requires minimal pruning.
Flower/Fruit Clusters of small white flowers in spring. The purple-black fruits are edible.
Maintenance May need thinning from time to time.

Flowering quince
Chaenomeles speciosa

A decorative shrub for a border or low ornamental hedge. The flowers are profuse in spring, but fairly short-lived. After flowering the plant can be used as a natural support for climbing annuals.
Flower/Fruit Bowl-shaped, predominantly red flowers are borne in early spring and followed by fragrant, green, apple-shaped fruits.
Maintenance Cut back shoots that have flowered in May. Grows best trained against a sunny wall.
Tip For more reliable flower colour choose one of the many cultivars.

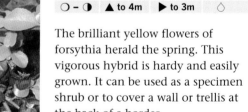

Forsythia
Forsythia × intermedia

The brilliant yellow flowers of forsythia herald the spring. This vigorous hybrid is hardy and easily grown. It can be used as a specimen shrub or to cover a wall or trellis at the back of a border.
Flower Golden yellow flowers from early to mid spring.
Maintenance To avoid straggly growth, prune flowered shoots to within two buds of old wood. Grows in any soil in sun or partial shade.
Tip Cutting back hard limits size, without causing damage.

Firethorn
Pyracantha cultivars

Kerria
Kerria japonica

○ – ◗　▲ to 2m　▶ to 2m　◌

A very easy-going shrub, kerria is a member of the rose family. Plant it and then just sit back and enjoy a golden burst of colour every spring.

Flower An abundance of yellow blooms appear from mid to late spring. Some cultivars such as 'Pleniflora' have double flowers.
Maintenance Pruning is not normally required.
Tip The slender arching stems can be trained up a trellis or fence.

Firethorn
Pyracantha cultivars

○ – ◐　▲ to 3m　▶ to 2m　◌

The firethorns are favoured for their glossy evergreen leaves and sumptuous autumn displays of brilliantly coloured berries. They can be easily trained up a wall to make dense, colourful hedging.
Flower/Fruit Frothy clusters of tiny white flowers appear in early summer, followed by berries that persist well into winter.

Maintenance Prune just before flowering to encourage a good show of berries later on.
Tip When pruning beware of the shrub's long, sharp thorns.

Mock orange
Philadelphus coronarius

○ – ◗　▲ to 4m　▶ to 3m　◗

Find this hardy deciduous shrub a sunny spot and it will reliably yield a glorious summer show of cup-shaped flowers with the heavenly scent of orange blossom.

Flower White semidouble blooms are borne throughout the summer.
Maintenance Cut back the flowering shoots after flowering to where a new shoot is developing.

Bridal wreath
Spiraea × arguta

○ – ◗　▲ to 2m　▶ to 2m　◗

Quick-growing and easy to cultivate, spiraea is deservedly popular. This cultivar forms a dense rounded

shrub. Clusters of early flowers smother arching sprays in spring.
Flower Tight clusters of dainty white-petalled flowers appear from mid to late spring.

Maintenance Prune back hard after flowering.
Tip Does best in a sunny spot.

Weigela
Weigela cultivars

○ – ◗　▲ to 3m　▶ to 2.5m　◗

Among the easiest and most popular of all the summer-flowering shrubs, weigelas are hardy, have attractive foxglove-shaped flowers and grow more or less anywhere. There are tall and dwarf varieties to choose from.
Flower Funnel-shaped flowers – in shades of red, pink or white – are borne in late spring and summer.

Maintenance Trim back just after flowering for a good display the following year.
Tip Benefits from mulching during very dry weather.

Common elder
Sambucus nigra

○ – ◗　▲ to 7m　▶ to 5m　◌

A shrub of wild hedgerows, common elder makes a trouble-free addition to the garden, although it is prone to be rather invasive. There are several cultivars available with attractive foliage that make better garden subjects, including 'Aurea' with golden foliage and the small, slow-growing 'Pulverulenta' with white-mottled leaves.

Flower/Fruit Flat creamy white clusters of delicately scented flowers appear in early summer followed by bunches of small black berries.
Maintenance Prune stems back to ground level in winter to prevent the plant becoming straggly and outgrowing its space.
Tip The flowers and berries can be used to make wine.

The 10 best easy-care evergreen shrubs

Evergreen plants make eye-catching splashes of colour even in the **winter months**. While the garden changes in the course of the seasons, these trees and shrubs can provide **continuity** throughout the entire year.

Mountain pine
Pinus mugo

Common box
Buxus sempervirens

○ – ● ▲ to 3m ▶ to 3m ◑

Small evergreen leaves, dense growth and tolerance of frequent clipping make box an ideal hedging plant. It will grow in shade or full sun, so can be utilised anywhere in the garden, the dark green foliage contrasting beautifully with flowers and gravel paths.
Flower Inconspicuous.
Maintenance Clip hedges two or three times a year.
Tip Can be grown for topiary.

Mountain pine
Pinus mugo

○ – ◑ ▲ to 6m ▶ to 4m ◌

A hardy, slow-growing evergreen that bears red female flowers among its densely packed long, dark-green needles. May form a large shrubby bush or a small tree. It is a good maintenance-free choice for awkward places.
Flower/Fruit Red female flowers, green male flowers. Blackish-brown cones ripen to yellow-brown.

Maintenance Remove any spindly lower branches.
Tip Grow in acid soil.

Hinoki cypress
Chamaecyparis obtusa

○ – ● ▲ to 20m ▶ to 5m ◐

The false cypresses are popular evergreens that are easy to grow and offer great choice in terms of size, habit and colour. There are varieties to suit every situation, including dwarf and slow-growing bushes, hedging and ornamental trees.

The tall, fast-growing Hinoki cypress has dense, deep green foliage and can be planted in rows for almost instant screening purposes or singly as an accent plant. Shorter, slow-growing varieties such as 'Nana Gracilis' (2m after 40 years) are available for smaller gardens.

Flower/Fruit Small orange male and pale brown female flowers; round, scaly brown cones.
Maintenance Remove any diseased or dead branches.
Tip Be sure to choose the right variety for your garden's size.

Common juniper
Juniperus communis

○ – ● ▲ to 6m ▶ to 4.5m ◌

Slow-growing and hardy, common juniper is a welcome addition to any garden. It thrives in almost any type of soil, except in water-logged conditions. Its habit varies from conical to creeping and this variability is seen in the range of cultivars bred from it. Some form elegant architectural columns while others are useful as ground cover on slopes and in hollows.
Flower/Fruit Tiny flowers at the tips of branches yield blue or black berry-like cones.
Maintenance Can be shaped in spring and autumn if required.
Tip The needles of this species are ferociously prickly.

Serbian spruce
Picea omorika

Blue holly
Ilex × meserveae

○ – ● ▲ to 3m ▶ to 2m ◑

With its brilliant berries and glossy, often spiky leaves, holly is one of the most care-free of all plants. This hybrid has blue-tinged foliage, best seen in cultivars 'Blue Angel', 'Blue Prince' and 'Blue Princess'.
Flower/Fruit Insignificant white flowers followed by red berries.
Maintenance Prune to shape.
Tip Tolerates pollution.

Common privet
Ligustrum vulgare

○ – ● ▲ to 5m ▶ to 3m ◑

Privet is a traditional choice for hedges, being hardy, fast-growing and able to withstand hard pruning.

Common privet has mid-green foliage, but there are golden or variegated varieties available.
Flower/Fruit White flower clusters appear from early to mid summer followed by shiny black autumn fruits.
Maintenance Prune hedges to desired shape in mid summer.
Tip Birds are attracted to the fruits.

Oregon grape
Mahonia aquifolium

○ – ● ▲ to 2m ▶ to 2m ◌

With its glossy dark green leaves and golden yellow, sweetly scented flowers, mahonia brightens up the garden in winter and spring. Some varieties such as 'Atropurpurea' have reddish purple leaves.
Flower Bright yellow flowers in mid to late spring are followed by small grape-like berries, hence the common name.
Maintenance No pruning needed except to remove any suckers.
Tip *M. aquifolium* is often grown as ground cover or as a low hedge.

Serbian spruce
Picea omorika

○ – ◑ ▲ to 35m ▶ to 3m ◑

An evergreen columnar tree that grows to a tapering point with pendulous branches turning up at the tips. It is very hardy and tolerant of pollution.
Flower/Fruit Red flowers produce narrow cones that fade to brown.
Maintenance The only pruning necessary is to remove dead twigs.
Tip The foliage is aromatic.

Common or cherry laurel
Prunus laurocerasus

○ – ● ▲ to 8m ▶ to 4m ◑

An attractive large evergreen shrub, this ornamental fruit tree has glossy mid-green leaves and bears attractive upright spikes of flowers in spring. It is robust and trouble free and grows to the perfect height for a screen or windbreak. The cultivar 'Otto Luyken' can be grown as low hedging or in a small border.
Flower/Fruit White flower spikes in mid spring followed by a profusion of black fruits.

Maintenance Generally trouble free, it needs only an occasional trim to keep it in shape.
Tip Will tolerate shade, but does not thrive on chalky soils.

Viburnum
Viburnum rhytidophyllum

○ – ◗ ▲ to 4m ▶ to 4m ◑

Viburnum is easily grown and suitable for almost every location. This species is a densely branched, round-headed evergreen with shiny, dark green, wrinkled leaves that are felted on the under side. It is an undemanding plant that makes a handsome addition to the back of a border or can be grown as a hedge.
Flower/Fruit Large clusters of yellowish-white flowers are borne in late spring and early summer. The bright red fruits turn black in autumn and winter.
Maintenance Prune immediately after flowering.
Tip *V. rhytidophyllum* and other large-leaved viburnums do not tolerate wind exposure. For a good show of berries, plant in groups of two or three.

The 10 best easy-care hedging plants

Hedges mark a boundary and provide privacy. A natural, informal hedge is less work than one that is neatly trimmed to shape, and also provides a haven for many birds and insects.

Barberry
Berberis thunbergii

○ – ◑ ▲ to 1.8m ▶ to 2.4m ◌

Colourful leaves, flowers and berries make *B. thunbergii* both versatile and excellent value. The densely packed reddish brown thorny branches of this neat, compact deciduous shrub form an impenetrable hedge. The cultivar 'Pow-wow' has bright yellow leaves that gradually turn green; 'Silver Beauty' has white and bluish green variegated leaves.
Flower/Fruit Pale, straw-coloured flowers suffused with red in spring. Small red berries in autumn.
Maintenance Encourage strong new growth by cutting out a few old stems each year. Trim hedges once a year in late summer or late autumn after the berries have fallen.
Tip Site in full sun for the best leaf coloration.

Spotted laurel
Aucuba japonica

○ – ◗ ▲ to 3m ▶ to 3m ◌

Glossy, deep-green, oval leaves give permanent value to the sturdy evergreen laurel. It is easy to grow, frost hardy and tolerates pollution. With a bushy, upright habit it can be planted in rows to create a formal hedge or screen. 'Crotonifolia' is an attractive variegated variety.

Flower/Fruit Small male and female flowers appear on different plants. Vivid red oval berries follow on fertilised female plants.
Maintenance Trim hedges during the growing season to maintain the desired shape.
Tip Plant male and female plants to ensure a good show of berries.

Cornelian cherry
Cornus mas

○ – ◑ ▲ to 5m ▶ to 4.5m ◌

A large hardy shrub with a spreading habit. Delicate clusters of tiny golden flowers can be seen on bare branches in late winter and early spring.

Flower/Fruit Yellow flowers in late winter and early spring are followed by bright red fruits.
Maintenance Pruning in late spring improves vigour.

Common hornbeam
Carpinus betulus

○ – ◑ ▲ to 6m ▶ to 3m ◐

This conical upright deciduous tree, makes a fine hedging plant, its leafy branches withstanding severe clipping. The dark green leaves are finely toothed and give a good display of yellow in autumn.

Flower/Fruit Green catkins in spring. Tassels of seeds in autumn.
Maintenance Clip hedges in mid summer – if left unpruned, plants can grow to a height of 20m.

Blackthorn, sloe
Prunus spinosa

  ○ – ◑ ▲ to 6m ▶ to 4m ◊

A hardy native shrub, frequently seen wild in hedgerows. Its densely branching habit and stout thorns make a suitably deterring barrier.

Flower/Fruit Small white flowers in early spring give way to small blue-black fruits in autumn.
Maintenance Trim in early summer to maintain size and shape.
Tip The fruit may be used to make sloe gin.

Mountain currant
Ribes alpinum

○ – ● ▲ to 2m ▶ to 2m ◑

The ornamental currants are hardy and easy to grow. This species is a tall shrub with leaves that turn bright yellow in autumn. The small greenish-yellow flowers provide interest in spring. The cultivar 'Aureum' has golden leaves that blaze in full sun.
Flower/Fruit Pretty greenish-yellow flowers are followed by red berries in summer.

Maintenance Trim immediately after flowering to keep in shape.

Spiraea
Spiraea japonica

○ – ◗ ▲ to 1.5m ▶ to 1.2m ◑

They are deciduous, but the dense growth of hardy spireas make them ideal as hedging plants. *S. japonica* is a medium-sized shrub that bears large rosy pink flowerheads in summer. There are various cultivars available for flowers and foliage in different colours.

Flower Rosy pink flattish clusters in mid to late summer.
Maintenance Cut back previous year's growth to 15cm above ground in second season. Thereafter shear to shape after flowering.

English yew
Taxus baccata

○ – ◑ ▲ 1.5m ▶ to 60cm ◊

Evergreen trees and shrubs, yews range in habit from low-growing, ground-cover plants to large trees. This species is useful as a hedging plant, its thick green foliage responding well to clipping.

Flower/Fruit After pollination the minute female flowers develop a single seed in a scarlet fleshy berry.
Maintenance Clip hedges twice in a season: a heavy cut in late spring and a light cut in late summer. If left it can reach a height of 20m.

American arbor vitae
Thuja occidentalis

○ – ◑ ▲ to 2m ▶ to 1m ◑

These evergreen conifers are clothed in densely covered slender branches. A row of specimens makes an effective hedge. The scale-like foliage is a glossy yellowish-green above and matt green below.
Flower/Fruit Yellow-green oblong cones turn brown in autumn.

Maintenance Clip once a year in early spring. If left the species can reach a height of 20m, so choose an appropriate cultivar for your garden.

Lawson cypress
Chamaecyparis lawsoniana

○ – ◑ In 10 years ▲ 6m ▶ 2.4m ◑

If you want a hedge in a hurry, the vigorous Lawson cyprus is a good choice since it gains 60cm in height every year. It may be too large for most gardens, but there are many smaller cultivars available.
Flower/Fruit Tiny female flowers form globular cones.
Maintenance No pruning needed.
Tip When choosing a cultivar take into account its mature height and the size of your garden.

The 10 best easy-care dwarf shrubs and trees

Many woody plants also have **low-growing** species and varieties. Due to their dwarf habit and **slow growth**, they are especially low-maintenance and make a decorative supplement to rockeries and heather gardens. They are also suitable for **tubs and containers**.

Barberry
Berberis × media 'Parkjuweel'

○ – ☽   ▲ to 1m   ▶ to 1m   ◊

A low shrub, forming a dense mound of oval, bright green glossy leaves that turn to a rich red in autumn. It reaches a height and spread of 60cm after five years, ultimately 1m by 1m.
Flower Yellow flowers appear in late spring.
Maintenance No need to prune.
Tip An alternative low-growing barberry is *B. thunbergii* 'Atropurpurea Nana', which has purple-red foliage and bright red berries in autumn.

Lawson cypress
Chamaecyparis lawsoniana 'Minima Glauca'

○ – ☽   ▲ to 2m   ▶ to 2m   ◐

Do not be put off by the species name. Although the species rapidly grows into an enormous tree, this cultivar forms a neat, unobtrusive spherical bush, eventually reaching 2m across. Its sea-green foliage is held in short, vertical sprays.

Flower Flowers followed by small globular cones on female plants.
Maintenance Pruning is not required.
Tip An alternative, even smaller variety is *C. pisifera* 'Golden Mop', which has a height and spread of 45cm by 30cm. As its name suggests it has attractive yellow foliage.

Cotoneaster
Cotoneaster adpressus

○ – ☽   ▲ to 30cm   ▶ to 1m   ◊

The cotoneaster is an undemanding, low, spreading shrub that is ideal for ground cover. Its dull green leaves turn a striking scarlet shade in autumn.

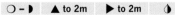

Flower Pinkish white flowers in summer are followed by red berries.
Maintenance No need to prune.

Spindle trees
Euonymus fortunei 'Emerald Gaiety'

○ – ●   ▲ to 1m   ▶ to 1.5m   ◑

With eye-catching, creamy white-edged leaves that turn an attractive bronze colour in winter, 'Emerald Gaiety' has year-round value in the garden. A dense, hardy evergreen, its compact height and spread make it a useful ground-cover plant.

Flower/Fruit Insignificant flowers; rarely produces berries.
Maintenance Pruning is not required except to keep plants within their allotted space. Do this any time except spring.

Juniper
Juniperus squamata

○ – ◑   ▲ to 1m   ▶ to 2.5m   ◊

An attractive, low-growing evergreen shrub with blue-green foliage. The species has several slow-growing cultivars that require minimal attention. The cultivar 'Blue Carpet' spreads into a blue-grey mat of sharp, pointed needles, reaching a height and spread of 30cm by 1.2m after 10 years. 'Blue

Star' grows even more slowly, taking 30 years to form a silvery blue mound 60cm by 1m.
Maintenance Pruning is not required, but plants can be shaped in autumn.

Privet

Ligustrum vulgare 'Lodense'

○ – ❶   ▲ to 70cm   ▶ to 1m   ◐

All the privets are hardy, fast-growing and trouble free. The semi-evergreen 'Lodense' is a dwarf, compact variety that is ideal for a low hedge. If left untrimmed it will form an untidy bush with a height and spread of about 1m.
Flower/Fruit White flowers in summer followed by black berries.
Maintenance Clip hedges twice in summer to maintain shape.
Tip Foliage, flowers and berries are poisonous.

Honeysuckle

Lonicera pileata

○ – ❶   ▲ to 80cm   ▶ to 1.2m   ◌

The honeysuckles are some of the hardiest shrubs found in the garden. This semi-evergreen species has a low, neat, spreading habit that is ideal for ground cover. Its tolerance of partial shade makes it useful for underplanting in mixed borders.

Flower/Fruit Yellowish flowers stand out against the dark green leaves in late spring. Transparent amethyst-coloured berries follow.
Maintenance Thin and cut back after flowering.

Spruce

Picea pungens 'Globosa'

○ – ◑   ▲ to 80cm   ▶ to 80cm   ◌

It may be hard to imagine a low-growing spruce, but this variety forms a flattened dome just 80cm high and wide. Its vivid blue needles bring colour to mixed borders and rockeries all year round.
Flower/Fruit Red and green flowers are followed by egg-shaped, pale brown cones.

Maintenance Confine pruning to removing damaged branches. Do this in winter to avoid resin bleeding, which can attract disease.
Tip The aromatic long-lasting foliage is good for decorations and flower arrangements.

Mountain pine

Pinus mugo

○ – ❶   ▲ to 2m   ▶ to 1.5m   ◌

Plentiful red female flowers are the best feature of the slow-growing evergreen mountain pine. The densely branched cultivar 'Mops' makes a neat, rounded bush that reaches a height and spread of 1m in 30 years, so grows well in even the smallest garden or in containers.

Flower/Fruit Red female flowers in spring. Blackish-brown young cones in autumn gradually ripen to yellow-brown.

Maintenance No pruning needed.
Tip An alternative choice for a container is 'Humpy', which reaches a height and width of 1m in 40 years. It has a conical habit and attractive red-brown winter buds.

Shrubby cinquefoil

Potentilla fruticosa

○ – ❶   ▲ to 1.5m   ▶ to 1.5m   ◐

Plant *Potentilla*, a hardy, compact, deciduous shrub, to bring a splash of long-lasting vibrant colour to a border or rockery in summer. There are many varieties to choose from and all they require to thrive is a sunny location.
Flower Yellow or white flowers are borne freely in summer and often well into autumn.
Maintenance Seldom needs pruning.
Tip The best cultivars include 'Goldfinger', an upright dwarf form bearing large, saucer-like yellow flowers that contrast well with its blue-green foliage. 'Red Ace' is low and spreading and produces bright red flowers.

The 10 best easy-care roses

As a species, this queen among flowers is often considered difficult to look after. However, there is a **multitude** of uncomplicated and **robust** roses that need little work, such as the **delicately** beautiful wild species.

English rose

Ground-cover roses

○ – ◑   ▲ to 1.5m   ▶ to 3m   ◐

With their low-growing arched shoots, ground-cover roses create a carpet of flowers. They look most attractive when allowed to tumble over a wall or sprawl down a bank.
Flower Pink, white, yellow or red.
Maintenance They do not usually need pruning, but can be cut back hard if necessary; do not prune varieties growing on their own rootstock by more than a few inches every few years.
Tip Robust varieties, which also do well in semi-shade, include 'The Fairy' (pink, double), and 'Surrey' (clusters of pink flowers). 'Kent' (white, slightly double) is scented, flowers in summer, and has glossy foliage. All three repeat flower.

English roses

○ – ◑   ▲ to 2m   ▶ to 2m   ◐

English roses, developed by the rose breeder David Austin, combine the achievements of modern breeding – repeat flowering, good health and modern colours – with the beauty and scent of older rose varieties. In addition, they are considered robust and fast-growing.
Flower May flower once or repeatedly, all colours except blue and black, usually scented.
Maintenance If not pruned back in spring, these roses will flower earlier; if pruned back, they become sturdier. Deadheading encourages repeat flowering.
Tip 'Abraham Darby', apricot to pink in colour, is an especially bewitching and robust variety.

Modern shrub roses

○ – ◑   ▲ to 2m   ▶ to 2m   ◐

With these slightly taller shrubs, you can admire their abundant flowers well into the autumn. They are good as specimen plants or to form loose hedges and also make ideal plants for smaller gardens.
Flower/Fruit All colours except blue and black, often scented; attractive red to black hips.
Maintenance Deadhead to encourage repeat flowering; cut out dead stems in the spring.

Tip Robust varieties include 'Centenaire de Lourdes' (pink), 'Mozart' (pink centres, carmine outside, single) and 'Westerland' (orange-pink).

Climbing roses

○ – ◑   ▲ to 4m   ▶ to 6m   ◐

Climbing roses provide a maximum of flowers in a minimum of space. Scrambling over house walls, pergolas or arches, they add a romantic touch to your garden. Climbers can reach a height of up to 4m, and the arching shoots of ramblers can grow longer than that.
Flower/Fruit Climbers are mostly repeat flowering, while most ramblers flower once, all colours except blue and black, single to fully double, some scented.
Maintenance Train side shoots horizontally to promote flowering; if necessary, thin out in spring.
Tip Best climbers include 'New Dawn' (mother-of-pearl coloured), and 'Compassion' (fragrant, salmon-pink). Best ramblers include 'Super Excelsa' (carmine pink, double, repeat flowering).

Scotch rose
Rosa spinosissima

Dog rose, hedge rose
Rosa canina

○ – ◐   ▲ to 3m   ▶ to 2m   ◐

A native of forest edges and wild hedgerows, the dog rose is as pretty as any cultivated variety but is easier to grow and more robust than most.

Flower/Fruit Pale pink blooms appear in June followed by orange-red hips from July onwards.
Maintenance Can be pruned back radically for rejuvenation purposes.
Tip Does well even on poor soil and is also suitable for informal hedges.

Apothecary's rose
Rosa gallica var. *officinalis*

○ – ◐   ▲ to 3m   ▶ to 2m   ◐

The robust, thorny Apothecary's rose, also known as 'Crimson Damask', is the original red rose of Lancaster and has been cultivated for more than 500 years. It flowers once a year in summer.
Flower/Fruit Large, deep pink blooms appear in June and turn into rounded hips.
Maintenance Thin if needed, can also be pruned back radically.

Tip There are numerous varieties available, for example 'Versicolor' (pale pink blooms, striped and splashed with reddish pink).

Father Hugo's rose
Rosa xanthina f. *hugonis*

○ – ◐   ▲ to 3m   ▶ to 3m   ◐

In spring numerous yellow flowers cover the gracefully arching branches of this hardy, robust rose that has its origins in China. In autumn its flowers transform into an abundance of brightly coloured fruits. Its leaves, light green when young, change to a duller green through the summer.
Flower/Fruit In May the first golden yellow flowers are seen; they are followed by an attractive display of spherical blackish-red hips.

Maintenance Thin out if needed.
Tip Allow this spreading rose plenty of space.

Multiflora rose
Rosa multiflora

○ – ◐   ▲ to 3m   ▶ to 3m   ◐

This vigorous wild rose lives up to its name, producing an incredible number of small flowers on its elegantly arched branches.

Flower/Fruit Clusters of white flowers in June. Small hips adorn the plant into the autumn.
Maintenance Thin if needed, can be pruned back radically.
Tip Tolerates partial shade, but will flower less abundantly.

Scotch rose
Rosa spinosissima

○ – ◐   ▲ to 3m   ▶ to 2m   ◐

If you are looking for an early-flowering rose this would be a good choice. A profusion of bowl-shaped flowers appear on this small to medium-sized bush from late spring. The branches are covered in prickles and spines.

Flower/Fruit Scented, creamy white flowers with partly pink edges occur in May; brownish hips are seen from September.
Maintenance Can be pruned back rigorously.
Tip Tolerates drier soils.

Rugosa roses
Rosa rugosa cultivars

○ – ◐   ▲ to 2m   ▶ to 1.5m   ◌

The many descendants of *R. rugosa* are robust and will grow in almost any soil. They are vigorous and colourful border plants and make a superb hedge with their prickly shoots quickly forming a dense, leafy thicket.
Flower/Fruit White, yellow, pink, red, single to semidouble, scented flowers; the large brightly coloured hips last well into the winter.
Maintenance Can be pruned back hard, according to need.
Tip Lime-rich soil will turn its leaves yellow. It can tolerate dry and even slightly salty soils.

The 10 best easy-care ground-cover plants

These creeping perennials and shrubs can be used as low-maintenance ground cover between taller plants, under shrubs, on slopes or as an attractive **alternative to a lawn**. They fill empty spaces with their **beautiful foliage** and often bear **charming flowers**.

Common bugle
Ajuga reptans

◗ – ● ▲ to 20cm ▶ to 1m ◗

A low, spreading evergreen that provides effective ground cover in any damp, lightly shaded spot. In late spring and early summer it is adorned with lovely blue flowers.

Flower Short blue flower spikes appear from spring to early summer.
Maintenance If it spreads outside its allotted space you can take brutal action without harming the plant. Slice through clumps with a spade in spring.
Tip Some cultivars have attractive foliage. 'Burgundy Glow' has creamy green and red leaves; 'Atropurpurea' has dark purple leaves.

Indian strawberry
Duchesnea indica

◗ – ● ▲ 5–10cm ▶ 10–50cm ◗

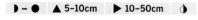

Resembling strawberry plants in fruit, leaf and habit, the herbaceous perennial Indian strawberries send out runners to form wide mats of foliage from spring to autumn. They look good in hanging baskets too.

Flower/Fruit Small yellow flowers open from mid spring to autumn, followed by glossy, bright red fruits.
Maintenance This vigorous plant spreads quickly and should not be placed close to small plants as it may smother them.
Tip The fruits are edible.

Yellow archangel
Lamium galeobdolon

◗ – ● ▲ to 50cm ▶ to 2m ◗

Not only will this spreading type of dead nettle keep down weeds, it also produces a lovely show of flowers in summer. Choose a variety with variegated leaves to add interest to shady borders. The leaves of 'Hermann's Pride' have dark veins that stand out against a silvery green background; 'Florentimum' has green leaves splashed with silver that turn purple in winter.
Flower Tubular, yellow flowers appear at the tops of the evergreen shoots in mid summer.
Maintenance Site in relatively poor soil to prevent plants becoming invasive. If the spreaders do get over vigorous they can easily be reined in by slicing off unwanted growth with a spade in spring.
Tip Plant three or four varieties to create an interesting display.

St John's wort
Hypericum calycinum

○ – ◑ ▲ to 40cm ▶ to 1.5m ◗

Hypericums are vigorous, hardy plants that readily suppress weeds. This species, also known as rose of Sharon, spreads rapidly and will even grow in deep shade. It has a tough, creeping rootstock, so can be somewhat invasive.
Flower Bright yellow flowers are borne throughout the summer.
Maintenance Prune back hard each spring.
Tip Bears highly decorative berries in autumn.

Creeping Jenny
Lysimachia nummularia

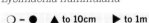

A rampantly spreading evergreen perennial, use Creeping Jenny as ground cover in shady places. Its prostrate mats of bright green foliage become studded with pretty yellow flowers in summer.
Flower Bright yellow flowers appear in early summer.
Maintenance Divide in autumn to control spread.
Tip 'Aurea' has golden leaves.

Pachysandra
Pachysandra terminalis

Another hardy, evergreen ground-cover plant for shady places. It spreads easily by means of creeping roots, forming a carpet of rich green leathery leaves. White flowers are dotted among the foliage in spring.

Flower Spikes of white flowers appear in late and early spring.
Maintenance None necessary.
Tip A useful choice for growing at the foot of shade-loving shrubs such as rhododendrons and camellias.

Stonecrop
Sedum kamtschaticum var. *floriferum* 'Weihenstephaner Gold'

Choose this tough succulent for effortless colour and interest in the less hospitable parts of the garden where there is little shade and the soil tends to be poor and parched. Its lax, fleshy stems bear mid green leaves and clusters of flowers at the tips in summer.
Flower A profuse display of yellow flowers begins in early summer and lasts well into the autumn.
Maintenance No care needed.
Tip The species *S. spathulifolium* (yellow flowers, grey-green leaves) and *S. spurium* (mauve flowers, dark green leaves) have a similar habit.

Periwinkle
Vinca major

Vigorous creeping periwinkles form extensive carpets of foliage in any location as long as the soil is not too dry. Thriving in partial or full shade, they will spread indefinitely, bearing masses of blue flowers.
Flower Blue, five-petalled flowers appear in spring and early summer. *V. major* var. *alba* has white flowers and var. *oxyloba* produces dark violet flowers.
Maintenance None, except to control size of plant.
Tip Useful under deciduous trees and shrubs and in wild gardens.

Lamb's ears
Stachys byzantina

Thick, woolly, silver grey leaves make this mat-forming perennial a popular choice in beds and borders. In a sunny spot it can be left to cover the ground in a dense carpet.

Flower Whorls of tiny mauve-pink flowers are carried on leafy spikes above the foliage in summer.
Maintenance None needed.
Tip 'Silver Carpet' is a particularly attractive variety and 'Primrose Heron' has unusual yellow-tinged furry grey leaves.

Knotweed
Persicaria affinis

Flowers in shades of pink and red appear late in the season on this hardy herbaceous perennial. The dark green leaves, which turn to shades of red and bronze in the autumn, form low ground cover.

Flower Dense, upright spikes of small pink or red flowers appear in late summer, often persisting through autumn into winter.
Maintenance Knotweed needs little attention, but spreads rapidly once established and for this reason may be more care-free in a wild, informal scheme.
Tip Will tolerate dry situations so is suitable for a rock garden or as edging to a path.

The 10 best easy-care climbers

Climbing plants can cover walls and fences in greenery and create a leafy roof over pergolas and arbours, providing both shade and privacy. Some have showy flowers or brightly coloured leaves and need very little space at ground level, or attention.

Clematis
Clematis tangutica

Rightly known as the queen of climbers, clematis brightens up a wall or trellis with sumptuous colour. There are hundreds to choose from. *C. tangutica* belongs to the particularly easy-to-grow orientalis group. As well as having fine flowers and foliage, their attractive seed heads provide autumn interest.
Flower Lemon-yellow lantern-shaped flowers in late summer followed by large, fluffy seed heads.
Maintenance Prune hard in February or March, avoiding strong woody stems.
Tip Other orientalis varieties include 'Aureolin' and 'Corry'.

Common passion flower
Passiflora caerulea

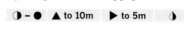

As well as the amazingly intricate, scented flowers, this hardy, vigorous climber also produces decorative, edible fruits. Given a well-drained spot it can be relied upon to haul itself up walls and over other shrubs and trees by means of its tightly clinging tendrils.
Flower Stunning large white flowers with a purple corona occur in mid summer, followed by orange, egg-shaped fruits.

Maintenance Shape in spring.
Tip The cultivar 'Constance Elliott' has ivory white flowers with conspicuous red stigmas.

Hydrangea
Hydrangea anomala spp. *petiolaris*

Climbing hydrangeas support themselves via aerial roots and do not need tying in. Use them to clothe a wall with greenery and adorn it with white blooms. Avoid planting against a south-facing wall.
Flower Large, flat, cream and white lacy flowerheads cover the plant in summer.
Maintenance Prune only to keep plant close to wall. Pruning not necessary when grown on trees.
Tip An alternative climbing species is the evergreen *H. serratifolia*.

Common ivy
Hedera helix

The profuse, evergreen foliage of ivy provides year-round cover. The plant is self supporting and will readily spread across walls, fences and pergolas. It is especially useful for shady places. The species has dark green leaves, but more colourful varieties are available. They include 'Caecilia' (creamy yellow and green leaves) and 'Eva' (grey-green and cream leaves) among many others.

Flower Clusters of small yellow flowers in autumn.
Maintenance Trim to control growth; restrict heavy pruning to spring.
Tip The late flowers of ivy attract wildlife into the garden when there is little else in bloom.

Common hop

Humulus lupulus

Hops are quick sprinting, twining climbers, grown for their bold, fresh green leaves. They make great temporary screening and will enliven dull hedging. On female plants papery hops add a decorative touch in autumn.

Flower/Fruit On female plants drooping cone-like flower clusters in summer turn to hops.
Maintenance Cut back to ground level in autumn.
Tip The plant's vivid summer foliage looks stunning against the backdrop of a darker shrub such as purple-leaved beech (*Fagus sylvatica* Atropurpurea Group).

Sweet pea

Lathyrus odoratus

The annual sweet peas bring a mass of delicate colour to the garden all summer long. Let them rampage through an established shrub – the stems die back in autumn and are

easily removed. There are numerous varieties to choose from, some of which are highly fragrant.
Flower Clusters of white, pink, or purple pea flowers are held on upright stalks.
Maintenance Clear to ground in autumn; the plant readily self seeds.
Tip The flowers are good for cutting and regular deadheading will prolong the plant's flowering period.

Woodbine

Lonicera periclymenum

A member of the honeysuckle family, woodbine will vigorously scramble over supports. Its flowers are sweetly scented.
Flower Creamy white flowers from early summer to early autumn.
Maintenance Thin after flowering.
Tip They do best with their roots in shade and their shoots in the sun.

Summer jasmine

Jasminum officinale
'Argenteovariegatum'

Trained around a pergola or patio, summer jasmine is a delight, with its highly perfumed flowers. Plant in full sun, to make the scent even more intense. In warm sheltered sites, the variegated foliage of this variety will last well into autumn.

Flower Fragrant clusters of white flowers appear from mid summer to early autumn.
Maintenance Thin out after flowering.
Tip Cut back *J. officinale* hard and regularly and it will form a self-supporting bush.

Morning glory

Ipomoea purpurea

Morning glory is grown for its abundantly produced trumpet-shaped flowers that may be red, purple, white or striped. It is a half-hardy annual in Britain that is best grown in a sunny, sheltered spot.

Flower Cheerful trumpet-shaped blooms appear in summer and autumn. They are very short-lived.
Maintenance Sow in mid spring directly where it is to grow.
Tip These make charming conservatory plants.

Crimson glory vine

Vitis coignetiae

Ornamental grape vines are at their best in autumn when they cover pergolas and trellises with colourful foliage and fruit. This species is a good choice for poor soil, which will bring out the best display of autumn colour in spectacular shades of yellow, orange-red and purple-crimson. It is best grown over trees or old buildings.

Fruit Clusters of inedible black grapes with a purple bloom hang decoratively in autumn.
Maintenance Thin out old growth in late summer.
Tip Choose a south-facing site.

The 10 best easy-care perennials for full sun and dry conditions

Sun, sun and even more sun, from early morning right on into the evening, is no problem for these perennials. Plants from the Compositae family, identified by their daisy-like flowers, are especially easy to look after and thrive in full sun.

Milfoil, yarrow
Achillea millefolium

Brightly coloured summer flowers and ferny, greyish-green foliage make these herbaceous evergreen perennials a popular choice for sunny borders and beds.

Flower Flat heads of white or pink flowers appear in summer.
Maintenance Lift and divide every three years.
Tip Colourful varieties include 'Lilac Beauty' (light mauve flowers) and 'Paprika' (orange-red and yellow flowers).

Pearly everlasting
Anaphalis margaritacea

Clusters of pearly white flowers glisten on this hardy, easily grown perennial. The silver-grey foliage is attractive too. This species is very drought tolerant so is ideal for the driest location in your garden.
Flower Loose heads of profuse white flowers appear in late summer and early autumn.

Maintenance Divide in autumn or spring.
Tip The blooms are excellent for cutting and drying.

Golden marguerite
Anthemis tinctoria

Marguerites are the perfect plants for borders and cottage gardens, with their pretty ferny foliage and masses of fresh daisy-like golden yellow flowers. Give them a sunny, well-drained site and they can be relied upon to produce a great show of flowers all summer long.

Flower Golden yellow flowers from early to late summer.
Maintenance Divide in autumn or spring every two or three years.
Tip Choose 'Alba' for white flowers.

Coneflower
Echinacea purpurea

In late summer the large daisy-like flowers of coneflowers make a bold addition to a sunny border. The flowers are long-lasting.

Flower White to purple flowers with an orange-brown centre appear from late summer into autumn.
Maintenance Divide in autumn or spring.
Tip The flowers are good for cutting and drying.

Michaelmus daisy
Aster ericoides

Choose asters for late season colour. This species survives drought better than many other asters. It forms a bushy plant, carrying masses of small daisy flowers in elegant, spreading sprays. Different cultivars offer flowers in a variety of colours: 'Blue Star' (lavender blue); 'Pink Cloud' (mauve-pink); 'White Heather' (white).

Flower Flowers are borne in autumn.
Maintenance Divide in spring every three to five years.
Tip For an eye-catching effect, plant in large groups of one colour.

Heliopsis

Heliopsis helianthoides var. *scabra*

The showy flowers of the hardy perennial, Heliopsis, stand out in a sunny border. The semidouble flowers of 'Goldgrünherz' are particularly striking with their lime-green centres.
Flower Upright daisy-like yellow flowers are borne in mid summer to early autumn.
Maintenance Divide dormant crowns in late autumn. Plants benefit from some support.
Tip Deadhead regularly.

Sundrops

Oenothera fruticosa

○ ▲ to 1m ▶ to 60cm ◇

This species of evening primrose adds grace and fragrance to the garden with its continuous supply of fresh yellow, scented flowers held on reddish upright stems. Its flowers stay open during the day.

Flower Cup-shaped scented yellow flowers are borne from mid to late summer.
Maintenance Divide in early spring.
Tip Not good for cutting, but will attract butterflies into the garden.

Sage

Salvia officinalis Purpurascens Group

Sage is an aromatic herb widely grown for its ornamental foliage as well as for its use in cooking. It is tough and tolerant of poor, dry soil. This particular variety has attractive soft, purple leaves that darken through the summer.

Flower Short spikes of purple flowers appear intermittently throughout the summer.
Maintenance Control the size of mature plants by cutting back in spring.
Tip Cutting back flowering stems encourages a second crop of blooms later in the season.

Mullein

Verbascum bombyciferum

○ ▲ to 1.8m ▶ to 80cm ◇

Showy spires of saucer-shaped flowers are produced by the compact evergreen, *Verbascum*. The leaves and stems are covered in dense white hairs, giving the plant an attractive silvery appearance.

Flower Spikes of sulphur yellow flowers are borne from early summer to autumn.
Maintenance Take root cuttings in late winter.
Tip Regular deadheading will prolong flowering.

Globe thistle

Echinops ritro

○ ▲ to 80cm ▶ to 60cm ◇

A stately plant that bears large spherical flowerheads on stout stems. The thistle-like, spiky leaves are divided, greyish green to dark green. It is a useful plant for the poorest and driest of soils, where its deep blue or purplish flowers will bring splashes of intense colour. As an alternative, the slightly taller hybrid *Echinops* 'Nivalis' has greyish-white globular flowerheads on grey stems with greyer leaves.
Flower Dark steel blue flowerheads from mid summer to early autumn.
Maintenance Divide in spring or autumn.
Tip Cut the flowerheads before they are fully opened and dry for use in flower arrangements.

The 10 best easy-care perennials for an open sunny garden

These undemanding perennials will thrive in an average garden soil. They **need good light**, but do best when not in full sun. Warmer places, too, are no problem for them, as long as they are **given sufficient water**.

Lady's mantle
Alchemilla mollis

○ – ◗   ▲ to 60cm   ▶ to 60cm   ◊

Fluffy yellowish-green flowers are seen above a low mound of silky green foliage in summer. The softly hairy, almost circular leaves have shallow lobes and serrated edges.
Flower Sprays of yellowy green flowers appear in summer and last for weeks, gradually turning brown.
Maintenance Divide in autumn or spring. Seeds itself freely.
Tip The flower sprays are good for cutting and drying.

Michaelmus daisy
Aster novi-belgii cultivars

○ – ◗   ▲ to 1m   ▶ to 60cm   ◊

Brightly coloured daisy flowers are held in branched sprays, often pyramid-shaped, on erect, branched, leafy stems. There are numerous cultivars available, giving a choice of colour from white to deep pink or lavender blue.
Flower Sprays of daisy-like flowers in late summer to autumn.
Maintenance Divide each spring.

Tip Recommended cultivars include 'Albanian' (white), 'Helen Ballard' (purple-red) and 'Rufus' (purple-red) and the dwarf (30cm tall), bushy cultivars of 'Chatterbox' (pale pink) and 'Lady in Blue' (lavender-blue).

Self heal
Prunella grandiflora

○ – ◗   ▲ to 45cm   ▶ to 30cm   ◊

Deep violet flowers provide a colourful and long-lasting display in summer. Self heal is a creeping perennial, useful at the front of a border or for splashes of colour among shrubs.

Flower Dense spikes of deep violet flowers appear throughout summer.
Maintenance Divide in autumn or spring.
Tip The flowers attract bees.

Mountain cornflower
Centaurea montana

○ – ◗   ▲ to 60cm   ▶ to 50cm   ◊

A profusion of large, thistle-like flowers are borne by this vigorous spreading perennial. It is a popular choice for cottage gardens.

Flower Blue thistle-like flowers in late spring and early summer.
Maintenance Divide in early spring.
Tip For a country cottage effect try a mixed planting of the cultivars 'Alba' (white), 'Carnea' (pink) and 'Parham' (light blue).

Dark-eyed sunflower
Helianthus atrorubens

○ – ◗   ▲ to 2m   ▶ to 60cm   ◊

Despite their name, sunflowers do well in partial shade as well as full sun. This species is a perennial and positioned at the back of a border or

against a wall, it will produce large flowers on tall stems year after year.
Flower Orange-yellow flowers with maroon centres are borne from late summer to early autumn.

Maintenance Can be invasive; curtail spread by lifting and replanting in spring.
Tip The seed heads encourage finches into the garden in autumn.

Catmint
Nepeta × faassenii

○ – ◗ ▲ to 60cm ▶ to 60cm ◗

Catmint adds a gentle touch as an edging plant with a soft haze of light-blue flowers against silvery grey leaves. It will also droop attractively over the edge of a pot.
Flower Pale lavender flowers appear in summer.

Maintenance Divide in early spring.
Tip Its aromatic leaves and flowers attract bees into the garden.

Day lily
Hemerocallis cultivars

○ – ◗ ▲ to 1.1m ▶ to 60cm ◗

The day lily's brilliantly coloured exotic flowers are available in an ever-increasing range of shapes and colours. They create a majestic summer display against a backdrop of strap-shaped, arching leaves.
Flower Pure white, orange, yellow, striped, red and much more.

Maintenance Divide in late summer to maintain vigour.
Tip The flowers last one day only but are continually replaced; deadhead daily for the best show.

Dotted loosestrife
Lysimachia punctata

○ – ◗ ▲ to 2m ▶ to 60cm ◗

Tall spires of bright yellow flowers add interest to the back of a border. Loosestrife needs fairly moist soil and will thrive if placed around a

pond or beside a stream. Its rampant habit is best suited to wild or cottage gardens where it will grow in broad swathes.
Flower Bright yellow star-shaped flowers appear in summer.
Maintenance Keep invasiveness in check by deadheading so that it cannot self-seed and cutting clumps back ruthlessly in spring.

Coneflower
Rudbeckia fulgida var. *sullivantii*

○ – ◗ ▲ to 1m ▶ to 80cm ◗

The sturdy golden flowerheads of the coneflower give a reliable display year after year. The prominent cone-shaped centre is

black, surrounded by gracefully drooping petals. Allow room for new plants to spread and clump.
Flower Golden yellow flowers with black centres appear in late summer to early autumn.
Maintenance Divide in spring or autumn. Deadhead to prolong flowering.
Tip Apply a mulch in spring to prevent plants from wilting in hot sun when in flower.

Stonecrop
Sedum telephium

○ – ◗ ▲ to 60cm ▶ to 60cm ◌

Sedums are easy to grow. Most prefer dry, hot, sunny locations, but this species needs a more moist environment. Its attractive reddish-purple flowerheads are carried at the tips of its fleshy stems, which also bear bright green, waxy, diamond-shaped leaves. The plants need good light and will lean towards it if positioned in too much shade.
Flower Reddish-purple flowers in late summer and early autumn.
Maintenance Divide in late autumn.

The 10 best easy-care flowering perennials for partial shade

These easy going perennials are suitable for places that only have **morning** or **afternoon sun** or are shaded by trees. They delight with their **charming flowers** and **beautiful foliage**.

Leopard's bane
Doronicum orientale

○ – ◗ ▲ to 50cm ▶ to 50cm ◊

Golden yellow daisy-like flowers bring colour to the garden in the spring. The plants grow in most soils and like a shady spot.
Flower Yellowy flowers are carried on slender stems above the bright green leaves in spring.
Maintenance Divide immediately after flowering.
Tip The cultivar 'Magnificum' has large yellow flowerheads.

Plume poppy
Macleaya cordata var. *cordata*

Plume poppy
Macleaya cordata var. *cordata*

○ – ◗ ▲ to 2.5m ▶ to 1m ◗

Rising majestically above most other plants, the feathery flowers and shiny leaves make the plume poppy ideal for the back of a border.
Flower Numerous creamy white flowers form large frothy plumes in mid summer.
Maintenance Divide in spring.

Tip Though tall, these plants rarely need staking.

Astilbe
Astilbe **x** *arendsii* 'Feuer'

◖ – ● ▲ to 1.2m ▶ to 75cm ◆

A gift in a tricky situation, astilbes thrive in damp shade. There are many easy varieties to choose from, all bearing tall, fluffy plumes of summer flowers above ferny foliage.

Flower Spires of deep red flowers appear in mid to late summer.
Maintenance Divide every four years to maintain vigour.
Tip Apply a thick mulch in spring to prevent plants from drying out.

Elephant's ear
Bergenia cultivars

◖ – ● ▲ to 40cm ▶ to 60cm ◊

Early spring flowers and large handsome leaves, which in some cultivars flare up red or purple in winter, give this plant year-round appeal. Place it at the front of a border for maximum impact.
Flower Pink, red, mauve or white bell-shaped flowers grow in loose

clusters above or among the foliage in early spring.
Maintenance Divide in autumn or spring.
Tip 'Sunningdale' has pink flowers on coral-red stems and its leaves are bronzed in winter.

Brunnera
Brunnera macrophylla

◖ – ● ▲ to 50cm ▶ to 80cm ◆

Brunnera is a handy ground-cover plant for any cool, damp, lightly shaded part of the garden. A clump will quickly form a lush, green carpet, its forget-me-not flowers nestling among the mid-green foliage in spring.
Flower Sprays of small blue, white, red or pink flowers appear from mid to late spring.

Maintenance Water plants regularly over their first summer. Divide in autumn.
Tip Plants will prosper in most situations except dense shade.

Black cohosh
Cimicifuga racemosa var. *racemosa*

) – ● ▲ to 2m ▶ to 50cm ●

Tall spires of white flowers stand above the compact clumps of delicate, deeply divided leaves in summer. This plant does well at the back of a border with some shade.

Flower Spikes of tiny white flowers are seen throughout the summer.
Maintenance Cut back to the ground in late autumn. Plants may need some staking.
Tip *C. simplex* is a smaller species that flowers later in the summer.

Windflower
Anemone hupehensis var. *japonica*

) – ● ▲ to 1.4m ▶ to 1m ●

Plant this spreading herbaceous perennial in dappled shade for a late show of flowers that will last into the autumn.

Flower Clusters of clear pink flowers appear from late summer to mid autumn.
Maintenance Mulch during the hot, summer months.
Tip When planting out add plenty of humus to the soil.

Cranesbill
Geranium × *magnificum*

◑ –) ▲ to 60cm ▶ to 50cm ◑

A medium-sized geranium that will grow happily in a partially shaded spot. It needs little attention, its dark green leaves providing good ground cover, livened up with bold violet flowers in summer.
Flower Rich violet-blue flowers appear in early summer.
Maintenance None needed. Divide in late summer or spring.

Columbine
Aquilegia vulgaris

◑ –) ▲ to 80cm ▶ to 40cm ◑

Dainty, nodding flowers are held on slender stems above lacy foliage on this easily grown plant. Native to British woodland, it thrives in dappled shade and humus-rich soil,

although it will tolerate drier soils. It flowers freely, seeding itself widely.
Flower Blue, purple, reddish purple, white or pink flowers in early summer.
Maintenance None needed.
Tip Recommended cultivars include 'Nivea' (white flowers) and *A. vulgaris* var. *stellata* 'Nora Barlow' (pompom-like pink flowers flecked with lime green and white).

Meadow rue
Thalictrum aquilegiifolium

◑ –) ▲ to 1.2m ▶ to 80cm ●

In summer a fuzzy aerial haze of flowers can be seen above lacy grey-green foliage. *Thalictrum* is a fairly tall plant that suits the back of a border or a woodland edge.
Flower Fluffy pink sprays of flowers appear in mid summer.
Maintenance Divide clumps and replant in early spring.
Tip The stems are sturdy and do not require staking. The blossoms make excellent cut flowers and the finely divided foliage is also useful for flower arrangements.

The 10 best easy-care flowering perennials for full shade

Perennials for shady places often have **especially decorative foliage**. They do well under the canopies of trees and shrubs or at **woodland edges**, where their flowers add colour to the greenery.

White baneberry
Actaea alba

》– ● ▲ to 1m ▶ to 50cm ◊

White, fluffy flowerheads stand above the divided and toothed foliage of these clump-forming plants. The white berries carried on fleshy red stems make an attractive display in late summer.

Flower/Fruit Spikes of white flowers appear in early summer followed by white berries.
Maintenance Rhizomes can be divided in spring.
Tip The berries are poisonous.

Goat's beard
Aruncus dioicus var. *dioicus*

》– ● ▲ to 2m ▶ to 1.2m ◊

Graceful light-green leaves are enhanced by elegant sprays of flowers in summer. Female plants develop dull green seedpods that dry well for indoor arrangements.
Flower Upright plumes of tiny creamy white flowers stand above foliage in mid summer.
Maintenance Lift and divide in autumn every two or three years.

Tip Thrives when grown around a pond or by a stream.

Bellflower
Campanula glomerata 'Superba'

》– ● ▲ to 75cm ▶ to 80cm ◊

The perennial bellflower will spread vigorously along shady borders, where its clusters of deep purple flowers, held on sturdy stems, will be noticed in summer. It has deep green, lance to heart-shaped leaves.

Flower Clusters of deep purple flowers are seen in early summer.
Maintenance It spreads by rhizomes and can be invasive. Lift and replant every three to four years after flowering or in autumn.
Tip The species *C. glomerata* has smaller flowers but blooms all summer long.

Epimedium
Epimedium grandiflorum

》– ● ▲ to 25cm ▶ to 20cm ◊

A clump-forming, herbaceous plant, grown for its superb foliage and intriguing, long-spurred flowers. The apple-green leaves flush bronze in spring and again in autumn. The ideal location for this plant is in a semi-woodland position with plenty of humus in the soil.
Flower White, pink, violet or rose-red flowers bloom in spring and early summer.
Maintenance Divide in autumn or early spring.
Tip Recommended varieties include 'Nanum' (pale purple flowers), 'Rose Queen' (deep pink flowers and copper-tinged young leaves) and 'White Queen' (pure white flowers and bronze-tinged young leaves).

Dame's violet
Hesperis matronalis

◗ – ● ▲ to 1m ▶ to 60cm ◊

Grown for its fragrant white or pinkish flowers, *Hesperis* is a short-lived perennial best suited to the shade of a woodland garden. Its scent is stronger in the evening.
Flower Long spikes of lilac or white flowers are borne in early summer.
Maintenance Divide in spring.
Tip The flowers attract butterflies into the garden.

Helmet flower
Aconitum napellus

◑ – ● ▲ to 1.5m ▶ to 1m ◊

In summer the violet pyramids of aconitum flowers look impressive at the back of a border. The hooded flowers are carried at the end of stiff, leafy stalks, which are usually self-supporting.

Flower Deep pinkish-violet flowers are borne from early to mid summer.
Maintenance Divide in spring.
Tip Cutting back flower spikes immediately after flowering encourages an autumn display.

Hosta
Hosta fortunei var. *aureomarginata*

◗ – ● ▲ to 60cm ▶ to 1m ◊

Hostas are grown for their sumptuous foliage. This variety has particularly attractive leaves with irregular yellow to cream edges.

Flower Lavender flowers are carried on upright stems above the leaves in early to mid summer.
Maintenance Mulch in autumn and keep well watered.
Tip Slugs and snails can be a problem. Catch them in beer traps.

Lungwort
Pulmonaria saccharata

◗ – ● ▲ to 30cm ▶ to 30cm ◊

Give them a shady, humus-rich spot and lungworts will reward you with attractive white-speckled foliage and

charming flowers. In borders or woodland edges they mix particularly well with primroses (*Primula vulgaris*) and hostas.
Flower Pale reddish-violet flowers appear from early to late spring.
Maintenance Divide in late autumn.
Tip Recommended cultivars include 'Frühlingshimmel' (brightly spotted leaves, pale blue flowers), 'Mrs Moon' (spotted pale green leaves, pink to violet flowers) and 'Pink Dawn' (wavy edged leaves blotched with pale green, large pink flowers).

Rodgersia
Rodgersia pinnata

◗ – ● ▲ to 1m ▶ to 1m ◉

Large, divided leaves, held on tall stalks give rodgersias architectural value in the garden. The flowers are held in plumes above the foliage in summer. They do well when sited in boggy ground beside ponds and streams.
Flower Plumes of tiny star-like flowers, in shades of white, yellow or pink, appear in mid summer.
Maintenance Divide rhizomes in spring or autumn.
Tip Recommended cultivars include 'Elegans' (cream flowers) and 'Superba' (rose-pink flowers).

Foam flower
Tiarella cordifolia

◗ – ● ▲ to 30cm ▶ to 1m ◊

This species of foam flower produces masses of spires of white frothy blossom in spring. Its pale green leaves are shallowly lobed and develop a bronze tint in winter. It is mat-forming, providing ground cover in damp, shady places.
Flower Spires of tiny white flowers appear in late spring and early summer.
Maintenance Spreads quickly and may need cutting back to control growth in spring.

The 10 best easy-care bulbs, corms and tubers

Unassuming bulbs and tubers, **simply planted** in the ground, can produce the most magnificent flowers. These plants are **virtually indestructible** adding colour to the garden year after year.

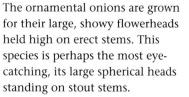

Allium
Allium giganteum

○ ▲ to 1.7m ▶ to 1m ◇

The ornamental onions are grown for their large, showy flowerheads held high on erect stems. This species is perhaps the most eye-catching, its large spherical heads standing on stout stems.
Flower Spherical violet flowerheads appear in early summer.
Maintenance In autumn plant bulbs 10–20cm deep and at least 25cm apart. Deadhead to prevent prolific self-seeding. Leave bulbs

undisturbed for several years. For propagation purposes, lift and divide after flowering.

Windflower
Anemone blanda

○ – ◗ ▲ to 25cm ▶ to 15cm ◇

Pretty starry flowers add interest to sunny borders in spring. The plant will tolerate a little shade, such as that found at a woodland edge.

Flower Blue, purple, pink or white flowers from early to mid spring.
Maintenance In autumn plant 5–10cm deep and 10–15cm apart. Lift and divide after flowering.
Tip Recommended cultivars include 'Charmer' (deep pink flowers) and 'Ingramii' (deep sky-blue flowers).

Montbretia
Crocosmia cultivars

○ – ◗ ▲ to 80cm ▶ to 50cm ◗

The montbretias quickly form large clumps and are ideal among shrubs. Their bright green, sword-like leaves form an attractive backdrop to the boldly coloured flowers. There are numerous cultivars to choose from.

Flower Yellow, orange or red flowers appear from late summer to early autumn.
Maintenance Between April and May plant bulbs 10cm deep and 20–35cm apart. Montbretias dislike long periods of frost, so a winter mulch is advisable in cold areas.
Tip Recommended cultivars include 'Canary Bird' (yellow flowers), 'Jackanapes' (flowers with yellow and dark orange petals) and 'Spitfire' (fiery orange flowers).

Meadow saffron
Colchicum autumnale

○ – ◗ ▲ to 20cm ▶ to 25cm ◗

Small goblet shaped flowers are produced from corms in autumn. The lance-shaped leaves appear later in the year, dying back in summer. Plant them at the front of a border.
Flower Up to six small lilac flowers are produced in early autumn.
Maintenance In July or August plant corms 5–10cm deep and at least 15cm apart. Remove offsets and replant in summer.
Tip The plants are poisonous. Choose 'Album' for white flowers.

Daffodil
Narcissus cultivars

Crocus
Crocus species and cultivars

○ – ◑   ▲ to 40cm   ◐

There are numerous crocus species and varieties to choose from. The early flowering *C. tommasinianus* increases rapidly and is good for naturalising in grass.
Flower Honey-scented flowers in white or shades of yellow, purple and blue appear in late winter and early spring.
Maintenance In autumn plant corms 5cm deep at 10cm intervals.

Spanish bluebell
Hyacinthoides hispanica

◗ – ● ▲ to 40cm ▶ to 30cm ◗

Carpets of intense blue spreading through light woodland are one of the delights of spring. This easy-to-grow species will readily naturalise under deciduous trees or shrubs in the garden to stunning effect.
Flower Large violet-blue bell-shaped flowers hang around an erect stem in late spring.
Maintenance In autumn plant 5–10cm deep and 15cm apart.
Tip The scented British bluebell, *H. nonscripta*, is also easy to grow.

Grape hyacinth
Muscari armeniacum

○ – ◗ ▲ to 20cm ▶ to 20cm ◌

This plant gets its name from the clusters of globular flowers that resemble a bunch of grapes. Looks attractive planted among daffodils.
Flower Purple-blue flowers in mid spring.
Maintenance In August plant 5–10cm deep and 5–10cm apart.
Tip Grows well in containers.

Daffodil
Narcissus cultivars

○ – ◗ ▲ to 60cm ▶ to 50cm ◌

One of the best known flowers of spring, daffodils are easy to grow and there is a wide variety to choose from.
They can be grown in a range of settings from natural drifts in a lawn to pots on a windowsill.
Flower The spring flowers come in white and shades of yellow, orange-red or pink; many varieties are bicoloured.
Maintenance In autumn plant 5–15cm deep and 5–20cm apart.
Tip The cultivar 'Geranium' is one of many sweetly fragrant daffodils.

Scilla
Scilla species and cultivars

○ ▲ to 20cm ▶ to 15cm ◌

Scillas, or squills, bring a touch of summer colour to the early spring garden with their luminous blue, bell-shaped flowers. There are species that flower earlier in winter (*S. bifolia* and *S. mischtschenkoana*) and one that flowers in autumn (*S. autumnalis*). They are best grown in loose drifts under shrubs or trees but are also good for containers.

Flower Generally blue, but also white or pink.
Maintenance In late summer plant bulbs 10cm deep and at least 10cm apart.

Tulip
Tulipa species and cultivars

○ – ◗ ▲ to 40cm ▶ to 30cm ◐

This is another bulb that has been bred into thousands of colours and forms. For example, the double early tulips have showy double blooms, while the Greigii tulips offer attractive foliage, their leaves marked with maroon mottling. The flowers are generally goblet shaped and the leaves are bright green and broadly lance shaped.
Flower Every conceivable colour except true blue, in late spring.
Maintenance In autumn plant bulbs 10–15cm deep at 10cm intervals.
Tip Tulips are a popular choice for containers.

The 10 best easy-care ornamental grasses

Versatile and easy to grow, tall and stately ornamental grasses bring movement into the garden as they sway in the wind. Some have decorative feathery ears while others form dense clumps and cushions. All have a long season and require little attention once established.

Calamagrostis
Calamagrostis × acutiflora

○ – ◗   ▲ to 1.5m   ▶ to 1m   ◊

Calamagrostis, a medium-sized grass, bears narrow, long-living, purple-green plumes on tall stems. It is a rhizomatous perennial with mid green leaves that form tufts.
Flower Purple-green plumes in early summer gradually turn brown.
Maintenance None needed.
Tip The cultivar 'Karl Foerster' has red-bronze heads that fade to buff.

Stipa
Stipa calamagrostis

○   ▲ to 1.2m   ▶ to 1m   ◊

A perennial with thin green leaves that form rounded mounds. In summer it bears greenish white feathery plumes on gracefully arching stems.
Flower Greenish-white plumes appear in mid summer to autumn and turn buff.
Maintenance Divide before flowering.
Tip A larger alternative is the species *S. gigantea*, which produces impressive golden plumes in early summer. They are carried on 1.8m stems and shimmer above dense clumps of dark green foliage.

Carex
Carex elata 'Aurea'

○ – ◗   ▲ to 60cm   ▶ to 1m   ◊

Plant this sedge for a splash of intense colour. The leaves, which form dense mounds, are bright yellow and narrowly edged with green. Like all the sedges it grows well in sun or shade but needs a moist soil.

Flower Dark brown flower spikes appear in early summer.
Maintenance Divide in spring or early summer.
Tip The plant is an attractive addition to a bog garden.

Fargesia
Fargesia nitida

◗   ▲ to 4m   ▶ to 3m   ◊

Belonging to the bamboo family, fargesia is fast-growing and robust. Many branches grow out from the nodes on the slender and often purple-tinged culms.
Flower Dark brown flower spikes appear in early summer.
Maintenance Divide large clumps in early spring.
Tip Another bamboo, *Phyllostachys vivax* f. *aureocaulis*, has thick, yellow stems attractively striped with green. At 7.5m tall, several plants will make a fast-growing screen.

Helictotrichon
Helictotrichon sempervirens

○ – ◑   ▲ to 1.2m   ▶ to 1m   ◊

Choose this grass for year-round interest provided by its striking steely blue leaves. The evergreen foliage forms tufts, above which feathery plumes of pale straw-coloured flowers appear in summer.
Flower Pale straw-coloured panicles appear in summer.
Maintenance Divide large clumps any time except mid summer.

Common woodrush
Luzula sylvatica

Woodrushes grow well in damp, shady places, where they make good ground-cover plants. This species has glossy, dark green, evergreen leaves that form low tufts. Delicate flower sprays add interest in spring and early summer.

Flower Chestnut-brown flower clusters are held on upright stems from mid spring to early summer.
Maintenance Divide clumps in spring.
Tip An alternative is the snowy woodrush (*L. nivea*), which carries pretty white flowers in summer on tall, slender stems.

Switch grass
Panicum virgatum 'Rubrum'

Switch grass makes good-sized clumps of medium height. In autumn it produces sprays of tiny flowers and the foliage ripens to a rich reddish colour.
Flower Panicles of tiny green spikelets appear in late summer.
Maintenance Divide clumps any time of year except summer.
Tip Use this stunning grass as a focal point.

Miscanthus
Miscanthus sinensis

The arching, slender, bluish-green leaves of this clump-forming perennial have silver midribs. From

summer onwards it has the added interest of long-lasting, purple-silver plumes of flowers.
Flower Purple-silver feathery panicles appear from mid summer and last into the winter.
Maintenance Divide in late spring or early summer.
Tip Other worthwhile varieties include 'Silberfeder' (silver to pinkish-brown panicles) and 'Variegatus' (leaves striped with creamy white and pale green).

Molinia, Moor-grass
Molinia caerulea subsp. *arundinacea*

A superb autumn plant, tall moor-grass makes an impressive show. The panicles are held high above the

foliage, giving a see-through effect. The foliage turns orange in autumn.
Flower Open panicles of purplish flowers in mid summer.
Maintenance Divide any time except mid summer.
Tip Useful for growing in boggy, acidic soils.

Fountain grass
Pennisetum alopecuroides

The most attractive feature of this grass is its bottlebrush-like flower spikes in late summer. The flowers are held on tall stems above the dense tufts of green leaves.
Flower Bottlebrush-like flowers appear in late summer.
Maintenance Divide in late spring.
Tip The cultivar 'Hameln' has reddish-brown flower spikelets and is slightly shorter.

The 10 best easy-care ferns

Diverse in shape and size, ferns can provide **architectural interest**, act as foils for flowering plants and form drifts of ground cover. They usually need only **slightly moist soils** in order to do really well, without too much attention.

Lady fern
Athyrium filix-femina

◗ – ● ▲ to 1m ▶ to 70cm ◐

The pale green, lance-shaped, bipinnate or tripinnate fronds of this deciduous fern die down in winter leaving a scaly crown. The fern is suitable for a variety of situations, from exposed walls to shady riverbanks. It grows best in an acid soil, although it will tolerate some lime.

Maintenance Divide in spring.
Tip Spreads freely but is intolerant of dry conditions.

Ostrich fern
Matteuccia struthiopteris

◗ – ● ▲ to 1.2m ▶ to 70cm ●

The elegant deciduous ostrich fern resembles a large shuttlecock with its upright, lance-shaped, pinnate fronds. The rich green sterile fronds surround light to mid green fertile fronds, which turn brown in late summer and persist throughout the rest of the year, creating a striking sculptural display. Plant this taller

fern for dramatic impact, either as a feature on its own or as a stunning backdrop to other plants.
Maintenance Divide in spring.
Tip Spreads rapidly, sending up new crowns from invasive rhizomes.

Scaly male fern
Dryopteris affinis

◗ – ● ▲ to 80cm ▶ to 70cm ◐

An easy-to-grow fern that grows naturally in woodland and is therefore best suited to the shadier parts of the garden. In spring the golden crowns unfurl to display dark green, bipinnate fronds with golden scales on the midribs. Planted near a pond, it makes a good backdrop to water plants.

Maintenance Divide in spring.
Tip Though it prefers shade, it will tolerate some sun.

Hard fern
Blechnum spicant

◐ – ◗ ▲ to 30cm ▶ to 30cm ◐

Plant easy-to-grow evergreen, acid-loving hard ferns in a shady border or woodland edge. The plant is made up of erect, dark-green, lance-shaped fertile fronds and arching, glossy, deeply lobed sterile fronds.
Maintenance None needed.
Tip Rather than division, this fern is propagated from spores.

Male fern

Dryopteris filix-mas

▶ – ● ▲ to 1m ▶ to 80cm ◐

The semi-evergreen male fern is useful for shadier parts of the garden where other plants won't grow, although it will tolerate sun. It is similar in appearance to *D. affinis*, but there are fewer scales on the midribs of the leaves.
Maintenance Divide in spring.

Royal fern

Osmunda regalis

▶ – ● ▲ to 1.2m ▶ to 80cm ●

A large, imposing fern, its erect lance-shaped, bipinnate fronds emerge brown, turn green and then

fade to yellowish hues in autumn. Many plants develop distinctive, upright, rust-brown fertile pinnae in summer. Thriving in a moist soil, the plant is particularly suited to waterside locations. It benefits from a mulch of well-rotted manure in spring. It also makes an excellent container plant, provided that it is regularly watered.
Maintenance None needed.
Tip Rather than division, this fern is propagated from spores.

Hard shield fern

Polystichum aculeatum

◑ – ● ▲ to 1m ▶ to 80cm ◐

An evergreen fern with elegant crowns of lance-shaped, pinnate or bipinnate fronds, which are glossy, dark green and leathery. The plant

Hart's tongue fern
Asplenium scolopendrium

requires a moist, shady area and an acid soil. The rhizome is short and thick and covered in large brown scales.
Maintenance Divide in spring.

Hart's tongue fern

Asplenium scolopendrium

▶ – ● ▲ to 40cm ▶ to 20cm ◐

A neat little evergreen fern that is useful for ground cover. It has a crown of simple, mid green, strap-like fronds. The crosiers look like small green cobras and are shown to best effect when the old fronds are removed from the centre of the plant in spring. It does best in a lime-rich soil, is drought tolerant and can be grown in crevices among alkaline rocks or in a prepared planting hole in a wall.
Maintenance Divide in spring.

Soft shield fern

Polystichum setiferum

◑ – ● ▲ to 1m ▶ to 80cm ◌

Intricately dissected, bipinnate, dark green fronds and densely scaled crosiers are produced by this

graceful evergreen. It tolerates direct sunlight, as long as the soil does not dry out. The rhizome is covered by papery orange scales.
Maintenance Divide in spring.

Sensitive fern

Onoclea sensibilis

▶ – ● ▲ to 60cm ▶ to 60cm ●

This moisture-loving fern produces triangular, pink-bronze, erect fronds that later become mid green and arching. The pinnate sterile fronds die back with the first frost while the more persistent bipinnate fertile fronds turn dark brown. Massed together they create a striking winter display.
Maintenance Divide in spring.

The 10 best easy-care rock garden plants

With their **abundant flowers**, some real treasures can grow between a rock and a hard place. **These tough little plants** are not only especially fast-growing, but also **very low maintenance**.

Tumbling Ted
Saponaria ocymoides

Alyssum
Alyssum montanum

○   ▲ to 20cm   ▶ to 30cm   ◊

Spreading mats of evergreen foliage become smothered in yellow flowers in summer. The plants can be used to soften the lines of a raised bed: position them at the front and they will tumble over the edge.
Flower Fragrant, deep yellow flowers are carried in clusters from late spring to mid summer.
Maintenance Trim back lightly after flowering to encourage bushy growth.
Tip Established plants often self-seed freely.

Tumbling Ted
Saponaria ocymoides

○   ▲ to 25cm   ▶ to 40cm   ◊

This vigorous species of soap-wort produces masses of pretty five-petalled pink flowers. Its evergreen leaves are hairy and form a low, spreading mat. It is ideal for growing along path edges or draping over a sunny wall.

Flower Loose clusters of pink flowers cover the foliage mat in early summer.
Maintenance None required.
Tip The cultivar 'Rubra Compacta' is a tight, slower-growing plant with profuse rich carmine blooms.

Bellflower
Campanula carpatica

○ – ◗   ▲ to 30cm   ▶ to 40cm   ◊

A clump or hummock-forming herbaceous perennial that produces a good show of bell-shaped flowers in summer. It is useful for rockeries or even a tiny gap in a wall. It also makes a fine pot plant for the conservatory or cool greenhouse.

Flower Large upright blue, violet-purple or white bells appear in mid to late summer.
Maintenance Lift and divide after flowering.
Tip For large, pure white flowers choose f. *alba* 'Bressingham White', while var. *turbinata* 'Isabel' has charming wide-spreading bells of deep violet blue. Cut plants back soon after flowering and they may produce a second flush of blooms.

Spurge
Euphorbia myrsinites

○   ▲ to 20cm   ▶ to 40cm   ◊

A low-growing biennial with leafy prostrate stems emerging from a woody crown. The yellowy green flowerheads are carried on the previous season's shoots. The thick blue-grey leaves spiral attractively around the stems.

Flower Yellowy green flowerheads appear from late winter to mid spring. Yellowy bracts may fade to orange during the summer.
Maintenance Cut back flowering shoots to ground level in late summer and leave current season's shoots (which will flower the following year).
Tip The milky white sap is toxic and so euphorbias should not be planted near a fishpond.

Cranesbill
Geranium renardii

○ – ◗   ▲ to 30cm   ▶ to 25cm   ◊

The free-flowering geraniums are among the easiest of garden plants to grow. This compact species is well suited to a rockery, thriving in full sun and well-drained soil. The grey-green leaves have a soft texture and scalloped edges.

Flower Off-white flowers with violet veins bloom in mid summer.
Maintenance Divide clumps at the end of summer.
Tip Alternative compact species include *G. cinereum* with pale pink flowers and *G. sanguineum* with bright purple flowers.

Alum roots, coral bells
Heuchera cultivars

Most of the cultivars have attractive foliage in purple, silver and coppery tones. Some bear airy sprays of tiny flowers above the leaves. They are best placed towards the front of a border or bed, where the flowers on top of the tall thin stems can be seen to best advantage.
Flower Red, pink or white flowers appear in early summer.
Maintenance Every few years dig up in early autumn and replant outer, more vigorous parts, discarding older woodier portions.
Tip 'Red Spangles' produces upright sprays of vivid red flowers.

Phlox
Phlox subulata, Phlox douglasii

Both these low-growing perennials produce a profusion of flowers above mats of evergreen, needle-like leaves. Plant at the edge of a rockery for a carpet of colour.
Flower White, pink, red, violet or blue flowers in late spring and early summer.
Maintenance Clip lightly after flowering to keep tidy.
Tip There are numerous cultivars to choose from, including *P. douglasii* 'Crackerjack' (magenta flowers) and *P. subulata* 'Red Wings' (rose-red flowers with a darker eye).

Speedwell
Veronica prostrata

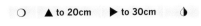

A profusion of blue flowers burst open in late spring, covering the mat-forming speedwell in vivid blue. It is untroubled by dry and impoverished soil and will happily cover an area of scree.
Flower Small dense spikes of bright blue flowers are carried from late spring to early summer.
Maintenance Divide every three years. Deadhead to increase vigour.
Tip For pink flowers choose the cultivars 'Rosea' or 'Mrs Holt'.

Aubrieta
Aubrieta cultivars

Compact cushions of grey-green foliage become smothered in brightly coloured flowers in spring.

They make ideal rockery plants and will grow on dry sunny walls or in the cracks between paving.
Flower Elongating clusters of pink, purple or blue cross-shaped flowers are carried throughout the spring.
Maintenance Divide in late summer or early autumn.
Tip There are numerous cultivars to choose from, including 'Belisha Beacon' (bright rose-red flowers), 'Doctor Mules' (rich violet flowers) and 'Triumphant' (blue flowers).

Houseleek
Sempervivum cultivars

All the plants in this genus of evergreen succulents are well suited to the rockery. They are mostly grown for their dense rosettes of fleshy leaves, often flushed with shades of purple or pink. The rosettes die after flowering but are constantly replaced by new rosettes.
Flower Sprays of small, starry, pink, red or white flowers appear above the foliage in summer.
Maintenance Plant ready-rooted offsets in spring or summer.

The 10 best easy-care aquatic and bog plants

Plants at the edges of a pond or stream are not just **pleasing to the eye**, they also **provide a habitat** for useful and interesting wild creatures. Once the plants are established the gardener can sit back, **relax and watch the wildlife in action.**

Siberian iris
Iris sibirica

○ – ◗   ▲ to 1m   ▶ to 1m   ●

Named for the Greek goddess of the rainbow, iris flowers combine an architectural flower form with a huge range of rich colours. This beardless water iris does well on the margins of ponds or streams but dislikes waterlogging.
Flower Up to five flowers, which vary from white to blue, are borne in early summer.
Maintenance Divide rhizomes after flowering every three years. Replant 2.4cm deep in moist soil.
Tip Irises are heavy feeders so spread compost or manure around the plants.

Flowering rush
Butomus umbellatus

○ – ◗   ▲ to 1m   ▶ to 70cm   ●

A deciduous hardy perennial, grown mainly for its twisted, rush-like leaves, which are bronze-green when young, and pale pink flowers. It is an aquatic plant and can be sited in water up to 25cm deep.

Flower Loose heads of pale pink cup-shaped flowers are borne from mid summer to early autumn.
Maintenance For strong flowering, divide or replant annually.

Marsh marigold
Caltha palustris

○ – ◗   ▲ to 40cm   ▶ to 40cm   ●

This herbaceous perennial grows best in very wet soil and is suitable for a bog garden or moist border. It will thrive in up to 15cm of water. Its attractive kidney-shaped leaves

form large, dark green patches, creating an attractive backdrop for its bright yellow flowers.
Flower Deep yellow cups appear on branching stems in spring.
Maintenance Lift and divide after flowering.
Tip White flowers appear on var. *alba* and var. *palustris* 'Plena' bears fully double 'button' flowers.

Joe Pye weed
Eupatorium purpureum

○ – ◗   ▲ to 1.8m   ▶ to 1.2m   ●

Although *Eupatorium* likes moist soil, it is not an aquatic so must be close to but not actually in a pond or stream. Its tall purple-tinged stems give height to a wild-flower garden or informal border, and are topped with large heads of purple-pink flowers in summer.
Flower Large, dense clusters of tiny pinkish-purple flowers appear during late summer.
Maintenance Divide in autumn.
Tip The flowers attract bees and butterflies into the garden.

Water forget-me-not
Myosotis scorpioides

◑ – ◗ ▲ to 30cm ▶ to 25cm ●

Carpets of delicate blue forget-me-nots are a favourite sight in spring. The moisture-loving water forget-me-not will thrive at the edge of a pond in up to 3cm of water.
Flower Sky-blue flowers with yellow eyes are borne in summer.
Maintenance None needed.

Leopard plant
Ligularia hybrids

◑ – ◗ ▲ to 2m ▶ to 1.5m ●

Site hardy perennial *Ligularia* in dappled shade by the side of a water feature, where their tall eye-catching spikes of orange or yellow flowers cannot fail to impress. Some have coloured foliage.
Flower Yellow or orange daisy-like flowers are carried on tall spikes in mid summer.
Maintenance Divide from autumn to spring. Stake tall plants.
Tip 'Greynog Gold' can withstand full sun.

Purple loosestrife
Lythrum salicaria

○ – ◗ ▲ to 1.5m ▶ to 1m ●

Slender wands of reddish purple flowers distinguish this upright, hardy perennial. The tubular-based flowers are carried on square stems above lance-shaped leaves that may turn yellow in autumn. It thrives in the boggy soil found at water margins, but can easily be grown elsewhere in the garden on rich moisture-retentive soil.
Flower Spikes of reddish-purple flowers appear in mid summer.
Maintenance Divide overcrowded clumps in autumn or spring.
Tip Deadhead to prevent the spread of self-sown seed.

Water lily
Nymphaea cultivars

○ ▲ to 2m ▶ to 3m ●

Grown for their waxy, star or cup-shaped summer flowers and floating foliage, water lilies are deciduous, perennial aquatic plants. The leaves shade the surface of the water and so help to reduce the amount of algae in a pond. There are varieties to suit every pond depth, including miniature varieties for planting in water tubs.
Flower White, pink, red, yellow or orange flowers open in summer.
Maintenance To avoid congestion, divide every three to five years.
Tip Recommended cultivars include 'Gonnère' (double white flowers) and 'Fabiola' (rose-pink flowers flushed red at the base).

Pondweed
Potamogeton species and cultivars

○ – ◗ ▲ to 3m ▶ to 3m ◑

Hardy aquatic pondweeds, with submerged and floating leaves, are often considered to be weedy and invasive, but some more restrained

species – such as *P. crispus* – make a useful addition to the pond. Though the flowers are not showy, the leaves help to oxygenate the water.
Flower Small spikes of greenish, inconspicuous flowers in summer.
Maintenance Remove any decaying foliage in autumn.

Umbrella plant
Darmera peltata

○ – ◗ ▲ to 1.8m ▶ to 1m ●

Enormous umbrella-like leaves create a magnificent mound of dark green foliage that turns bronze-pink in autumn. It is a hardy herbaceous perennial that thrives in damp, boggy soil. Planted next to a stream or pond, it makes an impressive backdrop for more colourful plants.
Flower Clusters of small white flowers appear on thick hairy stems before the leaves in early spring.
Maintenance Divide rhizomes in autumn or spring and replant.

Water lily
Nymphaea cultivars

The 10 best easy-care summer annuals

From spring until well into the autumn, these **abundantly flowering** annuals will add lots of **colour** to your flower beds. They are **easy to raise from seed**, fast-growing and very eager to produce a **good show of flowers**.

Painted daisy
Tanacetum coccineum

Pot marigold
Calendula officinalis

○ ▲ to 60cm ▶ to 25cm ◌

The daisy-like flowers of these fast-growing annuals can be relied upon to bring a burst of colour to a bed or border the whole summer long. The flowers peep out among thick, aromatic pale green foliage. There are numerous cultivated varieties to choose from with semi-double and double flowers.
Flower Yellow, orange, apricot or cream flowers are borne from late spring to late summer.
Maintenance None needed.
Tip Deadhead regularly to encourage more flowers.

Painted daisy
Tanacetum coccineum

○ ▲ to 80cm ▶ to 60cm ◑

Eye-catching large daisy flowers on robust erect stems add colour and interest to mixed borders. The numerous cultivars offer a great choice of colour, many with flowers that display concentric bands of contrasting colour.

Flower White, pink, purple, red, yellow and variously banded flowers appear in late spring and early summer.
Maintenance None needed.
Tip Flowers are good for cutting.

Cosmos
Cosmos bipinnatus

○ ▲ to 1.2m ▶ to 80cm ◑

Brightly coloured saucer-shaped flowers are carried on tall, slender stems above ferny foliage. The overall appearance is delicate and refined, yet this bushy annual is robust and easy to grow. It is excellent in areas of poor, dry soil, readily flowering where other plants may have trouble. There are several varieties to choose from, including 'Sonata White', which has shorter stems and white petals surrounding the yellow centre.

Flower Saucer-shaped flowers with yellow centres and rose, crimson, pink or white petals appear from mid summer to autumn.
Maintenance None needed.
Tip Deadhead regularly to encourage more flowers.

Sweet alyssum
Lobularia maritima

○ ▲ to 15cm ▶ to 50cm ◌

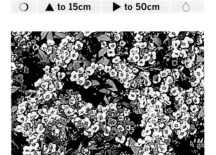

A great summer bedding plant, sweet alyssum produces masses of flowers all through the summer. The tiny flowers are produced at the tips of multi-stemmed branches clothed in greyish-green leaves. It is often used as edging, beside a path or at the front of a border.
Flower Tiny, four-petalled, white, pink or violet flowers are carried in dense fragrant clusters in summer.
Maintenance None needed.

Tree mallow
Lavatera trimestris

○–◐ ▲ to 1.2m ▶ to 80cm ◑

Lavateras are fast-growers, giving good value in the garden with a long-flowering season from mid summer until the first frosts in autumn. The large, showy rose-pink flowers of this species are borne freely among glossy, dark green leaves. All this bushy hardy annual requires is a sunny position, sheltered from the wind.

Flower Large rose-pink flowers are borne from mid summer to early autumn.
Maintenance None needed.
Tip Remove faded blooms.

Love-in-a-mist
Nigella damascena

O   ▲ to 60cm   ▶ to 40cm   ◗

Abundant summer flowers set against feathery, deep green leaves imbue this hardy annual with a dainty appearance. The plant also has inflated seed heads that are an attractive feature for some weeks after flowering has finished.
Flower Blue, pink or white flowers bloom in early or mid summer.
Maintenance None needed.
Tip Deadhead regularly to prolong flowering display.

California poppy
Eschscholzia californica

O   ▲ to 60cm   ▶ to 40cm   ◗

An easy-to-grow plant for poor, dry soil. It needs full sun, however, for its flowers to open fully. The bright poppy flowers are carried on slender stems well above the finely divided blue-green leaves.

Flower Yellow and orange flowers from early summer to mid autumn.
Maintenance None needed.
Tip Deadhead to prolong flowering.

Common nasturtium
Tropaeolum majus

O   ▲ to 3m   ▶ to 1m   ◗

This tender annual has a variety of uses. Its richly coloured trumpet-shaped blooms brighten up borders,

trellises, pots and hanging baskets. It does best in poor soil, where it will flower profusely. The circular leaves are also attractive.
Flower Yellow, orange or red flowers appear in summer.
Maintenance None needed.
Tip Plants in the 'Alaska Series' have cream-and-green variegated foliage and orange or red flowers; 'Hermine Grashoff' has double orange-scarlet flowers.

Zinnia
Zinnia angustifolia

O   ▲ to 50cm   ▶ to 30cm   ◗

A short species that is suitable for growing at the edge of a border or as a summer ground-cover plant. Its showy, dahlia-like flowers come in a range of vivid colours and last throughout the summer.

Flower Yellow, gold, orange, red, brown or multi-coloured flowers are borne from mid summer to the first frosts in autumn.
Maintenance None needed.
Tip This compact species also does well in a rock garden or a container.

Tagetes
Tagetes tenuifolia

O   ▲ to 20cm   ▶ to 20cm   ●

Crisp flowers in a range of bright yellow, orange and red shades are borne in profusion during the summer months. There are few bedding plants that can rival Tagetes in terms of ease of cultivation and length of flowering. The genus includes French and African marigolds (*T. patula* and *T. erecta*, respectively), admired for their golden double blooms. *T. tenuifolia* produces masses of small, single flowers in a range of bright colours. It has a very bushy habit and the blooms appear in such profusion that the plant can look like a ball of flowers. It is often grown to great effect at the front of a border and is best sited in full sun.
Flower Yellow, orange, red or brown flowers are borne throughout the summer.
Maintenance Water thoroughly during prolonged dry spells.
Tip The Gem Series has orange or yellow flowers, 'Lemon Gem' being a popular variety.

The 10 best easy-care container plants

Container gardening has an appeal all of its own – you can create little **patches of paradise** on a patio or balcony in a flexible and portable display. With a few thoughtfully planted pots you can **mix and match colour** and texture to your heart's content.

Treasure flower
Gazania cultivars

Asteriscus
Asteriscus maritimus

○ ▲ to 35cm ▶ to 30cm ◇

An abundance of sunny daisy-like flowers are borne amid silky greenish-grey leaves. As well as pots, this compact herbaceous perennial can be grown in rock gardens and does well in hanging baskets.
Flower Yellow flowers with finely toothed petals appear in summer.
Maintenance Place pots in a sunny, sheltered position.

Treasure flower
Gazania cultivars

○ ▲ to 30cm ▶ to 30cm ◇

The spectacular flowers of these easily grown pot plants are enhanced by the foliage, which in many varieties is silver or grey.
Flower White, yellow, red, orange or pink flowers (or a combination of colours) appear from mid summer to mid autumn.
Maintenance These tender perennials will only survive in

milder regions of Britain, but can be overwintered in a cool greenhouse.
Tip The cultivar 'Cookei' has grey foliage and orange flowers with an inner olive green ring.

Tickseed
Bidens ferulifolia

○ ▲ to 30cm ▶ to 30cm ◆

With a naturally spreading, thin stemmed habit, tickseed drapes prettily out of a hanging basket or container. In the summer the stems are covered in yellow flowers.

Flower Yellow flowers bloom from early summer to early autumn.
Maintenance Too tender to survive outdoors, but can be overwintered in a cool greenhouse.
Tip Though it prefers full sun, it will grow in light shade.

Swan River daisy
Brachyscome iberidifolia

○ ▲ to 30cm ▶ to 30cm ◑

This half-hardy annual produces a fine summer display of small daisy-like flowers. It is a bushy plant with green, deeply cut leaves.

Flower Blue, violet or white fragrant flowers appear in profusion throughout summer.
Maintenance Plants benefit from some support. Deadhead regularly.
Tip Can be grown as winter-flowering indoor plant.

Senna
Senna corymbosa var. *corymbosa*

○ ▲ to 2m ▶ to 1.5m ◇

A vigorous shrub grown for its pleasing divided foliage, pretty sweet-pea flowers followed by curious pod-like fruit. It is too tender for outdoors, but is ideal for a large container in a conservatory or greenhouse.

Flower Clusters of golden yellow flowers are borne from mid summer to early autumn.

Maintenance Plants can become leggy, so trim back regularly during the growing season. Apply a liquid houseplant feed regularly.
Tip The plant will be fully grown within five years.

Spotted laurel
Aucuba japonica

○ – ● ▲ to 2.5m ▶ to 80cm ●

Large, glossy, leathery leaves give permanent garden value to this robust evergreen shrub. It tolerates sun, shade and pollution. Grow it in large containers, placed in any inhospitable corner or on paved areas. Male and female flowers appear on different plants, so grow both sexes to ensure a good show of the vivid red berries in autumn.

Flower Insignificant pale purple flowers on short upright spikes appear in mid to late spring.
Maintenance None required.
Tip 'Crotonifolia' (female) is one of the brightest variegated forms; 'Golden King' (male) has splashes of gold on its leaves. Variegated varieties need to be sited in good sunlight for good colour.

Busy lizzie
Impatiens walleriana

◑ – ◐ ▲ to 30cm ▶ to 30cm ●

One of the most free-flowering bedding plants for shady sites, busy lizzie is a popular pot plant. Its many hybrids can be grown in containers indoors and outside. It is a perennial, but is normally treated as half-hardy annual. It is also a useful bedding plant for shady sites.
Flower White, pink, red, violet, orange or two-toned flowers appear from summer to autumn.
Maintenance Can be overwintered under cover.

Shrub verbena
Lantana camara

○ ▲ to 2.5m ▶ to 1.3m ◐

Grow this tender evergreen shrub in a greenhouse or conservatory, or in tubs for a summer display.

It produces large heads of flowers, sometimes with different colours appearing on the same plant. The oval, mid green leaves often have a pungent aroma.
Flower Rounded heads of tiny yellow, orange or red flowers appear throughout the summer.
Maintenance Trim back weak or dead shoots in spring. Outdoor specimens can be overwintered in a cool greenhouse.
Tip A recommended cultivar is 'Snow White' with creamy white flowers.

Rose moss
Portulaca grandiflora

○ ▲ to 20cm ▶ to 30cm ○

A popular half-hardy annual that produces brilliantly coloured flowers on low-growing reddish stems. It does well in a container placed in a sunny spot, but is also useful for covering a dry bank as a summer bedding plant.
Flower A succession of saucer-shaped flowers in shades of orange, pink, red, yellow or white appear from mid summer to early autumn.

Maintenance None needed.
Tip Site in full sun as flowers tend to close in shade or dull weather.

Pelargonium
Pelargonium cultivars

○ – ◐ ▲ to 60cm ▶ to 30cm ◐

The robust pelargoniums offer a huge variety of flower colour and handsome foliage. They are easy to grow and their ability to withstand some drought means that they can survive the odd lapse in watering. There are four groups: 'ivy-leaved' with a trailing habit for hanging baskets; 'regal' with large, richly coloured flowers; 'scented-leaved' with pleasantly aromatic foliage; and 'zonal' where the leaves are marked with a band of contrasting colour. All can be grown in pots or used in bedding schemes.
Flower Five-petalled flowers in shades of pink, purple, red, white and bicoloured appear from early to late summer.
Maintenance Deadhead to extend the flowering period. Repot in spring and replace every two years. Replace bedding plants annually.

The 10 best easy-care fruit-bearing plants

Fruit from your own garden **always tastes better** than that bought in the supermarket. In addition, you have the **mouthwatering anticipation** of watching your crop grow and ripen ready for harvesting.

Common hazel
Corylus avellana

Actinidia
Actinidia arguta

○   ▲ to 3m   ▶ to 3m   ◐

Admired for its flowers and foliage as well as its fruit, the deciduous climbing actinidia is great value. Let it ramble over a pergola where its scented flowers can be enjoyed in summer, followed by its decorative and edible gooseberry-like fruit.
Flower Clusters of fragrant white flowers in early to mid summer.
Maintenance Plants need initial training. Apply compost to mature plants in spring.
Harvest Autumn.
Tip For more reliable fruiting, grow in a cool greenhouse.

Common hazel
Corylus avellana

○   ▲ to 5m   ▶ to 3m   ◌

Hazel is easily grown and valued for it leaf shape and colour as well as its edible nuts. The nuts, surrounded by green bracts, form in autumn.
Flower Male catkins hang in clusters in early spring.

Maintenance None necessary except occasional prune in late autumn to control size of plant.
Harvest Autumn, when the nuts are brown and hard.

Common quince
Cydonia oblonga

○   ▲ to 15m   ▶ to 10m   ◌

Charming flowers, yellow autumn foliage and golden aromatic fruit are the chief attributes of this deciduous tree with attractively crooked

branches. In colder regions, quince requires the protection of a wall for the fruit to ripen.
Flower White to pale pink flowers appear in spring.
Maintenance In winter cut out any dead, diseased or crossing shoots.
Harvest Autumn, when the pear-shaped fruit are golden yellow.

Strawberry
Fragaria × ananassa

○ – ◐   ▲ to 30cm   ◐

Quick to produce a harvest, and compact enough for the smallest garden – it can even be grown in

containers – the strawberry is a most desirable fruit. Grow several varieties to prolong the fruiting season.
Flower Starry white flowers in late spring and summer.
Maintenance Protect flowers from spring frosts with straw or fleece. As fruits grow, protect from soil splash by tucking straw under them.
Harvest From early to late summer, depending on variety.
Tip After harvest cut back foliage to 10cm from the crown; remove it and burn with any straw and debris.

Blackberry
Rubus fruticosus

○   ▲ to 2m   ◐

With pretty flowers and autumn leaf colour, blackberries make an attractive display on an archway.

The long, rambling canes also bear an abundance of plump black berries in autumn.
Flower Clusters of white flowers in late spring and summer.
Maintenance Train canes between pairs of wires. Growth and fruiting follows a two-year cycle, so canes that have finished fruiting should be cut out at soil level in late autumn.
Harvest From late summer to early autumn, depending on variety.

Apple
Malus × domestica cultivars

Apples are the most widely grown fruit tree in Britain because they are hardy and easy to maintain. A huge choice of varieties offers fruiting from August to November.

Flower Clusters of five-petalled white or pinkish flowers in spring.
Maintenance Apply a compound fertiliser in late winter. Keep well watered. A few weeks after petal fall, thin young fruit to one or two per cluster. Prune in mid to late winter.
Harvest Autumn. Wait for fruit to ripen on the tree before picking.

Ballerina apple
Malus × domestica cultivars

This compact tree is the ultimate in care-free gardening since it requires little pruning and the fruits are easy to pick. Its vertical habit with few side shoots allows it to be sited in small gardens, borders and even tubs. Cultivars include 'Bolero' (green) and 'Flamenco' (red).
Flower Clusters of five-petalled white or pinkish flowers in spring.
Maintenance Care is the same as for all apple trees. Minimal pruning involves cutting back any side shoots to two buds in winter.
Harvest Autumn, when fruit is ripe.

Redcurrant
Ribes rubrum

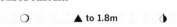

Redcurrant bushes or cordons are decorative and produce delicious fruit not often available in the shops. They are easy to grow, but the buds will need protecting from finches in the winter.
Flower Clusters of greenish yellow flowers in spring.
Maintenance Keep well watered when in fruit. Prune mature plants in early winter to remove old or diseased branches and to let in light.
Harvest Mid summer, when the berries have turned red.

Raspberry
Rubus idaeus

Raspberries are an easy and very rewarding crop. The tall upright canes require staking and a yearly prune, but the reward is an abundance of sweet juicy fruit year after year. Since they flower in early summer, frost damage is rare and the plants thrive in typically cool, wet British summers.
Flower Clusters of white flowers in summer.
Maintenance In autumn after harvesting, cut canes that have borne fruit back to soil level. Tie new canes to wires for fruit next year.

Harvest Mid summer to mid autumn, depending on the variety.
Tip Choose 'Glen Moy' for early fruit and 'Autumn Bliss' for a later harvest.

Gooseberry
Ribes grossularia

Gooseberries make compact bushes and can be grown almost anywhere in the garden where there is free-draining soil. In the winter protect the buds from finches.
Flower Clusters of small white flowers in spring.
Maintenance Prune mature plants just before harvesting to allow easier access to fruit. Remove diseased or dead branches and prune to let light and air into the centre of the plant.
Harvest Mid to late summer.
Tip There are dessert varieties that do not require cooking before eating.

The 10 best easy-care herbs and vegetables

Herbs and vegetables **earn their place** in the garden, providing flavour and sustenance. Some also have decorative appeal and can be grown **dotted about in beds** and borders. Just a little bit of care and these plants will **produce a bumper crop**.

Chives
Allium schoenoprasum

○ – ☽ ▲ to 30cm ◐

Grow chives in mixed borders, where their mauve-pink spherical flowers will add colour in summer, year after year. Hollow, cylindrical leaves have a mild onion flavour.
Maintenance Sow seeds outside in spring. Divide clumps every three or four years in autumn.
Harvest March to October.
Tip Remove flowerheads before they open if you want a plentiful and regular supply of leaves.

Borage
Borago officinalis

○ – ☽ ▲ to 60cm ▶ to 50cm ◐

The charming blue flowers of borage produce a decorative effect throughout the summer months. Its leaves and flowers have a mild flavour much like cucumber.
Maintenance Sow seeds outside in late spring. Thin seedlings to a spacing of about 50cm.

Harvest April to September.
Tip The flowers are often used to flavour summer drinks or candied for use as cake decorations.

Beetroot
Beta vulgaris

○ – ☽ ▲ to 40cm ◐

If space is limited, beetroots can be grown in a flowerbed, where their attractive red stems and glossy green leaves will not look out of place.
Maintenance Sow seeds outside in mid spring. Thin 2cm seedlings to a spacing of about 10cm.
Harvest From 12 weeks after sowing.
Tip Though usually deep red, there are pink, yellow and white varieties.

Broccoli
Brassica oleracea

○ – ☽ ▲ to 80cm ◐

A large, central head of purple, cream or green flowers forms the edible part of this highly nutritious vegetable. There are several varieties.
Maintenance Sow seeds in drills and transplant when 10–15cm tall. As with all brassicas, the crop will need protection from pigeons.
Harvest From February to November depending on variety.

Squash
Cucurbita pepo

○ – ☽ ▲ to 1m ▶ to 1.5m ◐

Perhaps the easiest of vegetables to grow, the squashes include marrows, pumpkins and courgettes. There are numerous varieties to choose from.

Their large leaves shade out weeds but their long creeping stems can sometimes become invasive.
Maintenance Choose a site with rich, fertile soil in good sun. Sow seeds in May.
Harvest July to October.
Tip Cut courgettes throughout the season to encourage more flowers.

Lettuce
Lactuca sativa cultivars

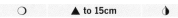

There are four types of lettuce: butterhead, crisphead, cos and loose-leaf. All have varieties that are sown outdoors for a summer crop. Some loose-leaf varieties are decorative enough to be used along border edges in the garden.

Maintenance Sow seeds outdoors in late March to July. Sow in short rows every two or three weeks to give a continual supply that does not mature all at once.
Harvest From June to October. With the loose-leaf varieties, take leaves as required or cut each plant at the base after six weeks and allow it to regrow.

Dwarf French bean
Phaseolus vulgaris var. *nanus*

A low-growing bean that does not require tying to supports. It is small enough to be grown in tubs and containers, where its heavy crop of slender beans can be easily accessed.

Maintenance Sow outdoors in late May or June in rows 45cm apart at 10cm intervals for easier picking.
Harvest As soon as first pods develop – from seven or eight weeks after sowing.

Radish
Raphanus sativus cultivars

Quick and easy to grow, radishes come in different colours and sizes. Summer salad varieties may be red, red and white or white, and either globe-shaped or cylindrical.
Maintenance Sow outdoors in March to July every two weeks for a continual supply. Sow thinly in drills and thin if necessary soon after seedlings emerge. Rows should be 15cm apart.

Harvest When young – three to six weeks after sowing.
Tip There are winter radish varieties for harvesting later in the season. Sow them in late July and August for a crop 10 or 12 weeks later.

New Zealand spinach
Tetragonia tetragonioides

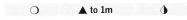

This half-hardy plant is not actually a type of spinach but is used in much the same way. Unlike true summer spinach, it thrives in hot, dry weather without running to seed. By regularly harvesting just the lower young shoots, the same plants should be able to regenerate to give you a crop all summer long.
Maintenance Sow outdoors in late May. It needs a sunny spot and rows

should be 60cm apart. As soon as they are large enough to handle, thin seedlings to about 60cm intervals.
Harvest Take a few leaves from each plant from June to September.

Lemon balm
Melissa officinalis

A cottage garden favourite, lemon balm gives off a delicious lemon scent when its leaves are crushed. It can be left to flourish in virtually any situation, and may even become invasive in some cases. It is useful as a herb, but also has decorative value. Its white tubular flowers crown the foliage in summer and early autumn, attracting bees. Let it billow out beside a path, where the aroma of its leaves can be enjoyed as people brush by.

Maintenance Promote fresh, leafy growth by cutting off flowering stems mid summer.
Harvest Take leafy tops throughout the summer.
Tip The leaves are used in cooking and can also be stewed to make a tea.

311

Index

Page numbers in **bold** type refer to entries in the directory of easy-care plants.